KT-144-435

2nd Edition

Business
Book 2

David Dooley • John Goymer
Philip Guy • Catherine Richards
Neil Richards

Askham Bryan
College
LIBRARY BOOK

www.harcourt.co.uk
✓ Free online support
✓ Useful weblinks
✓ 24 hour online ordering

01865 888118

05. 10. 07
059124

Heinemann

Heinemann is an imprint of Harcourt Education Limited, a company incorporated in England and Wales, having its registered office: Halley Court, Jordan Hill, Oxford OX2 8EJ. Registered company number: 3099304

www.harcourt.co.uk

Heinemann is the registered trademark of Harcourt Education Limited

Text © David Dooley, John Goymer, Philip Guy, Catherine Richards, Neil Richards

First published 2007

12 11 10 09 08 07
10 9 8 7 6 5 4 3 2 1

British Library Cataloguing in Publication Data is available from the British Library on request.

ISBN 978 0 435465 45 2

Copyright notice
All rights reserved. No part of this publication may be reproduced in any form or by any means (including photocopying or storing it in any medium by electronic means and whether or not transiently or incidentally to some other use of this publication) without the written permission of the copyright owner, except in accordance with the provisions of the Copyright, Designs and Patents Act 1988 or under the terms of a licence issued by the Copyright Licensing Agency, Saffron House, 6–10 Kirby Street, London EC1N 8TS (www.cla.co.uk). Applications for the copyright owner's written permission should be addressed to the publisher.

Edited by Sandra Stafford
Designed by Pentacor Big Ltd
Typeset by Tech-Set Ltd
Original illustrations © Harcourt Education Limited 2007
Illustrated by Tek-Art Ltd
Picture research by Helen Reilly
Cover photo/illustration © Alamy Images/Douglas Fisher
Printed by Scotprint

Websites
The websites used in this book were correct and up-to-date at the time of publication. It is essential for tutors to preview each website before using it in class so as to ensure that the URL is still accurate, relevant and appropriate. We suggest that tutors bookmark useful websites and consider enabling students to access them through the school/college intranet.

Contents

WITHDRAWN

Acknowledgements

The author and publisher are grateful to all those who have given permission to reproduce material. Every effort has been made to contact copyright holders of material reproduced in this book. Any omissions will be rectified in subsequent printings if notice is given to the publishers.

Photo acknowledgements

© Copyright 1994 The Board of Trustees of the University of Illinois / Created by the National Center for Supercomputing Applications (NCSA) at the University of Illinois at Urbana-Champaign by Donna Cox and Robert Patterson – page 2. Alamy/Jane Wiedel p.86; Arnos Design Ltd pp.107, 124, 173, 183, 311, 321; Corbis pp.44, 302; Corbis/Imre Feoldi/epa p.115; Dell Computers p.36; Fotolia/Janos Gehring p.169; Harcourt Ltd/Debbie Rowe p.258; Harcourt Ltd/Gareth Boden p.50; istockphoto/Brasil2 p.251; istockphoto/Erik Eilers p.225; istockphoto/Francisco Orellana p.218; istockphoto/Peter Mlekuz p.292; istockphoto/Stephen Finn p.119; McArthur Glen p.305; MG Rover Group p.285; Nissan Motor Co. Ltd p.96; Photos.com p.55; Rex Features/Arnold Slater p.248; Rex Features/SHOUT p.75; Rex Features/Stuart Clarke p.244; Royal Mail p.61; Sainsbury's p.29; Tesco p.129; Virgin Group p.63.

Text and screenshot acknowledgements

Acme Whistles – page 150 (reprinted with permission); Amazon.com Inc – pages 14, 321 (courtesy of Amazon.com Inc and its affiliates. All rights reserved); Apple – page 23; B&Q (www.diy.com) – pages 18, 140, 155; Bells Fish and Chips – page 149 (reprinted with kind permission); Body Shop – page 221; Borders Book Stores – page 74; BT Business Club – page 32; Business link (www.businesslink.gov.uk) – page 240; Channel 4 – page 26 (Channel 4 on Demand is available online at channel4.com/4od); Clickz.com – pages 12, 19; CNET Networks Inc – page 39 (reprinted with permission); Co-operative Bank – page 221 (reprinted with permission); Daily Telegraph – pages 26, 233, 236, 285; Dairy Crest – page 223; Dell – page 15. (Reproduced with permission); Egg (www.egg.com) – page 25; Environment agency – page 230 (www.environmentagency.co.uk. Reprinted with permission.); ERA (Environmental Rights Action) – page 252; Fairtrade Foundation – page 254; Fightback (www.fightback.com) – page 20 (reprinted with permission); Ford Global Technologies LLC – page 6 (reprinted with permission); Friends of the Earth – page 249; Go-Ahead Plc – page 226 (Extract from Go-Ahead Plc's 'Environment Report' on http://www.go-ahead.com. Reprinted with permission); Greenpeace – page 249 (logo reprinted with permission); Greenphase – page 133; Hammersmith and Fulham council – page 131 (reprinted with permission); Institute of Chartered Accountants – page 22 (statement reprinted with permission); Leighton Group – page 25 (screenshot from www.4projects.com); MB Web Design – page 33 (banner ad); Next Retail Ltd – page 151; NI Syndication – page 239 (extract adapted from 'Ethics debate booted about' from www.timesonline.co.uk. Reprinted with permission of NI Syndication); Nielsen NetRatings – page 10 ('Active Home Internet Users by Country, Aug and Sept 2006'. Reproduced with permission); Nottinghamshire County Council – page 272; PCpro (www.pcpro.co.uk) – page 143 (reprinted with permission); Point-topic.com – page 138 (reprinted with permission); Prentice Hall – page 179; Royal Institute of Chartered Surveyors – page 112; RS Components (www.rswww.com) – page 18; Sainsbury's – page 306 (reprinted with permission); Screwfix.com – page 24; Subaru UK – page 23 (reprinted with permission); Tesco Stores Ltd – page 22 (screenshot of Tesco Listens), page 29 (screenshot of Tesco pet insurance), page 223 (Tesco corporate governance). Reprinted with permission; The Guardian – page 133, 245, 268, 271; United Nations – page 241 (use of the UN logo, reprinted with permission); Walkers Crisps – page 237; www.othermedia.com – page 146.

Crown copyright material is reproduced under Class Licence No. C01W0000141 with the permission of the Controller of HMSO and the Queen's Printer in Scotland – pages 48, 68, 71, 76, 169, 210, 263, 269, 271, 276, 291, 312.

Introduction

BTEC National Business courses have been designed to be as practical as possible and allow you to get a good job with an employer or give you skills to enable you to progress on to university. Throughout your course you need to organise yourself, produce assignments and work with others – all using business-related materials. This book contains lots of very useful information with up-to-date real-world business scenarios to help you to become more aware of the business world around you.

Background to the BTEC National Business Qualifications

There are different types of BTEC National Business qualification that you may be studying – it could be a BTEC National Award that requires you to study 6 units, a BTEC National Certificate with 12 units or a BTEC National Diploma with 18 units. You may also have the chance to specialise, for example in Finance or Human Resources. Whichever qualification you are doing, you will find this book an invaluable companion to your study.

A BTEC National is a coursework-based qualification that requires a lot of time and hard work to achieve, but at the end of it you will have skills and ideas that will make you an asset to any business. Assessors will be checking that your work meets national standards throughout the year, and your work may be looked at by an external verifier as well.

You can access any extra information that you might need about BTEC National Qualifications at their website www.edexcel.org.uk.

About this book

This book is divided into 8 chapters covering all the core units and some specialist units. Each chapter represents a different unit. If you are following the BTEC National Certificate general pathway you will find enough information in this book to guide you to achieving the qualification at this level.

The 8 Units covered within the book are:

Unit 12	Investigating internet marketing
Unit 16	Human resource management in business
Unit 21	Aspects of contract and business law
Unit 30	Website design strategies
Unit 37	Starting a new business
Unit 38	Understanding business ethics
Unit 39	Exploring business and the economic environment
Unit 41	Understanding retailing

This book can be used in lots of different ways. You may wish to use it as a classroom-based resource by completing activities in class and sharing your ideas with your fellow learners, or you may also wish to use it to help you stay focussed and ahead within your learning. What is important is for you to make maximum use of the material provided in order for you achieve success within your BTEC National Business course.

This book has been endorsed by Edexcel, which means that it has been through a rigorous quality assurance programme to ensure that it is a suitable companion to the specification for both teachers and students.

What's in a Unit?

There are several new features in this book, designed to guide you towards success on your BTEC National course and help you achieve the best grade possible.

Introduction

Each chapter has an introduction to the unit, breaking it down into relevant areas that relate directly back to the specification (syllabus). This gives you an overall idea of what is covered in the unit.

■ Consider this

An activity is provided at the start of each unit – this is designed to get you to consider the broad issues that relate to that unit's business area.

■ Key Terms

Throughout each chapter there are explanations of important concepts as they occur.

■ Thinking Points

These activities are designed to help you reflect and build on your skills, and should help you when completing your assessed coursework. They will help you to broaden your knowledge and demonstrate your ability within business.

■ Practice Points

These activities are a bit more practical and may involve producing a poster, writing a letter or working out calculations. They allow you to continue to develop your skills and practise theoretical concepts.

■ Outcome Activities

Outcome activities are given within each chapter. These activities are taken directly from the unit performance criteria. That means that by completing these activities you will produce coursework that can be assessed as part of your BTEC National qualification.

To help you think about the level of qualification that you are working towards, each outcome activity is clearly marked with Pass, Merit and Distinction icons, mapped to the unit grading criteria.

To achieve a Pass for a unit, you will need to complete all the Pass outcome activities in that chapter. There will be different numbers of activities depending on the size and type of unit that you are studying. To achieve a Merit in a unit you will need to achieve all of the Pass *and* Merit outcome activities. Finally, to achieve a Distinction you will need to achieve all of the Pass *and* Merit *and* Distinction outcome activities in that unit.

■ Grading Tips

Each outcome activity comes with grading tips to give you extra guidance about what you need to do to achieve the individual criteria.

■ Case Studies

The most up-to-date case studies have been selected to increase your knowledge and awareness of current business trends and activities. Questions at the end of each case study are graded in difficulty, with one tick being the easiest and three ticks being the hardest. Case studies give you the opportunity to work on your skills before you complete your assessed outcome activities.

■ End of Unit Tests

At the end of each chapter, there is a test with questions that check your understanding of that unit's content. You may choose to complete the test before you decide to start work on the outcome activities.

■ Resources

A list of useful resources – such as books, magazines or journal articles and website addresses – is given at the end of each chapter. This provides you with the opportunity to do further research and gain understanding of the area that you are studying. This is particularly useful if you are aiming for Merit or Distinction level work.

■ Glossary

Finally, at the end of the book there is a glossary of terms. This contains all the key terms that you will have come across within the book. They have been put into alphabetical order in one place so that if a key term has been used in more than one unit but not explained in both chapters you can still easily access its meaning.

Investigating internet marketing

Introduction

The internet is capable of connecting devices of many kinds, including PCs, from all over the world. It is a powerful communications channel, increasingly used by businesses to deliver their marketing approach. By using the internet, businesses have acquired new tools to reach out, segment and target, and better serve their customers. The customer benefits by gaining the opportunity to interact with online content and to feedback to businesses. In this way, customers can help to shape products according to their exact requirements.

In this unit, you will explore the use of the internet in achieving marketing success. You will learn how the medium creates tremendous opportunities for businesses, helping them to find out exactly who and where their online customers are. You will see that internet marketing offers innovative ways of giving service and consulting customers.

Finally, you will learn that there are challenges too. Mistakes in the digital world can be costly. It is worth careful planning.

What you need to learn

On completion of this unit you should:

1. Know what role internet marketing has within a modern marketing context
2. Understand the benefits of internet marketing to customers
3. Understand the opportunities offered to businesses by internet marketing
4. Be able to investigate the challenges faced by businesses using internet marketing.

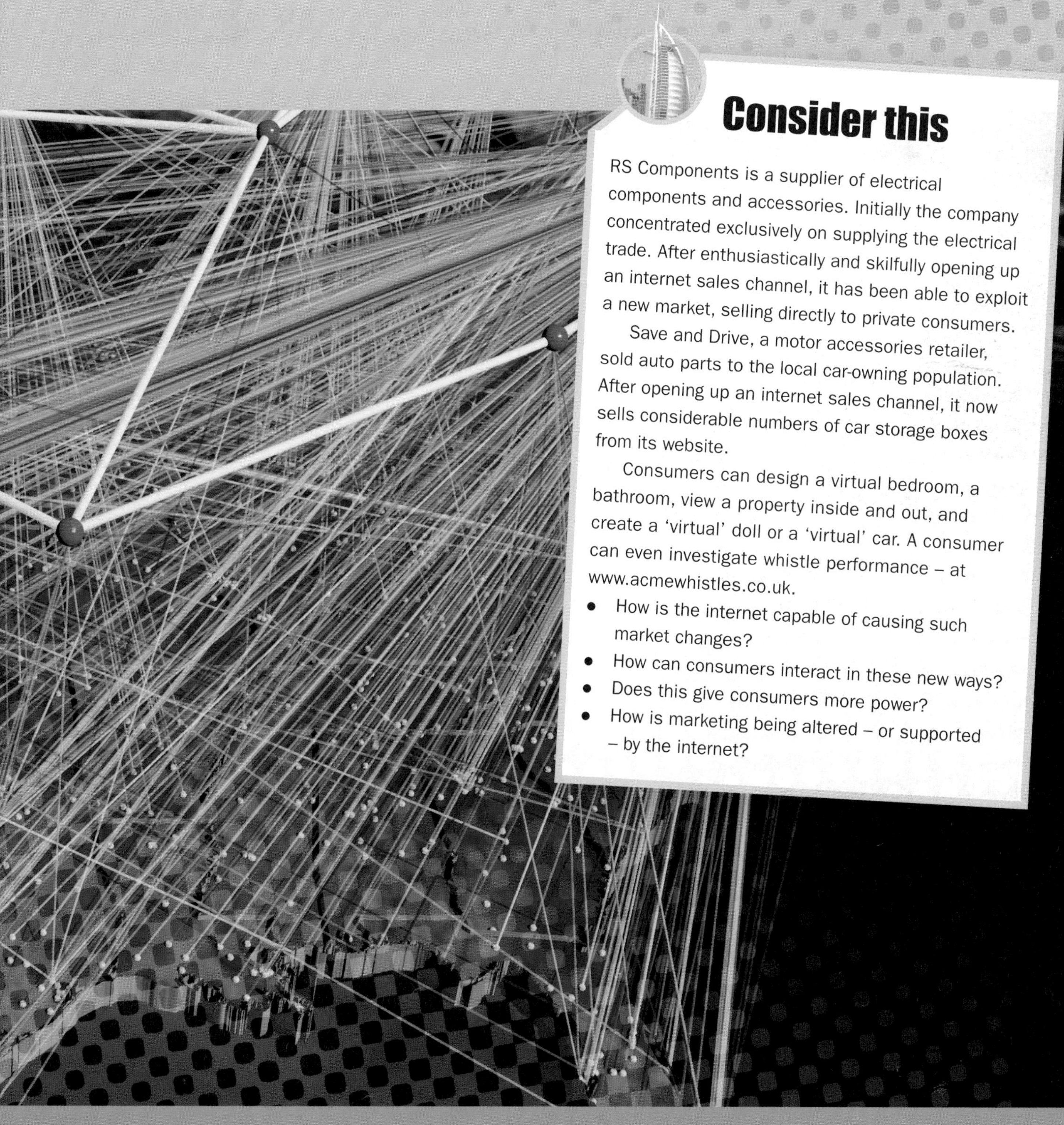

Consider this

RS Components is a supplier of electrical components and accessories. Initially the company concentrated exclusively on supplying the electrical trade. After enthusiastically and skilfully opening up an internet sales channel, it has been able to exploit a new market, selling directly to private consumers.

Save and Drive, a motor accessories retailer, sold auto parts to the local car-owning population. After opening up an internet sales channel, it now sells considerable numbers of car storage boxes from its website.

Consumers can design a virtual bedroom, a bathroom, view a property inside and out, and create a 'virtual' doll or a 'virtual' car. A consumer can even investigate whistle performance – at www.acmewhistles.co.uk.

- How is the internet capable of causing such market changes?
- How can consumers interact in these new ways?
- Does this give consumers more power?
- How is marketing being altered – or supported – by the internet?

12.1 Role of the internet in a modern marketing context

Modern marketing

The function of marketing in a private sector business, operating to generate profit, is to attract and keep customers. Customers might be private individuals, in so-called b2c (business-to-consumer) markets, or they may be other businesses in b2b (business-to-business) markets.

Markets exist wherever goods and services are bought and sold. There is a market for clothes and a market for cars; there are industrial markets and markets for food produce. Wherever people and organisations want, or need goods or services there is a market.

In the modern world, it is crucial for businesses to know about the markets they serve, so that they can work to serve them better. Marketing is the whole process of finding out what customers need or want, continually striving to meet their requirements in full and relating products to these requirements.

Marketing is a function within business that has become increasingly important over the years. Long before the growth of the web, it was essential for businesses – if they were to compete successfully – to think about how their products were going to meet the needs of the people who might buy them. If they failed to do this, people would stop buying them.

The internet is a medium that can help the marketing process. Not only does it help, it alters and re-shapes what businesses can do. However, before looking at the distinctive features of internet marketing it is necessary to have some grasp of traditional marketing principles and processes in the physical world. Unit 3 (in Book 1) introduces the marketing function and it is worth revisiting that unit before exploring the special features of internet marketing here.

The marketing mix

Classical marketing uses a 'mix' of tactics, based on a combination of the so-called four Ps. These are product, price, place and promotion. Marketers work with these to create a tactical mix, designed to achieve business aims and objectives.

Product

The marketing function considers the features of a product offered to a market or part of a market (called a segment). What is it? Who is it aimed at? What does it do? What *should* it do? Product development decisions are based on the answers to these questions. Some new cars feature improved benefits for drivers such as heated seats or adjustable mirrors. Shampoos contain new conditioners. These features rely on considerations of what customers require from products.

Price

The marketing function also considers the price a product should be pitched at. What sort of customers will buy at a particular price? What will be the best price to attract a particular kind of customer? What price might get more people to buy? What price might create the best image? What might be the effect of a change in price?

Different 'pricing strategies' are available according to what the business is aiming to achieve.

- **Penetration pricing** sets a price at a level that will gain a foothold in a market.
- **Destruction pricing** sets a price that will drive others out of the market.
- **Competitor pricing** bases the price on those of competitors.
- **Skimming (or creaming) the market** sets a high price because you have a unique product.
- **Discrimination pricing** sets different prices for different customers.

Place

Marketing specialists have always considered how a product will find its way to a *place* where consumers can make a purchase. This includes physical distribution and merchandising. Goods must be transported from the manufacturer into storage, through other distribution centres then to wholesalers, then to the high street retailer. Businesses working in between a manufacturer and a retailer are known as 'intermediaries'.

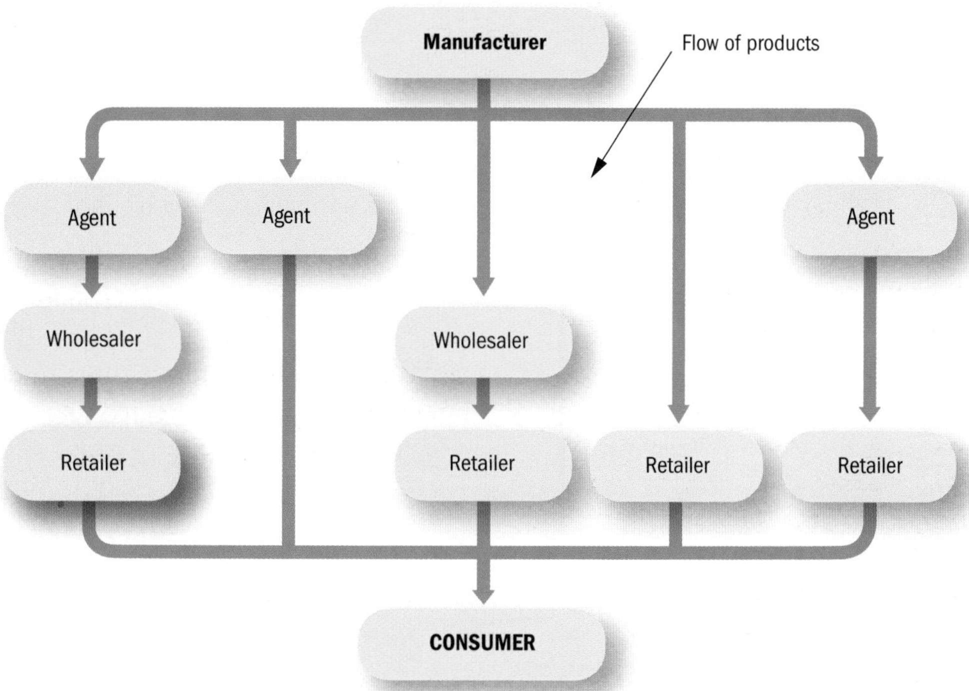

▲ Traditional channels of physical distribution

Promotion

Marketing professionals have to consider ways of bringing products to the attention of potential customers. This includes advertising in the various mass media, as well as other ways of promoting products in the eyes of consumers, such as special offers. These activities, in the physical world, are designed to 'push' products and services out towards the eyes and ears of potential consumers.

Remember

The four Ps are the basic set of marketing tactics that can be manipulated in order to attract customers.

The extended marketing mix

In our modern economy, many organisations do not sell physical products; they provide services that we cannot touch or feel. In fact, in the UK we now live and work in a 'service economy'. This means that there are more organisations and people working to offer services than work in manufacturing.

The marketing of services is different to the marketing of physical products. This has led some people to argue that the four Ps are not adequate by themselves to describe the marketing of services. They have added three further Ps to create an extended marketing mix. These are people, processes and physical evidence.

People

People are at the centre of service delivery. When we go to a restaurant, a shop, a café, a bank, or a school or college, our satisfaction hinges on how the people there deal with us. On the bus to school or college, if the driver is unfriendly or aggressive, that is what you remember.

Processes

When we use a service, we may have to take part in various activities or processes. For example a café may require us to use a self-service counter, or we may interact with a waiter. If we go to a bank, is it an attractive waiting environment? Do customers have to wait long to get service? Do we have forms to fill in?

Physical evidence

This refers to the environment in which the service is delivered. For example, we often check how restaurants look or how retail stores are laid out. Customers often look for tangible evidence to judge whether a service is what they want.

Remember

The **marketing mix** extends to seven Ps when discussing the marketing of services.

The marketing mix has to be put into practice by everyone in an organisation, guided and led (perhaps) by marketing professionals. Marketing consists of more than mere tactics; it is an entire style of doing business. The following sections show how marketing influences this style, and how internet technologies are changing this day by day.

Key Term

Marketing mix A combination of blended tactics used in delivering a marketing strategy.

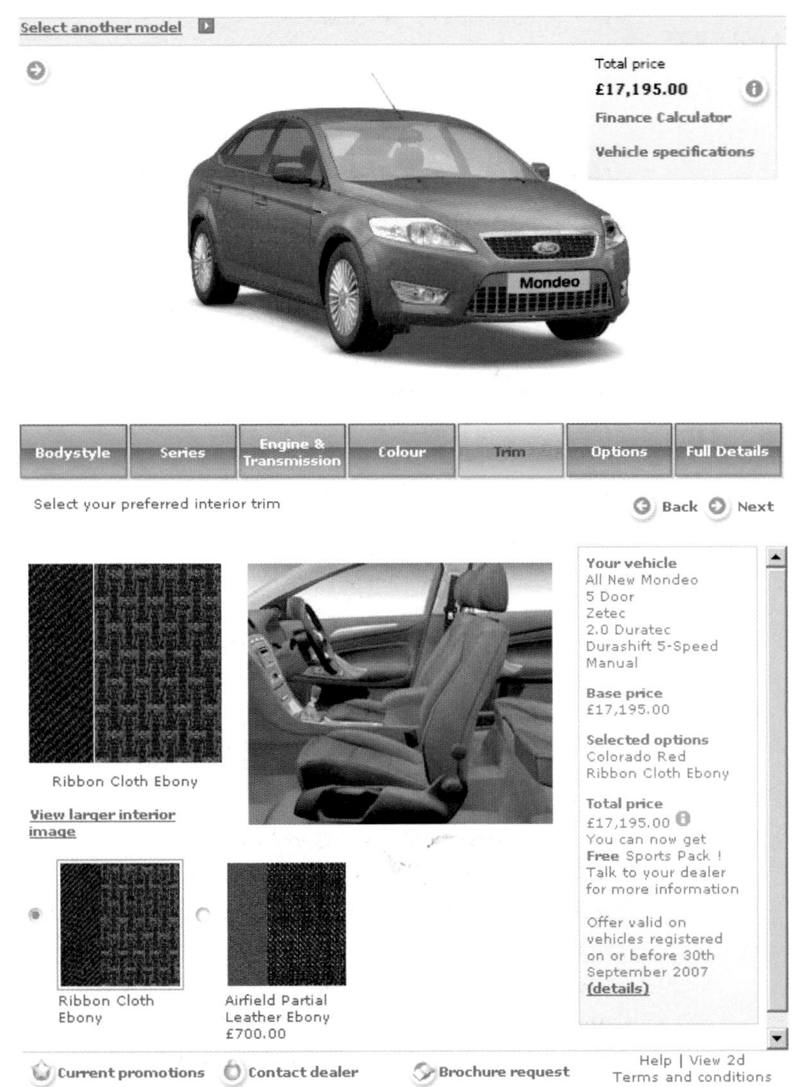

◄ Using the Ford 'car configurator', the customer can alter colours and fabrics

Relationship marketing

It is far more expensive to acquire new customers than it is to keep existing ones. For this reason, many businesses work hard to establish long-term relationships with their customers. This means that products and services offered to a market have to be highly appropriate. It is impossible to build a relationship with a customer who will never again return to your business.

Web technology is able to make use of detailed images and customer interaction. This allows customers to manipulate web pages and customise products to suit their preferences. One use of this is by allowing the customer to assist in the product design process. The Ford 'car configurator' is an example of this (www2.Fordconnection.com).

Web technology enables customers to interact with products and change them on screen to suit their own preferences. This is an added web benefit that even outperforms a physical environment. For instance, on its DIY website (www.diy.com) B & Q offers customers the opportunity to design their own kitchens, bathrooms and bedrooms.

Another technique in relationship marketing is to constantly monitor and analyse customer feedback and then respond flexibly to their wishes. Business websites usually offer 'feedback' mechanisms or 'contact us' links. These help the business to relate closely to customers.

Internet technology can help a business to target specific groups. This enables the business to develop goods and services that accurately meet customer needs. By discovering the preferences and wishes of a group, a business is more likely to be able to offer the best product. (See the section entitled 'Internet-enabled segmentation and targeting', pages 8–13.)

Remember

Marketing is often about long-term relationships. The web helps businesses to build these both in b2c and b2b markets.

Identifying new product and market developments

Because of the rapid explosion of the internet and its increasing (if uneven) penetration worldwide, business leaders today make important strategic decisions about the purpose and potential of an online presence. Managers have to take account of industry-wide factors to decide how effective or relevant the company's internet presence can be.

Web technology expands businesses into new products and markets and achieves significant aims and objectives. This can happen in a number of ways.

- **Market penetration** – businesses can increase their market share by offering better customer services or promotional information within the markets they already serve.
- **Market development** – businesses can enter new markets and potentially increase their market reach overseas because of the relatively low cost of advertising.
- **Product development** – a business can develop new information products and these can be digitally delivered over the web.

Remember

Business **strategy** and objectives are attainable by using the internet to enter new markets or develop products in existing markets.

Thinking point

Visit www.easyjet.com. How is the website helping EasyJet achieve its goals?

Using the internet to achieve objectives

When a business makes a strategic decision to create an internet presence, possibly to sell online, management will set objectives for the new channel. These objectives should be specific targets, designed to lead the company towards its overall aims.

Online business objectives could be:

- increase revenue from the internet by 10%
- achieve a top five ranking in market penetration in a particular country
- make cost savings of 10%
- increase customer retention by 20%
- increase sales by 25% to 25–40 year-olds
- improve customer response times to a two-hour limit.

Objectives should therefore be specific, measurable, achievable, realistic and time-related (i.e. SMART). To assist in this, the internet offers a number of methods for businesses to gain accurate measurements about how a website is performing.

Key Term

Marketing strategy The general direction in which marketing decisions take a business. For example, a business may be looking to increase its sales overseas or to target a smaller market segment.

Case study

B&Q Direct: online business objectives

When B&Q decided it was going to open an online sales channel through its website, www.diy.com, B&Q Direct, the subsidiary business managing the project, was given a four-year internet contribution target at the outset. The website had to reach specific levels of revenue.

Easyjet (www.easyjet.com) launched its online booking facility in 1998 with a two-year plan. The online revenue contribution needed to be 30% by 2000.

1. Why is it helpful for businesses such as these to set *specific* targets? ✓
2. What other specific objectives might a business establish for its website? Justify these suggestions. ✓✓

Segmentation and targeting

We saw at the start of the unit that there are markets for all goods and services produced, otherwise businesses would have no reason to produce them. However, markets do not contain individuals or businesses that are all the same. For example, although we say that there is *a* market for cars, cars come in all sorts of sizes, shapes, colours and styles. This reflects the fact that we as consumers have different preferences, different budgets, different tastes and different reasons for buying. I might buy a car because I want something reliable to get me to and from work; someone else might buy a car because they want people to know they are a success in their business.

One of the functions of marketing is to make sense of the different groupings within markets. This process is called segmentation. By segmenting markets, businesses are able to see particular characteristics within them and target products and marketing tactics to suit that segment. The process works like this.

Segment the market by using market research.
Identify customer needs within each segment.

↓

Target chosen **market segments**, using the tactics available from the seven Ps of the marketing mix.

Key Term

Market segment A subgroup within an overall market that has similar characteristics.

Internet-enabled segmentation and targeting

Segmentation and targeting online is undertaken using a number of different variables:

- demographic
- psychographic
- economic
- usage-based.

Case study

WebTrends marketing warehouse

With the latest release of WebTrends enterprise-class data warehouse for relationship marketing and business intelligence, marketers can easily capture visitors' online actions and correlate that with what they know about customers and prospects offline, such as demographic, psychographic and geographic information.

For example, a marketer could combine online behaviour such as how frequently someone visits the site, how recently they have visited, and product interest they exhibited with important offline characteristics such as past offline purchases, age or satisfaction rating, to create meaningful segments to target with relevant on-site offers or e-mail campaigns.

Additionally, a consumer products goods manufacturer could create a targeted list for a new product promotion, by identifying visitors who participated in an offline sweepstakes program who have been to the website three times in the last week and viewed information about the new product, but have not yet downloaded a coupon.

'The ability to understand customers across multiple channels is something marketers have been striving to achieve for years,' said Greg Drew, CEO and president, WebTrends Inc. 'Without this ability, marketers have had a fragmented view of their customers, thereby spending inordinate amounts of time and money aimed at acquiring and re-acquiring customers. Our solution changes all that by linking offline and online behavior together, and providing the facility to easily and instantly act on the insight to drive stronger, more profitable relationships.'

1. In what ways do you think a business will be able to 'target' customers more effectively using this WebTrends product? ✓
2. How useful do you feel that 'targeting' is to a business? Why is it important? ✓✓
3. Analyse the benefits from this kind of marketing intelligence for a business of your own choice. ✓✓

There are some comprehensive sources of web trends and analyses. Three of these are:

- www.clickz.com
- www.nua.ie/surveys
- www.webtrends.com

These online services provide business planners with detailed statistics and analysis of internet trends.

■ Demographic

Demographics are about the make-up of your population. We can study population trends all over the world. Another form of demographics is *internet* demographics and this directly relates to internet marketing. In internet terms, it is useful for businesses planning an online strategy to know how many internet customers there may be.

Potentially, a website gives a business global reach. However, levels of 'internet penetration' vary widely, depending on the proportion of the population within different countries and continents having access to the web. To make a well-informed decision about targeting requires an understanding of internet access and availability in different countries.

A number of services give comprehensive data about internet facts and figures. Nielsen NetRatings, for example, provides statistics on home internet use by country.

▼ Number of active home internet users by country, August–September 2006

Country	August 2006	September 2006	Change (%)	One-month difference
Australia	10,644,788	10,586,123	–0.55	–58,665
Brazil	13,641,174	13,639,042	–0.02	–2,132
France	18,914,885	19,291,466	1.99	376,581
Germany	33,129,089	32,981,612	–0.45	–147,477
Italy	16,544,902	17,015,825	2.85	470,923
Japan	44,520,096	43,799,569	–1.62	–720,527
Spain	11,803,428	12,812,106	8.55	1,008,678
Switzerland	3,807,822	3,757,992	–1.31	–49,830
UK	24,192,280	24,132,491	–0.25	–59,789
US	145,228,368	144,869,198	–0.25	–359,170
Total	**322,426,832**	**322,885,424**	**0.14**	**458,593**

Source: Nielsen NetRatings, 2006

■ Psychographic

This kind of segmentation uses lifestyle and personal characteristics as a way of segmenting a market. It addresses the question 'What are our possible customers like?' Using this basis, an online business can blend its marketing tactics to suit the segment. Psychographic profiles of different internet users are based on detailed research, carried out by marketing services companies. The case study below gives an example of this kind of segmentation.

Case study

Five personalities emerge from broadband users

Broadband users are often characterised as 'one homogenous group of people,' says Josh Crandall, Managing Director of Media-Screen, a strategic market research firm that published 'Netpop Portraits' as part of its Netpop Research series of data.

Broadband has continued at a 60% annual growth rate, reaching one-third of all Americans over age thirteen. Its adoption has created a population of five segments with unique characteristics: content king; social clicker; online insider; fast tracker; and everyday pro.

The 'content king' looks to the web for entertainment. Of this group, 76% play games online and 75% of website visits are for personal reasons. Content kings spend an average 2.5 hours online each weekday.

'Content kings are typically younger in age and really drive growth in entertainment activities online,' says Cate Reigner, Research Director at Media-Screen.

'Social clickers', who include both young and old, use the internet as a means of communication. The younger group uses social networking sites, IM and other messaging tools to socialise. The older group hinges its internet use and communications more on e-mail. Within the group, 78% contribute to internet content or information on a monthly basis. More than half of social clickers' time (57%) is spent on communications. The remainder is spent on news and information (10%) and shopping (8%).

The 'online insider' consumes content across the broader web. According to the report this person sees the internet as 'a rich personal and cultural phenomenon'. Behaviour among online insiders is like that of early adopters: 86% contribute to internet content or information each month, including posting to blogs, community sites and chat rooms. The group spends upwards of US$130 each month on e-commerce.

'This is the group that's going to vet new products and try things,' said Reigner. 'They will vet for other groups and users who come along behind them.'

'Fast trackers' typically use the internet to seek out news and information. Content categories include news, sports and weather. Fast trackers remain loyal to sources with frequent updates and real-time information. 'They are looking at a lot of pages online, consuming a lot of inventory, and are receptive to advertising as well,' says Crandall. '[With them] it's a little bit of an addiction, refreshing their browser window.'

The group reads news online (77%). It also typically looks up maps, directions and public transportation information (66%). Reigner says fast trackers use the internet to research products but typically buy in stores.

The 'everyday pro' is characterised by personal productivity and efficiency, and looks to the internet to fulfil those needs. The group adopts complex tools to simplify life. About 84% use online banking, and 68% purchase from online retailers.

'This group is older in age, and very much focused on the internet as a productivity tool,' says Reigner. 'They like to save money and time, and the internet is a tool for total efficiency.'

Media-Screen conducted an online survey of 4,190 members of the Global Market Insight panel. Respondents were thirteen years of age and older and were offered cash incentives to take the survey. Start rates for the survey were representative of the US internet population based on age and gender.

Source: Adapted from an article by Enid Burns on www.clickz.com, 16 November 2006

1. In what ways do you think that a potential online business might make use of this kind of psychographic profiling? ✓
2. Which profile, if any, would you place yourself in? ✓
3. Give examples of two online businesses that in your view could make valuable use of this psychographic profiling. ✓✓

■ Economic

On a global basis the economic prosperity and conditions within different countries determine the extent to which e-commerce (buying and selling on the internet) is likely to succeed in them. A business considering an online strategy that depends on an increasing volume of sales in, say, Eastern Europe, would do well to acquaint itself with economic data about the area. The Economic Intelligence Unit, available at www.eiu.com, provides detailed data.

Practice point

Produce a report for a business considering expanding into new markets in China and the Far East. In the report, summarise the main economic and demographic factors that you would suggest the business takes into account.

■ Usage-based

This kind of data informs business leaders about how the internet is being used in different parts of the world. The service provided by Clickz (www.clickz.com) offers detailed insights into traffic patterns on the web, as the example on page 12 illustrates.

▼ European internet usage by individuals, first quarter 2006 (%)

	Use the internet at least once a week					
	Total	Men	Women	16–24 years old	25–54 years old	55–74 years old
EU25	47	51	43	73	54	20
Belgium	58	62	54	82	67	27
Czech Republic	N/A	N/A	N/A	N/A	N/A	N/A
Denmark	78	80	76	94	86	56
Germany	59	65	54	83	69	30
Estonia	56	57	56	90	64	U
Greece	23	27	18	47	27	4
Spain	39	44	35	70	45	10
France	39	42	37	71	47	U
Ireland	44	45	42	59	48	17
Italy	31	36	26	55	37	9
Cyprus	29	32	27	55	31	7
Latvia	46	47	45	86	50	12
Lithuania	38	38	37	77	39	7
Luxembourg	65	76	55	89	71	37
Hungary	42	43	40	74	47	14
Malta	N/A	N/A	N/A	N/A	N/A	N/A
Netherlands	76	82	71	96	86	46
Austria	55	61	49	80	63	24
Poland	34	36	32	71	35	7
Portugal	31	35	28	68	34	6
Slovenia	47	51	42	81	54	12
Slovakia	43	47	39	72	47	9
Finland	71	72	70	94	82	38
Sweden	80	84	76	94	89	56
UK	57	63	51	72	66	33
Iceland	84	86	82	96	90	59
Norway	77	80	73	97	84	48

Notes:

1. EU25 excludes member states for which data is not available.
2. Individuals used the internet at least once a week.
3. N/A – data is not available.
4. U – data is not reliable.

Thinking point

How might a business looking to sell cosmetics and make-up accessories online find the table on page 12 useful?

Remember

Marketing techniques involve breaking a market up into smaller groups with shared characteristics. From this, marketers '**target**' these segments by blending the elements of the marketing mix.

Key Term

Target market The segment that marketers aim for when they create their marketing message.

Business interactions

Buying and selling involves interactions between different kinds of customers and suppliers. Business-to-business transactions are known as b2b. These are less frequent but of much higher value. Businesses purchase raw materials and buy services such as ICT from other businesses.

Private consumers are individuals like us. We need bread, carpets, pens, clothes and so on. We buy these things from businesses; hence they are referred to as business-to-consumer (b2c) transactions.

On the internet, consumers can buy from consumers. The most obvious example of this occurs on eBay. These consumer-to-consumer (c2c) transactions use bidding on an auction basis.

Disintermediation

In the physical business world a product originates with the raw materials from which it is made. Timber, for example, can be used to make garden furniture.

The timber is transported from its original source to manufacturers who produce the garden items. From the manufacturers the items may go to a distribution centre and from there to a garden centre, close to where customers live – the third 'P' marketing tactic of 'place' (see page 4). This describes a 'supply chain', which is the way that goods get to where you buy them.

The businesses that work between the original manufacturer of the furniture and the customer are known as 'intermediaries'. Their job is to move, store or package the items to be sold.

With the internet, there is often no need for intermediaries, as many products can be shipped directly to your home. This is '**disintermediation**'. One of the most well-known examples of an online business doing this is Dell Computers (see page 15).

Remember

The internet allows businesses to sell directly to consumers without using an intermediary. This saves both time and cash.

Direct market communication

A **direct** approach to **marketing** communications is now very common. Producers can directly mail potential buyers either online or through the post. Leaflets, booklets, catalogues and flyers are sent out daily, directly offering goods from manufacturers to end users.

Key Terms

Disintermediation The removal of intermediaries ('middle men') from the process of getting products to where consumers can buy them.

Direct marketing Sending messages directly to potential customers, e.g. by e-mail, without using indirect promotions such as advertising.

Internet marketing

Internet marketing can help businesses to deliver their strategy. Unlike traditional marketing communications media – TV, radio and printed material – which all *push* mass marketing messages out from a business, in one direction, the web is a pull medium. This means individual customers choose to visit a website when they feel like doing so. So, on the web, a marketing message is always delivered on a *one-to-one* basis.

Internet marketers use a number of techniques to take advantage of this. They re-mix the seven Ps described on pages 4–6 to offer different tactics.

Remember

The internet differs from traditional marketing communications because it is not a push medium, one to many; it depends on individual customers selecting a website and interacting one to one. Therefore, communication techniques are different and have to stimulate interest.

Online promotion

Promotion on the internet spreads widely. It relies on a combination of methods.

- **Search engine optimisation** – register with the big search engines such as Google, Yahoo! and make sure that the website contains the correct 'keywords' so the site appears high up in the relevant searches that people do.
- **Banner advertisements** – advertisements for products or services that appear at the head of a web page, often animated.
- **Affiliate programmes** – placing linked advertisements for products or services on another business' site.
- **E-mail promotion** – an easy but potentially damaging method of promoting a business. 'Permission-based' mailing works best.

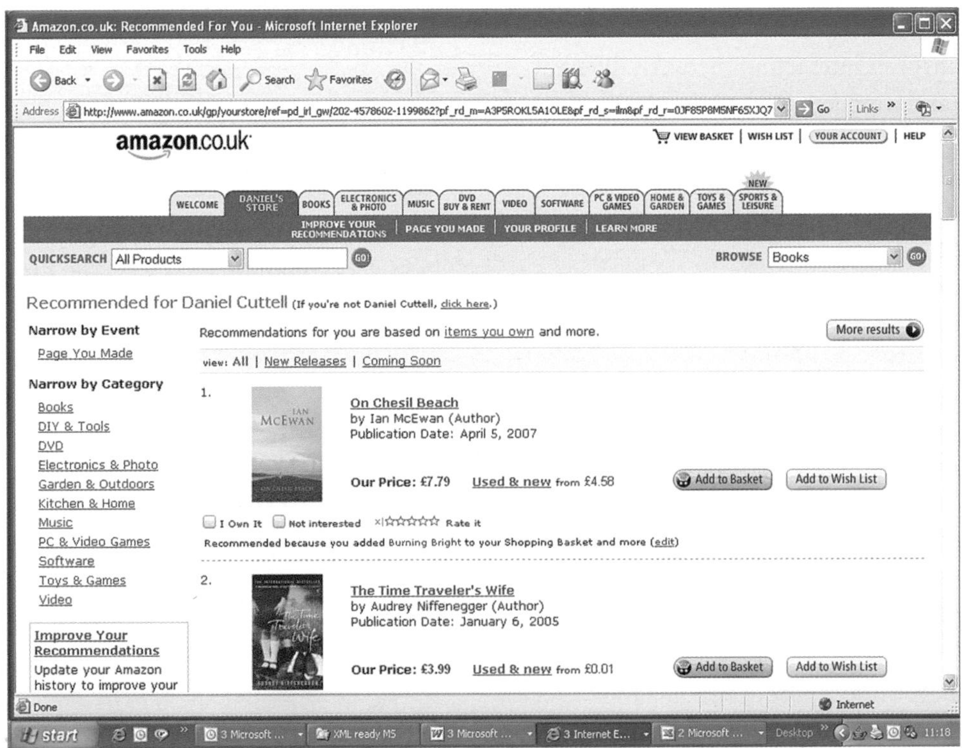

▲ A personalised web page

Individualising market attention

In b2c markets in particular, because a web visit is always an individual choice, a one-to-one 'relationship' is possible. Web technology means online businesses can personalise their response to suit an individual.

Amazon is the best-known online business for **personalisation**. The screen shot on page 14 shows a personalised Amazon page. Based on information about previous visits to the website, the next page makes individual recommendations, promoting other products that the individual customer may be interested in.

■ Mass customisation

The internet offers the opportunity for businesses to let customers tailor products to suit their individual tastes. In other words, we can 'customise' products according to our own preferences. An example is Dell computers, an online computer retailing service that allows customers to select the various components to build their own PC configuration. As this service is available from some businesses to *all* of their online customers, it is known as 'mass **customisation**'.

Practice point

Visit the following websites and write a report about 'customisation of internet products'.

- http://presentpicker.com/ppp/home.html
- www.ic3d.com/index.html
- www.nike.com/index.jhtml

In what ways, if any, do you feel that customers benefit from this?

Key Terms

Personalisation Adjusting the web page that is returned to a visitor so that it offers information that is personal, based on their previous visits to the website.

Customisation Opportunity for the customer to manipulate and change the online presentation of a product.

▲ Customising a Dell PC

Askham Bryan College LIBRARY BOOK

© 2007 Dell Corporation Limited. Dell and the Dell logo are either registered or unregistered trademarks of Dell Inc. Dell disclaims any proprietary interest in the marks and names of others. Dell Corporation, c/o Box 69 Milbanke House, Western Road, Bracknell, Berkshire. RG12 1RD

Increased information and product impact

There are obvious limitations in offering physical products for sale online. Depending on the product customers may prefer to examine the look and feel of products, the web allows businesses to compensate for this by *extending* products with added information and impact.

Extending online products is done by:

- extensive product endorsements from previous customers
- lists of customers
- warranties
- money-back offers
- additional customer back-up services
- 'cross-selling' of related or complementary products
- offering expert advice.

These facilities help to give customers confidence in an online purchase.

Thinking point

Explore the web and try to find examples of at least three sites where products are being sold using some of the above techniques. How effective do you feel these are? Would you recommend this to a business considering an online channel?

Websites usually offer detailed product information – including images and customer interaction – allowing customers to compare features, prices and costs (see, for example, www.diy.com).

Reaching wider markets

A glance at the table showing European internet usage (see page 12) is enough to show that by using the internet a business can instantly achieve a far wider and more distant geographic reach than by using other means of marketing.

Case study

Chinasearch

Chinasearch is a crockery and cutlery replacement service with an existing customer base of 75,000. The business has a 1 million square foot warehouse and is able to replace thousands of items of chipped or broken crockery items. The business has been relatively late in adopting an online strategy and has only now developed plans for an e-commerce site.

As Trevor Chappel, the company's general manager, says, part of this new online strategy will include a dedicated Japanese website to meet that niche market. 'We are looking to develop geographic markets,' says Chappel.

1. In what ways will 'develop[ing] geographic markets' help Chinasearch? ✓
2. What problems, if any, can you foresee from this strategy? ✓✓

Mix between online and offline activities

Much of the continued evolution of e-commerce has built on existing businesses that have established their reputations and customer bases in the physical world. Long-established names like Next, B&Q, Topshop and Tesco now combine offline and online sales channels. These are known as **'clicks and mortar' businesses**, as they have both physical buildings ('bricks and mortar') and an internet presence ('clicks' of the mouse). Many of these businesses also combine their offline and online promotional activities.

Key Term

'Clicks and mortar' business A business that has physical buildings and an internet presence.

Outcome activity 12.1

Describe the role internet marketing has in a modern marketing context using selected organisations as examples. 

Grading tips

Pass P1

Select at least two different types of businesses using an online channel to sell physical products or services. Identify and describe the ways the different businesses use the web to support their products or services. How do customers gain from the sites?

12.2 Benefits of internet marketing to customers

Customer benefits

The increasing availability of so many products and services on the internet has introduced many opportunities and benefits for customers.

Comparing and selecting providers

The internet allows a great deal of **price transparency** for consumers. This gives them an advantage because they can compare prices easily between many potential suppliers. Prices are stored digitally in databases, and software (robot shoppers, shopping bots or price search engines) is used to search for the best prices available on the web (see www.kelkoo.com). Some sites such as the BBC's internet shopping service at www.beeb.com provide instant price comparisons, and at www.letsbuyit.com customers can join together in order to lower prices. This has the effect of giving online customers much greater bargaining power.

Key Term

Price transparency When everyone who visits your website can see all of your prices.

Instead of prices being set by businesses and passively received by the market, the internet is capable of turning this situation upside down. Priceline.co.uk (www.priceline.co.uk), for instance, allows consumers to set their own prices, and at several online auction sites such as eBay (www.ebay.co.uk), consumers are able to place bids for consumer products after viewing the minimum (reserve) price acceptable to the seller.

Comprehensive and up-to-date product information

In both b2c and b2b markets, the internet offers businesses the opportunity to provide total product information. Private customers shopping online do not have the chance to touch, smell, taste or sample products; businesses looking for industrial components or business services might not have the chance to make contacts with a range of representatives. These drawbacks are bypassed because of the web's power to store and communicate information. RS Components' e-commerce site, for example, offers detailed information for business buyers of electrical parts.

For prospective buyers, the essential product details are:

- price
- descriptions of features and specifications
- colour swatches
- images
- drawings
- promotional deals.

From a well-designed website, customers can fully check specifications and quickly make e-mail contact with staff. The whole transaction process is quickly completed. In the case of RS Components, the site even offers a procurement software tool for use by a b2b purchasing organisation.

B&Q Direct offers a similar service in the DIY retail market. The diy.com website allows product comparisons across a range of DIY products.

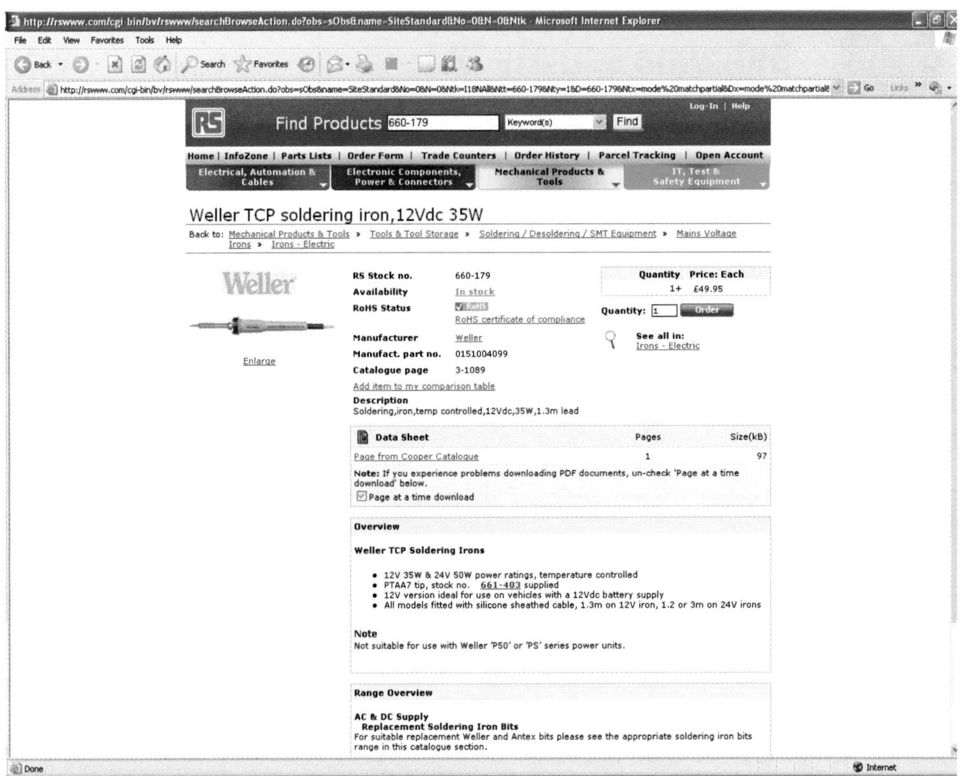

▲ Product information in a b2b context

▲ Product information in a b2c context

Case study

The importance of online product information

E-commerce sites lose as many as 67% of consumers; many abandon their shopping carts due to a lack of product information. The 'Online Merchandising Survey' research brief, released by Allurent, details consumers' perceptions of online shopping.

Increased interactive elements and innovative ways to display and purchase products would encourage internet purchasing for 83% of survey respondents.

Enhanced features that would also help could include mix and match outfits, where shoppers can put together an entire outfit on screen (44%); 360-degree product views (78%); side-by-side comparisons (63%) and personalisation or customisable products (53%).

Source: Adapted from an article by Enid Burns on www.clickz.com, 'Shoppers Seek Web 2.0 E-Commerce', October 2006

1. Consider as many business contexts as you can in which the factors mentioned in the above article could be usefully employed. ✓
2. Fully justify your recommendations and explain how customers might benefit. ✓✓

Case study

Dynamic pricing: PC vendors

PC vendors are planning to introduce dynamic pricing to sell more stock online. IBM, Compaq, Dell and Hewlett-Packard are among those 'actively investigating' dynamic pricing models, according to a report by InfoWorld.

Prices change as customers order multiple items on certain offers. Dell is considering extending the method to its whole product line by the end of the year.

All this means that system prices could change constantly, and catching a bargain would be down to surfers' lucky timing. Last year Amazon.com annoyed surfers when it was discovered to be using a dynamic pricing system that it had failed to publicise – the e-tailer used the system to make regular customers pay more than first-time users of the site.

1. In what ways might 'dynamic pricing' make buying online more appealing? ✓
2. Amazon annoyed regular customers with its use of dynamic pricing. Why? ✓

Dynamic pricing

Customers can gain excellent cost savings by making use of the internet's ability to alter pricing in real time to reflect market conditions. The airline industry and hotels are two examples where customers can save due to '**dynamic pricing**' (or 'fluid pricing'). When few seats are sold, availability is good and prices are set very low. As flight time draws nearer, and fewer seats are available, prices increase, depending on seat availability. The website and supporting technology can respond instantly to market changes. The price is constantly on the move.

Key Term

Dynamic pricing The facility of the web that enables online businesses to adjust prices quickly, according to market conditions.

Online auctions can make use of the same principle. Prices are open and available for all potential bidders to see. As bidding progresses, asking prices move according to the interest that is shown.

Responsive transactions

The internet offers customers the chance to conduct immediate transactions and immediately have the satisfaction of knowing that they have made a booking. Booking an airline ticket through an online facility such as the one offered by www.easyjet.com offers an easy process and great convenience.

Customer service

Marketers must constantly look at customer needs and wants. Customer service is of paramount importance if a business is to remain competitive in today's business world. Products and services may be very similar; it is customer service that can clinch the business, whether in b2c or b2b markets.

The internet offers businesses a number of ways of delivering improved customer services. Websites are available 24 hours a day. They almost all include links to FAQ (frequently asked questions) pages, 'About us' and 'Contact us' links. These all help to give online customers a better level of service.

Chat

The internet offers people the chance to participate in real-time online chat groups. This is especially useful to consumers who can add their opinions and read those of other consumers (c2c).

Outcome activity 12.2

You are working for a business consultant who has been asked to advise a client about e-marketing. Based on your research and investigations so far, respond to the following tasks in a report to your line manager.

1. Describe the principal benefits to consumers of internet marketing. 
2. Analyse the benefits of internet marketing for consumers. m1
3. Evaluate the effectiveness of internet marketing in meeting customer needs for a selected business. d1

Digital complaints

Online complaints services exist that can help customers to lodge a complaint about an online product or service. Consumers benefit because they can add their voice to those of others who have complained. This gives a collective view. A fee is paid to the complaints service company, which then contacts the business concerned and explains customer concerns.

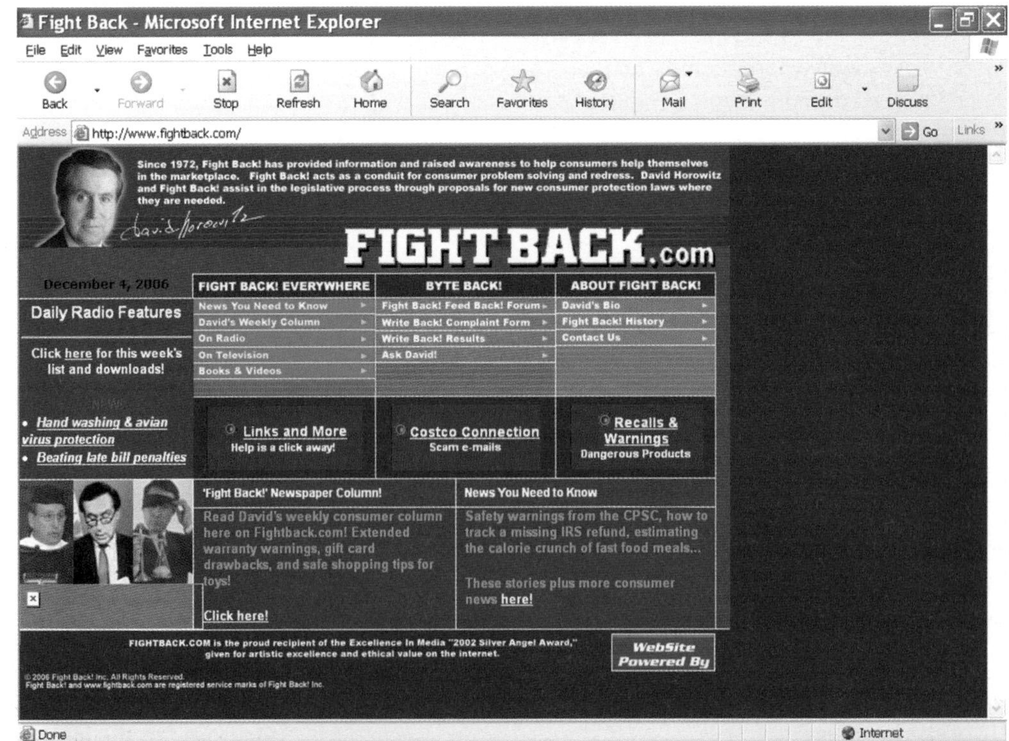

Online complaints service ▶

Grading tips

Pass 

Select at least three online retailing sites such as www.diy.com, www.topshop.co.uk and www.tesco.com. Using the main headings in the previous section, describe the features of these websites that offer benefits to their customers.

Merit

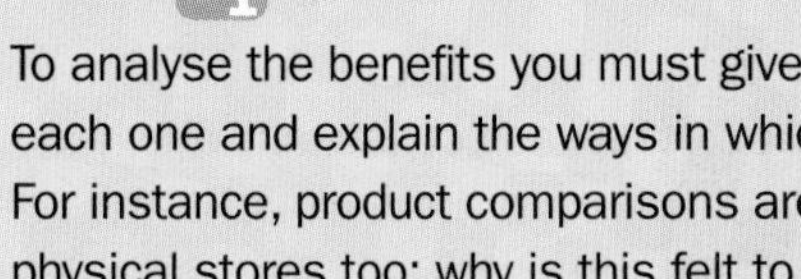

To analyse the benefits you must give full details about each one and explain the ways in which customers gain. For instance, product comparisons are available in the physical stores too; why is this felt to be 'beneficial' just because it is online? You might say that the features are available at the click of a button without any searching around, asking staff, etc. How have internet marketing activities built on conventional offline marketing activities? How is the mix exploited differently?

Distinction 

To evaluate means, in this case, you must review the information you have presented about one online business. This is a challenge because you must outline your own views based on your judgements about something. For example, you may decide to consider whether customers really benefit from having the chance to chat about products online. Your view may be that this is a gimmick. However, you must be able to fully justify that view. On the other hand, you may discover a 'chat' or 'discussion' service about a product that you think is very useful (e.g. Apple iPod discussion forum at www.apple.com). You must back up your views with evidence.

12.3 Opportunities offered to businesses by internet marketing

The internet presents businesses with great opportunities to improve their marketing effort and perhaps gain competitive advantage. However, the extent to which a business takes up these opportunities depends on some important considerations.

- Does the firm deal in appropriate products for online sales?
- Does the firm have the internal IT resources and skills to monitor and maintain a transactional website?
- Does the business leadership have a strategic plan for e-commerce?
- Are there competitive forces within the industry that are driving firms to e-commerce?
- What are the financial and technological capabilities of the business?

Assuming a business has considered these things and has a clear strategy for its online channel, then the marketing benefits available from the internet can be built into practice. Internet marketing can benefit a business in three main areas:

- communications
- product development
- business efficiency.

Opportunities for communications

Trading online gives businesses in both b2c and b2b markets the chance to develop new communications practices. Web technology allows a business to present products and services in detail, together with substantial supporting information. Once this is done, a well-planned website can be used to capture data about customers; their names, addresses, postcodes, telephone numbers and e-mail addresses. The business is able to build up a database of customers. From this point – as we saw earlier – the web page offered to return customers can be customised to give them an individual web page personalised according to their previous purchase history (e.g. www.amazon.co.uk.)

▲ Tesco: listening to customers

Once a business is able to make contact with a customer, e-mail can be used to send further product details or news about the business. Through its registration process and 'Clubcard' points system, Tesco.com tries to build a relationship with its online customers and is able to give them product offers and recommendations based on their buying history.

In b2b markets there is also a need for firms to use effective communications in order to build relationships. In industrial markets for example, b2b exchanges can be vital to the prosperity of a firm. Think of almost any business and there will be suppliers that are crucial. A printing business must have paper, ink, machine components, and soon; a fish and chip shop must have fish! It follows that communications between these partner businesses need to be good.

B2b relationships in general improve by establishing good online relationships. Businesses can co-operate better over a long term. Transactions can be quicker and the records of them more reliable and accurate. The whole question of dealing with customers efficiently can be handled online with the use of Customer Relationship Management (CRM) software. This is software that can automate sales responses, respond to customer queries, record visits, and manage e-mails, direct mails and campaigns.

Customer service is now a central element of a business' competitive drive. Prime considerations when choosing firms to work with are product suitability, reliability and quality; after these are established it is the quality of service that makes the difference.

Remember

It is more expensive to attract new customers than keep existing ones. Research quoted by Dave Chaffey in *Internet Marketing* (Prentice Hall, 2003) shows that by retaining just 5% more customers, online firms can boost profits by 25%–95%.

Communicating for promotion

A website is *itself* a promotional tool. Online businesses seek to create a look and feel that appeals to the self-image of their target market. Often, this is a hidden message to do with lifestyle.

New product launches are possible online. Software downloads can be made available on a trial basis and promoted widely online. The capacity of the web to carry lots of detailed product information makes it an ideal place to attract interest in new product developments. Businesses can use multimedia presentations, interactivity, movies as well as written information. In 2005 Subaru launched a new car in the USA using an interactive online tool.

Case study

Subaru's interactive product launch: the Impreza

Subaru needed to build awareness of its new luxury vehicle. The company hired an agency to develop an online campaign. Site visitors were encouraged to 'opt-in' to receive information by e-mail as soon as it became available.

Subaru then implemented a three-phase launch of the product online. There was a slow release of images of the new car. This occurred in the autumn. Then there was a staged reveal phase, when the official site was launched in the January.

Subaru's www.subaru-impreza.co.uk site featured video that was specifically shot for the site to capture the essence of the range of cars including its rally heritage.

Subaru intended to create a 'rich' experience for potential customers. Pictures and features were added to the site over time to stimulate interest and make people want to visit their local dealerships.

1. Why do you think Subaru chose to use an opt-in tactic for receiving e-mails about the new car? What is meant by 'opt-in' e-mailing? ✓
2. Can you think of another product type that could suitably use the internet for a launch? How might this help its launch? ✓✓
3. Why might a consumer wish to get 'interactive' with a product launch? Does it matter? Justify your response. ✓✓✓

Opportunities for product development

Due to the fact that customers on the internet initiate contact, the business immediately has – for a limited time at least – 100% of the customer's attention. To be successful, the website must present information that is both interesting and relevant to a visitor. Traditional marketing communications go out to everyone; internet marketing on the other hand can suit *individual* visitors, whether they are consumers buying leisure items or tradespeople on the lookout for tools or equipment.

Two online businesses that have made a special e-commerce effort and been recognised for doing so are RS Components (www.rswww.com) and Screwfix (www.screwfix.com). In both these cases, the buyer can register with the site and, thereafter, the site will record purchases and offer a customised set of menus to suit the next visit.

Key Term

Product development Taking an existing product and adding new features so that it sells more or appeals to different groups.

Thinking point

Investigate the services offered to trade customers from www.screwfix.com. In what ways does this site represent evidence of an online business taking full advantage of the internet's marketing opportunity? Justify your response with reference to the features of the website.

Identifying product development opportunities

The internet may be used by online businesses to gather detailed information about customer perceptions of an online product or service. Alternatively, it can be used to gather marketing research information. As an example of the former, Egg (www.egg.com) takes care to ask customers about their feelings about the online service. The business attitude is 'How can we improve things?'

Other online businesses have found that the internet has generated new business opportunities. RS Components was a traditional b2b wholesaler of electrical parts. The business discovered that 10% of its online sales were to private consumers. The internet allows businesses to target new subsets of larger markets that it may not have considered before.

The internet enables companies to offer digital delivery of new, information-based products. They can offer newsletters or services to meet new demands for web-based applications. Sunderland-based Leighton Group, for example, has developed an online collaborative service called 4Projects.

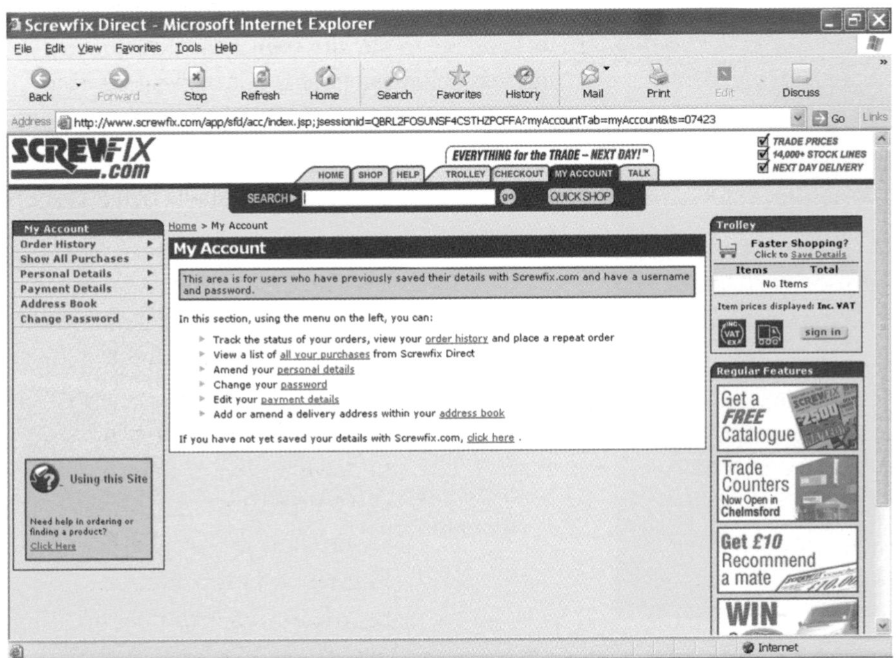

◀ A Screwfix customised buyer menu

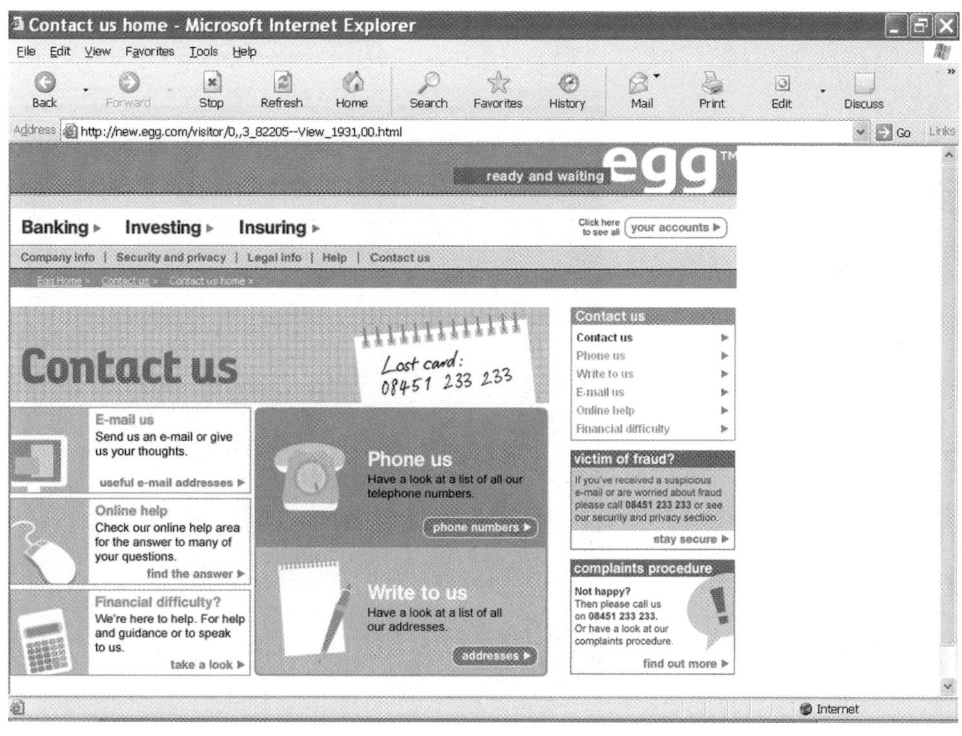

▲ Developing products using customer response

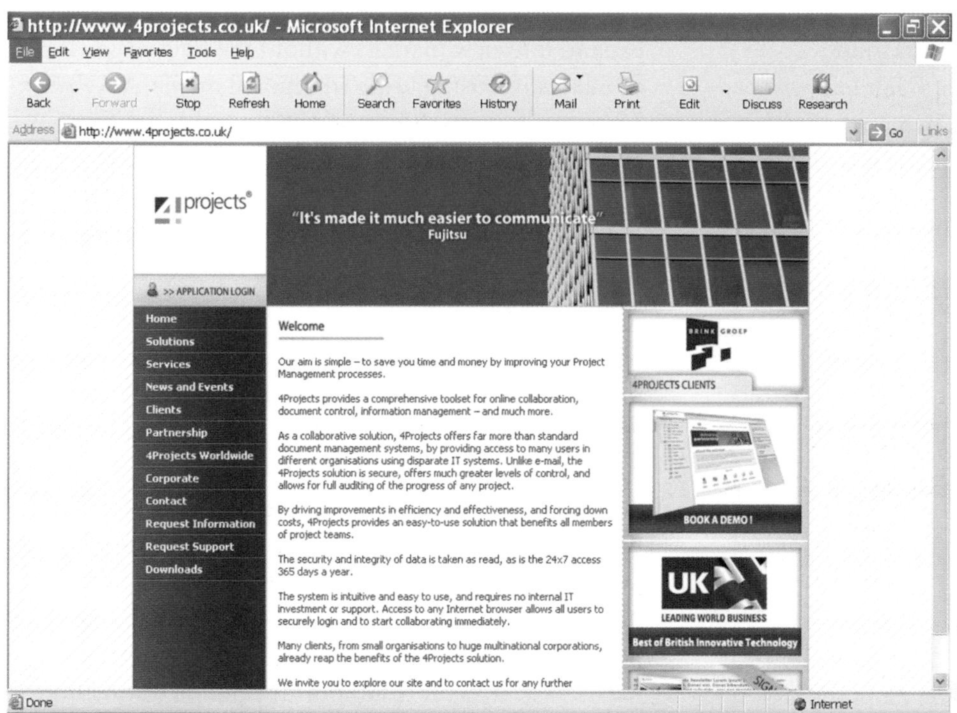

▲ 4Projects: a new online product

Immediate sales of products

Another advantage of the internet is that online services – particularly those that are information-based – are immediately accessible. People can use online insurance or banking services and gain peace of mind within minutes.

Substituting online products

The internet is a multimedia channel that is capable of delivering digital content in the form of downloads to a home device. It is now commonplace to download music, films, radio and TV programmes. These services are an easy alternative to visiting offline providers and, in the case of radio services or TV broadcasts, offer great flexibility.

Easy downloads online – Channel 4 on Demand is available online at channel4.com/4od

Podcasts

A podcast is a small multimedia file that can be downloaded using the internet. Podcasts are most commonly used by newspapers such the *Daily Telegraph* or by broadcasters such as the BBC, who can make podcasts of news summaries. In theory, any business can make use of podcasting to deliver marketing information.

Case study

Podcast for iPod

'Since 1 February we have been publishing a new, improved version of the *Daily Telegraph* podcast for iPods. The content is the same but we now use chapter markers. This means that you are able to skip around inside the podcast to your favourite bits. The new version works on all new iPod models, but if it doesn't work on yours you will need to resubscribe using the MP3 player link.'

Source: Daily Telegraph, 28 November 2006

1. In what ways might a business make use of podcasting as a marketing opportunity? ✓

Market development

The internet gives online businesses the chance to expand into new markets without the huge expense of mass advertising using traditional media. A website creates instant reach into wide geographic areas and is capable of generating new export sales. This opportunity must be balanced against the costs and the red tape involved in exporting to different parts of the world.

It is easy to assume that as the internet is a global phenomenon a business can launch its website and immediately generate immense sales all over the world. However, there are risks involved in an online strategy. Amazon.com did not achieve profitability for a long time, despite the fact that the business achieved multi-billion dollars' worth of sales. Online goods and services have to be delivered to consumers. Depending on the nature of the product, delivery involves shipping, packaging and acknowledgement, and the company needs back-up staff to support the online transaction. In some cases, however, the opportunities offered by the internet have transformed businesses. The cases of Save and Drive and the Card Corporation outlined on page 27 illustrate this.

Case study

Re-focusing a business

Save and Drive (www.saveanddrive.co.uk) is a 'clicks and mortar' motor accessories supplier based in the City of Sunderland, in north-east England. The business began in 1977 as a motorist discount centre (MDC), selling car accessories. In those days there was a strong market for car parts and accessories.

By the 1990s the market for car parts was in decline. Cars had become much more reliable. Design improvements meant that many replaceable components were obsolete. Engines had evolved into 'black boxes' that were computer managed. Modules could simply be unplugged and replaced. We had evolved into the era of the 'throw-away car'. People had stopped coming into the MDCs for do-it-yourself car maintenance and repair.

Save and Drive had to re-focus its business or close down. Proprietors Dave and Martin Robson decided to set up a website that promoted their full range of accessories. They found, for instance, that there was a market for roof boxes and that these could be marketed online. Indeed, the whole range of accessories could be offered online.

Today Save and Drive uses a promotional and e-commerce website. People can purchase online in a secure payments system. All of the information a customer needs is available from the site. If not, staff are available to give advice and personal assistance.

1. Describe how Save and Drive have used the internet opportunities available. Do you think that new skills would have been needed by the business? ✓
2. Explain why the owners of Save and Drive re-focused their business online. In what ways do you think the business will have benefited? What problems might they have had? ✓✓
3. How effective do you think that Save and Drive have been in using internet marketing? What evidence do you have for your response? ✓✓✓

Case study

Card Corporation

Card Corporation (www.cardcorp.co.uk) was founded in 1988 by Ivor Jacobs. The business set out to plug a market gap by producing short-run print items such as business stationery. These days the business is making extensive use of internet technology.

Card Corporation has very few direct competitors and, with sales snowballing, turnover is increasing at an annual rate of 80–90%. Its pioneering role in the industry has also allowed Card Corporation to grow through word of mouth, rather than through extensive marketing campaigns. 'People tell other people about our site because they've had such a good experience from it,' says Ivor. 'Other people's take-up of faster bandwidths and general misunderstanding of what technology is all about is a barrier.'

As an early adopter of an e-business strategy, Card Corporation's response is to help move its trading partners forward as well. It does this by building into its system simple but powerful features that will provide demonstrable benefits to clients. For example, the company has built in sufficient flexibility that it can develop new offerings in response to client requests, and has also set up an automated online approval tool. This adaptability helps clients to see the benefits of technology and encourages them to e-enable their own businesses.

1. Investigate Card Corporation through its website at www.cardcorp.co.uk. Produce a report outlining and evaluating the business' use of the internet. How does the business benefit from the internet? ✓✓✓

Lower entry costs for small businesses

The internet gives smaller businesses a relatively low-cost strategy for competing on the same online terms as much larger corporations. This is known as 'equality of internet presence' and refers to the fact that to internet surfers, all businesses can appear to be operating on the same scale.

'Virtual' services

Digital media are able to break down the barriers that naturally occur in the physical world. This is why it is common to speak of a 'virtual' world and a physical world.

We spend most of our lives in the physical world, in which we are bound by physical realities such as distance. In the virtual world, digital media can create a realistic impression of these physical realities, enabling the user to experience them without moving from their seat. This allows estate agents, for example, the opportunity to offer buyers 'virtual tours' of properties. Computer-generated images of rooms are uploaded onto the site. A prospective buyer can then select areas of the property and 'walk through' the rooms at the click of the mouse button.

24-hour service online

Not only do digital media break down physical constraints, but they also eliminate time constraints. A website is available 24 hours a day, 7 days a week. For service businesses this offers tremendous advantages, as clients with internet access can use the service any time, anywhere. Online services where this applies include:

- banking
- insurance
- education
- retail.

'Bricks and clicks'

Internet marketing is a strategic tactic that is dependent on the willingness and capacity of a firm to take advantage of the facilities that are potentially available from the web. Not all firms are ready for full participation on the internet. They can participate at one of various levels.

In their book *Internet Marketing* (Prentice Hall, 2003), Chaffey, Mayer, Johnston and Ellis-Chadwick, suggest a hierarchy of participation levels:

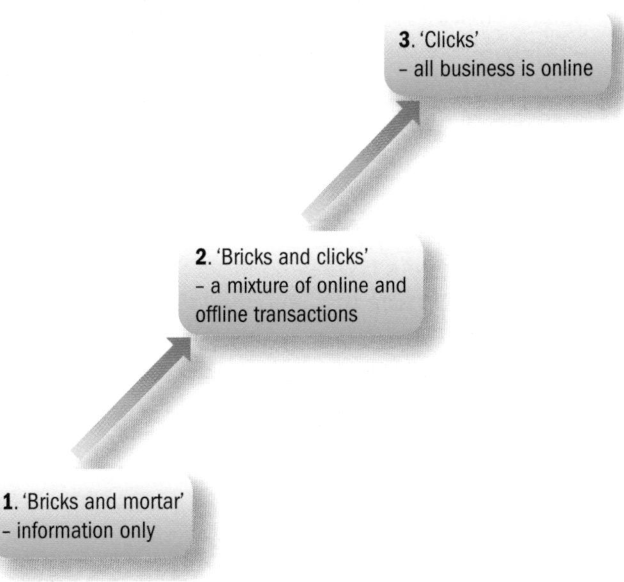

▲ Hierarchy of internet participation levels

The first level of internet activity consists of businesses that offer information only from their website. They do not offer sales of any kind and the site serves as a promotional tool only – for example, Bells Fish and Chips (www.bellsfishandchips.co.uk). The 'bricks and clicks' level consists of businesses that use both an online and an offline sales channel. This has been a growing category in recent years; well established names like Next, Topshop, Tesco and B&Q fall into the 'bricks and clicks' grouping. Finally, there are the so-called 'clicks'. These businesses, such as the insurance business elephant.co.uk, only trade online and have no physical sales operations at all. (It is worth noting that even Amazon uses some physical warehousing and distribution outlets.)

◀ Sainsbury's – a 'bricks and clicks' business

Market diversification

The internet's capacity to help offer services such as those mentioned earlier have allowed big retailers like Tesco to operate in new markets. In other words, they have been able to diversify by offering new online services.

Key Term

Market diversification Expanding a business by offering new products and services.

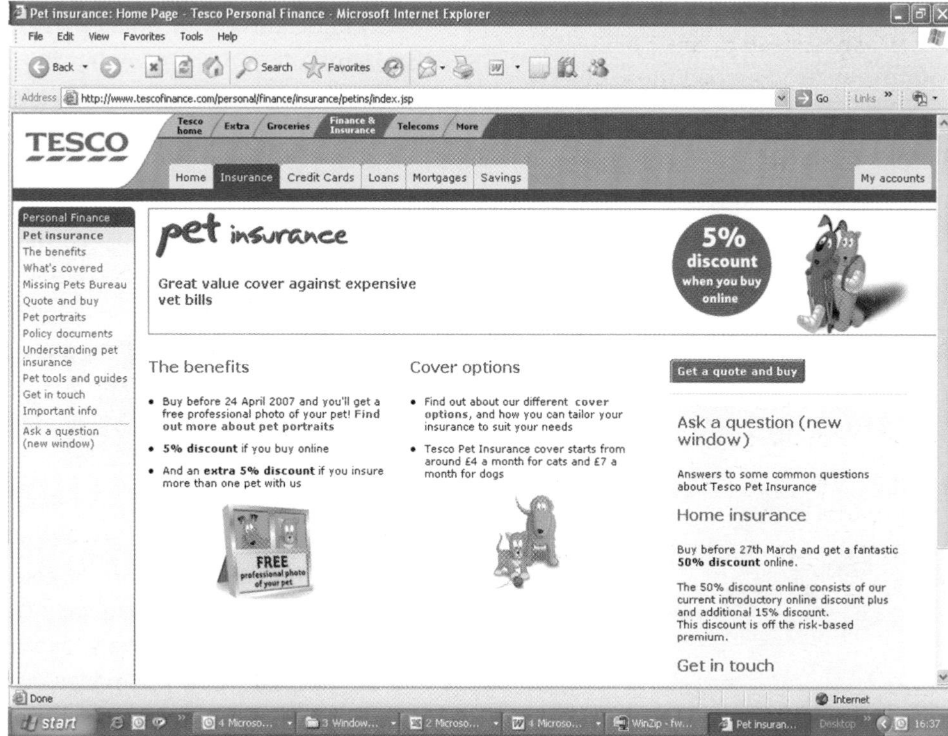

▲ Tesco offers pet insurance online

Opportunities for business efficiency

The increasing availability of the web gives businesses of all kinds the opportunity to speed up their interactions with both suppliers and customers. This can lead to a number of efficiencies.

Supply chain efficiencies

In b2b markets a business is often a link in a 'supply chain'. Such a business will be *both* a buyer and a seller, buying products *from* other businesses and selling *to* others, or private consumers.

A company that manufactures replica strips of football teams, for example, has to buy (or 'procure') the materials it uses before it can sell finished garments to the retail outlets. The Ford Motor Company uses in excess of 10,000 components for each car it produces. Outside firms manufacture individual car components, and they too use other components from other companies. Each company is a link in the supply chain.

For businesses working within supply chains, creating smoother, faster ways of dealing with the firms you regularly buy from – or sell to – can substantially save on costs and get your products to market more quickly.

Many people across an organisation are engaged in supply-chain activities. This involves delivering sales or services to customers, shipping products, negotiating with suppliers and trading partners, managing inventories, tracking orders or other critical tasks. The internet offers businesses a chance to manage the supply chain, speed up supplies and integrate businesses along the chain.

The case study on page 31 is about the Irish firm Kingspan. It is particularly related to how people can work together in supply by using the internet.

The Kingspan case shows how the internet can be used to enable all firms within a supply chain to share and communicate relevant information. Kingspan encourages its customers to use the web to specify their requirements clearly. This improves Kingspan's ability to give customers exactly what they need.

If Kingspan becomes aware of technical changes required in cladding or insulation, this information is made available where it is needed. In this way, an integrated response by the different participating firms is made possible. Important external factors such as local regulatory or economic changes that might affect demand (such as unemployment) can be identified, then *shared* and acted on.

The internet offers an ideal electronic link between organisations and it has the potential to eliminate distortions in information about market conditions that is crucial to proper business operation.

Participating as a *connected* business within the supply chain therefore offers businesses a real opportunity to be more informed, efficient and competitive.

One important way in which shared information can be useful is in *product planning*. Businesses need to make forecasts for buying (procurement) and replacing stocks, or for deciding whether stocks need replacing at all. They may need to make plans for increased (or reduced) production. Should *new* products be introduced to the market, or existing ones developed?

Remember

A supply chain moves goods along from business to business, eventually to the end consumer. The internet helps to manage and co-ordinate this and brings businesses closer together.

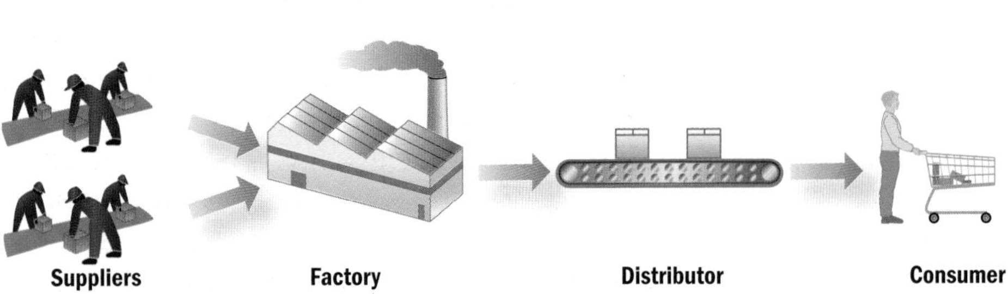

▲ Typical supply chain

Case study

Kingspan

Kingspan Insulated Roof and Wall Systems are part of the Kingspan Group PLC. They are market leaders in the manufacture of superior quality insulated roof and wall cladding systems for the building industry, and they are based in County Cavan, Ireland.

In 1998 Kingspan appointed a company called Cadapters to develop and launch the www.kingspanpanels.com website – a static site, simply designed to offer company and product information to the industry.

Market information

The market for roof and wall insulation systems works like this:

Building Owner/Investor

↓

Architects/Designers

↓

Consulting Engineers/Quantity Surveyors

↓

Main Contractors

Kingspan wanted to create an online ordering system that allowed for fast, accurate order processing. Roofing and cladding contractors, architects or anybody else considering Kingspan products needed to be made to feel that products could easily be researched and specified, and prices clarified, via the website. Added to this would be helpful detailed graphical images of panels and a range of complementary products.

The Kingspan online ordering system has dramatically reduced errors in order processing. The system highlights mistaken combinations in an order and automatically suggests corrections – impossible in a paper-based system. This helps to save time and make the supply of Kingspan products much more efficient.

While 45 out of 47 structural steel contractors in Ireland use the Kingspan ordering system, in the roofing and cladding sector, things have developed more slowly. This sector seems to be less IT literate, or confident. Kingspan therefore needed to be able to identify a customer's member of staff who could deal with the information about its products and use its system. IT literacy, combined with Kingspan product understanding, was important if the online system was to work properly.

Kingspan has been at the forefront in innovation using Internet technologies and is influencing the roofing/cladding market. It plans to develop further an entirely online cladding solutions package to meet the different needs of each customer in the market.

Source: developed with the permission of Tom Prendergast, Kingspan

1. Describe the ways in which the supply of Kingspan products has been made more efficient by use of the internet. ✓
2. In what ways do you think that Kingspan has used the internet as a marketing opportunity? ✓✓
3. Evaluate the Kingspan online experience from the point of view of customers. Do you feel they can gain real benefits? If so how? ✓✓✓

Practice point

Think of a manufactured product such as a piece of pine furniture. Try to consider the supply chain for this product. Where did the raw materials come from? Where were they assembled? How did the furniture find its way to where it was purchased? Draft a summary explaining how the internet can help with such a supply chain.

Opportunities to increase sales from existing customers

Businesses that adopt an internet marketing strategy do so because they can see opportunities to either improve sales within the markets they already serve or to enter completely new markets. As internet penetration increases and more businesses use an online strategy, the web will become the accepted method for marketing. The car accessories retailer Save and Drive at www.saveanddrive.co.uk (see page 27) secured its business and expanded into new product lines directly by using an internet strategy.

Case study

UK SMEs missing out?

Many of the UK's small businesses are falling behind the competition as technology progresses, according to a new comprehensive report launched and developed by the Centre for Future Studies, an independent forecasting think-tank.

By failing to recognise the need for the effective management and use of their IT and Communications (IT&C) many small businesses are unable to meet customer demands and expectations. In a world of e-business and converged networks the report shows that adopting a 'business as usual' approach could result in business failure.

With an estimated 4.3 million SMEs in the UK, accounting for half of the UK's turnover and employment, smaller businesses are now generating twice as many jobs as large employers and are providing real growth in the graduate job market.

Being able to get the most out of IT and services through good management is not just about gaining or maintaining competitive advantage, it is about keeping up with the demands and expectations of the customer. These factors now make IT skills mandatory: in particular, the rise of e-business and the growth in demand for online trading services from both customers and suppliers.

Dr Frank Shaw, Foresight Director, Centre for Future Studies, said: 'Consumer expectations are increasing as they experience a better level of service. All of this is driving IT investment and SMEs need to deliver on service while also accommodating changing work patterns which meet their employees' expectations. Innovation is the key if SMEs want to compete in today's domestic and world markets.'

Source: Adapted from IT and Communication Technology Report, BT Business Club, 15 November 2006

Note: An SME = a small- to medium-sized enterprise, which is defined by the Companies Act 1985 as: small = not more than 50 employees, turnover less than £5.6m; medium = not more than 250 employees, turnover less than £228m. There is an EU definition too.

1. What advice would you give to an SME manager who simply said, 'Let them get on with ICT; it's business as usual for us'? ✓
2. Write a summary explaining how such a business might increase sales from internet marketing opportunities. ✓✓
3. In what ways do you think an internet marketing business must 'accommodate changing work patterns'? ✓✓✓

Opportunities to monitor competitor activity

Businesses must constantly monitor the external forces around them so that they can follow strategies and objectives that will enable them to stay competitive. In an increasingly global business world, competition can come from anywhere. It is best to stay informed.

In 1980, Michael Porter set out a 'five forces' model for business managers to use to watch out for external threats. (See also page 339.) These were:

- the bargaining power of buyers
- the bargaining power of suppliers
- the threat of substitute products
- barriers to entry
- rivalry between existing competitors.

The internet offers business leaders a quick and cost-effective way of monitoring what competitor businesses are doing. The case study on Euromonitor (see page 33) illustrates how it is possible to check trends and developments in the market for a single product line.

Opportunities to buy online promotion

There are various forms of online promotion that businesses can buy.

■ Search engines

An internet visitor might type 'flight tickets India' into (say) www.google.co.uk. On the right-hand side of the screen will be a panel showing a list of businesses that

Case study

Deodorants in France

Euromonitor International's 'Deodorants in France' report offers a comprehensive guide to the size and shape of the market at a national level. It provides the latest retail sales data, allowing you to identify the sector's driving growth. It identifies the leading companies and brands, and offers strategic analysis of key factors influencing the market, be they new product developments, packaging innovations, economic/lifestyle influences, distribution or pricing issues. Forecasts illustrate how the market is set to change.

Source: adapted from www.euromonitor.com

1. What sort of useful data do you think a service such as Euromonitor can offer a business? How do you think this could be used? ✓✓

have 'sponsored' that link. Many businesses pay for **search engine advertising** so that their business shows up on the first page of a relevant search.

Key Term

Search engine advertising Paid-for links that are presented by a search engine when a user requests a particular search.

Promotion on websites

Online advertising is now an important component of some of the most successful campaigns. In just ten years it has overtaken cinema and surpassed radio. It now reaches 67% of the UK's population – that's 31.7 million people.

The most obvious form of advertising is banner ads. If you've spent any time surfing the web, you will have seen plenty of these small rectangular advertisements. Although they vary considerably in subject matter, they all share a basic function: if you click on them, your web browser will take you to the advertiser's website.

▲ A typical banner ad ©MB Web Design

Online advertising facts

- Online reach in Great Britain already stands at 67% – that's 31.7m people (2006).
- Among internet users, more than 20% of all time spent exposed to media is now spent online (BMRB Internet Monitor 2005).
- 79% of users access the internet at least once a week, with 52% online everyday/most days (2006).
- 55% of users state they would be lost without online access (Millward Brown/EIAA Media Consumption study November 2004).
- The internet today is demanding more than a quarter of weekday media time (Aged 15+ online, BMRB Internet Monitor Q3 2005).
- Online advertising topped £653.3 million in 2004, a year-on-year increase of 60% that pushed the market share to 3.9%. By comparison, radio's market share during the same period was 3.8%. Rapidly rising demand for broadband internet access and increased advertiser confidence have pushed online's market share beyond that of radio.

Sometimes a business can misjudge the power of the internet in its promotional effort. The off-licence chain Threshers thought it had a winning idea. However, as the case study on page 34 shows, the internet can be a monster if marketing ideas go wrong!

Links

Businesses can use other low-cost methods of generating traffic to their websites by making sure they have links on other sites.

- **Reciprocal links** are two-way links between two businesses and, as such, they are free.
- **Affiliate links** are agreements whereby a link to your site is placed on another site. In return, the site receives payments for 'click-through' sales.

Case study

Threshers discount vouchers

The Thresher Group was bracing itself for an unprecedented rush at its shops in December 2006, after millions of bargain hunters downloaded an online discount offer.

The 40% discount offer was for champagne and wine purchases at 2,500 stores nationwide and applied between 30 November and 10 December 2006.

Spokesman for the business, Dirk Kind, said: 'The initial e-mail was sent to our suppliers and we did say it could be sent to friends and family. We knew it was a bit of a grey area but it has just absolutely snowballed way beyond anything we anticipated.'

The chain initially mailed the coupon to a limited number of suppliers at the end of November. It then appeared on the website of Stormhoek, a South African wine company which estimates it has been downloaded more than 800,000 times. The voucher quickly spread among the public by e-mail.

All recipients have to do is print off the coupon, fill it in and present it at a store. Threshers has said it will honour all vouchers presented.

Kind said the business had not made it clear on the coupons that the offer was intended for limited use.

Robert Dirkovski, head of interactive media at the Direct Marketing Association, said the case demonstrated the power of the internet.

'The internet lends itself perfectly to passing things on from your friends and relatives. This "viral marketing" is a very good way for a business to collect data. Once you have taken up the offer, a business can send you e-mails.'

1. What do you think the Thresher Group had to gain from offering the downloadable 40% vouchers on the web? ✓
2. What lessons (if any) do you think Threshers will have learnt? What would you advise? ✓✓
3. Given the situation Threshers has been faced with in relation to the vouchers, what advice would you give it in the situation it faced in early December 2006? ✓✓✓

Practice point

Write a report on at least five different forms of online promotion activity. You should include banner ads, pop-ups, affiliates, reciprocal links and search engine advertising (try to illustrate the latter using examples from three different searches).

Grading tips

Pass 

Success for this outcome hinges on a description of both benefits and opportunities for a business. A clue to the structure might be given in the reference to the marketing mix. You might describe the various tactics under the seven Ps and outline benefits and opportunities for each one.

Outcome activity 12.3

A local entrepreneur has approached the consultancy firm you work for and requested a report on internet marketing. Describe the benefits and opportunities to the business of using internet marketing within the marketing mix of a selected business. 

12.4 Challenges faced by businesses using internet marketing

While the internet offers marketing benefits and opportunities, it also throws up many challenges. These challenges have to be prepared for, faced and overcome if a business is to successfully compete in the online world.

Traditional thinking about business activity looks at the chain of value-adding processes the organisation undertakes, e.g. acquiring materials, storing materials, working with materials to produce something, packaging the product, warehousing (storing) the product, marketing the product, selling it, moving it.

Many modern businesses have grown to encompass several of these spheres of activity within the one single organisation. By networking these systems and being able to draw on accurate digital data, a business can connect with the outside world with increased confidence. However, just as the internet represents a new channel of opportunities, so it causes potential conflict and challenges. Internet activity is measured by the value it adds to the business. If it fails to add value, then the strategy has been either poorly thought through or it is inappropriate for the business anyway.

Competition through global website visibility

The following 'challenges' are threats that online businesses must face.

Disintermediation and channel conflict

The internet offers the chance to use a *direct* channel of supply to clients or customers. This process, called 'disintermediation', is the tendency to cut out the 'middle-man', as illustrated here:

Manufacturer → Distributor → Wholesaler → Retailer → Consumer

Direct selling

This creates obvious efficiencies and savings, but at the danger of de-stabilising many older traditional channels that might still be valuable sources of revenue to the business. Several scenarios will show how this can occur.

- **Example 1**: A manufacturer (e.g. Dell) sells PCs directly to customers. Several long-established and valued retail outlets for the product object to this and refuse to sell it any more.
- **Example 2:** A distributor is employed to deal with physical placement of products and is made redundant for some products but not others.

Established businesses considering adding an online distribution channel (either to their 'buy-side' or 'sell-side' channels) therefore have to consider the impact such a move may have on existing methods of distribution. If a new online channel causes problems with an established set of business relationships, this is known as '**channel conflict**'.

> **Key Term**
>
> **Channel conflict** Where the introduction of an internet sales channel threatens relationships with businesses working in existing channels.

Dave Chaffey argues in *Internet Marketing* (Prentice Hall, 2003) that today's firms have to identify what their 'core competency' is. What do they do best? Once their core business is identified, they can then build key channel partnerships, collaborating with other firms who do other things better. Consider these examples.

- **Example 1:** A manufacturer works with a retailer to offer better online customer support. Both share customer data. Both work to create the brand identity.
- **Example 2:** B&Q Direct (at www.diy.com) work in partnership with Spark Response, the latter providing customer service, call centre, warehousing and product fulfilment .

Case study

Dell Computers: direct selling from the internet

In 1984, nineteen year-old student Michael Dell founded Dell computers, buying surplus IBM PCs and upgrading them in his room at the University of Texas. His success soon encouraged him to leave college. The Dell concept was to sell directly, at first through catalogues.

Today, Dell achieves 60% of sales through the internet, 30% by phone.

Soon Dell was manufacturing PCs, working on a just-in-time principle which meant carrying the minimum stock and using a very short lead time (this helped when technology was changing fast). The direct sales meant that profits were not shared with intermediaries.

However, in 2005 sales growth slowed and complaints about customer service increased. Dell reduced prices even further to maintain market share, but margins were squeezed. Dell issued two profit warnings.

This year, problems with Sony-manufactured batteries in Dell laptops flared up (literally!). As a result, Dell recalled four million batteries. Added to this, Dell has lost out on its long-held market leadership to Hewlett-Packard.

In December 2006, Dell was considering opening computer shops – a complete reversal of Chairman Michael Dell's founding philosophy. Chief Executive Kevin Rollins claims that as long as the company still owns the shops, it is still 'selling directly'.

1. What is the main justification for Dell's policy of direct selling? ✓
2. Why do you think Dell considered opening its own retail outlets? What do you feel are the advantages and disadvantages of such a move? ✓✓
3. Evaluate the idea of selling direct to consumers from a website. What problems might arise? ✓✓✓

- **Example 3:** Ford Motor Corporation in the USA work in collaboration with its dealer network on an 'Internet Approved' programme, giving training and expertise to promote internet-based customer relationships. In this way, Ford has developed direct customer relationships over the internet without conflicting with its highly valued dealership network.

Practice point

Read the Dell Computers case study above and create a report about its online business. Evaluate its online strategy and marketing, and conclude by assessing whether, in your view, the company's current thinking about introducing physical stores will be helpful to it.

Remember

Selling directly to consumers cuts out intermediary businesses. This direct channel might cause conflict if you use intermediary businesses for other products you sell.

Payment security

Consumers are often concerned about the **security** of transactions via the internet. There are frequent stories about attacks by hackers, 'identity theft', etc. – all of which leave us feeling vulnerable. Therefore, many people are reluctant to give their credit or debit card numbers online, which deprives them of access to products and services that cannot be found elsewhere. Whether a business sells to private consumers or other businesses, payment transactions are necessary. It is a matter of management policy how payments are to be taken, and how to reassure potential customers. Cost considerations, security considerations, customer service and image considerations have to be taken into account. If a business refuses credit cards, there will always be other businesses that will accept them. It is a question of keeping up with the competition.

Key Term

Payment security Setting up online payments systems so that customers' personal details remain hidden.

Remember

The major issue for many consumers and corporate organisations is security. For online customers to verify that they are in a secure connection mode, it is necessary to take two elements into account.

- If the page is in secure connection mode, the URL begins with 'https' ('s' for secure).
- A padlock icon, which indicates security in the closed position, is present on the browser and shows the level of 'encryption' (for Internet Explorer). This means the data has been scrambled so it cannot be read by a third party.

Meeting customer expectations

The internet continues to raise customer expectations and this is a challenge to all online business. The 24/7 availability and convenience of the internet has been reinforced with increased personalisation and price transparency. Even more importantly, customers are starting to expect higher levels of reliability, responsiveness, convenience and speed – speed in terms of both the time taken visiting the website and in delivery of items once the order is placed. Taken together, these are heavy demands on the online business.

We have seen that through the internet, merchandise is becoming available in *mass customised* form, enabling customers to enter personal measurements online (for, say, a pair of jeans) before ordering or to configure their machines (such as a computer) as they order. Customers will increasingly demand or expect this one-to-one online attention.

The process of engaging the customer is fundamental to good online marketing. Yet it generates a fierce level of expectation that what is asked for *is* delivered and that every scrap of supporting information is available – and that it is correct. A beautifully constructed website, with tremendously informative content, competitive prices, smooth and easy transaction arrangements, all count for zero (or *less* than zero!) if a customer's product or service expectations are not fulfilled.

A Forrester Technographics survey of 9,000 users who had made online purchases found that 80% of them had visited a manufacturer's site *first* before visiting the retailer selling the item. These people then re-visited throughout the buying cycle and knew exactly what they wanted. Buyers on the internet are increasingly showing this willingness to bypass the retailer to get product information. They are usually well informed.

Remember

Online customer expectations are very high – higher than in the offline environment.

The challenge for online marketers is to anticipate and understand what customer expectations will be, whatever the market context. One of the best-known failures of the dot.com boom was a US online delivery service called Kozmo. This was a retailer promising free delivery of *any* online order. The idea was born in New York City, where many people living in high-level apartments might decide they suddenly want a DVD or a pizza *at any time*. The business proved to be neither realistic nor cost effective.

Marketing should lead to customer expectations being satisfied *profitably* – so, the moral is, do not make outrageous promises.

A business strategy for managing customer expectations has been suggested by Chaffey in *Internet Marketing*.

- Find out what customers expect by doing some research. Include in the site a feedback form if necessary. Always work to rectify any shortcomings.
- Make realistic promises and communicate them clearly. Do not make impossible promises.
- Deliver commitments with the help of staff as well as physical fulfilment.

Overload of market feedback

Internet marketing opens up a business to the entire market it hopes to serve, its customers and its competitors. As a result the business will accumulate a massive amount of data, and its employees and systems can quickly be overloaded. There is therefore a need, at the outset, to consider the kind of data that is crucial to the business and from that, to think of the processes and information systems necessary for handling that data.

In b2b markets especially, customer profiles are usefully built up. Customer profiles characterise each customer in terms of the products they have bought. This sort of information helps to place customers in their 'market segment' and the business can form an appropriate marketing relationship with them. It is vital to capture the relevant information and act appropriately on it.

Businesses need to be aware that 'information' is not 'knowledge'; data has to be interpreted and made sense of. What does it mean? Managers and individual staff within the organisation should have good access to relevant data, assistance with its interpretation and the ability to act on it. This of course generates more information and so the cycle goes on. Eventually, however, the sheer volume of profiles and the complexity of the data can create overload. This is known as '**information fatigue**'.

There are many specialist marketing advisory services available to help businesses make good use of marketing information.

Key Term

Information fatigue Having so much data that it becomes meaningless and impossible to use.

Many organisations incorporate a FAQ (frequently asked questions) panel on their website. Most serious online businesses also include an e-mail contact and telephone number within a 'Contact us' link. This facility is likely to generate a considerable degree of customer feedback. The online business must be prepared to allocate resources designed to effectively deal with this, otherwise it risks damaging its reputation. If necessary, large portions of an internet marketing strategy may need to be revised in response to aspects of feedback. The business must process feedback and be prepared to act on it if required.

Remember

Online businesses can successfully acquire a lot of market data. However, this has to be sorted and prioritised before being acted on.

Keeping pace with technological change

As internet business gathers pace, most businesses in competitive markets are facing up to the challenges of whether to go online, what to do, when to do it and how. Technological change has always been with us. Without it there would have been no progress at all. Our own economy has evolved from agriculture to manufacturing, and in recent times to services. These days we are evolving into a digital economy in which change is accelerating at a quicker pace than ever before. Businesses are under pressure to *innovate* (find new ways of doing things) in virtually all markets. They

Case study

Publisher gets smart about marketing

Publisher Wolters Kluwer has invested nearly £1m in business intelligence tools that are increasing the effectiveness of its marketing campaigns.

The company, which publishes both print and electronic materials on health, safety, legal and finance issues, has grown by acquisition and in the process acquired several sets of customers that it didn't necessarily know a lot about. Data existed about which publications and services customers subscribed to, but it was locked up in separate systems which made it difficult to get a quick view of each account.

Because of this, Wolters Kluwer's marketing team had a difficult time working out which of its products to pitch to which customers.

In early 2006, the company was using the data analysis tool Faststats from Apteco – but felt it was limited in what it could do for it.

Mike Turner, Business Systems Manager at Wolters Kluwer, said the challenge with considering a new software option was: 'How would we build on this to give us a complete view of the customer?'

The company asked for quotations from software suppliers and chose SAS marketing automation software. Turner said: 'It could do all we needed it to do.' He also liked the 'joined-up approach' of the SAS products. The other short-listed option entailed buying software components from a lot of different vendors and 'gluing them together', he said.

The result has been more targeted and lucrative marketing campaigns – during a seven-week pilot of the SAS software earlier in 2006, response rates went up and one campaign returned three times the expected revenue.

The availability of up-to-date customer profiles means marketing staff are able to plan more strategically, said Wolters Kluwer's Turner. They can now figure out which products customers might be interested in and which formats – e-mail, direct mail, telemarketing – are most effective.

Turner said one key advantage of the SAS system is the 'clarity of knowledge' it provides for marketing campaigns. Wolters Kluwer's marketing team is able to see immediately whether a campaign is effective or not and react accordingly – if it's succeeding, they can do more of what's working, and if it's failing, they can stop it and cut their losses.

The new system has proved fairly easy for workers to learn – after just a few months, the vast majority of users are comfortable with it and 'can't imagine life without it', said Turner.

Another benefit is that staff will no longer be needed to maintain older databases which contained customer info, as all the data has been migrated to the new system – and these staff can now be re-deployed elsewhere.

Turner said if the company continues to see the benefits and savings they've experienced so far, it's on track to meet the board's goal of a return on investment over the next three years, which is worth 'just short of £1m', according to Turner.

'So far the project has stuck to our schedule, goals and objectives,' he said.

Source: Adapted from 'Publisher gets smart about marketing', by Sylvia Carr, 28 November 2006, www.silicon.com

1. In your opinion, why does Wolters Kluwer feel it needs better 'business intelligence'? ✓✓
2. Explain how Wolters Kluwer have been able to use the better business intelligence to their marketing advantage. How, in your view, has their marketing work improved? ✓✓

must respond to new ways of working, both of their partner firms as well as their competitors. The digital economy is a **knowledge-based economy**, based on providing better products, faster and more efficiently than others. In this economy, speed wins – and for management this adds pressure.

Key Term

Knowledge-based economy An economy that is based on the creation of advanced information services that inform both businesses and citizens.

Askham Bryan
College
LIBRARY BOOK

Remember

Businesses today must constantly keep pace with change. Look back at the case study on page 32 about UK SMEs.

Ensuring maximum exposure through ISPs and search engines

Internet Service Providers

Internet Service Providers (ISPs) are firms that offer an internet connection service to both private householders and businesses. Their primary function is to provide a link to the internet and many ISPs also host websites on their own servers.

The crucial point for business management is to ensure that the ISP is offering a satisfactory level of service for a reasonable price. ISPs have to be able to deal with fluctuating and perhaps growing traffic. Speed of access is crucial. We have seen earlier that customers online demand speed. One way of helping in this respect is to have a dedicated server – that is, one which is serving only content from your business. Additionally, bandwidth is an important factor in governing the speed of content delivery. The bigger the bandwidth, the quicker data can pass (like a pipe). Bandwidth is measured in kilobits (1,000 bits) per second and is written as Kbps. A typical modem operates at 56.6 Kbps. This is the bandwidth that small businesses often use. ISDN is usually twice as fast.

A further issue with ISPs is the amount of time that a website is made available to customers. Ideally a business needs to ensure that the site is available 24/7. Not all sites are made available 100% of the time and of course this is lost revenue.

Search engines

Search engines are extremely important for the promotion of a website, as we saw earlier. More than 80% of web users are known to use them and if a business hasn't registered with the search engines it is unlikely to be found unless it has an extremely well-known brand name. Registration and website design are basic and fundamental to the site profile – the former for making the search engines aware of the site and the latter for elevating the site in the search engine listings. There has been a growing trend, too, for businesses to use paid-for listings ('sponsored links').

Security and payment systems

The internet has become a global phenomenon *because* it is an open network, but it is also an insecure network. Despite this, millions of internet-based business transactions are taking place every minute. Confidential, sensitive and potentially damaging company data is increasingly accessible over the internet. Viruses, hackers and other undesirables are a constant danger. Malicious individuals or firms can attack a business' data; they can make fraudulent claims or simply attempt to steal it.

Almost 50% of all credit card fraud is known to be internet-related; for the e-tailor (retailer selling on the internet) there is a significant risk of fraudulent purchases. Repudiation of orders (ordering goods online, then denying it) is a common problem. Private consumers are just as open to attack. Consumer reassurance is a primary marketing task of an online business.

The challenge for business leaders is therefore to *plan for security*. This means, right at the outset, devising an e-business strategy that takes security issues seriously. There are several ways of doing this.

- **Authorisation** – determine who has access to certain applications and information. Establish a consistent policy and ensure this is centrally controlled and monitored.
- **Encryption** – this is a method of changing data into a hidden format. The actual meaning of text, numbers or symbols becomes almost impossible to recognise by anyone other than those who have access to the 'key'. Businesses in the digital world *have* to embrace encryption. Confidential documents such as contracts, personal data, pricing details, and

product research data are vulnerable to theft or attack. Encryption of e-mails is the equivalent of slotting a document into a sealed envelope to keep it private. Both SSL (Secure Sockets Layer) and SET (Secure Electronic Transactions) are standards that ensure the encryption of internet traffic. SET encompasses a whole payments system, while SSL encrypts only traffic between a web browser and server.

- **Authentication** – customers must identify themselves through a login and password procedure.

Remember

Online consumers are naturally worried about security of personal information as they make purchases. An online business must reassure customers that the order process is secure and safe.

Legal complexity

If you buy a product from an online retailer based in the USA and it is shipped to you, only for you to find that you are not satisfied with the product, whose legal system applies – the UK's or the USA's? What rate of taxation, if any, applies to the purchase?

A business setting up a website to sell across Europe, possibly worldwide, must satisfy the legal requirements that might exist in the different European or other nation states. What laws exist covering online promotions or offensive material?

In 2002 the European Union enforced an Electronic Commerce Directive designed to set a framework for electronic commerce in the EU. (See www.berr.gov.uk/files/file14635.pdf for a useful summary.) There is little doubt that legal regulations need to be considered for any business intending to sell online. The UK government's BERR website offers information services for small businesses (www.berr.gov.uk).

Linguistic and cultural sensitivity

As use of the internet continues to grow, more and more users are expected to be non-English speakers. According to Jupiter Research, almost 60% of the internet population is likely to live outside the USA by 2005. English-speaking audiences are unlikely to dominate the internet for long. Obviously it is important for any business that is seriously attempting to expand to consider translations on their site. However, creating literal *linguistic* translations – that is, from one language to another – isn't as straightforward as it might appear. Here are a few examples of translations that went disastrously wrong!

- The Pepsi slogan 'Come alive with the Pepsi generation' was translated into Taiwanese as 'Pepsi will bring your ancestors back from the dead'.
- The Kentucky Fried Chicken slogan 'Finger-lickin good' came out as 'Eat your fingers off' in Chinese.
- US car manufacturers General Motors realised why it wasn't selling any of the Chevrolet Nova in South America when it found out that 'no va' meant 'it won't go'. The company re-named the car the 'Caribe' for Spanish markets.

It's also important to be aware that adding translations is only the first step. A website must also take account of users' cultural expectations, which vary around the world.

Remember

Cultural differences need to be taken into account when a business sets up a website that is intended for overseas markets.

Cultural attitudes to payments

A report in 2000 by NetSmartAmerica ('America.com: What makes America click') showed that 70% of online shoppers in the USA paid by credit card. In Japan, the most common payment method (in May 2000) was cash on delivery. This is said to reflect the Japanese preference for cash-based payment. A spin-off from this was that in Japan many more websites were obliged to be membership-based, as this enables members to pay by direct bank deposit.

■ Cultural issues for designers and marketers

Web designers of the future will increasingly need to consider cultural differences at great length. Differences in perception are significant. Oriental scripts (Japanese, Korean, Chinese) are justified and read vertically, and Arabic is read from right to left whereas English is read from left to right. These differences *are* very significant. Will a Chinese user find a left-justified web page appealing?

Some societies can be said to be very family- or group-oriented (China, for example), while others are much more individualistic (USA, UK, Western Europe). This difference needs to be reflected in marketing communications. Get the message wrong and real long-term online damage can be caused. In marketing, as you know by now, it is vital to know your market.

Outcome activity 12.4

In your work for a consultancy firm, prepare some background information in readiness for a meeting with the management of a local SME by responding to the following tasks.

Pass

Describe the challenges facing a selected business when using the internet as a marketing tool.

Merit m2

Analyse the marketing opportunities and challenges faced by a selected business when using internet marketing within its marketing mix.

Grading tips

Pass p4

One way of approaching this task might be to carry out a review of online businesses that you have encountered in this unit. Select one of these and carefully describe the ways in which the challenges outlined here might apply to it.

Merit m2

To achieve this grade outcome you need to offer a detailed analysis of both the opportunities and the challenges that an online business has encountered. You are required to relate these to the 'mix' of tactics the business appears to use, e.g. products, pricing, placement, promotion etc.

End of unit test

1. What do you understand is the main purpose of marketing?
2. List at least four ways in which the internet helps a business to find out about its customers.
3. Describe what is meant by 'targeting' customers.
4. Describe what is meant by 'segmenting' a market.
5. Describe and give three examples of 'personalisation' of web pages.
6. What do you understand by 'mass customisation'?
7. How may the internet offer customers improved value?
8. What is 'dynamic pricing'?
9. List and describe three ways in which businesses can use internet marketing opportunities.
10. Describe three challenges that a business going online might have to face. Why are they challenges?

Books

Chaffey, Mayer, Johnston and Ellis-Chadwick, 2003, *Internet Marketing, Strategy, Implementation and Practice*, Prentice Hall
Goymer, John, 2004, *BTEC National e-Business Book 1*, Heinemann,

Websites

http://presentpicker.com/ppp/home.html – A site providing customisation of its products
http://searchenginewatch.com – Search engine marketing
www.acmewhistles.co.uk – Lets you investigate whistle performance 'virtually'
www.amazon.co.uk – An extremely successful online store
www.beeb.com – BBC's internet shopping service, providing instant price comparisons
www.bellsfishandchips.co.uk – A 'bricks and mortar' company, with an information-only website
www.berr.gov.uk – The Department for Business, Enterprise and Regulatory Reform, offering information services for small businesses
www.cardcorp.co.uk – Card Corporation
www.clickz.com – Useful for internet trends and statistics
www.diy.com – B&Q's online service, which has a variety of interactive features
www.easyjet.com – The low-cost airline's dynamic pricing facility
www.ebay.co.uk – Online auction site connecting private customers
www.egg.com – Egg's website collects detailed information about customer perceptions of its financial services
www.eiu.com – The Economic Intelligence Unit
www.fightback.com – A consumer response service
www.4projects.com – An online collaborative service
www.ic3d.com/index.html – An interactive shopping site that lets the customer modify clothing before ordering
www.kelkoo.com – An online service listing the best prices available on the web
www.nike.com/index.jhtml – The Nike sports footwear group
www.norton.com – The website for Norton, selling anti-virus software online
www.priceline.co.uk – A site that allows consumers to set their own prices
www.rswww.com RS – Components, a supplier of electrical components and accessories, with a successful b2b and b2c website
www.saveanddrive.co.uk – Save and Drive, a successful 'clicks and mortar' motor accessories supplier
www.screwfix.com – A DIY business, with a successful customised buyer menu
www.statistics.gov.uk – A rich source of government statistics
www.tesco.com – Tesco, a very successful 'bricks and clicks' supermarket
www.webtrends.com – WebTrends, an analytics service

Grading criteria	Outcome activity	Page number
To achieve a pass grade the evidence must show that the learner is able to:		
P1 Describe the role internet marketing has in a modern marketing context using selected organisations as examples	12.1	17
P2 Describe the principal benefits to customers of internet marketing	12.2	20
P3 Describe the benefits and opportunities to the business of using internet marketing within the marketing mix of a selected business	12.3	34
P4 Describe the challenges facing a selected business when using the internet as a marketing tool	12.4	42
To achieve a merit grade the evidence must show that, in addition to the pass criteria, the learner is able to:		
M1 Analyse the benefits of internet marketing for consumers	12.2	20
M2 Analyse the marketing opportunities and challenges faced by a selected business when using internet marketing within its marketing mix	12.4	42
To achieve a distinction grade the evidence must show that, in addition to the pass and merit criteria, the learner is able to:		
D1 Evaluate the effectiveness of internet marketing in meeting customer needs for a selected business	12.2	20

Human resource management in business

Introduction

Human resource planning is the work that businesses do in planning for their future workforce, inside and outside the company. It is a really important aspect of how a business is run or managed. In this unit you will learn about all aspects of human resource management in business, including the different factors that are taken into account.

First, you will consider the impact of internal and external planning factors on the human resource management of the business such as new technology, products and trends in skills or unemployment levels.

You will then consider how organisations can make their employees even more productive by motivating them. You will consider appropriate theories and reward systems.

As well as motivating them with rewards, employees also need to be co-operative, so you will consider the implications of contracts of employment and different ways of working to encourage employees to get involved, such as suggestion schemes.

Finally the unit ends by considering how important managing employee performance is at work and the different measures that can be used to help manage that performance.

What you need to learn

On completion of this unit you should:

1. Know the factors that are involved in human resource planning in organisations
2. Know how organisations motivate employees
3. Understand how to gain committed employee co-operation
4. Understand the importance of managing employee performance at work.

Consider this

The Confederation of British Industry estimated in 2006 that £11.6 billion is lost every year due to absenteeism in the workplace. At the same time, British employees are working long hours, with one in three fathers working more than 48 hours per week, every week. Helping employees to balance their work and home life is becoming more and more important as part of human resource planning, to ensure that fewer days are taken off due to stress or illness.

Looking after employees by motivating them, rewarding them and monitoring their performance in a way that they can understand is becoming more and more important for UK businesses, if they are to compete within the UK, EU and world at large.

Consider your own work–life balance by thinking about how many hours you:

- are at school or college including travelling time
- are doing homework or study at home
- work a part-time job
- have to manage home responsibilities such as looking after a relative or cleaning
- have for hobbies or special interests
- have left over to relax.

How is your work–life balance, and are there improvements you can make?

16.1 Factors that are involved in human resource planning in organisations

Human resource planning looks at the current workforce skills and motivation and compares them with what is going to be needed in the future. To do this the business has to take into account internal (inside the business) and external (outside the business) considerations as well as the skills that are needed. These factors can be divided into three main areas:

1. Internal planning factors
2. External planning factors
3. Employee skills

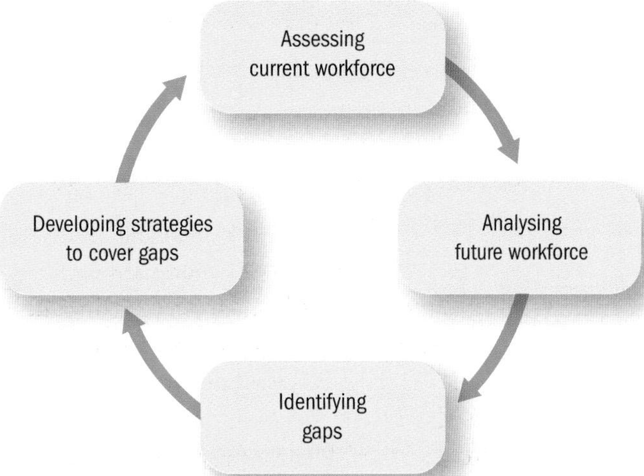

▲ **Human resource planning cycle**

Internal planning factors

Internal planning factors are those that relate to what is happening inside the business and how the organisation is changing itself to cope with new methods of working or new demands being made on it, such as the introduction of technology or new products. It is also a way of considering the new skills that will be needed in the future and those that existing staff already have, so that the gap can be measured.

Organisational needs

Organisations are constantly changing and therefore their human resources (workforce) need to be able to adapt as part of this. The demand for products and services will affect the number of employees needed for that role. Organisations need to plan for these new products and services and make adjustments to their workforce either by reducing the workforce (contraction) or by expanding the workforce (expansion).

The changing organisation will need to look for different ways to increase business by considering new markets that they may not have thought about before. This could mean expanding into different countries or targeting different groups of people to buy the products. They may require different types of employees working there, those who are able to speak foreign languages, for example, or work in different locations. It may also have an impact on the number of people involved in distribution (transporting goods from the organisation out to the customer).

Technological change also affects the internal working arrangements of an organisation. Fewer or different types of staff may be needed to do a particular job, so existing staff may have to move jobs, which in turn may involve additional training. Many large supermarkets have introduced self-scanning and payment into their stores. It's predicted that this will become an increasingly popular way for customers to pay for their shopping. Customers also frequently want to make use of the internet to buy products and services. These trends may reduce the need for in-store staff, while more staff will be needed in centres responding to online orders and arrange for deliveries.

Recently many large organisations have taken this further by moving their factories or businesses to other countries, to make use of different skills and cheaper labour. This helps them to be more cost-efficient and potentially make larger profits.

Skills requirements

Assessing the skills of the current workforce is an essential part of human resource planning as it enables the business to build up a profile of the training,

Case study

Cadbury

Cadbury will open a new factory in Poland by 2008 to supply the increasing demand for its brands, particularly in Europe, the Middle East and Asia, which gave Cadbury a turnover of £349 million in 2004. The factory in Poland will create 300 jobs at first and there may be the possibility of expansion there at a later date. Cadbury chose Poland as its base for new manufacturing plants for a number of reasons including the fact that the country offered a 'low cost base' and a good central position for distribution throughout Europe, Asia and the Middle East. This is not the first venture for Cadbury in Poland. In 1999 it acquired the Polish chocolate brand Wedel, which trades in Poland as Cadbury Wedel.

1. In terms of human resource management and production, what do you think is meant by a 'low cost base'? ✓
2. What advantages might Cadbury have by being centrally located in Europe in terms of staffing and distribution? ✓✓✓
3. How might Cadbury acquiring the Wedel chocolate brand in Poland have helped them to expand there, from the point of view of both the workforce and distribution points? ✓✓✓

experience and qualifications that the employees already have. This is very important, whether the business is **capital**- or **labour-intensive** (these terms are discussed further on page 49).

Key Terms

Capital-intensive Describes a production process that requires a lot of machinery and technology.

Labour-intensive Describes a production process that requires a lot of human resources.

As the nature and type of work changes, so do the skills requirements that are needed. The organisation must make sure that it measures the skill levels of its workforce and plan for any future training or recruitment it may need in order to remain competitive. Some organisations that have rapid changes in demand or technology may need to plan for the next 12 months, while others will look at the longer term, such as over the next 10 or 20 years.

Workforce profiles

Producing a workforce profile means that business managers can see the types of employees that are working for them, including details such as their age, gender, ethnicity and ability.

Knowing the age of the workforce is important as it can indicate whether there are likely to be recruitment problems in the future, such as if lots of employees will be retiring at the same time. It is also important because it shows the extent to which the organisation is fairly recruiting its staff. The Employment Equality (Age) Regulations 2006 mean that organisations must show that they are not discriminating against potential employees because of their age. By profiling the workforce it is possible to see the number of older and younger workers that are employed. This can help in planning, as any gaps in the number of younger or older workers can be identified and recruitment practices can be put into place to reduce them.

Gender and ethnicity are also included within a workforce profile. Measuring these numbers can again demonstrate whether or not there is equality of opportunity.

The final aspect of measuring the workforce is to profile their qualifications and experience or skills – that is, the level of ability. Some organisations use online human resource information systems to keep a record of all the training, experience and skills of their workforce so they can measure any training gaps or find employees who have training in one job that may be of use in another.

Remember

Workforce profiling is one way of measuring an organisation's level of skills and abilities.

External planning factors

External planning factors are those that influence the business from outside its direct control. These factors include the type and availability of employees to work for the organisation and the amount of money that is needed to pay them.

Supply of labour

An important consideration is the supply of labour on a local, national and international scale.

Some parts of the UK have changed as a result of a shift in the nature of work. In the north-east of England, for example, employment has changed from mostly primary and manufacturing industry jobs to new industries, such as microelectronics, and biotechnology, and there has been growth in service industries, including retail, education and tourism.

Practice point

- Using the National Statistics website www.statistics.gov.uk, have a look at what is happening in your neighbourhood by doing research on your postcode. This will help you to find out information about employment levels and types of jobs in your area.
- Look at the national statistics on the number of hours worked on average, and the types of employment for the nation as a whole.
- Make a note summarising your findings on both your local area and the national employment situation.

This presents a huge training issue for the area as there may be a high number of people with skills in manufacturing but fewer skilled in retail where jobs are available. This training gap needs to be dealt with by both local businesses and agencies, so that local people can acquire the skills they need.

From a national perspective the supply of labour is dependent on trends in unemployment and the type of skills that employers need. Unemployment has been increasing over the past two years, which means there are potentially more employees available for employers to choose from if they have suitable skills and experience.

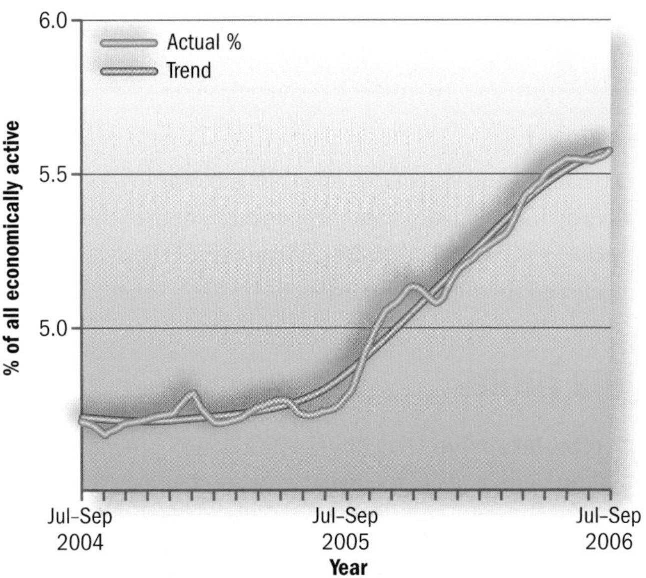

▲ **Unemployment rates affect the supply of labour**

If suitable employees are not available it is important for the government and employers to invest in training and education to help unemployed people become more employable and thus fill available vacancies. This is good for employers and the government, as it means that there are fewer people claiming benefits and there is more productive work taking place.

There is also an international perspective to the supply of labour, because more people are moving to the UK from other countries to work. Since the major expansion of the EU in 2004, when the number of member countries grew from 15 to 25, the number of workers moving between countries to find work has risen. With more countries joining in the future, this trend will escalate. This can affect the level of wages that employers offer in order to attract candidates and the types of training and skills that might be needed for these new workers. The difference in wages is shown in the table below. The figure can be as much as ten times more in some EU countries compared to others.

Country	Annual gross average earnings per person for businesses employing 10 or more people in 2002 in euros
Denmark	€43,577.17
UK	€40,533.02
Germany	€39,440.00
Poland	€7,172.43
Hungary	€5,870.66
Slovakia	€4,582.29

Source: Europe in Figures Eurostat Yearbook 2005

Thinking point

The income and pay levels in countries throughout the EU are changing all the time. The table above gives a snapshot of how things looked in 2002. Look up the latest data on pay levels between the EU member states by using resources such as www.europa.eu.int to get the latest research and statistics that you can use to develop your strategy.

Trends in the supply of labour have to be looked at from two points of view – short term and long term. Short term means looking at numbers of possible employees in the next year or two. Employers may need to incorporate emergency measures such as emergency training or temporary contracts to cope with these immediate changes. Long term refers to initiatives and changes that need to be made in the next 5, 10 or even 20 years. Both the government and industry need to invest in education and training to make sure that people with appropriate skills are available to work in the future.

Labour costs

The cost of labour is an important element of human resource management. As a percentage of the other costs within a business, it will depend on whether the type of work needed is capital- or labour-intensive and the extent to which the necessary skills are available and accessible. You have already learned that there are international implications for labour costs but the level of labour needed for an organisation to operate also has implications. In organisations like colleges and schools, at least 70% of costs are labour costs. This is because the main resource needed is teaching staff, who are present in classrooms. For organisations that make use of robots and machinery, the labour costs may be much lower – for example 20%.

In the UK, labour costs are also governed by legislation such as the minimum wage. The minimum wage is the lowest hourly rate of pay that employers are allowed to pay by law. They can of course pay more but they must not pay less. Human resource planning must include adjustments for increases to the minimum wage, which happen every year. (You can get more information about the minimum wage in Book 1, Unit 13, page 363.)

Workforce skills

A business can examine its local area to see the types of skills levels that are available by using national statistics published by the government. This information is available on an area and sector basis. To use this information to their best advantage, businesses need to consider their future needs and those of their competitors in order to make sure they attract the right people to work for them, especially if they are working in a skills shortage area. This may mean they need to offer extra benefits or better working conditions in order to get the right people. In some areas it may not be possible to get people with the right skills, and then the business may need to recruit abroad in order to get suitably qualified staff. Skills shortages in 2005 included doctors, nurses, teachers and IT staff. To fill these gaps, doctors and nurses were being recruited from developing countries such as India or the Philippines and teachers from countries such as Australia and Canada.

Case study

Plumbing skills shortages

Plumbing is one of the skills areas that is facing a real shortage. In fact it has been estimated that over the next few years there will be a shortage of 1,300 plumbers in Wales alone.

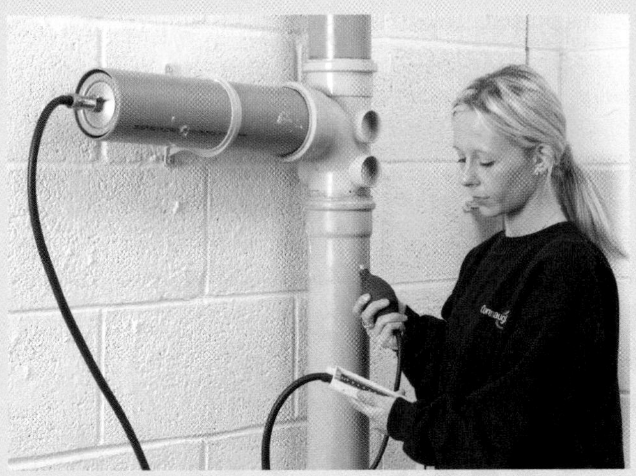

The vast majority of plumbers have traditionally been male and white, so there has been a concerted effort to get more women and ethnic minorities into the workforce. Coleg Gwent in Pontypool has tried to address the balance by setting up a female-only plumbing course, increasing the number of skilled plumbers but at the same time encouraging women to come into the trade.

Plumbing is just one of a number of skills areas experiencing trouble recruiting people with the right skills. Others include teaching, social work and nursing.

1. In small groups, using text books and internet resources, produce a mind map of all the areas of work that appear to be experiencing a skills shortage. ✓
2. What are the implications of these skills shortages? ✓✓
3. How can encouraging female or ethnic minority workers into these industries help the situation? ✓✓

Government policy

The UK has a skills shortage at the moment and relies on a low-skilled workforce. This can be demonstrated by research from the CBI, which states that one in three employers found it necessary to give extra training to their staff in English and Maths in March 2006. Other figures announced by the government's Department for Education and Skills in February 2005 suggest that around 33% of the UK workforce possess low-level qualifications; of that figure, under 13.6% have no qualifications at all. This makes it difficult for employers to recruit suitably qualified staff, and grow their businesses and the economy as a whole.

As a result, the government published the Further Education (FE) Reform White Paper 'Raising Skills, Improving Life Chances' in March 2006 to improve the numeracy and literacy skills of school-leavers. This is introducing into schools and colleges specialised diplomas in the curriculum for students aged 14–19.

The introduction of policies for education, work and training has implications for the number of potential employees available and their level of ability when they leave school.

Labour market competition

As an individual business plans its workforce for the future, so do other businesses within that industry. If the industry is expanding there may not be enough potential employees to supply all the businesses that are interested in recruiting in the future.

Companies in industries facing labour shortages are more likely to need to pay higher wages in order to attract the right people to work for them. If one organisation pays less than others in the same industry they are not likely to be able to attract new recruits. At the same time, an increase in the level of pay a company offers may then lead to less profit in the future. This

Case study

Whitbread Plc

Whitbread Plc is one of the leading hospitality companies in the UK and employs around 40,000 people. Whitbread manages some of the leading hotels, restaurants and health and fitness clubs including Premier Travel Inn, Brewers Fayre, Beefeater, Costa, TGI Friday's and David Lloyd Leisure.

Across the chain, 10 million customers are served each month and in the year to March 2004 Whitbread had a pre-tax profit of £240.8 million.

Whitbread's businesses are all very labour-intensive, as they provide services. David Lloyd Leisure needs employees to run every aspect of the fitness club, from working in the restaurants, to coaching tennis, giving advice on fitness or maintaining the facilities. Premier Travel Inn is a hotel chain and, again, it needs a large staff to look after guests and keep their rooms in working order. The other part of Whitbread's chain is the restaurant business, again relying on staff to produce and serve food in more than 1,000 outlets across the UK.

Whitbread shows that using labour-intensive working methods can be very successful and very profitable.

1. Why does Whitbread's chain of companies need to be so labour-intensive? ✓
2. What possible problems might Whitbread have when operating in this way? ✓✓
3. What are the implications for the training budget of being so labour-intensive? ✓✓
4. How might low levels of unemployment affect Whitbread? ✓✓✓

means that the company must strike a very careful balance between paying the appropriate rate for the job and managing its funds carefully in order to make profit.

Remember

The availability and supply of labour affects the cost of that labour and the likelihood that an employer can recruit employees with the appropriate skills and knowledge required by the business.

Key Terms

Flat-structured organisation One that has fewer hierarchical layers and therefore fewer levels of management.

Hierarchical or pyramid-structured organisation One that has many hierarchical layers and therefore many levels of management.

Case study

Changing nature of work

As you have already learnt, there are many influences on human resource management from changes in technology to where employees can be recruited from. As these changes are implemented into the business world employees need to be flexible and able to cope with rapid change. In the past, employees were often recruited from school or college and remained with their employers for the whole of their lives. These days, employees need to have a wider range of skills and be willing to change employer and job role in order to stay in work.

Many business organisations have also opted to become **flat structured**, with fewer levels of management. This means that when an employee wishes to experience different work, they may either have to find another job at the same level within the organisation or, in order to be promoted to a more senior post, consider finding a new employer.

Case study

Jarrang

Jarrang (www.jarrang.com) is a national company that designs and sends out e-mail marketing information, including questionnaires. The company, based in Cornwall, only employs people to work from home or in their customers' workplaces rather than in an office. The managing director of Jarrang took this decision as it meant that he could run a business without paying rent and other office expenses. Employees do not have to pay to get to work and can spend the time they would have taken commuting working with their customers and achieving results. It also means that there is less impact on the environment from vehicle pollution.

Using the information from this case study and other research on the web answer the following questions.

1. Why did Jarrang decide to close its office in Cornwall? ✓
2. What are the possible advantages of working from home for employees and employers? ✓✓
3. What are the possible disadvantages of working in this way? ✓✓
4. To what extent is home-working changing the nature of work? ✓✓✓

Working flexibly from home is another way in which the nature of work is changing. This is influenced by technology. Employees may use a laptop or PC from home rather than go into an office, which reduces travelling time and can lead to an increase in productivity. This type of work is known as tele-working.

Employee expectations

Work expectations are also changing for employees as well as organisations. Employees may be employed for a whole range of different contracts for the employer and employee's benefit.

Many employees now work a full-time week (35 hours or more) for an employer on a permanent basis. This means that their contract stays in place unless the employee decides to leave or the employer dismisses them. Employees wanting more flexible working arrangements so that they can look after young children or elderly relatives may ask their employers if they can work part-time instead. Part-time can range from just a few hours a week to every day, depending on the type of job and the employer involved.

There has also been a move towards more temporary or casual work. Temporary work means that the work is not permanent, and the start- and end-date for the work is known by the employer and employee. Casual work is similar to temporary work, in that it is not permanent, but it is usually required at short notice or for just a short time. Casual work is difficult to rely on, as the employee does not know the start- and end-date in advance, but this type of flexibility can help employers to become more efficient in covering sickness or other absences by their permanent employees.

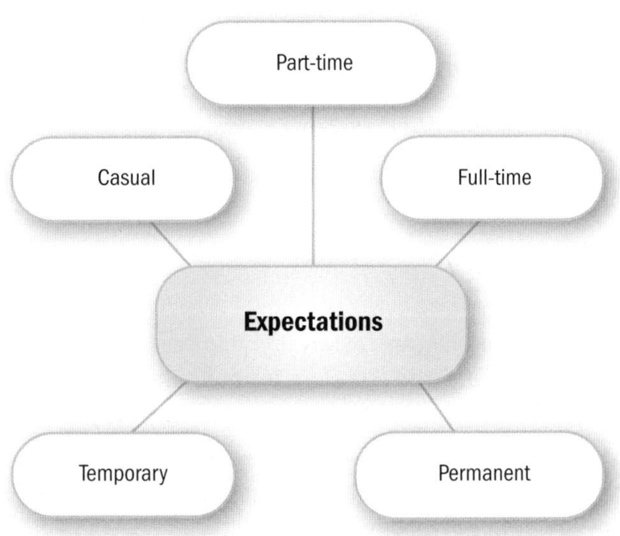

▲ **Employee expectations of work**

Impact of automation

Over the past 50 years there has been a shift towards greater use of technology and the internet in the workplace. This has changed the way employees work and the type of work they do.

In the past, telephone operators connected all telephone calls, but technology now does this automatically. Data entry clerks used to be employed in great numbers to input order information into computers, but now many customers order for themselves online. Managing orders online is about managing the overall process and identifying problems, rather than just inputting data. Such changes in working methods are happening on a national scale, and people with IT skills are in demand for a huge variety of jobs.

Demand for products and services

The external demand for products and services can also have a big impact on human resource management. This is because changes in demand can affect the level of service or products that are required and in turn affect the number of employees that are needed. Unexpected shifts in demand can be difficult to cope with and may be outside the control of the business.

Organisations such as hotels and travel agents may be affected by natural disasters, when demand for their services is likely to decline and they have **excess capacity**. In such circumstances they are likely to reduce the number of staff (making them redundant) with the expectation of employing more staff when things pick up again.

Key Term

Excess capacity When an organisation has too many goods or services on offer compared to the number of customers.

Employee skills

The skills and talents of employees are very important to organisations as they can be used to add value. Human resources, like finance or buildings, need to be used efficiently. They need to be paid and planned for, especially if the skills required are hard to find.

People as organisational resources

As human resources are just one part of the set of resources available to an organisation, people should be considered in an objective way and treated like any other resource. However, this is easier said than done because, unlike other resources, humans have feelings and should be dealt with sensitively in order to achieve the best outcomes and maximise efficiency for the business. This means that plans should be in place to help employees who are no longer needed, either through redundancy or by re-training them for future projects.

Remember

People are resources that need careful management, as reducing and expanding the workforce has a huge impact on the lives of individual employees and their families.

Skill sets

The type of work that an organisation does will affect the level of human resources needed and the level of skill required. Some organisations invest heavily in machinery and have fewer employees. As we have seen, these types of businesses are known as capital-intensive, because lots of financial resources, known as capital, are invested in machinery or technology to support production. Examples of capital-intensive businesses include food manufacturing and car-making.

Other organisations need human involvement rather more than machinery. Such organisations are known as labour-intensive, which simply means they need a lot of people to provide their service. Examples of labour-intensive businesses include hairdressing and house-building.

Key Term

Skill sets Groups of competencies and skills that employees need to have in order to be able to carry out a job.

■ Levels of skill needed

Different jobs have different levels of skill. A complicated job that requires a high level of education and training is said to be a highly skilled job. A job that can be performed with a minimum amount of training is more likely to be low-skilled. Taking into account the range and complexity of skills that are needed is an important task for management.

A porter's job in a hotel might require a low level of skill, but it includes a range of tasks such as carrying luggage, giving directions, opening doors and being polite to customers. An employee in a highly skilled job, such as a programmer for a specific piece of software, might centre on only one task but needs to be an expert in that field. A senior occupational therapist, on the other hand, might need to be highly skilled and be able to demonstrate a range of complex skills including leadership, supervision, planning, development, management of patient case loads and appraisals. These types of skills are job-specific, which means that they are particular to this type of work.

There are also common skills that are transferable to many different types of work. These are known as generic skills and include the ability to use IT, answer the telephone or produce written documents. You can learn more about transferable skills opposite.

Skill acquisition

Acquiring skills during work is extremely important for employers and employees. Employers must make sure that they have got new people being trained to do jobs in case employees leave the organisation. They need to invest money and time in training young people to take over from older people who are going to retire. Unless skills can be acquired the organisation is likely to face shortages in the number of people available to the jobs they require, both inside and outside the organisation.

Skills audit

Employers can establish future training needs by completing a skills audit with employees. This involves auditing employees to see if they already have the skills needed to do a job that covers new organisational objectives. Some employees may have those skills but are not using them. The organisation may refocus these employees instead of employing new staff.

Organisations may also routinely carry out skills audits to work out the skill level within the organisation. A firm of solicitors, for example, may analyse how many junior solicitors they have in training and how many are fully qualified, so they can plan for the future needs of the business. Sometimes organisations will use specialised software packages called Human Resource Information Systems (HRIS) that keep records of the skill levels of all employees in the organisation. This is particularly useful for project work, when people with specialist skills or qualifications need to be found very quickly. Employees may be able to work for the organisation in more than one job area.

Skill transferability

Some specialist jobs such as doctor, teacher or quantity surveyor involve skills that can easily be transferred from one organisation to another. This means that it is relatively easy for employees to leave and get a job elsewhere. Organisations have to look after employees who have highly transferable skills, to try to make sure they don't leave. Some organisations have a high dependence on specific workers and if they cannot get them within the UK, they may need to take steps to source such workers from other parts of the world. Employees can also experience problems if their

Case study

Hair-cutting industry

In the hair-cutting industry there is a growing shortage of skilled hairdressers. Unless salons have the right number of staff they are likely to lose money, so they need to ensure that they are constantly updating the skills of their employees and have good sources of recruitment.

The website www.hair-recruitment.com was set up to help hairdressers throughout the UK and the world get in touch with trainers, trainees and potential staff to fill vacancies. Before the online system was used the main way that vacancies were advertised were in the local paper or shop windows. This online system centralises that process.

Habia (www.habia.org) set the standards for the hair and beauty industry and identified, in its July 2006 report, that the acquisition of skills from NVQ Level 2 to Level 3 for hairdressers is an issue. Habia also identified that only 28% of hairdressing salons were making use of IT. If greater use of IT is to be made in the future for bookings and customer support this may be an area where more skills need to be acquired.

1. What happens to a business with a shortage of skilled staff? ✓
2. Why might there be an issue for hairdressers acquiring skills from NVQ Level 2 to Level 3? ✓✓
3. What are the advantages and disadvantages of making greater use of IT in hairdressing? ✓✓
4. Discuss the view that increasing skills in the hair and beauty industry is the responsibility of business owners and not the government. ✓✓✓

Case study

Network Rail

In August 2004 Network Rail faced the problem of not having enough staff to carry out important work on signal boxes in the Stockport area.

Essential operations had to be completed quickly in order for work totalling £8 billion to be completed on time, but the company was unable to recruit enough rail engineers. The whole project was in danger of being delayed.

As no rail engineers were available in the UK because of a skills shortage, Network Rail's solution was to fly in twelve mechanical engineers from India to work alongside the UK Network team.

This is an example of the fact that skills cannot always be transferred from one industry to another. An aircraft engineer may not be able to transfer their skills to work as a rail engineer, and this can make organisations very dependent on specialists. Problems arise if companies cannot recruit and retain the right staff.

1. What was the problem for Network Rail in 2004? ✓
2. What are the disadvantages of having to bring in specialist staff from another country to carry out essential work? ✓✓
3. What might the benefits be? ✓✓
4. How could this situation have been prevented in the first place? ✓✓✓

skills are so specific that they cannot be transferred to another organisation or if they are employed by the only organisation of its type in the area. For example, in April 2005 it was announced that the car-maker Rover was to close, with the loss of around 6,000 jobs. As Rover was the only company manufacturing cars in the Longbridge area of Birmingham, workers were unable to transfer their skills to another business in the same industry. Instead they were encouraged either to relocate (as far away as Australia), to take their skills to other manufacturers, or to consider retraining in other types of manufacturing that were experiencing skills shortages in the area.

Impact of technology

As technology is changing it is important that employees gain new skills so they can make best use of that technology. If employees cannot use new systems or equipment they will not be as productive as they should be. You will have seen in your own lifetime how fast technology is changing and how new ideas and concepts are being developed all the time – MP3 equipment being updated to MP4, the use of text messages and e-mail at work. Employees have to have the skills to work with new technology as and when it becomes available.

Outcome activity 16.1

Pass

1. Describe the internal and external factors to be considered when planning the human resources requirements of an organisation. 
2. Describe how the different skills that are needed by employees to do the jobs in the organisation are identified. 

Merit

3. Conclude your report by explaining why human resource planning is so important to an organisation.

Grading tips

Choose an organisation that you know well and consider how it is developing and any changes that may affect the direction of the organisation, for example technology or demand for its products or services. You will need to consider the gap between the skills that employees currently have and what is needed in the future. You should make sure you include information on:

- demand for products or services (internal and external)
- markets
- technological change
- production location
- workforce profiles
- supply of labour including trends
- competition within the labour market
- changes in the nature of work
- employee expectations
- automation.

Pass  

Consider the skill sets required by employees to work in that organisation and the influences on those, such as changes in working practices and technology. You should comment on the ability of staff to acquire additional skills and to transfer those skills to other parts of the business. You should also examine the use of skills auditing to make judgements about the level of skills within the organisation.

Merit 

Explain why human resource planning is needed to ensure an organisation has employees with the right skills, knowledge and experience to be able to meet its aims and objectives. You may wish to give examples of how successful human resource planning has made organisations become more efficient and why ineffective resource planning may have affected the performance and results of other organisations.

16.2 How organisations motivate employees

Motivation is about having the will or desire to do something or to work that little bit harder. You need a degree of motivation to get out of bed every morning and go to school, college or work. Motivation theories identify aspects of motivation that can be enhanced through pay or responsibility. You will learn about the work of a number of theorists and different reward systems that can be put into place to enhance the effort and therefore the productivity of employees.

Motivation theory

Motivating staff is an essential part of management and there are a number of theorists who have researched how this can be done. The main theorists are:

- Taylor
- Mayo
- Maslow
- Herzberg
- McGregor
- McClelland
- Vroom.

Motivation means the influences on and within people that encourage and sustain them to work to the best of their ability – giving them the 'will to work'. The extent to which the employee can feel motivated in the workplace will be influenced by the culture and techniques that managers use to improve motivation within their workforce. Improving motivation will mean that employees are happier in their jobs and this should increase productivity. Motivated and productive employees are more likely to make higher quality products, answer more telephone calls or provide better customer service. This should lead to an improved company image and, in profit-making companies, to increased sales – hopefully leading to bigger profits. In non-profit making organisations, having a motivated workforce should lead to a better return, in other words improved service for the same amount of money.

Taylor

Frederick Taylor studied motivation at the Bethlehem Steel Company in the USA in the late 1800s and believed that there was a more efficient way for employees of the Steel Company to work using shovels. He worked out that 21.5 pounds of weight was the ideal weight of material for an employee to lift in order to work at their best level, and that all employees should be given targets of material to move in order to earn their wages. He suggested that the role of management was to decide what a worker should do, how they should do it and when. Taylor put forward the case that workers were only motivated by money, so work must be linked to payment. A manager should motivate a worker by using pay as an incentive and threaten them with less money or the sack if they did not work to the best of their ability.

Using Taylorist principles, the more an employee works the greater their pay and the less they work, the less they get paid. This type of payment scheme is also known as piece rate, which means that an employee is paid per piece of work that they do – for example, paying a hairdresser per haircut or a tailor per suit. Henry T. Ford, the famous car producer, used Taylor's method of motivation to mass-produce Ford cars in the 1900s.

The positive side of this form of motivation, which relies solely on money, is that the more you produce, the better your pay. But this can lead to issues around quality. If you are hurrying and trying to get as much produced as possible, you may make mistakes or your work may not reach a high enough standard to maintain customer satisfaction.

Practice point

Consider the following occupations and how well Taylorist principles could work for each:

- bricklayer
- toy maker
- musician
- doctor
- pilot
- teacher
- car maker.

Which professions would work well and which not so well?

Mayo

In the 1920s and 1930s, Elton Mayo took Taylor's ideas and tried to explore them further, as he recognised that there may be more to motivation than just financial reward. He carried out a study known as the Hawthorne Study, in Chicago, USA, and found – after experiments testing incentive schemes, rest periods, hours of work, lighting and changes in lighting and heating – that whatever changes were made, output continued to rise. Mayo found, therefore, that rises in productivity were not only due to financial rewards but also due to management involvement, teamworking and communication. Mayo's new insights into motivation became known as the Human Relations School. Mayo suggested that workers should:

- be given a say in what happens to them
- have improved communication
- be organised into teams
- be given social facilities such as clubs or sports facilities.

Maslow

Abraham Maslow suggested that the needs of individuals were based on a set of needs that could be ranked into a hierarchy. The lower-ranking needs, such as the need for food, water and then shelter, were more basic. He outlined that basic needs have to be met first before employees can be motivated. His theory is known as the Hierarchy of Needs.

From the diagram opposite you are able to see that as the lower-level needs are satisfied, the employee can then be motivated to the next level of the hierarchy. Maslow's ideas can be usefully applied by managers in a number of ways and are influenced by the structure and culture within the organisation.

- All employees have a range of needs to be satisfied. Any unsatisfied lower-level needs will mean that employees cannot be motivated.
- Offering pay rewards or increasing salary may not motivate employees but inadequate pay will demotivate them.
- Strategies such as increasing responsibility may be used to motivate workers but if basic needs such as safe working conditions are not met, workers will remain demotivated.

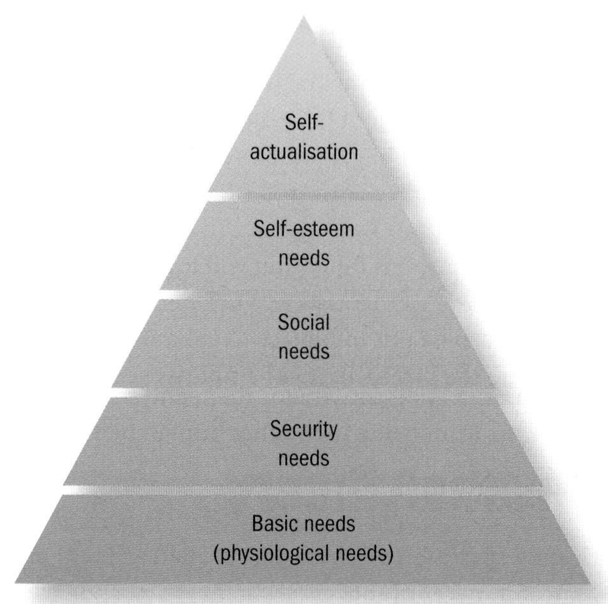

▲ Maslow's Hierarchy of Needs

Herzberg

Like Maslow, Frederick Herzberg believed that pay was not the only motivator and came up with his theory, which had two elements to it – hygiene factors and motivators. For an employee to be motivated, all the hygiene (maintenance) factors have to be met first and then the motivators can be used to make them work harder.

Hygiene factors	Motivators
Level of supervision Too much = demotivation	Achievement
Administration Too much = demotivation	Recognition
Pay Too low = demotivation	Advancement
Working conditions Unsafe = demotivation	Responsibility

From the table above you can see that Herzberg's theory works in a similar way to Maslow in that, even if recognition and advancement are offered, if the working conditions are unsafe an employee will still remain demotivated. A culture that rewards safe working and pays well is likely to have staff who are ready to be motivated.

McGregor

Douglas McGregor took the idea of motivation and applied it to management theory. He believed that there were two main ways of managing employees:

1. **The Theory X** *way*, where employees are managed as if they are lazy and need to be punished and threatened if they don't work hard enough
2. **The Theory Y way**, where employees are managed as if work is a good activity for them and they will get reward from being with other human beings and doing a good job.

The type of management style that is used with employees can make a difference to the level of motivation that they feel. Some employees may work harder if they are threatened with punishment but for others this can lead to demotivation and therefore they will either produce less work or eventually leave.

Theory X managers believe	Theory Y managers believe
Employees want to avoid work Employees are not ambitious Employees need punishments Employees don't want responsibility Employees want to be told what to do	Employees naturally want to do well Employees like responsibility and challenge Employees want to be able to utilise their creativity Employees don't need punishments Employees want to achieve

Thinking point

Consider the two types of manager: Theory X and Theory Y.

1. Which type of manager do you think you work with best? Do you need to be told what to do or do you always try to do a good job?
2. Which type of manager do you think get the best results? Why do you think this?

McClelland

David McClelland took the idea of motivational needs and expanded them further. He suggests that there are three main types of motivational need.

1. The need for achievement.
2. The need for authority and power.
3. The need for affiliation.

Each employee and manager has different levels of these needs, and this influences their style and behaviour as managers or employees.

1. A person who is *achievement-motivated* wants challenging goals and to be able to reach them. They need to receive feedback on how they are doing and to feel that they are a success.
2. A person who is *authority-* and *power-motivated* needs to have a big influence on others and tries to make an impact. They want and need to lead, as this helps them to feel better about themselves
3. A person who is *affiliation-motivated* wants friendly relationships and likes being with other people. They are team players and are often popular at work.

As most people possess a mixture of all three sets of characteristics the style a manager uses is influenced by the dominating style that they experience.

- A manager who has strong *affiliation motivation* will want to be liked and they may find it difficult to make unpopular decisions.
- A manager who is *authority-* and *power-motivated* will take control and want to lead the organisation, but may not be good with people.
- A manager with strong *achievement motivation* is the best type of manager, as they want to achieve and therefore will use results and people to achieve this. The only issue with achievement-motivated managers is that they may ask too much of their staff, which may cause motivational problems in itself.

Vroom

Victor Vroom's theory of expectancy argues that people are motivated according to the effort, performance and outcome that they expect as a result of completing a task. This means that if they believe the effort to be worth putting in they will be motivated to do it; if they believe they are able to do the task they will be motivated to do it; and if the final outcome is something that they value they will be motivated to do it. He produced an equation that is used to calculate motivation:

$M = E \times I \times V$

M = motivation
E = expectancy (the likelihood that effort will be followed by personal achievement)
I = instrumentality (the likelihood that performance will lead to outcomes)
V = valence (the value to the individual of an outcome)

By multiplying these factors together Vroom says it is possible to work out how motivated someone is likely to be. If each of the variables is high then motivation is likely to be high, but if one is low, then overall motivation will be lowered.

Remember

There are seven different influencing theorists that you may wish to consider when you are thinking about motivation and performance.

Reward systems

You have learnt about the different issues associated with motivation and that some theorists believe that pay is the most important factor (Taylor), whereas others believe it is something that must be given to avoid demotivation but does not motivate in itself (Herzberg). You will now learn different ways that rewards can be given to employees to make them work harder in the workplace.

Pay

For many employees, pay is the reason why they attend work. They may not feel motivated to work harder for more pay, but they need it to cover the bills and expenses required for everyday life. Some organisations will use pay to reward their employees. This may be by giving additional pay in the form of a one-off bonus or it could be by giving employees a pay-point rise each year to reward them for their loyalty to the company. Many companies use pay scales to do this, so a junior employee may start on Point 1 and then, if they stay five years, will leave on Point 6.

Employees must be paid at least the minimum wage, so by paying an employee above the minimum wage the employer may be able to suggest they are rewarding the employee. Pay is also linked to qualifications and experience. Pay can be used to attract and reward employees who want to take on additional responsibility such as team leadership or development. Giving an enhancement to their pay is one way to do this.

Performance-related pay

Performance-related pay (PRP) is a way of giving employees extra money depending on their performance in the previous three-, six- or twelve-month period. Many types of employment offer PRP. Linking pay to performance is relatively simple when considering a manufacturing or sales business; the more products that are made or sold, the higher the performance level.

In some industries, applying PRP is a much more complicated business. One such area is education. Many teachers and lecturers receive PRP on the basis of keeping students in classes and on those students passing their courses. If their performance is above what is expected at a national level they are likely to be rewarded with a performance-related element to their pay. Some students may not stay on a course because of very difficult personal problems that are nothing to do with the teacher but this will still affect the results of that class.

The main point to remember about PRP is that the method used to calculate the pay must be easily measurable and avoid any type of inequality. It must be accessible for all employees regardless of race, gender or religion.

The Royal Mail started a scheme to reward employees who had good attendance records and had not taken time off sick by putting their names into a prize draw to win cars or holiday vouchers. As a result, sickness levels between August 2004 and January 2005 were reduced because employees aimed to earn more opportunities to enter the competitions. This saved the company money and improved customer satisfaction as the business was able to complete more work. Such incentive schemes are designed to help certain behaviour at work and to change the culture.

Key Term

Pension A payment that is given to a person when they retire. The pension may be a company scheme that the employee has paid into during their employment, a private scheme that they sort out themselves or the state pension, which they pay into through national insurance contributions.

▲ Royal Mail delivery staff

The share of the profit is distributed between employees depending on the number of years they have worked there and their level in the organisation. If the business is doing well, employees will benefit, but if the business is not doing as well, then payments will be small. The positive side of profit sharing is that it rewards employees if the business does well. The negative side of it is that profits may be linked to other forces such as world events or disasters over which employees have no control, so it can be difficult for employees to see how their individual contribution leads to a change in profits.

Pension schemes

Some organisations offer **pension** schemes as a reward for employees. These usually come in two types: contributory or non-contributory. A contributory pension scheme means that the employee and employer both put money into a pension scheme for the employee when they retire. A non-contributory pension scheme means that only the employer puts money in for the employee when they retire.

Profit sharing

Profit sharing is when a business gives their employees a share of the profits based on how the business is doing.

Employee share options

Like profit sharing, employee share options can be a way to reward employees based on company performance. Share options may be given to employees as free shares that they can sell during a set period of time or as an option, allowing them to buy shares in the company at a fixed rate which is often lower than the current value of the shares. Either way, as shareholders the employees own a small part of the company and therefore may have a greater interest in its performance. As with profit sharing, it can be difficult to see how an individual employee's contributions make a difference to overall company performance, so this may not be a huge motivator.

Mortgage subsidies

Mortgage subsidies are payments that are given to employees towards their mortgages. These sorts of payments are commonly used in areas where housing is expensive or as incentives for employees in areas where there may be a shortage of people with appropriate qualifications. Some institutions such as banks use mortgage subsidies as part of their package for employees.

Relocation fees

Relocation fees are paid to employees to help cover their costs of moving to a new location either as part of their current job or to start a new job. There is no automatic right to receive relocation fees and some organisations will willingly pay for all expenses while others have a set amount they are prepared to pay. Either option will be based on the type of position the employee has or is going for and the level they represent within the organisation. Some examples are given opposite to give you an idea of the amount an employee might receive. Some companies offer a minimal amount as a percentage of the total cost of moving.

Name of organisation	Amount given
E.ON (energy company) www.power-to-inspire.co.uk	£1,500 joining fee given to graduates towards relocation expenses
Haringey Council www.haringey.gov.uk	Up to £5,000 towards stamp duty, fees and relocation expenses
West Hertfordshire Hospitals (NHS) www.westhertshospitals.nhs.uk	Up to £7,500 after quotations and receipts have been provided plus employees must continue to work for the Hospitals for a minimum of two years or pay back the money.

Bonuses

Bonuses can be a good way of giving employees extra money without including them as a payment that has to be given every year. Often linked to a particular level of performance as a result of reviews or as a one-off special bonus for the completion of a project or piece of good work, they are a reward that many employees enjoy. As with pay, employees must pay tax and national insurance on their bonus.

Case study

Essex teacher recruitment

Essex County Council offers incentives including rent and mortgage subsidies for teachers in certain subject areas or at certain levels. The mortgage subsidy scheme offers monthly payments towards mortgages for five years for teachers moving from other cheaper housing areas to Essex. The amount of money paid to the individual teacher is not based on the difference between their mortgage in the old location and the one in Essex but is a set amount, fixed by the local education authority. The payments are made to secondary school teachers who offer subjects such as English, Maths or ICT. These payments are made on condition that the teacher stays and works for the council or area for a specified amount of time and that they live within 25 miles of the organisation for which they are working. By offering mortgage subsidies Essex County Council is likely to attract more applicants for jobs than it would otherwise.

1. What is meant by a mortgage subsidy and how does it work? ✓
2. What are the benefits of offering such a scheme? ✓✓
3. What are the limitations of the scheme? ✓✓
4. To what extent can mortgage subsidies reward teachers? ✓✓✓

Company vehicles

Company vehicles may be given to employees as a reward. This means they can use the vehicle in their working and personal lives, so they do not need to have their own vehicle. As with bonuses, tax must be paid on this type of benefit.

Loans/advances

If employees have large expenses to pay in their personal lives, employers may offer to pay part of their wages in advance, to help them out during this time. Other employers also offer loans, often with a special low rate of interest to help their employees out when they need it.

Childcare

Childcare is a reward that can be given to staff with children. Some employers offer childcare within their own buildings by providing a nursery or crèche. Others pay towards the fees of private or council nurseries in which the children are placed. For older children, after-school and holiday clubs may be paid for or subsidised. A further way that employers may offer help with childcare is in the form of childcare vouchers. These vouchers are often offered on a tax-free basis and allow employees to save money on tax and national insurance contributions for childcare. In April 2005, employees were able to receive up to £243 per month, which results in a saving in tax and national insurance contributions of £962 per year. This can make a big difference to employees.

School fees

Some employers may also choose to pay for school fees as a reward for employees, particularly if they are teaching or working for the school that the child is being sent to. If an organisation has a number of employees sending their children to a particular school they may be able to gain discounts and therefore make it even more cost effective.

Corporate clothes

Some organisations offer corporate clothes as a reward for employees. This might be in the form of a uniform to wear as part of the job or by offering them discounts on clothing they can buy from the business. Some organisations use corporate clothing as part of their identity, for example you can recognise staff that work for organisations like ASDA or McDonald's when they are in uniform even if they are not in the store. Other businesses use clothes as a way to advertise to customers the different types of clothing they have on offer. Some clothing chains offer 50% or even 75% off their clothing for employees, providing they wear the clothes to work.

Staff discounts

You have already learnt about discounts on clothing, but many businesses offer staff discounts across the range of their products or even have negotiated discounts on the products offered by other businesses they work with. The Virgin Tribe Discount card is an example of a discount card that is given to staff working for the Virgin Group of companies that gives them money off everything from plane tickets to CDs sold by Virgin companies and other companies that Virgin work with.

▲ **Richard Branson uses the Virgin Tribe Card to reward staff**

Flexible working

Other ways to increase the motivation of employees in work include making them feel more valued by giving them special working arrangements to help them balance their work and home life, known as the 'work–life balance'. To do this some employees prefer flexible working practices. This might be flexi-time, which means working a certain number of hours per week but choosing the hours within guidelines set by the employer, for example between 6 am and 8 pm.

Leave

Offering paid leave for employees each year is another way of rewarding employees. Every employee is entitled to four weeks paid leave per year as part of the Working Time Regulations 1998. If employers decide to offer a more generous amount of holiday per year, they can use this as a reward for their staff. The number of days that employees receive from their employers can vary enormously from the minimum four weeks to thirteen weeks per year. It will depend on the type of job that the person is doing, how difficult it may be to recruit for that role and the level of expertise that is needed to do the job. In businesses where self-employed workers are used to conduct the day-to-day work (e.g. a self-employed hairdresser working in a salon), there is no entitlement to holiday, as they need to arrange to pay themselves during this period.

Thinking point

In 2005 a survey was conducted by the Chartered Management Institute (CMI) into the number of days that managers took as part of their annual leave. Most UK managers admitted they continued to work during their holidays and a third did not take their full entitlement. This saved companies around £900,000,000 per year. When managers do go on holiday they found they often checked their e-mail and voicemail and found it hard to relax.

- What effects might there be on managers who take reduced holiday times?
- What impact would this potentially have on the business?
- What can employers do about this?

Healthcare

Many employers now offer free or subsidised healthcare for their employees and often their families as well. This means if they are ill they can claim from organisations such as BUPA to have private healthcare treatment. The healthcare may also be given in the form of vouchers for related treatment such as discounts on massages, visits to the osteopath or beauty therapist. The employee may receive the treatment either at the premises of the therapist or at the employee's workplace. Organisations such as www.onsitemassageco.com offer massages and treatments in the workplace. By receiving such services at work employees may take less time off sick and are more motivated, as they are less stressed. This saves money for the employer and makes employees happier.

Extended parental leave

Extended parental leave is leave that employees can take to look after their children in addition to the paid leave they are entitled to as part of the Work and Families Act 2006. Often the extended parental leave is not paid but the employer keeps the employee's job open for them to return to.

Career breaks

Career breaks are a way of offering extended parental leave for parents if they wish to take a number of years off work. Some employers offer to give their employees career breaks so they can stay at home and look after their children until they go to school. Others offer career breaks to give their employees the chance to do something that they have always wanted to do. There is a huge variety of reasons that employees might have for taking time out, such as travelling the world, doing charity work, studying a language in a country where

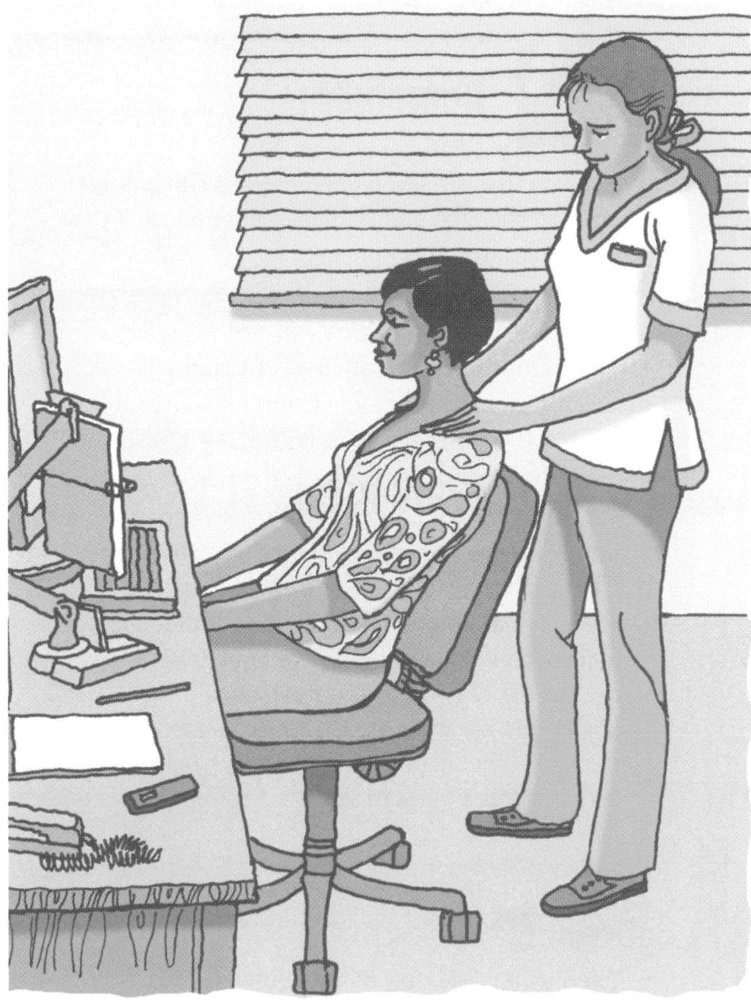

◀ **Massage treatments are one type of reward that may help employees to reduce their stress levels and feel looked after**

it is spoken, or going on an expedition. According to www.careerbreak.com, career breaks are more common for employees over the age of 35 than for those who are younger. While it may seem disadvantageous for employers to allow their employees to have breaks from the workplace, there are some advantages.

- The employee may learn new skills and ideas they can bring back to work.
- The employer may avoid losing key staff, who simply need a short period to do something different.
- The employee is likely to return to work happy, refreshed and motivated.
- The employee's confidence level may also have increased, if they have achieved a personal goal during their break.
- It may enhance company image, as the company is seen to care about its employees.

Cafeteria incentive schemes

Cafeteria incentive schemes work much like any food cafeteria you have been into. Employees are offered a selection of different rewards and benefits, and they choose which ones that they want. For example, the choice may include:

- holidays
- company car
- bicycle loan
- insurance, e.g. medical or house
- loans
- childcare
- health screening
- season tickets for sporting events
- computers
- discounts
- pension.

Some employees may wish to have longer holidays as one of their rewards whereas others may want a company car. As well as the obvious benefit of the scheme to the employee, it also benefits the employer in that the employee will be happier and more motivated, and the organisation avoids spending money on rewards that are not wanted or needed. However, there are some potential difficulties for employers. First, it may be difficult to compare the value of various benefits. This may mean that a system using points or tokens needs to be included. Second, the system can be very complicated to set up, so it will require more time and effort in the early stages.

Salary sacrifice schemes

These schemes allow employees to give up part of their **gross salary** to receive some kind of benefit instead. One example of this is a pension salary sacrifice scheme. The employee gives up some of their pay and, in return, the employer donates more money on their behalf into a pension. The advantage of using this type of scheme is that the employee and employer will not have to pay as much tax or national insurance. Salary sacrifice schemes can also be offered on a range of other benefits such as computers, mobile phones or childcare.

Key Terms

Gross salary Salary before any deductions, such as tax or national insurance, are made.

Net salary Salary that is put into the employee's account after deductions are made from gross salary.

Outcome activity 16.2

Produce a case study about the organisation you used for Outcome activity 16.2 or another organisation with which you are familiar. Include details within the case study of how this organisation motivates its employees, making use of theory and practice.

Pass P3

In your introduction outline how the organisation's motivational practices and reward systems are informed by theories of motivation.

Merit 

Compare the use of motivational theories in your chosen organisation.

Distinction 

Suggest, with justification based on your findings, ways of improving motivation in the organisation.

Remember

Benefits that are given to employees can only be used to enhance and increase performance if they are valued by those employees.

Grading tips

Pass 

You will need to show how the ideas from motivational theorists you have learnt about, such as Maslow, Mayo or Taylor, have shaped the way that employees are motivated in the organisation you are studying. You should make clear links between the use of a type of reward and the motivational theory that links to it, e.g. the use of childcare vouchers to satisfy affiliation needs.

Merit 

You should show how different theories of motivation contribute to employee motivation techniques in the organisation in more detail, building on your answer to question 1. You should show how some motivational theories are more relevant in this organisation than others as a result of the reward systems they use.

Distinction 

You should conclude your case study with suggestions, based on justified conclusions, of how the organisation could improve motivation. Focus on the type of reward systems that could be introduced, e.g. a cafeteria incentive system. You should also outline any issues that might arise in the development and introduction of such reward systems.

16.3 How to gain committed employee co-operation

You have already learnt about employee motivation and rewards. Employee co-operation is a related feature of human resource planning. It aims to involve employees in what is happening within the workplace by outlining the entitlements and expectations of both employer and employee and the different groups and schemes that can help both parties to work effectively together.

Contracts of employment

The contract of employment is the contract that is made between the employer and employee. The employer agrees to offer a salary in return for the employee performing duties. Types of entitlements, rights and procedures associated with employment contracts are described in the text that follows.

Remember

Although most contracts of employment are written statements, they do not have to be provided within the first two months of work. After two months a written statement, outlining the main terms, must be provided.

Contractual entitlement

Contractual entitlements are outlined within the contract so that the employer and employee know what is expected of each other. They include arrangements for the employment such as:

- hours of work
- sick pay
- holiday pay
- amount of pay and when it is paid
- notice period
- type of employment, e.g. temporary or fixed
- disciplinary rules.

Employee and employer rights

Some of the entitlements that are written into the contract are statutory entitlements (legal rights for the employee), while others are voluntary. Terms that are written very clearly and directly within the contract, such as '25 days holiday per annum', are known as 'express terms'. There is also a set of terms within the contract known as 'implied terms'. These are implied expectations such as the employer's trust and the employee's co-operation.

As a result of changes in the law there is also a huge list of statutory rights that an employee and employer must adhere to within the contract. These are just a few of the employee's rights:

- equal pay
- not to be subject to discrimination
- not to be unfairly dismissed
- an itemised pay statement
- maternity or paternity pay
- notice of termination of employment
- redundancy pay
- statutory sick pay
- annual leave
- minimum wage.

As well as the employee having rights, the employer has rights too. It is written into the contract that the employee will work within Health and Safety legislation, that they will give notice to the employer if they decide to change employment and that they give notice before they go on paternity or maternity leave.

Types of employment contract

Like the different types of working arrangements that you learnt at the start of this chapter, there are also different types of employment contract.

Permanent contracts are common. They contain information about the pay and conditions that are offered and accepted by the parties until further notice.

Temporary contracts are becoming increasingly popular as they can help businesses to manage costs more effectively. A temporary contract may be offered on a fixed-term basis, for example for 35 hours a week for 12 months.

A zero hours contract offers more flexibility for an employer as it means the employer only pays for the hours that have actually been worked rather than agreeing to a specific number of hours. Zero hours contracts are often used in industries such as retailing where casual labour is required on a flexible basis.

Annual hours contracts work in a similar way to zero hours except that a set number of hours are guaranteed over the year (or whatever length of term has been agreed) and the employee works them at times that suit the employer, e.g. working more hours during busy times and fewer hours when things are less busy.

It is also possible to have part-time contracts. These may just involve one person doing the hours or can be offered as part of a job-share arrangement, where two people do half a full-time job between them. There is also the possibility of having a fractional contract where one person works part-time, doing part of the contract, e.g. 50% or 60%. This can be a good way to divide up a full-time job with one person doing 40% of a full-time contract and the other doing 60%.

To help parents, term-time only contracts are often offered in schools and colleges to help employees who need to look after their own children during holidays. Some employers also offer flexi-time contracts so that employees work a set of core hours and then work additional hours beyond those, according to their needs and those of the business.

Self-employed contracts are a further option that can be used by businesses. This is when a person is asked to do a job but on the basis that they are doing it as if they are running their own business. This means that they have to sort out their own national insurance, tax, sick pay and holiday pay. Self-employed contracts may be used for electricians, builders or beauty therapists who go into a workplace offering services. Using self-employed contracts can be complicated for employers, as it may be difficult to prove whether the person is actually offering services or is in fact an employee by working for the business.

Disciplinary procedure

By law an employer must give an employee a written copy of their disciplinary procedure. This sets out the rules and guidelines concerning any breach (breaking) of contract by the employee.

Statutory minimum procedure

The disciplinary procedure includes a minimum number of steps that must be followed before the employee can be dismissed. This is known as a statutory minimum procedure. If employers do not follow their disciplinary procedure carefully they can be accused of unfair dismissal and taken to an industrial tribunal. The minimum three steps are shown below. (Some employers may have more steps in their procedure but there must be these steps as a minimum.)

Standard (three-step) dismissal and disciplinary procedure	
Step 1	The employer must set down in writing the nature of the employee's conduct, capability or other circumstances that may result in dismissal or disciplinary action, and sends a copy of this statement to the employee.
Step 2	The employer must invite the employee to a hearing at a reasonable time and place where the issue can be discussed. The employee must take all reasonable steps to attend. After the meeting, the employer must inform the employee about any decision, and offer the employee the right of appeal.
Step 3	If the employee wishes to appeal, he/she must inform the employer. The employer must invite the employee to attend a further hearing to appeal against the employer's decision, and the final decision must be communicated to the employee. Where possible, a more senior manager should attend the appeal hearing.

Source: Employment Act 2002 Guidance, www.berr.gov.uk

Warnings

There are also some different types of warning that can be given to employees, depending on the action of the employee that has made it necessary to start disciplinary procedures.

Verbal	The employee is told about their behaviour orally.
Written	The employee is told about their behaviour in writing – usually for more serious offences.
Final written warning	A final written warning is issued after previous warnings to get the employee to improve have failed

▲ Types of warning

Gross misconduct

Sometimes employees do things that are so serious they are described as 'gross misconduct'. Here are some examples:

- violence
- drug or alcohol abuse
- damage to property or equipment
- serious breaches of Health and Safety regulations
- fraud
- theft
- harassment or discrimination
- negligence with serious consequences.

In such cases, an employer may need to ask the employee to leave the company straight away, while an investigation takes place. During that period the employee will still be paid. This enables the employer to follow the minimum statutory procedure and to arrange a meeting with the employee to talk about what has happened. If the employer does not follow the procedure very carefully, the employee could sue them for unfair dismissal.

Grievance procedure

A grievance procedure is the process that can help an employee bring something to the attention of their employer that they are not happy about. The grievance procedure should be given to an employee within their contract of employment or published in the company handbook or website. It can be used by employees to highlight any issues regarding their working arrangements, e.g. pay or working hours. A typical process for the grievance procedure in an organisation is shown opposite. The employee must try each stage in turn, continuing if they do not meet with success at the previous stage.

Talk through the problem with the line manager, human resources person or trade union to ask for help to solve it informally.

Make a formal complaint in writing.

Attend a hearing with your employer and wait for them to give the employee a decision.

Appeal against the decision and wait for further outcome.

Take the grievance to an Employment Tribunal where the problem will be dealt with independently. (This can be a costly undertaking.)

▲ The grievance procedure

Practice point

Find out more about Employment Tribunals by conducting research on the government's website (www.employmenttribunals.gov.uk/claim/hearing.htm).

- What are the procedures that happen there?
- Who can attend?
- What documents are needed?
- How much does it cost?
- Who can help with payments if you are on a low income?

Take it further

Produce a worksheet or information pack that could be given to employers, helping them to understand more about what happens in an Employment Tribunal and how they may be affected.

Remember

Employers must be aware of the latest changes in legislation to make sure that their procedures and policies are up to date and comply with the law.

Union membership

Trade unions can play an important role in a business. Unions will negotiate with management on behalf of a number of workers about pay or working conditions. Some organisations may not want to recognise a union and this may demotivate employees, as they may feel they have no one to speak on their behalf. ACAS (Advisory, Conciliation and Arbitration Service) can try to help employees get union recognition in their workplace by law, but this can be complicated and take a long time.

Practice point

Copy the following table about trade unions. Complete it to show the advantages to both the employee and employer of having a recognised union. What are the possible disadvantages?

You may find it helpful to use websites such as ACAS (www.acas.org.uk), Business Link (www.businesslink.gov.uk) and the Department for Business, Enterprise and Regulatory Reform (www.berr.gov.uk).

	Trade unions
Advantages to the employer	
Advantages to the employee	
Disadvantages to the employer	
Disadvantages to the employee	

Codes of behaviour

To avoid any confusion that may arise between employers and employees about what is acceptable behaviour and what is not, many employers now publish a code of behaviour giving clear guidelines. These codes can include details on everything from the use of internet and e-mail in the workplace to how to speak to other employees. An example of a code of behaviour used by HM Treasury is given opposite.

Employee involvement techniques

The aim of employee involvement techniques is to get workers more involved in decision-making at work, so they feel more motivated and happy.

Membership of work groups

Employers may have work groups, where workers get together and make recommendations about changes in the workplace. They might look at areas of the business such as health, technology at work or working parents. Some work groups may also have a task to look at, e.g. quality issues within the company. They meet to discuss activities related to their job or even to the company as a whole. The outcomes of the work group meetings are fed back to senior managers in the business, who can help to implement changes based on the recommendations.

Quality circles

Like other work groups, quality circles are groups of workers who meet to discuss ways of improving the workplace, but their focus is on safety, product design and manufacturing. They are able to make suggestions that could make workers' jobs easier and more effective, and by having greater responsibility for quality they are likely to be motivated to work harder.

HM Treasury Code of Conduct

Aim

- To provide a framework which delivers to every member of staff the feeling that they are a valued member of the department.
- By recognising staff who treat colleagues and business contacts properly. And by refusing to employ, promote or reward staff who consistently do not meet these high standards and who will not accept guidance or training in order to do so.
- So as to create an atmosphere of harmony and co-operation.

Code

You have the right to:

- be spoken to politely
- be treated with respect
- have your life and commitments outside the office respected
- be assertive
- expect colleagues to treat you as a fellow professional
- speak out if you are the victim of bullying, vindictiveness, verbal or physical aggression and to expect your complaint to be taken seriously.

You have a responsibility to:

- treat all colleagues as individuals and show sensitivity to their needs
- praise work done well and balance praise against any constructive criticism of work that could have been done better
- be assertive and not aggressive
- listen to what others say and respect their point of view
- take action swiftly if you witness or are made aware of unreasonable behaviour; you should not assume it is someone else's problem
- try to learn from your mistakes in handling relations with others
- take every complaint or disagreement seriously and work to find common ground.

Source: www.hm-treasury.gov.uk

Intra-organisational groups

Having intra-organisational groups can help businesses by allowing different areas of the organisation to meet and share their experience and ideas. For example, there may be a simple procedure that is being followed within one area that is causing problems for another area. Getting groups together that represent the different areas can help to avoid this and encourage greater understanding of how the business works as a whole.

Suggestion schemes

Suggestion schemes are another way that employees can communicate with their employer. Simple suggestions by employees can sometimes save organisations large amounts of money. Occasionally the schemes give out awards (Bronze, Silver and Gold) or money prizes for an employee suggestion that has been successfully implemented.

▲ Employee suggestions can prove invaluable

Thinking point

Does your college or school have a suggestion scheme? If yes, what is good about it and how can it be improved even more? If not, could one be introduced and how could it be put into place to make effective solutions of ways to improve?

Delegated authority and responsibility

Giving authority and responsibility to more junior employees is a way of getting them more involved in the business. It means they have the power to make decisions themselves and be responsible for them. Delegating (passing on) authority and responsibility in

Case study

Vodafone reported that its employee suggestion scheme 'My big idea' had generated more than 500 relevant ideas from employees that were to be used for improving customer experience and the products and services offered. From these, the top ideas will be picked and then a final winner chosen and implemented. The competitive element in this scheme helps to motivate employees, and the result may be of considerable benefit to Vodafone and its customers.

1. What is meant by an employee suggestion scheme? ✓
2. Which different methods can be used to run a scheme, based on evidence from the case study and this chapter? ✓✓
3. What might the issues be when implementing such a scheme? ✓✓

this way can help to motivate an employee. However there are a few issues that need to be considered.

- The employee may not want to take on the authority and responsibility without extra payment.
- They may feel under additional pressure and therefore potential stress.
- They may need extra training to be able to cope.
- They may not be suitably qualified for the additional role and may have the potential to negatively affect the running of the business.

Open communications

Open communication at work means having two-way communication so that employees feel they are involved and aware of what is happening in the company. By having open communication and letting employees know how things are going and of any possible changes or issues, employees are helped to feel that they are an important part of the organisation. If communication with employees is not open, problems can arise, as they are likely to feel they are being excluded from issues that are relevant to them. This is when the 'grapevine' – the unofficial communication channel that operates in a business – can develop, leading to the circulation of rumours. Keeping communication open is an attempt to avoid this. It is also likely to lead to more trust and understanding between employer and employee.

Open communication can take place in different ways within an organisation, and it is important to ensure that a variety of methods is used. Some of these methods are shown in the table below.

Types of communication

The type of communication used within an organisation can affect the message that the employees receive. Employees are likely to feel more trust in the organisation if information is communicated in a relatively personal way, such as in a discussion, rather than through e-mail or text. The table on the following page lists the advantages and disadvantages of each type of communication.

Organisational culture

Organisational culture is often described as 'the way we do things around here'. It is like a set of rules that employees learn and abide by that influences their behaviour. It could be as simple as using first names for the company directors or bringing cakes in on your birthday. The culture can influence whether the business operates in a forward-thinking or traditional way.

▼ **Methods of communication**

Method	Meaning	Examples
Formal	Official method of communication between employer and employees.	• Company newsletter • Staff briefing
Informal	Friendly, relaxed communication between employees.	• Chat with another employee • Group discussion over coffee
Top-down	Communication that comes from the highest point in the organisation, e.g. managing director, which is passed down to other managers before reaching employees.	Company speech or announcement of sales targets
Bottom-up	Communication that starts with employees and then works its way up the organisation, so an employee tells their manager and then it goes to the manager's manager and so on to the top of the organisation.	Employee suggestions for improvements
Lateral	Communication between employees at the same level – sometimes called horizontal communication.	A team meeting of employees who are all at the same level

▼ Advantages and disadvantages of different types of communication

Communication type	Advantages	Disadvantages
Face-to-face meeting	• Gives the employees the option to ask questions. • Immediate form of communication where everyone can be involved. • Everyone is present so it avoids miscommunication or rumours developing. • Fast method.	• May be difficult to arrange. • May be confrontational if there is bad news to communicate. • Employees may not hear everything that is said or may misunderstand something.
Telephone	• Fast method. • Gives employees the chance to reflect on what is being said without being directly in front of the manager.	• May interrupt the employee working and therefore lose working time. • Does not give any visual clues such as body language to support the message.
Memo	• Written, so can be clearly stated.	• Subject to personal interpretation. • Takes time to photocopy and send out. • May take time to reach all employees if sent to their home addresses or via work postal system. • Does not directly permit the asking of questions, so may need a follow-up meeting. • May not be possible to see whether someone has read it or not.
E-mail	• Fast to use. • Immediate response is possible. • Receipts can be issued to show that it has been read. • Can include links to relevant information and other media, e.g. video clips.	• May be too informal, depending on the information to be communicated. • May not be accessed by employees who dislike e-mail. • May be easily forwarded to people outside the organisation, which may not be appropriate. • May be ignored by employees if this method is used very often.
Text message	• Fast. • Easy to use. • To the point.	• Brief, so may not be able to communicate enough information. • Only useful if everyone has access to a mobile phone. • Can seem too informal if serious information is being sent.
Company newsletter	• Room to include lots of information in an attractive/glossy format. • Can highlight good practice and reward employees for good service.	• May be costly to produce. • May seem irrelevant to employees if appropriate information is not chosen. • Can quickly go out of date.
Company intranet	• Easy to update. • Can include other forms of media, e.g. video clips. • Can include all the information that employees might need in one place.	• Needs regular updating or employees will not keep accessing it. • May be too informal for certain types of information. • Does not usually incorporate online discussion.

The ethos of the organisation represents the beliefs, values and attitudes held by the organisation. Ethos and culture are closely linked. In some organisations the ethos and values are rooted in particular religious or charity-based values. Cadbury, for example, was set up by Quakers and has been influenced by Quaker values in the way it looks after its employees and invests in the local community. Many organisations use their mission statement to outline their values and culture, to make it clear to employees what their organisation represents.

Mission statement for Borders book stores

Our mission is more than just a statement. Everything Borders Group sets out to achieve begins with the core values at the heart of our mission.

'To be the best-loved provider of books, music, films and other entertainment and informational products and services. To be the world leader in selection, service, innovation, ambiance, community involvement and shareholder value. We recognise people to be the cornerstone of the Borders experience by building internal and external relationships, one person at a time.'

Source: www.bordersstores.co.uk

Case study

Fire fighters' culture

Some aspects of corporate culture can work across whole industries, as well as within individual organisations. One example is the culture of fire fighters. Their culture is based on tradition and values that have been passed down over generations.

When dealing with dangerous incidents, fire fighters have to have complete confidence in their colleagues, as they must trust each other with their lives. Their culture is therefore based on strong leadership and respect, and as each fire fighter joins the service they become part of that culture. Some of the influences on the culture come from the need to wear a uniform and follow orders as part of drills and safety checks each day.

There are approximately 38,000 full-time fire fighters and 15,000 part-time fire fighters in the UK, most of whom are members of the Fire Brigades Union (FBU). Between 2002 and 2003, members of the FBU agreed by ballot to take industrial action. They went on strike for varying lengths of time. They were protesting that:

- their pay was inadequate
- changes were being made to their jobs, such as different shift patterns and arrangements for overtime
- fire fighters were due to lose their jobs.

During the strikes the police and armed forces undertook fire-fighting duties, but some fire fighters helped out at very serious fires while they were officially on strike. This was partly to do with the culture of the organisation. Fire fighters feel a very strong duty to protect each other and the general public. Therefore, although they were willing to take industrial action, they were prepared to assist in difficult situations.

▲ Fire fighters staging a protest

1. What do you think is meant by a culture of 'strong leadership and respect'? ✓
2. Why do you think it is so important to have a strong culture in an organisation such as the fire service? ✓✓
3. How could changing working conditions affect the culture of an organisation? ✓✓✓

Remember

The culture of an organisation affects the way that communications are sent and received by employers and employees.

National accreditation

Some companies hope to prove their commitment to their employees by winning relevant status awards.

Investors in People

One of the best-known awards is Investors in People (IiP). IiP is based on four key elements:

- commitment to employees
- planning for their development
- taking action to develop them
- evaluating success.

In 2002 IiP conducted research with employers that showed that by gaining IiP status there was an increase in employee commitment and productivity.

Askham Bryan College LIBRARY BOOK

Charter Mark

Charter Mark is the national standard for customer service excellence within the public service. The scheme is owned by the Cabinet Office. Achieving the Charter Mark standard encourages the public service to be the very best, to focus on its customers, to constantly improve and give value for money. All are key to the efficient delivery of public services. By reaching the standard, organisations show that they put their customers first and go that extra mile.

International Standards Organisation

The International Standards Organisation (ISO) has brought into force a number of standards associated with quality procedures and working methods that can be met by organisations. In order to gain the standards, organisations need to get staff more involved with making suggestions and decisions, and offer them the necessary training and support to help them put their ideas into practice.

Outcome activity 16.3

Pass P4

Produce a briefing pamphlet for your chosen organisation describing how organisations obtain the co-operation of employees through the contract of employment and employee involvement techniques.

Grading tips

Pass 

You will need to divide your pamphlet into two sections.

1. Describe what is meant by a contract of employment and what must be contained within it, including the rights of employees and employers.
2. Go on to outline different ways that employees can be involved in communication with their employer including employee suggestion schemes, work groups, unions and additional responsibility. You should consider the culture of an organisation and how that affects employees, including links between the employer and the local community.

16.4 The importance of managing employee performance at work

Encouraging employees to be more involved and motivating them is likely to increase the amount of work that they do. To check that this is happening, employers need to measure and manage employee performance.

Measuring performance

While motivation is the key to encouraging employees to work as hard as possible, a business can only find out how hard employees are working if it measures their performance to see how productive each employee is.

Performance indicators

Businesses have different ways of measuring employee performance. For example, they might calculate how many customers an employee has served on a till per day, how many products they have made in a factory or how many reports they have written in a week. Measurements like these give management a tool for comparing employees.

Some industries find it more difficult to measure productivity than others. If employees are sewing slippers in a factory, it is relatively easy to compare the number made; e.g. Sunita made 20 pairs and James made nine – Sunita has been more productive than James. But in some industries, such as service industries, it is difficult to draw accurate comparisons. This is because some measurements are quantitative (linked to numbers and statistics), whereas others are qualitative (based on opinions and judgements). In service industries, more qualitative measurements are made. Each method has its place but they must be used carefully and appropriately so both the employee and employer feel their needs are being met.

In the National Health Service, for example, it may be possible to compare bed occupancy rates of hospitals throughout the UK, but some may be in areas of greater ill health. This may mean one area appears more productive than another, and may not be a good way of comparing the efficiency of the service. Healthcare is difficult to measure as it is not just about numbers and processing 'products' – it is about offering people care and attention.

Achievement against targets

Worker performance measurements will be different, as you have already learnt, depending on the type of industry. In banking and other office-based environments measurement is often linked with the employer's appraisal system. Under this system the employer and employee measure performance against objectives or targets that were set in a previous review. These reviews can take place at different intervals such as three, six or even twelve months. Examples of targets that may be set for an employee might include learning a new software package or taking part in a training day and putting a new skill into practice.

Some employers may give an employee six or eight relatively simple targets, whereas others may concentrate on only one or two more difficult targets that require a high level of performance.

It is important that targets are relevant to the employee as well as the employer, so that everyone is aware of what needs to be achieved and the way in which the targets will help to meet the business' and employee's needs. At the review meeting, those targets will be measured against what has actually happened and a judgement will be made.

Goal theory

Goal theory is about setting goals for employees to achieve. The best set of goals is produced when the employer and employee work together to set them.

Practice point

Consider the following businesses. What type of measurement could be used for productivity, and which method of performance management could be used? The first example is completed for you.

Organisation	Measurement of performance	Method of review
Restaurant	Number of dishes produced Number of customers served Spend per customer Amount of waste produced Mystery shopper results	Daily target setting with weekly review by restaurant manager Mystery shopper results analysed monthly Action plans drawn up weekly for shortfalls Annual appraisal of individual staff performance
Police force		
Bank		
Charity		
Estate Agent		

Employees then have the incentive to meet their goals in order to achieve the performance that is required. Working towards goals can increase the motivation of employees and therefore make them more productive. It is also important that employees want to achieve the goals and that they value the rewards for achieving their goals. These may not be monetary rewards but could be in the form of recognition or praise.

SMART targets

SMART is a business tool that is used to work out how useful a set of objectives actually is. Judging objectives according to how 'SMART' they are means testing how focused those objectives are.

SMART means:

- **S**pecific – objectives should have a focus and not be vague
- **M**easurable – objectives should include something that can be measured
- **A**chievable – if staff don't think they can achieve the objectives they will be demotivated
- **R**ealistic – objectives should be realistic in relation to both the resources and skills available, and the overall goals of the organisation
- **T**ime-related – objectives must have an end so that success can be measured.

SMART targets may be used to give employees set amounts of work that need to be achieved or levels of sales that need to be set by a certain date. After the targets are set, measurement and review dates may be added, so that progress can be monitored and checked at the end.

Benchmarking

One way for a business to gain a basis for the comparison of performance is through the use of industry-wide benchmarks. Benchmarking seeks to provide data in an industry so that competitors within that industry can judge how they are doing against the best possible standards. The best organisation in an industry becomes the standard to which all other competitors should aspire.

Benchmarking can be used to compare the performance of different employees with national standards, for example the level of sales an employee is making per month, or the number of calls or customer complaints received. It can then be used to give employees a level of performance that they need to match or exceed for comparison purposes.

Managing performance

Managing performance is about taking the measurements and ideas that employees have been given and keeping an eye on how they are progressing.

Probation

When an employee starts a new job they are often put on probation for a certain amount of time so they can be monitored more closely. This gives the employee the opportunity to demonstrate their suitability for the job but also allows an employer to dismiss the employee if they are not suitable for the job. The amount of time an employee is on probation depends on the level of job they have been appointed to do, and can be anything from one week to one year. It is unusual to be on probation for longer than this.

Having an employee on probation allows more feedback meetings and intervention to take place, which can be useful for the employer and employee to help them constantly improve.

Appraisal

Appraisal systems in any organisation should be designed to motivate and encourage employees to give their best performance. The targets that are set by employer and employee should strike a balance between what is needed for the business and what the employee needs. An employee may feel they would like to attend a particular course in the coming appraisal period, but if it does not meet a business need the manager may need to persuade them to undertake different training.

Advantages of appraisal systems	Disadvantages of appraisal systems
Allow an employer and employee to discuss and work together on improving performance, leading to better use of resources or more profits.	Need tight control so that all appraisers set the same level of target, and standards are fair.
Provide a formal system for monitoring and measuring performance.	Targets need to be achievable, but if they are too easy costs may go up.
Rewards can be given for good performance such as pay rises, prizes or time off.	If targets are too high, employees may feel demotivated.
Allow business objectives to be filtered down and 'owned' by all employees, therefore more likely to be achieved.	Will only be useful if both the employer and employee believe in the system and regard it as valuable.
Allow the employee and employer to learn more about each other and therefore improve their working relationship.	Need time and effort to be done successfully – a bad appraisal interview is far worse than none at all.
Allow the business to plan training and development so that future needs can be met, e.g. planning for someone to take over when someone else is about to retire.	Budgetary constraints may mean a limited amount of money is available for training and therefore needs identified within the appraisal system cannot be met.

Some appraisal systems include self-appraisal. This is an opportunity for the employee to consider their own performance and to set themselves targets to achieve. By doing self-appraisal employees can help to manage their own performance and make improvements. As a result of this, they are more likely to be motivated in the workplace.

Take it further

Produce a self-assessment document that could be used by future students on your course in order that they can improve their productivity and performance.

Practice point

Complete the mini self-assessment below by considering your performance so far on your BTEC National course. Be honest with yourself – have you given your best performance, or have there been times when you could have made improvements or given extra effort?

Read each of the following statements and tick (in pencil) which most applies to you.

Statement	Very like me	A bit like me	Not like me	Very unlike me
I have been excellent at planning and have always handed my assignments in on time.				
I have coped with various difficulties during the course but have overcome them.				
I have spent time giving detailed analysis within my work.				
I have developed my listening skills during the course in order to more fully understand what I am being asked to do.				
I am gradually developing more skills in order to succeed at the higher levels on the BTEC National course.				
I am determined to get a Merit or Distinction on this course.				

This mini self-assessment should have given you some idea of why reviewing yourself can be important. Discuss your results with your teacher so that you can set targets for your course that will help you to achieve the highest level possible.

Remember

The best appraisal systems include opportunities for employers to comment on performance and for employees to reflect on how they feel they have performed themselves.

Supporting employees

Supporting employees to make sure their performance is managed effectively takes two main forms: mentoring (where an employee is given access to another employee for help and advice) and monitoring (where employee performance is measured and analysed).

Mentoring

A manager may act as a mentor – someone who supports and encourages someone else within the workplace to achieve the best performance possible. The person the manager is supporting, known as a mentee, may be a subordinate or someone on the same grade. The relationship is one to one, in that the mentor tries to pass on all their knowledge and experience to the mentee. The mentor also helps to support the mentee by encouraging them to break down barriers and achieve their full potential. A key benefit of having a mentor is that a mentee can discuss their ideas and be helped to make judgements made about their best way forward within the industry. The mentor may also be willing to share business contacts and to help their mentee form new social networks.

Monitoring

Monitoring is the process of checking back with an employee to see whether they are making progress. Monitoring takes two main forms: formal monitoring (whereby a manager uses an established method of checking the employee's progress), and informal monitoring (whereby a manager makes subtle judgements about how the employee is fitting in to the workplace or noticing if that employee has some kind of work-related problem).

Occupational health

Humans, unlike machines, may feel stress in the workplace. While employers want employees to work as hard as they possibly can, they also need to understand and put into place methods of helping their employees deal with pressure. There are many different ways this can be done. For example, in the Netherlands something as simple as increasing the number of plants put in offices has been found to increase productivity and reduce stress. Similarly, government jobcentres in the UK were given softer décor to make the environment more relaxing for both staff and customers.

Making the environment at work as healthy and relaxing as possible should help employees to feel happier while they are there, but they also need to feel safe in order to feel less stressed. Stress may be reduced

▲ A plant-filled environment can lower stress levels

for bank workers if they are behind security screens, or for bus drivers if two-way radios are available. In many large cities taxi drivers not only have two-way radios but also have CCTV in their cabs to make them feel safer when they are transporting passengers. These measures all help to make employees feel safer and therefore less stressed.

Managing workloads

One of the ways of making sure that employees don't feel under too much pressure at work is to ensure that everyone has a fair share of the workload. Employees should not be given too much while others have little to do. This sounds very easy in theory but requires careful management to make sure it is done properly. Flexible working hours and the use of part-time staff may also help to even out the workload, as extra employees can be brought in to deal with a higher workload at certain times in the week or month on a permanent basis.

Delegating authority and responsibility

You have already learnt that delegating authority and responsibility can be a way to reward and motivate employees in the workplace. Monitoring how well an employee is coping with their increased responsibility is extremely important – both for the employee, who could lose their job if they make a serious mistake, and for the employer, who could lose a substantial amount of money or their reputation if something goes wrong. An extreme example of what can happen when delegated authority and responsibility is poorly monitored took place in the 1990s. A Barings Bank employee called Nick Leeson was able to overtrade for a number of years on the Far East Stock Exchange. It caused the eventual collapse of the bank.

Capacity

Capacity, as you have learnt, refers to the amount of work or product that can be produced and is being produced. Using as much of a business' capacity as possible should lead to lower costs for the business, so employers need to ensure that employees are working at their highest level. However, measuring and monitoring capacity in occupations where services are offered can be complicated to manage. It is important to ensure that everyone is working equally hard. However, this should not involve so much pressure on employees that they suffer with stress and become ill.

Competence

If someone is competent in their job, it means that they are fully trained and experienced enough to be able to carry out the tasks that are associated with it. Having competent staff leads to a more efficient organisation and one that can provide better services or products to customers. If an organisation has a fully competent staff it is likely that it provides good value for money or makes large profits.

Competency at work is achieved through experience and training, so employers must be prepared to invest in both. Organisations have a set of competencies that are considered essential to job performance against which they can evaluate employees, usually using observation, exercises or tests such as psychometric tests. In this way they can monitor the competence levels of staff and make adjustments to the training process as necessary.

Practice point

As a BTEC National student, there is a set of competencies that you need to work towards or already have in order to achieve the qualification, e.g. having a good attendance record or research skills.

- As a class or in small groups, produce a list of the core competencies that you think are needed
- Rank them in order of importance.
- Now measure your own performance against them. Are there areas you need to work on?
- If you have achieved them all, how could you move from being competent as a BTEC National student to being excellent? How could this be measured?

Autonomy

Autonomy means that the individual worker or team of workers has the necessary power and control over decisions in order to get a job done. This is likely to mean that the worker or team is also responsible for monitoring their own performance. By giving employees this power, they are often motivated to work as hard as they can to achieve their targets and goals. However, there is also the possibility of giving employees too much autonomy, as they may be tempted to set lower goals or to try and 'cheat' the system by seeking shortcuts.

Linking rewards to performance

You have already learnt about the different types of rewards that are available (see pages 60–66), and how employees can be encouraged to work harder. When there are direct links between rewards and performance, performance needs to be monitored in order to check that the outcomes have been achieved. Monitoring outcomes is as important as actually setting the target and measurements in the first place, as giving a reward for performance is only beneficial if the outcome was desired from the beginning.

Discipline

Discipline is relevant to employee monitoring because it is part of a process that may come into effect when employees are not working to the desired level. Disciplinary procedures set out the process for what should happen to an employee if they are not working to the desired level. Employees usually receive verbal warnings in the first instance followed by written warnings if there is no evidence of change. After a specified number of warnings without change, an employee may be dismissed. If an employee does something in the workplace that is particularly serious (for example, stealing) they may face instant dismissal. Discipline helps to maximise the efficiency of the organisation by dealing with poor performance.

Employee development

Employee development is the final area to look at when considering employee performance and monitoring, because it means employees can continue to improve their performance at work. Employee development can take a number of different forms.

■ Training

Training may involve going on a course away from work (known as off-the-job training), or take place while the employee works (known as on-the-job training). Both can help employees to develop and improve their job performance.

■ Learning

Learning ranges from studying for a high-level qualification to developing personal skills such as team-building. Developing technical skills such as greater use of IT can make employees more flexible in the workplace, giving them access to different types of work.

■ Job rotation

This is when employees are moved from one job to another at the same level within an organisation. In a restaurant, for example, an employee might be moved from washing up, to waiting on tables, to preparing drinks and then to preparing starters. These jobs are roughly at the same level and by increasing the variety in their work it can increase employees' motivation.

■ Accelerated promotion

Some organisations have accelerated promotion programmes. This means that employees receive additional training and courses to help them to progress through the management levels more quickly than they normally would. This is often offered to graduates leaving university who want to progress to more senior positions very quickly. The police force offers a scheme called the Police High Potential Development scheme(s), which seeks to find high achievers and move them quickly through the police ranks into senior positions.

Personal development

Sometimes employees want to take time off to develop themselves personally. This might be a formal career break, such as the options you learnt about on pages 64–65. Alternatively, employees might need help in order to function more effectively at work, so personal development can take the form of stress or time management training.

Professional development

Employees may receive training that is directly related to their employment or type of career. This is known as professional development. Many organisations offer continuing professional development (CPD) programmes, which enable staff to constantly update their knowledge about what is happening in their industry. CPD may take the form of seminars, workshops or even industrial work experience for adults.

Employee development is extremely varied, as what suits one individual will not suit another. Developing employees and monitoring their progress can help them to achieve their maximum performance. This naturally benefits both the employee and the organisation they work for.

Remember

Giving employees opportunities such as job rotation or training may help to reduce staff turnover (the number of employees who leave the organisation each year).

Outcome activity 16.4

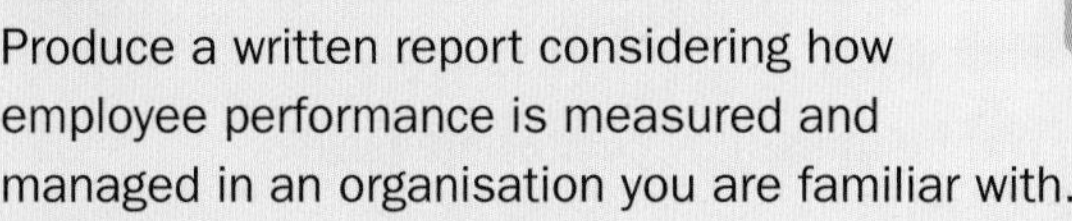

Pass P5

Produce a written report considering how employee performance is measured and managed in an organisation you are familiar with.

Merit M3

Explain how the results from measuring and managing performance can be used to plan and influence the employee development used in that organisation.

Distinction D2

Conclude your report by assessing the importance of measuring and managing employee performance at work.

Grading tips

Pass 

You will need to describe the different measurements used by employers to see how workers are performing – including specific competencies that are needed for that role. You should consider the use of SMART targets and goal-setting in helping to measure and manage performance.

Merit 

You need to show how suitable performance indicators can be used by employers to show how an employee's performance can be raised through performance management. You should consider the individual indicators for that role and the influences on the planning of employee development – including monitoring, occupational health, workloads and responsibility.

Distinction 

Your conclusion should show how important measuring and managing employee performance is within the workplace. Base your judgements on the evidence that you have collected about the value of monitoring and managing employees, and include the consequences of not managing employee performance effectively.

End of unit test

1. Name two internal factors affecting human resource planning.
2. What is meant by capital-intensive?
3. What is a workforce profile?
4. What is meant by short-term labour supply planning?
5. How might labour shortages change the cost of labour in a particular industry?
6. How can producing a skills audit help a business to plan for the future?
7. Name two benefits for an employer of giving their staff a career break.
8. What is the difference between an annual hours and a zero hours contract of employment?
9. Describe the work of three motivation theorists that you have learnt about.
11. How does a cafeteria incentive scheme work?
12. Describe the minimum number of stages that must be present in the disciplinary process of any organisation.
13. To what extent does the method of communication affect the way messages are received by employees from their managers?
14. What is meant by occupational health?
15. Name two different types of employee development.
16. What is meant by autonomy in the workplace?

Books

Alred, Garvey and Smith, 2006, *The Mentoring Pocket Book*, Management Pocket Books

Bartol and Martin, 1997, *Management*, McGraw-Hill

Chaffey, Dave, 2002, *E-Commerce and E-Business Management*, Pearson Education Limited

Gillespie, Andrew, 2002, *Business in Action*, Hodder & Stoughton

Harvey-Jones, Sir John, 2003, *Making It Happen: Reflections on Leadership*, Profile Business

Kirton, Michael (ed.), 1989, *Adaptors and Innovators: Styles of Creativity and Problem-Solving*, Routledge

Martin, Malcolm and Jackson, Tricia, 2002, *Personnel Practice (People and Organizations)*, Chartered Institute of Personnel and Development (CIPD)

Parsloe, Eric and Wray, Monica, 2000, *Coaching and Mentoring*, Kogan Page

Journals

Business Review

Personnel Management

Websites

www.acas.org.uk – The Advisory, Conciliation and Arbitration Service

www.adviceguide.org.uk – Citizen's Advice Bureau with guides to the workplace

www.berr.gov.uk – The Department for Business, Enterprise and Regulatory Reform, giving information on coaching and mentoring

www.businesslink.gov.uk – Business Link Advice for businesses

www.cbi.org.uk – Confederation of Business and Industry

www.cipd.co.uk – Chartered Institute of Personnel and Development

www.coachingnetwork.org.uk – Useful tips

www.investorsinpeople.co.uk – Investors in People website

www.managementqualifications.co.uk – Management Qualifications website giving advice

www.mindtools.com – Tools that can be used to help managers

www.mybusiness.co.uk – My Business provides information on management issues for small businesses including resources

www.personneltoday.co.uk – Personnel Today human resource information provider (UK)

www.statistics.gov.uk – National Statistics published by the government

www.thecareerbreaksite.com – Website giving lots of information about career breaks

Grading criteria	Outcome activity	Page number
To achieve a pass grade the evidence must show that the learner is able to:		
P1 Describe the internal and external factors to be considered when planning the human resources requirements of an organisation	16.1	56
P2 Describe how the different skills that are needed by employees to do the jobs in an organisation are identified	16.1	56
P3 Outline how an organisation's motivational practices and reward systems are informed by theories of motivation	16.2	66
P4 Describe how organisations obtain the co-operation of employees through the contract of employment and employee involvement techniques	16.3	76
P5 Describe how employee performance is measured and managed	16.4	83
To achieve a merit grade the evidence must show that, in addition to the pass criteria, the learner is able to:		
M1 Explain why human resources planning is important to an organisation	16.1	56
M2 Compare the use of motivation theories in an organisation	16.2	66
M3 Explain how the results from measuring and managing performance inform employee development	16.4	83
To achieve a distinction grade the evidence must show that, in addition to the pass and merit criteria, the learner is able to:		
D1 Suggest, with justifications, ways of improving motivation in an organisational setting	16.2	66
D2 Assess the importance of measuring and managing employee performance at work	16.4	83

Aspects of contract and business law

Introduction

Contracts exist in every aspect of the business world, from buying paperclips for your office to creating multi-million pound deals. Contracts are *the* essential business requirement. The whole basis of business has been underpinned by agreements made between traders and individuals. The law relating to these agreements is contract law. It developed from the business dealings of nineteenth-century traders to protect businesspeople and purchasers from unfair deals. This is still the basis of contract law today. Whether you are a sole trader selling apples from a market stall or a tycoon like Richard Branson buying new aircraft, the essential elements of the contract will be the same, with the same rules and ideas of fairness between the parties. As businesses have become more powerful, traders and consumers have been given protection by Parliament, which has created laws to control aspects of contractual agreements to protect those in potentially weaker positions.

What you need to learn

On completion of this unit you should:

1. Be able to apply the requirements for a valid contract
2. Understand the impact of statutory consumer protection on the parties to a contract
3. Understand the meaning and effect of terms in a standard form contract
4. Be able to apply the remedies available to the parties to a contract.

Consider this

Contract law is one of the many elements of business law that a business will need to consider when dealing with customers and suppliers. Imagine that you are running a business as a fruit and vegetable shop. The importance of contract law will be seen in many aspects of the day-to-day running of the business. How could contract law be important? How would it protect both your business and the people and organisations who would be likely to trade with it? It may be that as a budding entrepreneur you may not have considered exactly how important contract law is for your business.

Consider who it is that your business will be trading with. You will hopefully have customers who will buy your product. You will have to ensure that your goods are sold at the correct price and in the correct condition. You, as a person who is supplied with stock, will want goods delivered at the correct time, for the right price. You will also want to know what to do if things go wrong. All of the above, including remedies that are available to you, are governed by the law of contract. From the point of view of a new business, consider the following questions.

- What contractual situations might arise?
- How is a valid contract formed?
- What type of contract might you use?
- Who can you make contracts with?
- How are both you and customers protected if things go wrong?
- Why is contract law so important for businesses?

21.1 Requirements for a valid contract

In this chapter you will be able to understand the key elements of a valid contract and factors that might invalidate them, and apply these points to business situations.

Contracts

The main point of running a business is the formation of business transactions. The business will require premises, staff, plant or machinery to produce goods and (of course) the business will also require buyers or users of the product or service the business provides. At the heart of these business dealings is the contract. Contract law will allow the business to secure premises, hire staff, buy equipment and allow it to trade legally.

The key elements of a **contract** that will need to be applied are an offer, followed by an acceptance, together with consideration and capacity.

Types of contract

A contract can exist in a variety of ways (as the sections that follow show). Contracts exist in everyday transactions (such as buying a newspaper or sandwich) to more complex transactions (such as buying a mobile phone). In the business world the range of contractual agreements can be vast from buying photocopier paper to placing orders for multi-million pound contracts. Contracts can take a variety of forms.

■ Verbal

A verbal contract exists where two parties agree through the spoken word to be bound by a verbal agreement. This is often done between friends or businesspeople who know each other well enough to agree to be legally bound on a spoken word or a handshake.

Key Term

Contract An enforceable agreement made between parties.

■ Written

In the business world it is more common for parties to be bound by the terms of a written contract, where the details of the contract are included in a document signed by each party. These can range from relatively simple agreements to much more formal contracts signed by the parties.

Some contracts must be written and signed by the parties.

- The law relating to the sale of land requires that the contract must be written together with all terms agreed by the parties, and be signed and dated by them.
- Under the Consumer Credit Act 1974 all regulated credit and hire agreements must be in writing.
- It is a requirement of employment legislation that all employees are given a contract showing terms and conditions of employment within two months of starting work. However, a contract need not be formally issued providing that the employer informs the employee of things such as working conditions within the first two months.

▲ Do you think a handshake constitutes a legally binding contract?

The legal effect of verbal and written contracts are exactly the same in that the parties agree to be bound by the contract. However, there are many benefits of having the contract in writing.

- A well-written, clear, concise contract can avoid, or at least lessen, customer disputes and complaints. It should, if the parties are clear about their respective rights and obligations, minimise litigation on contracts, which can be extremely expensive and time consuming.
- Disputes can be avoided if the specifications of the product are carefully and accurately described, or if the services being provided are set out in full.
- It details delivery times and/or deadlines for performance of service(s).
- It outlines remedies for defective products or inadequate performance.
- It gives payment terms.
- It can provide alternative methods for the settlement of certain disputes, such as by arbitration or a system of 'alternative dispute resolution' (ADR). For some types of dispute, such a method may be quicker and cheaper than going through the courts.

Standard form contracts

Companies often use their own **standard form contracts**. These forms often contain terms that amount to custom-made offers and acceptances that fit individual business needs. So it is quite possible for one company to make an offer on its own standard form contract and the other company to accept it on its own standard form contract.

The benefits from using standard form contracts include:

- cost reduction
- avoiding the need for individual negotiation
- regular parties such as producers and suppliers who contract on a frequent basis become familiar with their rights and obligations.

However, there are some disadvantages.

- They can appear one-sided and heavy-handed, particularly when one of the contracting parties is an individual not acting in the course of a business and the other has a stronger bargaining position.
- Where one party is an individual (not acting in the course of business) the terms must be written in easy-to-understand language so that all sides can understand the contract.
- There are certain statutory controls regulating standard form contracts, and some terms will be subject to a reasonableness test. Also, where one of the parties is a private individual, in general, terms must be 'fair'. Otherwise, they will be declared invalid and unenforceable by the business.
- A business may come to rely too much on its standard terms and does not bother to negotiate individual contracts for customers.

Any standard terms must clearly form part of the business arrangement, so that the other party is given notice of the terms before the contract is entered into so that they can be accepted or rejected.

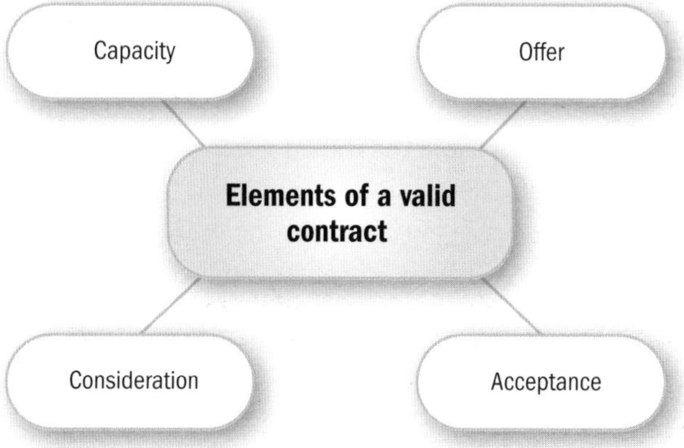

Offers

An offer is a definite promise from one of the parties to the agreement made with the intention that it will become binding or legally enforceable on the person making it as soon as it is accepted by the person receiving.

Key Term

Standard form contract A contract made between parties using their standard set of terms.

Invitation to treat

It is important that you know the difference between an offer and an invitation to treat. The **invitation to treat** is nothing more than an indication that a person is prepared to receive offers from another person. In this sense, 'treat' means 'trade' or 'do business'. The person who is available to receive such an invitation to treat can accept or reject the offer until the final moment of acceptance.

An invitation to treat can exist in many ways.

- **The display of goods with a price ticket attached in a shop window or supermarket.** These are not an offer for sale but are an invitation to treat. The customer must make an offer to buy that can be accepted or rejected by the seller at any time until it is accepted.
- **Products displayed in advertisements, catalogues, brochures and the internet.** These will be deemed to be invitations to treat even if the word 'Offer' is used by sellers to promote their goods.
- **A company prospectus issued when a company is selling its shares.** This is an invitation to treat, as potential investors offer to buy the shares at a price that the directors can accept (through allocation) or reject.

Invitations to treat can sometimes cause confusion and embarrassment where mistakes have been made about product information. This has resulted in businesses having to tell disappointed customers that, strangely, their products are 'not for sale'. This is because the information given is classed as an invitation to treat, and the items do not have to be sold.

It is important to recognise at an early stage in any negotiation whether you are intending to form a contract (by making a definite offer) or whether you are merely making enquiries about making a contract in the future (e.g. an invitation to treat).

One way to do this is to look at the intention of the parties and, from their actions, decide whether a definite offer has been made or whether the parties are still negotiating. This can be very difficult to establish and it is normally up to the person relying on the offer to prove that a contractual intention was to be formed.

Case study

Kodak: 'The right price'

In 2002 the camera firm Kodak made a mistake on its website when it priced a camera worth £300 at £100. At first the company refused to honour the thousands of orders that were placed by customers. It argued that it had no legal duty to sell the camera at the incorrect price, as this was an invitation to treat and as such was not actually for sale at this price. After huge media interest, the threat of legal action and a concerted act of pressure from angry customers, Kodak agreed to honour all of the orders for the camera.

1. Do you think this was the correct decision? ✓
2. Legally, what could the company have done? ✓✓
3. Assess the business reasons for the company's actions. ✓✓✓

Key Term

Invitation to treat Indication that a person might be open to receive an offer. Not legally binding.

Counter-offers

One factor that indicates the offer has not been accepted is the existence of a counter-offer. The principle of acceptance is that the offer must be accepted on the same terms as it was made.

Communication of offers

An offer must be communicated to the other party, usually in writing (although verbal communication will still be valid).

However, there is an exception to this rule about communication. In certain situations known as 'reward cases', an offer to make a contract can be made to many people or even, in theory, the whole world. The term has come from the idea that if you were to lose your dog and put 'lost' cards in shop windows with a reward for its safe return, you would be making a universal offer to any person in particular who might accept the challenge and begin to look for the dog.

The offer must also be certain and not too vague or it will be invalid. A person entering into contract negotiations must know what it is they are agreeing to in certain terms.

Case study

Hyde v Wrench (1840)

Mr Wrench offered to sell some property to Mr Hyde for £1,000 on the 6 June. Two days later Mr Hyde made a new offer to buy the property at a lower price of £950. This was a counter-offer and was rejected by Mr Wrench. Mr Hyde then said he would accept the original price of £1,000, but Mr Wrench refused to sell.

1. Explain what is meant by a counter-offer. ✓
2. Do you think Mr Hyde's original offer was still valid or has it ceased to exist? ✓✓
3. Evaluate the effect of a counter-offer on an original offer. ✓✓✓

Acceptance

A valid offer must be accepted by the other party (known as the **offeree**) to the contract. Several important factors should be considered when looking at acceptance.

- **Acceptance** of the offer must, in normal circumstances, be communicated to the person making the offer (known as the **offeror**). Silence to an offer is not acceptance of that offer.

Case study

Carlill v Carbolic Smoke Ball Co (1893)

The Carbolic Smoke Ball Company placed advertisements in various newspapers advertising its new remedy for 'flu. The advertisement stated that it would pay £100 to any person who used the smoke balls for fourteen days and still caught 'flu.

The claimant, Mrs Carlill, used the remedy but unfortunately still caught 'flu. She made a claim against the company for the money. The company refused to pay, so she took legal action against it. Among many arguments put forward by the company was that the advertisement was an attempt to make an offer to the whole world, which meant communication of it was impossible.

Finding in favour of Mrs Carlill, who was able to claim her money, the Court of Appeal stated that the company had made an offer to the whole world that was capable of being accepted by anyone coming forward to perform the required conditions of the offer.

1. Explain how an offer was made in this case. ✓
2. Give examples of other types of 'reward cases'. ✓✓
3. Evaluate why businesses would create such offers and analyse the problems they create. ✓✓✓

- Acceptance of an offer must be in the form (if any) specified in the offer.
- There is a presumption that if the offer is silent as to the method of acceptance, then only written or oral acceptance will suffice.
- Acceptance need not necessarily be in the specified form as laid down in the offer, as long as the method of acceptance used satisfies the offer and the offeror is not prejudiced in any way.
- Acceptance of an offer must be absolute, unqualified and without condition. The effect of a change in acceptance will have the effect of cancelling the original offer. It creates a counter-offer.

Acceptance by post is an exception to the rule that acceptance must be communicated to the person making the offer. Here, acceptance is considered to be effective as soon as a correctly addressed, stamped envelope is posted in a letterbox. (It is not acceptable to hand the letter to the postman.) Acceptance will be valid even if the letter is delayed or never reaches its destination. Proof of postage will be required.

Case study

Adams v Lindsell (1818)

On 2 September 1817 the defendant (Lindsell) wrote to the claimant (Adams) offering to sell them wool. Lindsell wanted a reply 'in the course of the post'. The letter was wrongly addressed and was misdirected; it did not arrive at the claimant's until 5 September. On the same day the claimant posted a letter of acceptance, which arrived on 9 September. On 8 September the defendant sold the wool to someone else. The defendant argued that he had wanted matters concluded 'in the course of the post' and that that would have been the 7th. The defendant lost the case. The court held that the contract was created when the claimant posted the letter of acceptance on the 5th.

1. Describe the normal rules of acceptance. ✓
2. Explain the effect of the postal acceptance rules. ✓✓
3. Evaluate the effect of this rule on other forms of instant communications. ✓✓✓

Key Terms

Acceptance A formal agreement to accept the offer.

Offeree The person receiving the offer.

Offeror The person making the offer.

Battle of the forms

Particular difficulties have arisen in business law when companies deal with one another using standard contracts (see page 89). When businesses contract with each other they may make an offer and acceptance on their own forms. These standard form contracts often contain terms that conflict with each other. In the event of a dispute, the courts have to decide which standard form contract applies to the transaction. It is not an easy decision and it may be very difficult to determine whose terms have prevailed. Sometimes there may not be a valid contract at all, due to the conflict.

Consideration

Under contract law the agreement between the parties will not in itself create a legally binding contract. One of the things there must be for a valid contract is some degree of consideration between the parties. Consideration is defined as something given, promised or done in exchange by each party to the agreement. It can take two forms.

- **Executed consideration.** This is an act in exchange for a promise such as a reward case. The promise of the person making the offer to pay the reward is consideration for the act of completing the task to have earned the reward.
- **Executory consideration.** This is a promise yet to be fulfilled. It is where the parties exchange promises to perform acts in the future. Most contracts begin in this way.

Case study

Butler Machine Tool Co Ltd v Ex-Cell-O Corp (Eng) Ltd (1979)

The claimant (Butler Machine Tool Co) offered to supply machinery to the defendant (Ex-Cell-O Corp) for £73,535. The quotation included a term in a standard form contract called a variation clause that would allow the sellers to increase the price of the quotation. The defendant accepted the offer on its own standard form contract that was silent as to variation clauses.

An agreement was made and on delivery the claimant had increased the price by £2,892. The defendant refused to pay this. The Court of Appeal decided that the defendant's form had been accepted by the claimant, so the defendant's terms governed the agreement, which meant the claim to recover the extra money failed.

1. Explain why businesses use standard form contracts. ✓
2. Consider how the courts decide which standard form contract should be used. ✓✓
3. Can you propose a better way of dealing with such disputes? ✓✓✓

An example of the promise of a seller to deliver to a buyer is consideration for the buyer's promise to buy at the agreed price. Consideration from the buyer is the promise to pay the price on completion.

There are various rules of consideration, as the section opposite and on page 94 shows.

Practice point

In groups, list different examples of:

- executed consideration
- executory consideration.

Past consideration

Consideration can never be past, so something already completed by a party can never be deemed to be consideration for a promise made later by the other party.

Case study

McArdle (1951)

Mr McArdle died leaving his wife a life interest in their house, after which it was to be given to their children. While the widow was still alive one of the children and his wife moved in and voluntarily made improvements valued at £488 to the house. The other children agreed to reimburse them for the work done. Later a dispute arose and they refused to pay. It was held that the promise to pay was not legally binding as the promise to pay was made after the work had been done, so consideration was in the past and invalid.

1. Explain what consideration means. ✓
2. Why was consideration not valid in this case? ✓✓
3. Analyse what could have been done to satisfy the requirements of consideration in this case. ✓✓✓

Thinking point

Jane is away on business and Paul, without being asked, puts up a new fence for her. On Jane's return, Paul asks for payment and Jane refuses. Has Paul provided any consideration?

The rule that **consideration** must always move from the Promisee emphasises the idea that there must be consideration in form from both parties to a contract.

So if person X makes a promise (the **Promisor**) to person Y (the **Promisee**), Y must also show consideration for that promise. Consideration cannot be one-sided.

Consideration must not be illegal; a contract will not be valid if the consideration involved is illegal or considered immoral.

Key Terms

Executed consideration An act in exchange for a promise.

Executory consideration Set of promises yet to be fulfilled.

Consideration Something of value done by the parties.

Privity of contract The relationship between parties to a contract. It is a legal concept denying third parties the right to sue on a contract.

Promisor The person making the promise.

Promisee The person receiving the promise.

■ Adequacy of consideration

In all valid contracts, consideration must have some value, but there is no requirement for that consideration to be adequate. The value of consideration is agreed by the parties. The court will not help parties who agree consideration, then complain of making a 'bad bargain'.

Privity of contract

The traditional position in contract law regarding contract formation has been that the contract only created rights between the parties. This meant that a third party could not acquire rights under the contract. The relationship between parties to a contract is known as **privity of contract.**

So for example: 'Person A promises to person B that they will pay a sum of money to person C. Here the contract is between A and B, so that C cannot sue for the money.'

Privity of contract is firmly linked with consideration as one of the most important ways a third party can either become liable or gain rights on a contract.

Case study

Chappell and Co v Nestlé and Co (1959)

As part of a promotional campaign, Nestlé (the defendant) offered to supply a record to consumers who sent in a postal order for 1s 6d plus three wrappers from six penny bars of Nestlé chocolate.

A copyright dispute arose between Nestlé and the owners of the record (Chappell, the claimant). The owners claimed that Nestlé was selling it for money, which would require a separate agreement. Nestlé claimed it was not selling it for money, so under the Copyright Act 1956 it was only required to give the owners notice and 6.25% of the retail selling price as payment. Nestlé argued that the wrappers had no value and could not be consideration in the agreement.

The House of Lords disagreed and held that the wrappers were consideration in the transaction as the offer by Nestlé was to supply the record in return for cash plus the wrappers.

1. Explain what consideration was given in this case. ✓
2. Do you think the consideration was sufficient? ✓✓
3. Can you think of any other similar types of promotion and the types of consideration provided? ✓✓✓

Case study

Dunlop Pneumatic Tyre Co Ltd v Selfridge & Co Ltd (1915)

Dunlop (the claimant) sold tyres to Dew & Co (a distributor) on condition it would not sell the tyres at less than the prescribed retail price. The contract also imposed a condition that if Dew & Co sold the tyres to a third party, it should obtain a similar undertaking from them.

Dew & Co sold the tyres to a third party, Selfridge & Co (the defendant), which agreed to follow the conditions imposed. It agreed to pay Dunlop £5 for each tyre it sold below the prescribed retail price. Selfridge & Co then sold tyres to customers below the list price.

Selfridge & Co refused to pay the penalty. Dunlop sued for breach of contract. Selfridge & Co argued that it could not be liable, as no contract existed between them.

The court agreed with Selfridge & Co, and held that there was no privity of contract between the parties, so no contract could exist.

1. Explain what is meant by privity of contract. ✓
2. Why did Selfridge refuse to pay up in this case? ✓✓
3. Comment on whether or not you think privity of contract is a fair rule. ✓✓✓

The Contracts (Rights of Third Parties) Act 1999

There is a Statutory exception to the idea of privity of contract. That is the Contracts (Rights of Third Parties) Act 1999. This creates the law that allows third parties to have rights in a contract that affects them.

To gain rights under the Act the third party must be clearly identified by name, class or description but need not (in the case of a company) be in existence yet so long as it is clearly identified.

The third party rights under the Act are limited by the terms and conditions in the contract. The parties must limit and define what rights they want to give the third party at the negotiation stage.

All remedies will be available to a third party as if that person was a party to the original contract made between the original parties.

Case study

Tweddle v Atkinson (1861)

The claimant's father and father-in-law exchanged promises by which each was to pay the claimant (Tweddle) a sum of money in consideration of the claimant's intended marriage. The marriage went ahead, then the father-in-law died without making a payment and the claimant sued the executors of his estate. It was decided by the court that the claimant's action should fail, as the claimant (who was a third party in this case) had given no consideration for the contract.

1. What might the consideration be in this case? ✓
2. Why did the case fail? ✓✓
3. Should agreements like these form valid contracts at all? Justify your answer. ✓✓✓

Capacity as applied to business situations

Having looked at offer, acceptance and consideration, it is also important to consider whether a person has the legal capacity to enter into an agreement. This is vital if a contract is to exist between the parties.

Capacity means whether or not a person has the legal power to enter into a contract. There are certain classes of person that only have limited capacity to enter into legal agreements.

Key Term

Capacity The legal ability or authority to make a valid contract.

Minors

Legal rules have been developed to protect minors (those aged under eighteen) from contractual liability and to allow them also to enter into agreements in limited circumstances.

Generally there are two types of contract that will bind a minor when dealing with adults:

- contracts for the supply of necessary goods and services
- beneficial contracts of service.

These are binding on the minor and the position is clarified under the Sale of Goods Act 1979. Under this Act necessities are defined as: 'Goods suitable to the condition in life of the minor and to his actual requirements at the time of sale and delivery.'

Here the definition will be looked at by the courts in context of the social and financial background of the minor involved.

Luxury goods are generally excluded, as are items or services that the minor already has. Duplicate items and services are not seen to be necessities of life.

A minor is also bound by contracts of employment, apprenticeship and education as long as the whole contract is for the benefit of the minor. This will include contractual matters such as football apprenticeships and music scholarships.

Minors who set themselves up in business will not be bound by their trading contracts, even if the contracts are deemed to be for their benefit. The exception is contracts created out of fraud, in which case the contract will be binding on the minor. So minors who set themselves up in business will not be liable to repay the price of goods if they fail to deliver them!

Practice point

If a minor made contracts to purchase the following, which do you think would be legally binding?

- A set of tailor-made suits.
- A motor car.
- A copy of this text book (for a business studies student).
- A mobile phone.
- A new coat.
- A train ticket to attend a hospital appointment.
- A holiday to Australia.
- Emergency private dental treatment.

Case study

eBay boy buys sports car

In September 2006, a three year-old boy used his parent's home computer to buy a £9,000 Nissan Figaro car on the internet site eBay. The boy had somehow got onto the site and placed a successful bid for the sports car. Having received the confirmation message from eBay, the boy's parents believed they were about to receive the new car!

As soon as the seller was told what had happened he immediately rejected the boy's 'offer' and put the car back up for sale. In reality, the seller could not have gone through with the bargain due to the issue of capacity.

1. What is meant by capacity? ✓
2. Does a three year-old have legal capacity? ✓✓
3. Consider the age that a person should have capacity to enter into valid contracts. ✓✓✓

Incapacitated persons

People who are diagnosed with a mental disability cannot enter into a valid contract, as they do not have sufficient mental capacity to understand what they are doing.

However, under the Mental Health Act 1983 the court may enter into valid contracts on the patient's behalf and continue contracts entered into before the illness came to the person and before the person was sectioned under the above Act.

If a person is suffering from a temporary insanity, or a drink or drug-related problem, any contract made by that person during that time will be voidable by the person providing they can prove that at the time of negotiation they had no understanding of what was going on and the other party to the agreement knew, or should have known, this.

Organisations

It is necessary to consider the legal position when entering into an agreement with various types of organisations.

Registered companies

Companies are created by registration under the Companies Act 1985 (as amended). The company in law has a legal identity of its own, and can sue and be sued on contracts made in its name. Under this Act the company's power or capacity to contract was limited to those powers in its Memorandum of Association in the Objects Clause.

The Companies Act 1989 has amended the 1985 Act allowing a company to change its Objects clause by Special Resolution so that it can carry on 'any trade or business whatsoever'.

A company has no legal power before it is formed to enter into binding contracts.

Any person 'acting on behalf of the company' before the date of incorporation will be personally liable on the contract. (Incorporation means the date when the company came into existence.)

Case study

Kelner v Baxter (1866)

The promoters of a proposed hotel, an unincorporated company, agreed to buy a stock of wine on its behalf. After the company was incorporated, it tried to enforce the contract in the name of the company, but a dispute arose. The court had to decide whether a contract existed at all, and if so, between whom.

1. Explain how companies can enter into contracts. ✓
2. Describe what a company's Objects clause does. ✓✓
3. Evaluate who you think was liable for the contracts before the company was incorporated. ✓✓✓

Unincorporated associations

These are groups of people joined to further a common interest such as a sporting, social or political group. In general terms, these groups are not considered legal entities; capacity to contract belongs to members jointly and not with the group or association in its own right.

Partnerships

Many partnerships are, in fact, associations formed for business purposes and are governed by the Partnership Act 1890. Under this Act each partner has capacity to contract on behalf of all the partners. Therefore each is liable jointly on any contract entered into on behalf of the partnership. Here it is not the partnership that has legal capacity but the individual partners themselves.

Local authorities

Local authorities have power from either Royal Charter or the Local Government Act 1972. Local authorities are separate legal entities and have capacity to contract in their own right. They are subject to the ***ultra vires*** rule and can be found to have acted beyond their powers.

Key Term

Ultra vires To act outside one's powers.

Remember

The key requirements for a valid contract are:

- offer
- acceptance
- capacity
- consideration.

Take it further

Research the area and make your own notes on any other key requirements of a valid contract.

Factors that invalidate/ vitiate contracts

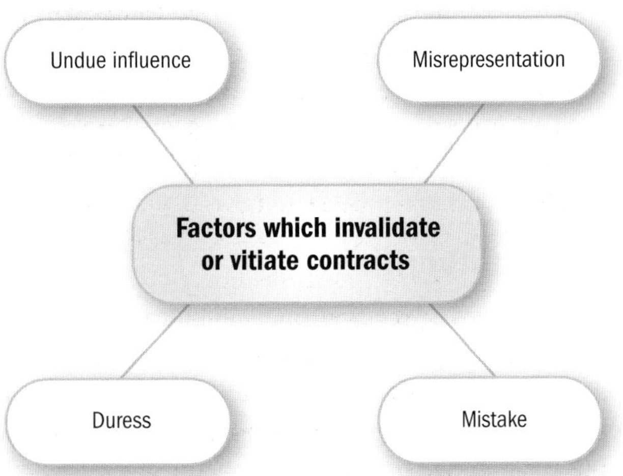

We have already seen that a binding agreement between two or more parties forms a valid contract. Along with the other vital elements of a valid contract a binding contract will only be formed when there is consent between the parties (i.e. that the contract was entered into voluntarily and freely). It is only when this genuineness of consent exists that a valid contract will exist.

However, there a number of factors that will invalidate or vitiate (corrupt) an agreement:

- misrepresentation
- mistake
- duress
- undue influence.

Each of these is covered more fully in the sections that follow.

Misrepresentation

Contracts are often preceded by a series of negotiations made between the parties. These negotiations are a series of representations forming the basis of the contract itself. If these representations are in fact misrepresentations, then the contractual position between the parties is in doubt.

Thinking point

If you were selling a car, what representations might you make about it to the seller and how would you make sure of your facts?

A misrepresentation is a false statement of fact (not law) made by one party to a contract to the other party before the contract is made with a view to inducing the other to enter it.

As a general rule of law, for misrepresentation to exist a positive statement must be made by a party making the representation. There is no general duty to disclose facts, and silence will not normally amount to a misrepresentation. But gestures, smiles or a course of conduct may amount to a representation.

Case study

Spice Girls Ltd v Aprilia World Service BV (2000)

Spice Girls Ltd (SGL) was formed to promote the Spice Girls. At the beginning of May 1998, SGL entered into a contract with the defendant. The defendant was Aprilia, an Italian company that manufactures motorcycles and scooters. An agreement was made between the parties for the Spice Girls to take part in a TV commercial promoting the scooters.

At the time of the contract the Spice Girls had five members. However, a month before the contract was signed Geri Halliwell had told the group she was leaving it in September 1998. The group had decided to keep the information secret; the defendant was not informed and the contract was signed.

The group went ahead with the shoot, and this was seen to be a representation by conduct that no one was intending to leave. The fact that the group knew Geri would have left by the time the commercial was due on air meant that the conduct of the group amounted to a misrepresentation because, according to the defendants, the commercial showing the five girls was subsequently of little value.

1. What representations did the Spice Girls make to the defendant? ✓
2. How was it claimed that the representations were broken? ✓✓
3. Critically assess how far a person is under a duty to disclose the facts in a contract. ✓✓✓

Silence is not enough in the case of contracts made in the utmost good faith where one party alone is in possession of all the facts that form the basis of the contract. Here there is a duty to disclose relevant information in full. These include:

- contracts of insurance
- contracts for the sale of land
- contracts of family arrangement
- contracts to purchase shares.

The misrepresentation must involve a statement of fact, not a statement of law or intention. However, if a person misrepresents what they intend to do in the future they may be liable for misrepresentation.

A statement of opinion will not normally be a misrepresentation because a statement of belief is not capable of proof. There may be occasions when a statement of opinion may become a representation of fact. This is the case where it can be proved that the person was in a position to know facts on which the opinion was based.

It must be shown that the statement has induced the person to whom it was made to enter into the contract. If it is a false statement it can be a misrepresentation. However, if the person to whom the statement was made attempts to check the truth of what has been said to them, then clearly they have not relied on that statement and the statement cannot be a misrepresentation.

There are various types of misrepresentation, each resulting in a voidable contract.

- **Fraudulent misrepresentation.** A person will be liable for fraud if they make a statement which they know to be false, or they have no belief in its truth, or they are reckless or careless whether it is true or false. In such a case an injured party may reject the contract and sue for damages for the tort of deceit.
- **Negligent misrepresentation.** This is when a person makes a false statement having no reasonable grounds for believing the statement to be true. The effect of such case is that damages can be awarded for negligent misstatement. There is now also statutory negligent misrepresentation under S2(1) of the Misrepresentation Act 1967. Under this Act the burden of proof is on the defendant to show they are not liable and to show they had a reasonable belief in the accuracy of their statement. Negligent misstatement will entitle the other party to rescission or damages or both.
- **Innocent misrepresentation.** An innocent misrepresentation is a false statement made by a person who had reasonable grounds to believe that it was true, not only when it was made but also when the contract was entered into.

Case study

Hedley Byrne & Co Ltd v Heller & Partners (1963)

The claimant (Hedley Byrne & Co) was asked for credit by a particular company. It asked for financial advice on the company's standing from the company bankers (the defendant). The defendant negligently stated that the company was financially sound. It was held that the defendant was, in principle, liable as it had a duty of care to the claimant.

1. Describe how a duty of care existed in this case. ✓
2. What type of misrepresentation existed here? ✓✓
3. Evaluate the different types of misrepresentation and the effect they have on the contract. ✓✓✓

There are various remedies for **misrepresentation** including:

- rescission, where the injured party refuses to carry out the contract and the parties are returned to their pre-contract position
- the injured party claims damages.

Mistake

In general terms a rule of common law is that **mistake** as to the agreement will not affect the validity of the contract. The common law principle applied here is the maxim of *caveat emptor*, or 'let the buyer beware'. This means that it is, in reality, up to the parties to accept the contract even if there had been a mistake.

This means that if a person agrees to pay £500 for a second-hand car when it is only really worth £100, a valid contract for £500 will be created. The buyer must be aware of such factors as they will suffer any loss incurred.

However, there are circumstances when mistake will invalidate a contract, e.g. the situations below.

- Where the parties make a mistake about the subject matter of the contract.
- Where there is a mistake over the identity of the parties.
- Where a document has been signed in error.

Duress

As already stated, the parties must enter freely into a contract. If one of the parties has been forced into it as a result of violence or threat of violence to themselves or their family, the contract may become invalid. In such circumstances the affected party can avoid the contract on the grounds of **duress**.

Key Terms

Misrepresentation A set of untrue facts made by one party relied on by the other when entering into the contract.

Mistake Where a person enters into a contract after getting the facts in the negotiation wrong.

Duress Where a person enters into a contract against their will.

Undue influence

Undue influence occurs when one party to the contract has a dominant position over the other. Where this type of relationship exists there is a presumption that the more dominant party will have used undue influence and the weaker party may avoid the contract due to undue influence.

Thinking point

Discuss what type of dominant relationships might exist in business and how undue influence might occur.

Case study

Barton v Armstrong (1975)

The defendant (Armstrong) was the chairman of a company and the claimant (Barton) was the managing director. The defendant threatened to have the claimant killed unless the claimant signed an agreement buying the defendant's share in the company at a highly inflated price. The claimant signed the contract, but the court decided that this contract could be avoided by the claimant due to duress.

This has now been extended to include threats of economic harm.

D & C Builders v Rees (1965)

D & C Builders (the claimants) undertook work for Rees (the defendant) valued at £482. The company was in severe financial difficulties at the time. Mrs Rees got to know of this and offered £300 in full settlement of the work, which was reluctantly accepted. The company then sued for the balance. Rees tried to say she should owe nothing. The court disagreed and said she had held the company to ransom and they could not rely on the duress.

1. Explain the idea of duress ✓
2. Describe the effect of duress on a contract. ✓✓
3. Compare and contrast the different types of duress shown in these cases. ✓✓✓

Key Term

Undue influence One party exerts pressure on another to enter into a contract due to the nature of their relationship or position.

Take it further

You might also like to look at the effect of entering into an illegal contract and whether or not the illegality invalidates the agreement.

Remember

A contract can be invalidated by:

- misrepresentations
- mistake
- duress
- undue influence.

Outcome activity 21.1

Pass P1

Prepare a factsheet in your own words describing the essential elements of a contract in an area of your choice, e.g. your own mobile phone contract.

Merit M1

Prepare a presentation to analyse the impact of the requirements of the contract you have chosen. You may wish to work as part of a group to produce the presentation, but remember to write up your own ideas and presentation individually.

Grading tips

Pass 

For pass make sure you include both when and how a contract would come into existence. You should include a description of:

- invitations to treat
- how the contract comes into existence
- the offer, acceptance and counter-offers.

Merit 

You should consider the strengths and weaknesses of the formation of a contract including relevant problems that you have already studied such as:

- what is good or weak about the offer
- implications of pricing through the invitation to treat
- clarity of communication and capacity for acceptance
- likelihood of counter-offers.

21.2 Impact of statutory consumer protection on the parties to a contract

While many contracts are concerned with agreements between businesses, many others are made between a business and a member of the public. The text that follows will help you to understand how statutory consumer protection law will protect the parties in such contracts by looking at the Sale of Goods Act.

Sale of goods

The key piece of legislation which controls such contracts and protects consumers is the Sale of Goods Act 1979. This Act covers all types of **consumer contract**.

Thinking point

Try to think of different types or examples of consumer contracts. Challenge your team-mates to find the largest type of contract and the smallest!

Definition of 'goods'

S2(1) of the Sale of Goods Act 1979 defines a contract of the sale of goods as one by which 'the seller transfers or agrees to transfer the property in goods to the buyer for a money consideration called "price"'.

This definition is very important because only those contracts that fall within it will be covered by the Act. 'Goods' include all tangible items of property such as:

- food
- clothes
- furniture.

Land and money are excluded from the definition.

Key Term

Consumer contract Contract made between a business and members of the public for consumer goods such as food, clothes and furniture.

Implied terms

Parties are generally free to agree between themselves the details of their contract. But the Act automatically includes a series of conditions in every contract for the sale of goods dealing with:

- title
- description
- fitness
- satisfactory quality.

These are known as implied terms and are dealt with in sections 12 to 15 of the Sale of Goods Act 1979, discussed below.

Title

In S12(1) there is an implied condition on the part of sellers that they have the right to sell the goods. For example a car dealer impliedly confirms that the cars it sells actually belong to it and that it can legally pass ownership (**title**) to another person. If sellers cannot pass good title (the right of ownership) to buyers, they will be liable for breach of contract.

Key Term

Title The legal right of ownership.

Description

Where there is a contract for the sale of goods by description, there is an implied term that the goods will correspond with that description. The description of the goods may cover such matters as:

- size
- quantity
- weight
- ingredients
- origin, and
- even how they are packed.

The slightest departure from this description will entitle the buyer to reject the goods for breach of condition of the contract.

Case study

Moore & Co v Landauer & Co (1921)

The claimants (Moore & Co) agreed to supply 3,000 tins of Australian canned fruit, packed in cases containing 30 tins each. When the goods were delivered it was discovered that about half the consignment was packed in cases of 24 tins. The court agreed that the claimant could reject the whole contract.

1. Why are terms about quantity, quality and description important in a contract? ✓
2. Explain why you think the law implies such terms into a consumer contract.✓✓
3. Comment on whether you think it is correct that a contract should be ended due to minute deviations from what is expected. ✓✓✓

Fitness and satisfactory quality

There is no general duty placed on sellers who sell in private to ensure that the goods sold are of correct quality and suitability. This preserves the principle of ***caveat emptor*** (or 'let the buyer beware'). This means that if you buy a camera from a friend and it does not work you will have little remedy available. However, if your friend was selling the camera in the course of their business, S14 implies two conditions:

- that the goods are of satisfactory quality
- that they are fit for a particular purpose.

The Sale and Supply of Goods Act 1994 provides that where sellers sell goods in the course of their business there is an implied condition that the goods supplied are of satisfactory quality, except to the extent of defects which are brought to the buyers' attention before the contract is made, or ought to have been noticed by buyers if they have examined the goods.

Key Term

Caveat emptor Latin term meaning as a buyer you should be aware of defects in a product when you buy it.

The quality of goods includes their state and condition. Fitness for the purpose for which goods of the kind in question are commonly supplied means that they are:

- safe
- free from minor defects
- durable (long lasting).

The Act does not impose absolute standards of quality with which all goods must comply. However, goods must be satisfactory to a reasonable person. This means that goods do not have to be absolutely perfect but satisfactory in the usual run of events.

Case study

Rogers v Parish (Scarborough) Ltd (1987)

The claimant (Rogers) bought an expensive new car for £16,000. Within six months of delivery the engine became defective and the bodywork began to deteriorate. The claimant wished to reject the vehicle, and it was held that they were entitled to do so. The vehicle was not of merchantable quality, as the buyer did not receive the appropriate degree of comfort and reliability from the new car.

1. What sort of quality standards are implied into a consumer contract? ✓
2. How long would you expect a new car to be free from defects? Would this time period change depending on what product was purchased? ✓✓
3. Analyse whether this level of protection is necessary for purchasers. ✓✓✓

Where the seller sells goods in the course of a business there is an implied condition that these goods will be reasonably fit for the purpose that the buyer had expressly or impliedly made known to the seller. It is vital that a seller is told if a particular product is to be used for a particular purpose, as this will offer them a degree of protection under the legislation. Compare the cases of Grant vs. Australian Knitting Mills and Griffiths vs. Peter Conway.

Case study

Grant v Australian Knitting Mills (1936)

The claimant (Grant) bought a pair of woollen underpants from a shop. The pants contained a chemical that should have been removed before sale, and the buyer contracted dermatitis. It was held that the items were not fit for the purpose, as the buyer had impliedly made known to the seller that the pants were to be worn next to the skin.

Griffiths v Peter Conway (1939)

The claimant (Griffiths) bought a tweed coat from the defendant (Peter Conway). Unknown to the defendant, the claimant suffered from exceptionally sensitive skin. She also contracted dermatitis. In this case it was held that the defendant was not liable, as the buyer had not made her condition known to the sellers and the coat was a normal coat fit for ordinary wear.

1. What general principle of law do these cases raise? ✓
2. How do they differ from each other? ✓
3. Comment on whether or not the buyer should have to declare any special requirements as to fitness for purpose. Analyse whether this places the seller at a disadvantage or not. ✓✓✓

Sample

The Sale of Goods Act 1979 provides that in a contract of sale by sample there is an implied condition that:

- the bulk will correspond with the sample in quality
- the buyer will have a reasonable opportunity of comparing the bulk with the sample
- the goods will be free from any defect making their quality unsatisfactory which would not be apparent on reasonable examination of the sample.

▲ According to the Sale of Goods Act 1979, the bulk must correspond with the sample

Take it further

You might like to look at some consumer websites or journals to research some real cases where consumer contracts have led to real disputes and real court cases.

Supply of goods and services

The sale of goods legislation only applies to contracts where goods are sold for a money consideration. It does not cover other methods of obtaining goods by means other than money purchase; nor does it cover the provision of services.

The Supply of Goods and Services Act 1982 was passed to place on a statutory footing terms that had previously been implied by common law in contracts for services.

Definitions

Legislation has been passed to protect commercial transactions that are not covered under the sale of goods including:

- contracts for work and material (building work, car repairs, installation work such as central heating and double glazing, hairdressing and gardening)
- contracts where no money changes hands (exchange or barter)
- contracts for 'free gifts' (where buyers are given a free product if they buy another) and contracts for hire of goods (including the hire of cars, machinery and clothing).

Implied terms for supply of goods and services, work and materials

- S2 contains an implied condition that the transferor (the person who is providing the goods or services) has the legal right to transfer the property.
- S3 provides that where the transfer is for goods or services by description there is an implied condition that the goods will correspond to that description. For example, if your computer broke down and it was sent to a computer repair shop to be repaired, when the invoice described the work and the parts fitted it would be implied into the contract that the actual work and parts had been provided.
- S4 provides that where goods are transferred in the ordinary course of business there is an implied condition that the goods are of suitable quality and fit for the purpose.
- S5 provides that where there is a transfer of goods by reference to a sample, there is an implied condition that the bulk will correspond with the sample.

Implied terms for hire of goods under Supply of Goods and Services Act 1982

These apply to contracts when one person agrees to bail (hire) goods to another – e.g. the hire of cars or machinery. Again the Supply of Goods and Services Act deals with this.

- S7 provides that there is an implied condition that the bailor (the person providing the hire) has the right to transfer the goods. For example, if a person hires a car from Hertz for their holiday via the internet, it is implied that the car they pick up from their holiday destination will be owned by Hertz, which will allow the hire to take place.
- S8 provides that where there is a contract for the hire of goods by description there is an implied condition that the goods will match that description.
- S9 provides that where goods are hired in the course a business, there is an implied condition that the goods are of a satisfactory quality and reasonably fit for the purpose.
- S10 covers implied conditions in relation to contracts for the hire of goods by sample whereby the bulk must match the sample.

Remedies for breach of contract will be broadly the same as for contracts for the sale of goods.

Thinking point

How do these implied terms compare and contrast with terms in a consumer contract?

False trade descriptions

When the parties to a contract begin negotiating and start to form a contract, there will be several representations made by the seller about the items being sold. Those representations may involve a description of the product. Any descriptions of goods and services given by a person acting in the course of a trade or business should be accurate and not misleading. Misleading descriptions of this type are called false **trade descriptions** and are against the law.

Key Term

Trade description A description made by sellers about the goods they are selling.

Trade Descriptions Act 1968

This Act makes it a criminal offence to mislead a consumer by a false description, which means a description of goods sold or hired must be accurate. That description could be:

- in writing
- in an advertisement
- in an illustration
- given orally, e.g. in a sales pitch.

The description itself covers a range of factors, including:

- quantity and size
- composition
- method, place and date of manufacture
- fitness for stated purpose
- endorsements by people or organisations.

If offering to supply services, accommodation or facilities, it is a criminal offence to:

- make a statement that is known to be false or misleading
- 'recklessly' make a false or misleading statement about the provision, nature, manner, location or approval of the services, accommodation or facilities.

Those guilty of an offence under the Act could receive an unlimited fine or up to two years imprisonment.

Link to misrepresentation

Breaking the Trade Descriptions Act creates a criminal offence but also makes the person liable for misrepresentation for which damages may also be awarded.

Remember

Consumer contracts for goods and services are strongly protected and terms are implied into contracts by law. Businesses that break these terms will be in breach of contract and in certain cases might face criminal prosecution.

Case study

Marks & Spencer

In September 2005 Marks & Spencer was fined £10,000 for breaking the Trade Descriptions Act. It was found guilty for making misleading claims about a new collection of men's clothing.

The high street chain was found guilty after it admitted five breaches of the Trade Descriptions Act by suggesting that items in its new Italian range were made in Italy. This was untrue.

Trading Standards investigated complaints from customers and found clothes in the company's Birmingham store clearly labelled 'Made in Italy'. Investigations found that the clothing was, in fact, from Egypt, India and Romania.

The store was fined £2,000 per offence and received some unwanted publicity.

Its clothing range now states 'Inspired by Italy', rather than made in it!

1. Why was Marks & Spencer found guilty? ✓
2. Do you think firms like Marks & Spencer should be criminally prosecuted for such acts? Justify your answers. ✓✓
3. Discuss the 'Inspired by Italy' branding and how far that still might be misleading. ✓✓✓

Take it further

Keep up to date with news stories about businesses and how they commit trading standards offences. You might like to look at your own local Trading Standards Office for details of local companies or look at www.tradingstandards.gov.uk for a national picture.

Outcome activity 21.2

Pass

1. Prepare a report in your own words describing the effect of legislation on contracts for the sale of goods to protect consumers. P3
2. Describe how consumers might be protected in a contract for the supply of goods and services such as faulty plumbing of a new kitchen. P4

Merit

3. Analyse how consumers are protected in the event of breach of contract for the supply/sale of goods or services. M2

Grading tips

Pass P3

You should describe the Sale of Goods Act 1979, including quality and fitness for purpose, making sure that you relate them to the goods that you have chosen.

Pass P4

You should describe the Supply of Goods and Services Act 1982, including the quality and delivery of services, relating them to the service that is required.

Merit M2

You should analyse (including the benefits or weaknesses) specific issues relating to the creation of the contract, e.g. exclusion clauses and how consumers might be protected in the event of a breach of one of these contracts, and discuss how effective the legislation is.

Askham Bryan
College
LIBRARY BOOK

21.3 Meaning and effect of terms in a standard form contract

A contract is a set of mutually agreed promises made between parties with the intention of creating a legally binding agreement. However, it is important to analyse exactly what it is that parties are agreeing to do.
In the sections that follow, we will examine what parties are bound to do under the contract, e.g. the **terms** of the contract.

Types of terms

Those things that parties are bound to perform under the contract are called terms of the contract. The statements made by parties under negotiation that are *not* meant to form part of the contract are called representations. There are two types of term found in a contract:

- the express term
- the implied term.

Express terms

Express terms of a contract are statements actually made by the parties, either by word of mouth or in writing, intending these terms to create the fundamental part of the contract. It will be these terms that the parties will be forced to stick to under the contract. They can be either **conditions** or **warranties**.

■ Conditions

A condition is a fundamental part of the agreement and is something that goes to the root of the contract. For example, if the parties agree to buy and sell a brand new car and the actual item supplied is a motorbike, then there is a clear breach of contract as the supply of a car was a condition of the contract. A breach of condition will entitle the injured party to repudiate (treat it as at an end) and claim damages.

■ Warranties

A warranty is a less important term that does not go to the root of the contract. Breach of a warranty will only give the injured party the right to claim damages; the contract cannot be rejected.

For example, consider the issue of buying a new car. You agree with the supplier that it will be fitted with a particular model/brand of DVD player. The car arrives, so the supplier has completed the main condition of the contract to supply of the car. But it has been fitted with the wrong type of DVD player. The DVD player is not the vital part of the contract and will be seen as a warranty.

This failure, although annoying for the person buying the car, will still allow them to sue the supplier for damages. It will not mean the contract can automatically be ended.

It is common in business contracts not only to have express terms relating to conditions and warranties but also to have common express key terms included in the contract. These might include:

- exclusion clauses limiting the parties' responsibilities under the contract
- terms relating to the amount of damages that the parties might receive if things go wrong
- terms allowing parties to vary the contract price known as a price variation clause.

Key Terms

Terms Parts of the contract agreed by the parties.

Express terms Clauses in the agreement actually agreed by the parties.

Conditions Essential parts of the contract.

Warranties Important terms of the contract but not so important as to be classed as essential.

Implied terms

Implied terms are not actually stated in a contract but are introduced into the contract by statute, custom and common law.

Terms implied by statute

To protect parties, terms are implied into a contract by virtue of legislation. The best example is the Sale of Goods Act 1979, which is implied into contracts for the sale of goods. In every contract for the sale of goods you'll find the following implied terms.

- Every seller has the right to sell goods.
- Where there is a sale of goods by description there is an implied condition that the goods will correspond with that description.
- Goods sold are of a satisfactory condition and fit for a particular stated purpose.
- In sales by sample there is an implied condition that the bulk order will correspond with the sample.

Terms implied by custom

An agreement may be made subject to customary terms not actually specified by the parties. These could be historical, and a person making a contract should try to establish if any such terms are in existence. However, it should be noted that such a custom will be overruled by any express clause to the contrary.

Terms implied by the common law

Courts will be prepared to imply a term into the contract in order to give effect to the obvious intentions of the parties. This may be a point that has been overlooked or may not have been clearly stated by the parties. In such circumstances the court will imply such a term in the interests of 'business fairness' so that the contract makes commercial common sense.

Distinction between express and implied terms

- **Express terms** are those in the contract that the parties have negotiated and expressly agreed. Parties can strike out these terms and re-negotiate other ones until all terms have been agreed. The parties have total control over the type of express term their contract contains.
- **Implied terms** are those where the law insists certain terms are included in the contract. Here the parties have no say in the matter; if they wish to do to business with each other they must follow these implied terms precisely.

Key Term

Implied term Parts of the contract not necessarily included by the parties but automatically included by law to protect the parties.

Impact of contractual terms

When parties create a contract, its terms are expected to be followed by both sides. Probably the most important terms of the contract are those relating to the seller's delivery of goods and the buyer's payment for them, together with the quality of the goods delivered, issues relating to title (ownership) and how the parties can avoid or exclude responsibility on the contract.

Time for performance and rejection of goods

Usually the parties will have agreed a date for delivery of the goods. This is known as a fixed delivery date. Failure to deliver on time will allow the other person to repudiate (reject) the contract and sue for damages.

Where there is no such fixed date the law implies into the contract that delivery will take place within a reasonable time.

Price variation

Many businesses will include in their contracts a term that is known as a price variation clause. The price first agreed when the parties negotiated may have changed

Case study

Ever hopeful

Several years ago, plans were announced to build a new national football stadium at the site of the old Wembley Stadium (London). The principal contractors, the Australian firm Multiplex, assured the FA (Football Association) that the new Wembley would be completed by 31 March 2005 in order to host the 2005 FA Cup final in May.

The stadium was finally 'open for business' in 2007, and did eventually host the FA cup. However, Multiplex is still liable for many millions of pounds of damages for failing to deliver the contract on time.

1. How is Multiplex in dispute with the FA? ✓
2. What could the FA now do? ✓✓
3. Consider why in a project this size time delays are common and why the injured party seldom rejects the contract. ✓✓✓

due to unforeseen rises in, e.g. inflation, fuel costs and production costs. Clearly a business will not want to lose out financially and will cover such a rise by a term allowing it to increase the contract price.

Payment terms

The payment for goods delivered by the seller is a very important part of the contract. These terms will normally be agreed between parties when the contract is negotiated. It is usual to expect payment on delivery, payment by instalments or payment by any method agreed by the parties.

Quality and quantity of goods delivered

When the goods are delivered it is expected that what was agreed to be delivered will in fact be delivered. The goods will be expected to match in terms of quality and quantity. In terms of quality, the law implies into contracts that the goods delivered are:

- fit for their intended purpose
- free from minor defects in terms of finish and appearance
- safe and lasting.

A person will have time to examine the goods on delivery before deciding to reject them if they fail to meet the required standard, as previous examples in this unit have shown.

If the wrong quantity is delivered, then the buyer has various options regardless of what was agreed between the parties.

- If the seller delivers a smaller amount than was expected, the buyer will be allowed to reject the entire delivery. The buyer will, however, be allowed to accept the smaller quantity for which full payment will be expected.
- If the seller sends a larger quantity, the buyer can:
  - accept the quantity expected and reject the rest
  - reject the entire delivery
  - accept the entire delivery at the new contract price.

However, if the difference in quantity is so slight that it would make no difference to the contract, then the buyer will be prohibited from rejecting the delivery.

Reservation of title

It is not unusual for sellers, wishing to protect themselves, inserting a clause into the contract that ownership of the goods is not to pass to the buyer until the seller has been paid. This is known as a **reservation of title** clause.

Key Term

Reservation of title Retaining ownership of the goods until the contract is completed.

Practice point

Imagine that you have to draw up a contract to sell and deliver 1,000 computers to NHS hospitals. What key terms would you include in the contract?

Exclusion clauses

An exclusion clause is a term in a contract that tries to exempt or limit the liability of a party in breach of that agreement. Parliamentary controls over the law relating to exemption clauses comes in the form of the Unfair Contract Terms Act 1977. It is a vitally important piece of legislation but is not applied universally to all contracts. It was intended to be used primarily for contracts of sales by commercial organisations and businesses rather than by individuals.

There are some contracts where the Act does not apply. These are contracts for land, insurance, company promotions, shares and debentures, and patents (copyrights). Exemption clauses under the Act are regulated in two ways.

- Either they are rendered void and ineffective automatically because they are unfair.
- Or they are made subject to a test of reasonableness. Should they fail the test, they will be deemed unfair.

Again, the reasonableness of an exemption clause will be a matter for the court to decide in the light of all the circumstances of the case such as the relative strength of the parties concerned.

Standard form contracts

Businesses will almost certainly try to limit their liability when things go wrong during business with consumers on their standard term (pre-written) contracts. Page 112 shows an example of a typical standard form contract. Look at the way it is written and in particular notice how the surveyor excludes liability.

The impact of statutes on common contractual terms

Generally, businesses have been free to create contracts on whatever terms they wish. The law has never stepped in to protect parties who had created 'bad bargains'. However, as businesses have become more powerful with stronger bargaining positions, Parliament has passed more laws that have had an impact on business contracts.

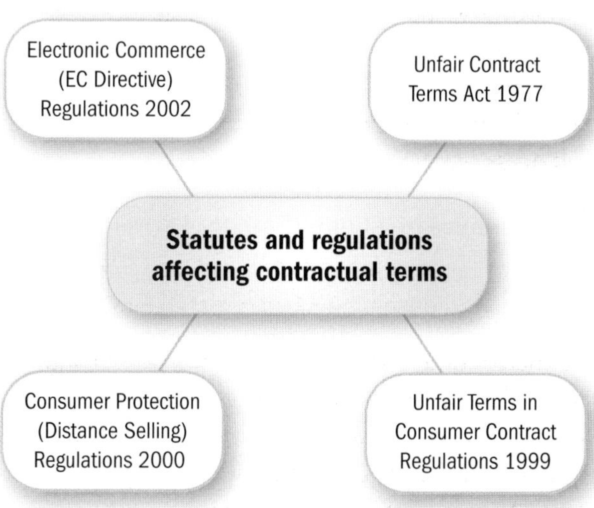

STANDARD TERMS OF ENGAGEMENT

PART 1: GENERAL

1. **The Service**. The standard HOMEBUYER Survey & Valuation Service ('the Service') laid out in the preceding *Description of the Homebuyer Service* ('the Description') applies unless an Addition to the Service is agreed in writing before the Inspection. (An example of such an Addition is reporting upon parts which are not ordinarily inspected, such as the opening of all windows.)

2. **The Surveyor** who provides the Service will be a Member of the Royal Institute of Chartered Surveyors who is competent to survey, value and report upon the Property which is the subject of these Terms.

3. **Before the Inspection**. The Client will inform the Surveyor if there is already an agreed or proposed price for the Property and if there are any particular concerns (such as plans for extension) which the Client may have about the Property.

4. **Terms of payment**. The Client agrees to pay the fee and any other charges agreed in writing.

5. **Cancellation**. The Client will be entitled to cancel this contract by notifying the Surveyor's office at any time before the day of the Inspection. The Surveyor will not proceed with the provision of the Service (and will so report promptly to the Client) if, after arriving at the Property, he or she concludes:
   - a that it is of a type of construction of which he or she has insufficient specialist knowledge to be able to provide the Service satisfactorily, or
   - b that it would be in the typical Client's best interests to be provided with a Building Survey, plus valuation, rather than the HOMEBUYER Service.

In case of cancellation, the Surveyor will refund any money paid by the Client for the Service, except for expenses reasonably incurred. In the case of cancellation by the Surveyor, the reason will be explained to the Client.

6. **Liability**. The Report provided is solely for the use of the Client and the Client's professional advisers and no liability to anyone else is accepted. It may not be provided to anyone else.

Source: http://home.clara.net/pauljspence/STOE.htm

Case study

R W Green Ltd v Cade Brothers Farm (1978)

A farmer bought seed potatoes from a supplier. An exclusion clause in the supplier's standard form contract stated that any complaint had to be brought within three days of delivery of the product. When the seeds grew, the potatoes were not the correct quality. The farmer complained but the supplier tried to rely on the exclusion clause in the contract.

1. Explain how an exclusion clause works. ✓
2. How did the supplier try to limit liability in this case? ✓✓
3. Consider how far you think this clause was reasonable. ✓✓✓

Unfair Contract Terms Act 1977

The Unfair Contract Terms Act 1977 (UCTA) is a vitally important piece of legislation intended to protect innocent parties from unfair exclusion clauses. Examples of simple exclusion clauses are:

- 'The management accept no responsibility for loss or damage'
- 'Cars parked at owner's risk.'

Here the Act ensures such clauses satisfy the test of reasonableness by making sure that those relying on them for protection adequately display such signs so users know of their existence. (Page 111 discusses exclusion clauses under the Act.)

The Act does lay down some interpretation guidelines for judges when deciding this question.

- Reasonableness will be judged in light of all the circumstances of the case.
- It is up to the person claiming reasonableness of the term to prove it is.
- Availability of resources to cover liability such as insurance.
- The relative strengths of the parties.
- Any inducements offered.
- Whether the customer should have known about the term.
- Practical considerations such as time factors.
- Any special circumstances requiring special terms.

For the purpose of the Act 'consumer' means:

- the person who makes a contract other than in the course of a business
- the other party makes the contract in the course of a business
- goods that pass under the contract are the type of goods that are usually supplied for private use or consumption.

The Act itself lays down some very important rules relating to exclusion clauses.

- S2 states that a clause restricting liability for death or personal injury is void.

Liability for any other types of damage caused by negligence are subject to the reasonableness test.

- S3 restricts the exclusion of liability in standard form and consumer contracts.
- S4 deals with unreasonable **indemnity clauses**.

Exclusion clauses restricting liability must satisfy the reasonableness test.

- S5 deals with guarantees of consumer goods.

A manufacturer or distributor cannot restrict their liability in negligence for losses arising from defective goods by means of a term in a guarantee.

- S6 and S7 deal with implied terms in contracts of sale and hire purchase.
- S8 deals with Exemption of liability for misrepresentation.

Any clause that excludes or restricts liability for misrepresentation will be ineffective unless it satisfies the reasonableness test.

Key Term

Indemnity clause Term in a contract between two parties in which one of the parties agrees to indemnify the other party for liabilities in respect of a third party.

Case study

Mitchell v Finney Lock Seeds (1983)

A farmer (Mitchell, the claimant) bought cabbage seed from the defendant (Finney Lock Seeds). When the cabbage grew it was inferior and the wrong type. The defendant relied on an exclusion clause in its standard form contract excluding his liability. The House of Lords held that the clause was unreasonable as the purchaser would have no idea of the defective nature of the crop until it grew.

1. Explain how the seed company was trying to limit liability on the contract. ✓
2. Explain why the House of Lords viewed this as unreasonable. Do you think this is a correct approach? ✓✓
3. Analyse the way liability could be excluded in similar types of contract and whether the exclusion clauses would be fair or not. ✓✓✓

Unfair Terms in Consumer Contract Regulations 1999

The law relating to exclusion clauses has been added to by the creation of the Unfair Terms in Consumer Contracts Regulations 1999, which applies only to consumer contracts and means the court can strike out any term in a contract it deems to be unfair. The idea of unfairness looks at whether:

- the parties have acted in 'good faith', a judgement that will be made on the basis of the strength of the parties
- any inducements were offered to make the consumer agree to the contract
- the seller had dealt fairly with the consumer.

Case study

Dell scraps the small print

In September 2006 Dell, the world's largest computer maker, was persuaded by the Office of Fair Trading to remove unfair small print in its contracts relating to faulty goods. The OFT discussed a number of terms with Dell that it considered to be inconsistent with the Unfair Contract Term Act 1977 and the Unfair Terms in Consumer Contracts Regulations 1999.

1. Why do parties include exclusion clauses in their contracts? ✓
2. Can parties exclude all liability? ✓✓
3. Evaluate some of the reasons why Dell might have scrapped this particular exclusion clause. ✓✓✓

The Consumer Protection (Distance selling) regulations 2000 (as amended)

The Unsolicited Goods and Services Act 1971 – now updated by the Consumer Protection (Distance Selling) Regulations 2000 – makes it a criminal offence for suppliers to demand payment for unsolicited goods and services to unsuspecting consumers.

Worse than this for the supplier is that the receiver of these goods or services:

- is under no obligation to return the items
- may treat them as an unconditional gift
- will be under no duty to pay for them.

The supplier will be committing a criminal offence by demanding payment for them.

The Electronic Commerce (EC Directive) Regulations 2002

According to Verdict Research, web-based online retail sales in 2006 will produce sales amounting to around £10 billion in the UK. This is an ever-growing market, and more and more businesses are looking at this area to increase their turnover. As more businesses trade online, inevitably problems will arise and laws will be introduced to control them and protect consumers. (See www.verdict.co.uk for more details, online sales figures and retail sales generally.)

At present there are various regulations that control the use of online selling. The main law is found in the Electronic Commerce (EC Directive) Regulations 2002. These regulations stipulate information that must be included on a business website, such as:

- full company identity details (name, a geographic address and an e-mail address)
- terms and conditions that are easily accessible and fair to consumers
- a description of the goods or services being offered for sale
- pricing information, including of any delivery charges or tax
- information about how long the offer or price applies
- details of stages involved in the ordering process, including any additional costs of delivery
- the steps to follow to conclude a contract, so that consumers are made aware of what the process will involve and the point at which they will commit themselves and a contract is formed
- information about the availability, delivery and dispatch of goods
- information about substitutes in the event that goods or services are not available, including telling the

Case study

The perils of online buying and flying

As the growth of online holiday firms continue, so too do the risks associated with the failure of those businesses. Consumers are at extreme risk of losing their money with little comeback.

A good example of this is the risk of low-cost airlines going out of business. According to the Transport Select Committee, around 40% of all holiday flights in the UK are booked via the internet – many on low-cost airlines that are not members of government-funded schemes for compensation such as the Air Travel Organiser's Licence (ATOL).

In January 2005 Air Polonia, which flew from Stansted to destinations in Poland, collapsed and disappeared from the internet. More than 50,000 passengers lost their bookings and several others were left stranded at airports. There is little chance of any of them receiving back any money from the airline, leaving them to claim the money from their holiday insurance.

1. What could customers check before they book online? ✓
2. Explain how customers might try to get their money back. ✓✓
3. Evaluate whether controls on internet selling are adequate. If not how would you strengthen them? ✓✓✓

consumer that the cost of returning unsatisfactory substitute goods will be refunded

- a clear complaints procedure and policy on returning goods
- information about withdrawal/cancellation rights
- a statement that UK law is the applicable law
- a statement indicating that, when buying goods and services on the internet, the consumer is entering a legally binding contract
- the technical means for identifying and correcting input errors prior to the placing of the order
- a data protection statement
- a privacy policy and information about security issues
- a cookie (unique identifier) policy
- details of any registration scheme to which the seller belongs and its registration number
- details of relevant professional bodies through which the business is registered
- details of any code of practice to which the business subscribes
- VAT number (if appropriate).

These regulations place restrictions on businesses that use electronic commerce as a way of selling items on the internet, and it is difficult to ensure that all of the law has been followed.

Consumer organisations are increasingly concerned about the growth of this area of business. In October 2006, the OFT announced that it would be investigating whether or not stricter controls might be required to protect the consumer (see www.oft.gov.uk for more details).

REAL LIVES

'Stay Legal' checks business websites

To overcome the problem of legal compliance for internet businesses, the 'Stay Legal' logo has been developed by solicitor Michael Coyle. His firm will assess a business website, certify that it complies with the law and allow its logo to be added to the website to reassure customers (see www.stay-legal.com for more details).

Take it further

You can watch developments in controls over e-commerce transactions during your study and comment on any new laws that are introduced.

Outcome activity 21.3

Pass p2

Prepare a briefing sheet explaining how statutes affect contractual terms and the meaning of the key terms in a contract. You should use the contract you studied for Outcome activity 20.1

Distinction d1

Complete your briefing sheet with an evaluation of how effective, in your opinion, the terms of the contract are for the needs of the parties involved.

Grading tips

Pass 

You should describe the express and implied terms in the contract from Outcome activity 20.1 and how they are each affected by statute.

Statutes are Acts of Parliament, e.g. Sale of Goods Act 1979 or Unfair Contract Terms Act 1997. You should make direct links between the terms and the statutes you have learnt about.

Distinction 

You should reach a justified conclusion on how well the business protects itself from things like loss from non-payment or failure of delivery.

You should consider how the buyer is to be protected adequately from issues such as late delivery or poor quality.

Remember, 'evaluation' means 'judgement', so you should look at what is positive about the terms and what needs to be improved before you judge how well the terms meet the needs of both parties.

21.4 Remedies available to the parties to a contract

When contracts go wrong, injured parties will want to know that there is an opportunity to gain compensation. In the final part of this unit you will look at the remedies available to help the injured party.

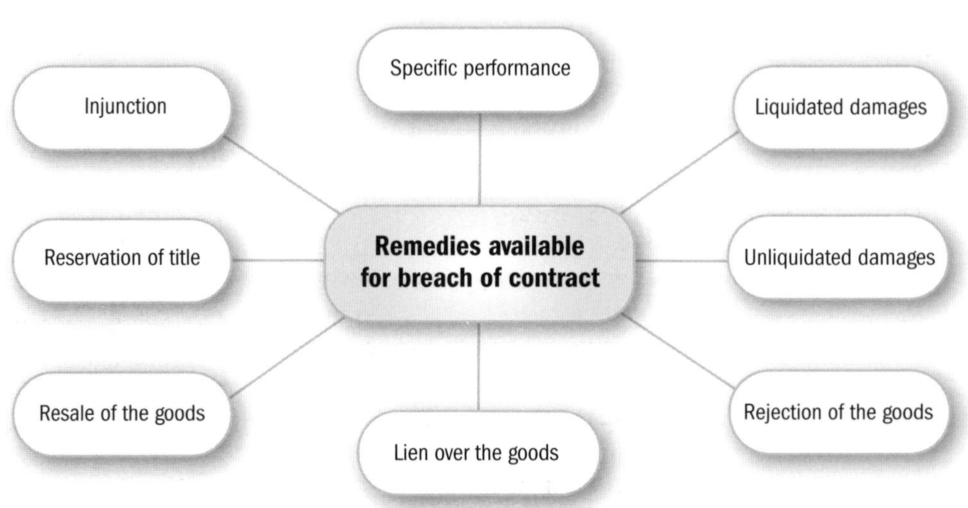

Remedies

When one of the parties breaks the terms of a contract, the injured party will be able to gain some form of compensation for the loss of the contract. This is known as a **remedy**; it is aimed at ensuring that the injured party has not lost out. These remedies can be written into the contract or exist as what are known as equitable remedies (coming from the historical idea of equity or fairness). The main remedy available is damages. These are split into two types:

- liquidated damages
- unliquidated damages.

Key Term

Remedy Solution for the victim of a breach of contract.

Liquidated damages

In the business world it is quite common for parties to agree in advance the amount of damages that will be paid in the event of a breach of contract. These are known as **liquidated damages**.

An example of a common form of agreed damages can be found in most holiday booking confirmation forms. Below is a set of cancellation charges relating to money that will be paid in the event of a firm cancelling a customer's holiday.

Period before departure within which notice of cancellation or major change is notified to you	If we cancel your holiday amount you will receive from us
More than 56 days	Deposit only
More than 28 days	100% of holiday cost + £5
More than 14 days	100% of holiday cost + £10
More than 1 day	100% of holiday cost + £15
Less than 1 day	100% of holiday cost +£30

Unliquidated damages

Unliquidated damages are those damages awarded for breach of contract where there is no prior agreement between the parties as to the amount of damages to be awarded.

The aim of unliquidated damages is to restore the person to the position they would have been in had the contract been carried out correctly. The damages are designed to compensate only for loss suffered. That means if no loss has been suffered, damages awarded will only be nominal to recognise that there has been a breach of contract.

Courts use the following guidelines when awarding damages.

- The damage can include sums for financial loss, damage to property, personal injury and distress, disappointment and upset caused to the claimant.
- An injured party cannot necessarily recover damages for every kind of loss.
- Breaches of contract can cause a chain of events. In law, there has to come a point after which the damage becomes too distant from the original damage to be recoverable.
- Provided the loss is not too distant, courts have to decide how much is payable by way of damages.
- Once a breach of contract has occurred, the innocent party is under a duty to mitigate or lessen their loss.

Mitigation of loss

A victim cannot simply stand back and allow his losses to get worse. So for example a seller whose goods have been rejected, must attempt to get the best price for them elsewhere. This is **mitigation**.

Key Terms

Liquidated damages Damages agreed at the negotiation stage.

Unliquidated damages Damages awarded that were not agreed.

Mitigation To reduce your loss.

Rejection

A party who is the victim of a breach of contract may reject the entire contract. You will already have come across circumstances where the contract fails because of:

- not delivering on time
- delivering the wrong quantity
- delivering goods of poor quality.

Rejection of the goods will still allow the injured party to claim damages as well.

▼ **A party can reject an entire contract if it has been breached – for example, not delivered on time**

Lien

The owner of goods may be able to exercise what is known as a lien, which is a right to retain possession of the goods until the contract price has been paid.

An example of this would be where a person leaves a television set to be repaired. A contract is formed that the set will be repaired and the owner will pay for the service. The television repairer now has a lien over the television and can retain possession of it until the bill is paid.

Case study

R v Turner (no. 2) (1971)

Mr Turner (the defendant) left his car for repair at a local garage. The garage telephoned to say it was ready for collection. Mr Turner told the garage (the claimant) to leave it outside on the road and he would come in the next day to pay the bill and collect it. Using his spare keys he collected the car later that evening and refused to pay the bill. The garage had a lien over the car and called the police. Turner was arrested and convicted of stealing his own car!

1. Explain what a lien is. ✓
2. What other remedies were available to the garage? ✓✓
3. Discuss the fairness of this type of remedy. ✓✓✓

Resale

Where a seller of goods remains unpaid, re-selling of the goods will be allowed:

- when the goods are perishable and likely to be spoiled
- where the seller has told the buyer of the resale and the buyer fails to respond
- where the term of the contract allows the seller to do this.

This resale will not affect the seller's right to claim damages.

Reservation of title

A remedy that is often expressly written into the contract is the right of the seller to reserve title (or to retain ownership of the goods) until the contract price has been paid. This will enable the seller of the goods to recover them in the event of the liquidation or bankruptcy of the buyer, so that the seller's goods are not lost to the buyer's creditors.

Injunctions

This is an order of the court requiring the party at fault not to break the contract. Its main use is to enforce promises in certain contracts such as employment contracts restraining employees working in a similar capacity for rival employers.

Specific performance

Specific performance is an equitable remedy granted instead of damages in cases where damages are not considered an adequate remedy. Specific performance requires the party in breach of contract to carry out their contractual promises. An example of this is where a person who is compelled to make a personal performance (a nightclub DJ, perhaps) refuses to work.

Case study

Shining stars?

A music promoter called Star Enterprises has booked a famous singer to perform as the main act in a large concert. Everything is in place – the venue, the supporting acts – and all of the tickets have been sold. But the singer has had a row with one of the producers of the show and has refused to perform. The star's lawyers have gone to court to gain a remedy.

1. What is the contractual position between the parties? ✓
2. What remedy will the star be trying to get? ✓✓
3. Are damages suitable here? ✓✓✓

Application of remedies

In the earlier examples, where a breach of contract has occurred, the parties will be able to claim one or more of the remedies described. This is not an automatic right and the injured party (known as the claimant) will have to go to court to get their remedy.

Courts

In the event of a contractual dispute it may be necessary to apply to the civil courts for your claim to be heard and hopefully resolved to a satisfactory conclusion.

The civil court system was transformed under the Woolf reforms, a series of changes to the civil courts made under Lord Woolf when he was Master of the Rolls in the late 1990s. This resulted in the Civil Procedure Act 1997 and Civil Procedure Rules. The three main civil courts that can hear cases initially are:

- the Small Claims Court
- the County Court
- the High Court.

If you are in dispute with an individual or company, you must apply to the court and your case will be passed to a judge who will be assigned as case manager for your case. It will be allocated to the correct court depending on the seriousness of the case. This is known as the 'track system'.

The small claims track deals with small claims court cases; the fast track deals with County Court cases; and the multi-track system deals with complex High Court cases.

The Royal Courts of Justice ▶

Small claims court

The small claims court is a special part of the County Court which deals with minor claims, including contractual and business disputes where the claim does not exceed £5,000. This includes claims such as:

- failure to supply goods
- failure to pay for goods
- other business disputes.

These cases are not expected to raise any difficult questions of law.

If the case is a simple one and both parties agree, the district judge may make a decision on the documents alone, without a hearing. Otherwise, the judge gives directions (e.g. about producing certain documents in advance, and about the number of witnesses allowed) and sets a date for a hearing.

It is usual for parties to be encouraged not to have legal representation from a solicitor or barrister, as help for payment of legal fees is not allowed. The courts try to reduce both parties' cost burden.

If the case goes to full hearing, the proceedings are very informal and are often uncontested – meaning the other party does not disagree.

Help with a claim is available on www.hmcourts-service.gov.uk.

County Court

The County Court deals with fast-track cases worth between £5,000 and £15,000. The County Court also has jurisdiction (power) to hear cases concerning the recovery of land, bankruptcies, company wind ups, consumer credit and copyright matters. Jurisdiction means they have the power to hear those cases.

A case at the County Court is more formal and will be heard by a circuit judge and it is normal for the parties to have legal representation.

However, as with the small claims court, help and advice are available from the court itself and a person can now even make a claim against another person online (using www.moneyclaim.gov.uk).

High Court

The High Court is the most senior of the first-instance civil courts. Based in London and other larger cities, it is split into three divisions dealing with different branches of civil law.

- **Queen's Bench division.** This will hear contract cases – multi-track cases involving large sums of money or involving complex points of law. It sits as a commercial court dealing with business matters such as insurance, banking and the meaning of commercial documents. Its Divisional Court will also hear civil appeals from the County Court.
- **The Chancery division.** This deals with matters of equity (or fairness) including trusts, mortgages, partnerships, companies, bankruptcies and taxation.
- **The Family division.** This deals primarily with family law matters such as divorce and adoption, so has little role to play in the law relating to businesses.

Thinking point

Using the court system can present problems for parties. Look at the problems for parties using the civil courts and suggest alternative methods of resolving disputes. (See www.acas.org.uk for more details.)

Time limits

The right to claim for breach of contract does not last forever. The Limitation Act 1980 imposes time limits to bring an action.

- Simple contract dispute must be brought within six years of the breach.
- For contracts made under deed (such as the sale of land) the time limit is within twelve years of the breach.

This time limit can be extended where fraud is involved, or where the person making the claim is suffering from a disability or lacks capacity.

Remember

All breaches of contract will allow parties to claim remedies. These remedies may have to be claimed via a court case.

Outcome activity 21.4

Pass

Using the contract that you explored for Outcome activities 21.1 and 21.2, describe the remedies available for a breach of contract.

Merit

Analyse the remedies available to a business provider in the event of a breach of contract for the supply of goods or services.

Distinction

Evaluate the statutory protection given to a consumer in their dealings with a business and the remedies available.

Grading tips

Pass 

You should include a description of damages, how these damages are assessed and the different types available. You should briefly include a description of other remedies available. You should be able to describe issues such as reservation of title and issues of retention of ownership until the contract has been paid. You need to demonstrate understanding of the distinction between ownership and possession.

Merit 

Using the damages and remedies you have described for task 1, you should now consider the strengths and weaknesses of each when applied to a breach of contract situation. How well do they seek to resolve the situation?

Distinction 

You should give a judgement, based on evidence you have collected for M3, about how well the law protects the consumer and business including damages and equitable remedies.

You should include evaluation of the court process, features of the process and suggesting ways to resolve the dispute.

End of unit test

1. What is the definition of a contract?
2. What is the difference between an offer and an invitation to treat?
3. What is 'consideration'?
4. Explain 'capacity'.
5. What is the small claims track?
6. How are purchasers on the internet protected?
7. If a sample and the bulk order do not match, what can the buyer do?
8. What is an express term? Give an example.
9. Explain the difference between liquidated and unliquidated damages.
10. What implied terms are in a contract for sale of goods?
11. What remedies are available for breach of a consumer contract?
12. What is the purpose of an exclusion clause?
13. What punishment might a seller of a defective product receive?
14. Explain a false trade description.

Books

Abbott, K, 1994, *Business Law*, DP Publications

Chitty, J, 1994, *Contracts*, Sweet & Maxwell

Keenan, D and Riches, S, 2002, *Business Law*, Longman

Sparrow, A, 2001, *The E-Commerce Handbook*, Fitzwarren Handbooks

Statutes and legislation

Companies Act 1985

Companies Act 1989

Consumer Credit Act 1974

Consumer Protection (Distance Selling) Regulations 2000

Contracts (Rights of Third parties) Act 1999

Copyright Act 1956

Electronic Commerce (EC Directive) Regulations 2002

Local Government Act 1972

Misrepresentation Act 1967

Partnership Act 1890

Sale of Goods Act 1979

Sale and Supply of Goods Act 1994

Supply of Goods and Services Act 1982

Trade Descriptions Act 1968

Unfair Contract Terms Act 1977

Unfair Terms in Consumer Regulations 1999

Unsolicited Goods and Services Act 1971

Case references

Adams vs. Lindsell (1818)

Barton vs. Armstrong (1975)

Butler Machine Tool Co Ltd vs. Ex-Cell-O Corp. (Eng) Ltd (1979)

Carlill vs. Carbolic Smoke Ball Co (1893)

D & C Builders vs. Rees (1965)

Dunlop Pneumatic Tyre Co Ltd vs. Selfridge & Co Ltd (1915)

Grant vs. Australian Knitting Mills (1936)

R W Green Ltd vs. Cade Brothers Farm (1978)

Griffiths vs. Peter Conway (1939)

Hedley Byrne & Co Ltd vs. Heller & Partners (1963)

Hyde vs. Wrench (1840)

Kelner vs. Baxter (1866)

Mitchell vs. Finney Lock Seeds (1983)

McArdle (1951)

Moore & Co vs. Landauer & Co (1921)

R vs. Turner (No.2) (1971)

Rogers vs. Parish (Scarborough) Ltd (1987)

Spice Girls Ltd vs. Aprilia World Service BV (2000)

Tweddle vs. Atkinson (1861)

Websites

http://home.clara.net/pauljspence/STOE.htm – Example of standard form contract

www.acas.org.uk – Arbitration advice and guidance

www.hmcourts-service.gov.uk – Information about court proceedings

www.moneyclaim.gov.uk – Advice for making civil court claims.

www.oft.gov.uk – Office of Fair Trading; government department ensuring businesses trade fairly

www.stay-legal.com – Firm carrying out checks into the legality of website traders

www.tradingstandards.gov.uk – Government website checking trading practices

www.verdict.co.uk – Business research consultants

Grading criteria	Outcome activity	Page number
To achieve a pass grade the evidence shows that the learner is able to:		
P1 Describe the requirements for a valid contract	21.1	101
P2 Describe how statutes affect contractual terms	21.3	116
P3 Outline how consumers are protected in contracts for the sale of goods	21.2	107
P4 Outline how consumers are protected in contracts for the supply of goods/services	21.2	107
P5 Describe the remedies available for breach of contract	21.4	121
To achieve a merit grade the evidence shows that, in addition to the pass criteria, the learner is able to:		
M1 Analyse the impacts of the requirements for a valid contract in a given situation	21.1	101
M2 Analyse how consumers are protected in the event of a contract for the supply/sale of goods or services	21.2	107
M3 Analyse the remedies available to a business provider in the event of breach of a contract for the supply of goods or services	21.4	121
To achieve a distinction grade the evidence must show that, in addition to the pass and merit criteria, the learner is able to:		
D1 Evaluate the effectiveness of terms in a given contract	21.3	116
D2 Evaluate the statutory protection given to a consumer in their dealings with a business and the remedies available	21.4	121

Website design strategies

Introduction

New figures suggest that online sales in the UK are due to rise by 40% next year, to a total of £42 billion. The Interactive Media in Retail Group (IMRG) found that October 2006 was the biggest ever month for online sales in the UK, with customers spending a record £2.7 billion.

These figures demonstrate the growing willingness of UK shoppers to use their bank cards in online transactions, with the wider use of broadband a major factor. 'More consumers are getting broadband,' said IMRG chief executive James Roper. 'It is huge. When people have broadband they shop online; it is as simple as that.'

A strategy for excellence in web design is vital for any business hoping to tap into the growing world of online sales.

In this unit you will examine the huge range of organisations now using their own websites for a variety of business purposes. You will examine the various features that have an impact on usability and appeal for users of websites. Finally, you will look at the practical matters to be addressed in designing a modest website of your own.

What you need to learn

On completion of this unit you should:

1. Be able to define the purposes of a range of websites
2. Understand the main elements in web design for usability and visual appeal
3. Know some of the issues to be considered when developing an e-business website.

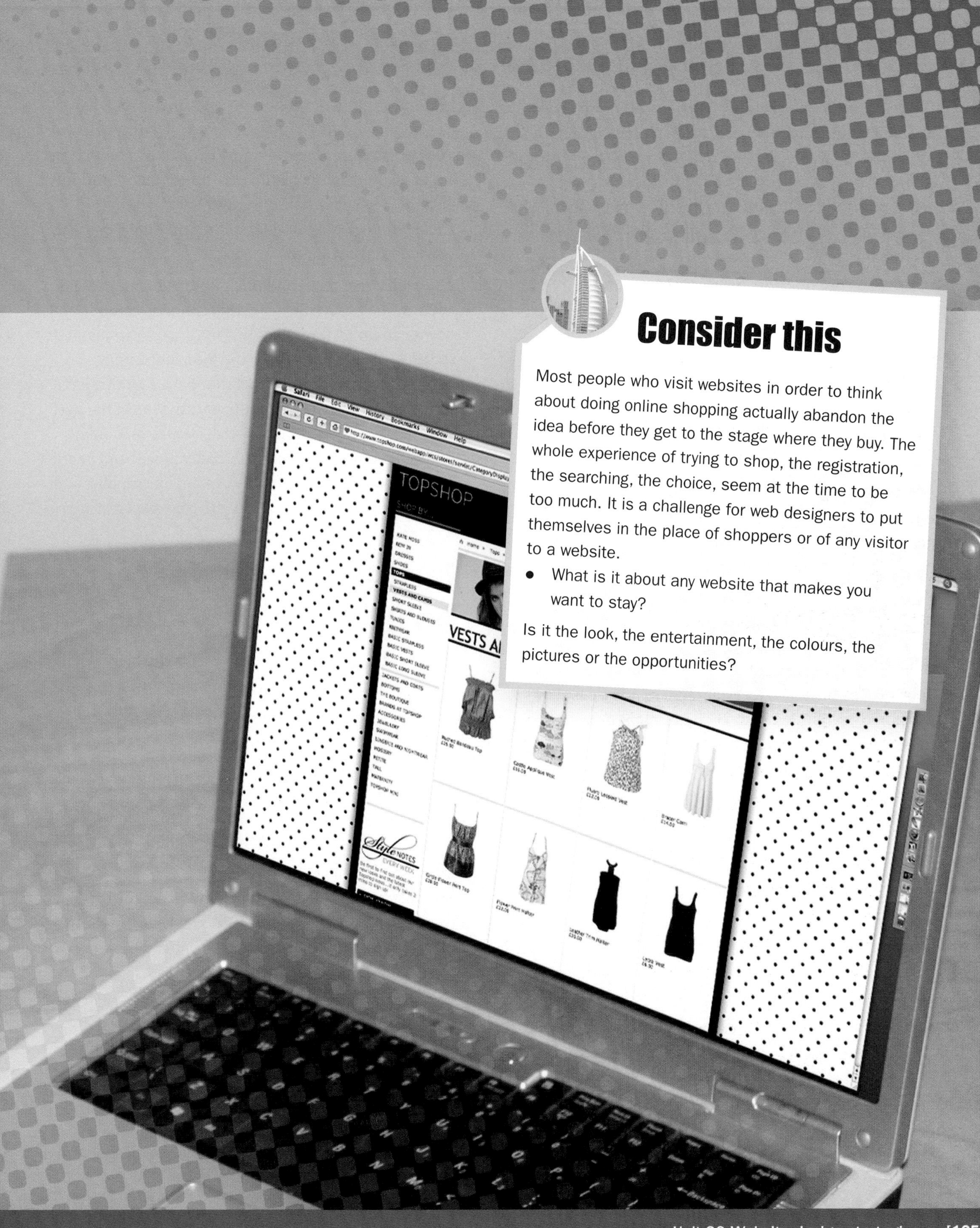

Consider this

Most people who visit websites in order to think about doing online shopping actually abandon the idea before they get to the stage where they buy. The whole experience of trying to shop, the registration, the searching, the choice, seem at the time to be too much. It is a challenge for web designers to put themselves in the place of shoppers or of any visitor to a website.

- What is it about any website that makes you want to stay?

Is it the look, the entertainment, the colours, the pictures or the opportunities?

30.1 Defining the purpose of a range of websites

It is sometimes said that there are now more web pages available online than there are stars in the sky. Certainly, in the UK alone, several thousand organisations have websites that act as global shop windows. Today, there are so many different kinds of organisation using the web that it is helpful to try to make sense of this by placing them into categories.

In broad terms, it is possible to distinguish two kinds of *commercial* (i.e. buying and selling) relationships online. The two most common interactions occur on business-to-consumer sites (b2c) and business-to-business (b2b) sites.

Business-to-consumer (b2c)

A b2c website offers to sell or provide a service to private consumers rather than other businesses; b2c businesses service *consumer* demand.

Walk around any shopping area and you will see a range of retail outlets offering goods for sale to us, private consumers. Before the development of the internet, shopping was restricted to particular times and places. Shops were only open at certain times and you had to *travel* to them. By contrast, an online shop is unlimited in time or space and there are no limits to what an internet retailer (known as an 'e-tailer') can *offer* to consumers. (There are only limits as to what they can practically do, as some early dotcoms found out.)

One thing worth noticing is that these e-tailers are usually part of an established retail firm (as you will discover later). There is a big difference between adding an online sales channel to an existing firm and trying to set up a completely new online retail outlet. Most of the growth in e-business is due to physical businesses adopting an e-strategy.

Amazon is one of the most successful online businesses and a model for every online firm. Amazon started off as a bookseller and today offers nearly 5 million books, together with information about them all, as well as personalised recommendations based on past choices from the site (see more on this on pages 157–158). Amazon.co.uk has diversified its product range to become a multi-product online business: as well as books it now sells CDs, DVDs, toys, electronic items and sports equipment to name just a few. The internet – a brilliant carrier of information content – not only gives e-tailers the chance to offer a wider range of choices, but also it allows them to offer more back-up services to consumers.

The problem of the abandoned shopping cart is a major issue for the e-tailer. Slow internet connections and download times, fears about intrusion and fears about security will often drive even the most enthusiastic consumers away from internet shopping. Research has shown that 67% of online shoppers drop out at the cart stage because of lack of speed. Despite this, online shopping continues to increase. Faster broadband internet connection may be the solution, but online suppliers still have to make a real internet offer to gain sales.

Business-to-business (b2b)

In the online world, b2b is reported to be bigger than b2c. Transactions between businesses may be less frequent over the internet, but they account for more in terms of money value.

The b2b business is buying from *and* selling to other businesses. It is buying either for its own internal maintenance, repair and operations (MRO) purposes, or for items used as part of what is sold to another business in a supply chain.

A report by *eMarketer* (www.eMarketer.com) predicted that these kinds of transactions would soon amount to almost 90% of total e-commerce. In 2006, it was reported that:

- 93% of business decision makers used the internet every day
- 70% thought their use of b2b websites would increase.

Why has b2b internet trade become so significant? The reason is that there are many more opportunities for big-deal transactions between businesses than there are for transactions with private customers. The diagram on the following page illustrates this.

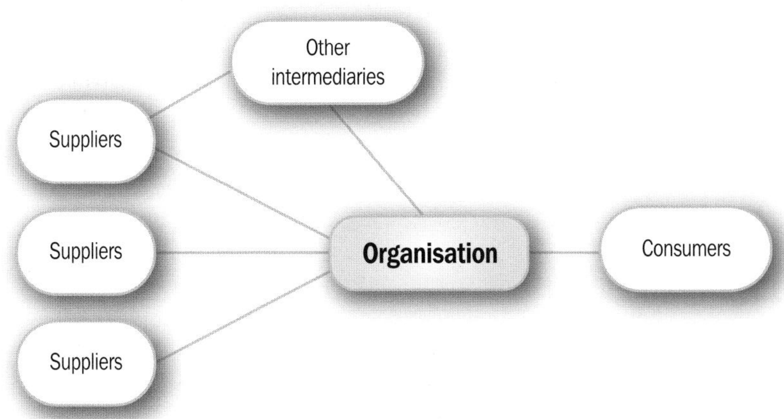

▲ b2b and b2c interaction compared

Business organisations are likely to have several suppliers and the suppliers themselves will have suppliers.

Online marketplaces for components are becoming more common. For example, Ford and General Motors have joined forces and moved their US$300 billion and US$500 billion supply chains online (see www.covisint.net).

Remember

For commercial websites offered by profit-seeking organisations, a basic distinction can be made between b2c websites targeted towards private consumers and b2b websites aimed at business buyers.

Purposes of commercial websites

The basic purpose of a commercial website is, of course, to generate revenue from sales. There are a number of business models achieving this online. We saw on page 126 that many long-established retailers have added an online sales channel to their existing offline (physical) stores. There are some notable businesses (Amazon being the most well known) that have established a purely online presence. In other words, you won't (yet) find an Amazon shop down your road.

Direct online sales

The internet offers the ability to sell directly to consumers from a website, thus bypassing other intermediaries (e.g. wholesalers).

Computers and software

One company that built its business solely on this model is computer manufacturer Dell (www.Dell.co.uk). The strategy adopted by Dell Computers was that it would not have any physical retail outlets. Consumers would simply visit Dell online, specify their computing requirements, and Dell would build and deliver on this basis.

In 2007, Dell seems to be changing its strategy by considering a move into high street retail sales. It has recognised that private consumers need to experience through 'touch and feel' the products they are considering buying.

Music and software products lend themselves to purely digital formats. These can therefore be sold and delivered solely via the web. In the case of expensive software, individuals and business customers appear to be less willing to pay large sums up front for a CD packed with coding. The preferred model is to buy a contracted deal whereby the software is offered on an ongoing maintenance arrangement. This way, purchasers would pay as they use, with support offered via a contractual agreement. The software industry is changing.

This is an important development. For businesses, software products are a means of making far better use of the internet. Software applications such as customer relationship management, database management and project management can help firms to automate their processes and gain a competitive advantage.

The Leighton Group's 4Projects application is an example of the kind of software that businesses can purchase with ongoing maintenance and support.

Case study

The Leighton Group: 4Projects application

The Leighton Group is a Sunderland-based company operating in the UK, Canada and Belgium. Starting in publishing, the firm has branched out to become a leading-edge provider of web-based applications, one of the most innovative being 4Projects (www.4Projects.com).

4Projects is a comprehensive software application designed to enable partner companies to effectively collaborate using an extranet across the web. It particularly applies in a construction context, where a number of firms must work closely together to see a building project come to fruition.

4Projects is an extranet-based platform. This means that firms buying into the application enter into a secure wide area network along with other partner companies. Immediately the problems inherent in the internet or public e-mail accounts are overcome. Extranets are robust, secure and flexible.

The software is designed to be totally flexible and capable of being configured to meet many requirements. The application consists of a number of component modules including:

- document management
- task management
- versioned forms
- calendar management.

If Tesco (for example) plans to build new stores – from initial design concepts to groundwork and roof work, fittings and electrical – each firm contracted to work on the project is able to log on to 4Projects and make use of relevant facilities. 4Projects gives potentially full access to all drawings, documents and contacts. The software creates a virtual project environment, bringing all parties together (if necessary, literally while online).

If people working on a project – wherever it may physically be – need to see images of a site, a building or a room, then thumbnail images can be stored and distributed via the web.

1. 4Projects is an example of software application and Leighton Group is an application service provider (ASP). Software applications can be sold via the web directly to users. Can you describe another example of software available directly on the web? ✓
2. What are the advantages of this kind of software for a business in construction? ✓✓
3. In what other contexts do you think that software like 4Projects could be used? Do you think it adds value to a business? How? ✓✓✓
4. How are demand and supply inter-related in the marketplace? ✓✓✓

■ Music

Music downloads are now an absolute must for many, if not all, teenagers. The Apple iTunes application and others such as Napster, Limewire and AllofMp3 allow for both peer-to-peer file sharing and music purchases directly online.

Online sales with physical delivery

Retail stores such as Tesco, ASDA, Sainsbury, Next, Marks & Spencer, B&Q and many more have opened up online sales channels, adding to their physical stores. Clearly the goods they sell are incapable of direct delivery over the web, so they have to be physically delivered, sometimes using a third party service.

In the case of PC World, the sales strategy has included online promotion with offline collection. This is a helpful sales strategy combining the convenience of the web with the practicality of physical collection.

Pre-sales models

All pre-sales business models can make excellent use of the web because of its suitability to carry detailed information about products. Internet shoppers can get as much information as they could possibly require

Tesco.com deliveries ▼

before making a decision to buy. This means that brochures and online catalogues are very suitable vehicles for product promotion. Businesses seeking to generate sales from a website can embark on e-mail campaigns too.

It is important for any business looking for sales via an e-mail campaign to recognise that unrequested e-mails are a source of great irritation to many people. **Spam** is a nuisance. Research has shown that where permission has been sought and agreed, e-mail campaigns can be very fruitful. The message for online businesses is: always request permission to e-mail before sending out a campaign.

Key Term

Spam Unsolicited e-mails, often referred to as junk mail.

Post-sales models

The web is useful for helping communications between customers and the selling business. The customer is in a stronger position to give feedback once a sale has been made. As businesses adopt an online business approach, some feel that automated responses in customer services can be a help.

Software applications are now available to manage the entire relationship with customers. This means that two businesses that work closely together in partnership within an industry (e.g. a fence manufacturer always purchases the wood from a particular producer) can be digitally bound together. There are databases of, for example:

- staff
- product codes
- technical support staff
- technical information
- sales staff.

If someone wishes to make contact, the software can easily allow this to happen.

Remember

The relationship between businesses in a b2b context can be helped by the use of customer relationship management software. These are applications that manage the interactions between two businesses, making sure that each one is satisfied.

Websites not related to sales

Although the web is a proven vehicle for generating sales, there is also a use for the medium in supporting other activities of the core business.

Most websites include pages that are intended purely for corporate communications. Some websites (e.g. Bells – see 'Real lives', page 149) have no intention of generating sales because of the nature of the business.

The B&Q owned e-business Screwfix uses its website for some PR work, as do many others. It is worth remembering that the web is a vehicle for carrying information. Clearly it is in the corporate interest of all businesses to sell themselves as well as their core products.

Other websites exist to inform the consumer about the available choices. The CNET website offered at www.computers.com only contains reviews and price comparisons.

Non-commercial business relationships

Whereas commercial websites set out to generate consumer interest and (hopefully) sales, non-commercial websites set out to do something else. This depends on whether they are:

- local government
- national government
- voluntary sector bodies
- campaigning groups.

Local goverment

Local government is delivered through local councils. Local councils are democratically elected bodies that have the responsibility to offer local services according to the wishes of Parliament. All local councils get their powers from Parliament. Services such as education, social services, planning, trading standards and rubbish

▲ Notice how many links from this home page are intended purely for communications purposes

clearance are all carried out by your local council because they are required to do so by Parliament.

Local government is important. We tend to ignore our local council. But think about the following.

- If your neighbours decided to build a big extension to their house, it would be the council that would give or refuse permission.
- If a road was to be built near you, it would be the council making that decision.
- If you wanted your child to attend one school rather than another, it is the council that finally decides.

It follows that if your local council has a website, it is likely to carry information that is important to you.

These days, most local councils have a website. The purpose is to provide information about services they provide and, in some cases, to make services available online. Of course, apart from information about services, councils know that the local electorate have the power to vote them out of office. It is therefore in their own interest to promote the work they do. Local voters are aware that councils cost them money. Tax payers like to know what the council is doing and a website is an ideal way of communicating.

Remember

Local councils use websites to promote their services and inform people about what is going on in their area.

National government

National government offers services and deals with concerns that affect us all. The internet is a great way to offer certain services across the country in an efficient and cost effective way. Because national government covers so many issues and concerns, many government departments have their own website. Some typical government websites are:

- www.berr.gov.uk (Department for Business, Enterprise and Regulatory Reform)
- www.dfes.gov.uk (Department for Education and Skills)
- www.defra.gov.uk (Department for Environment, Food and Rural Affairs).

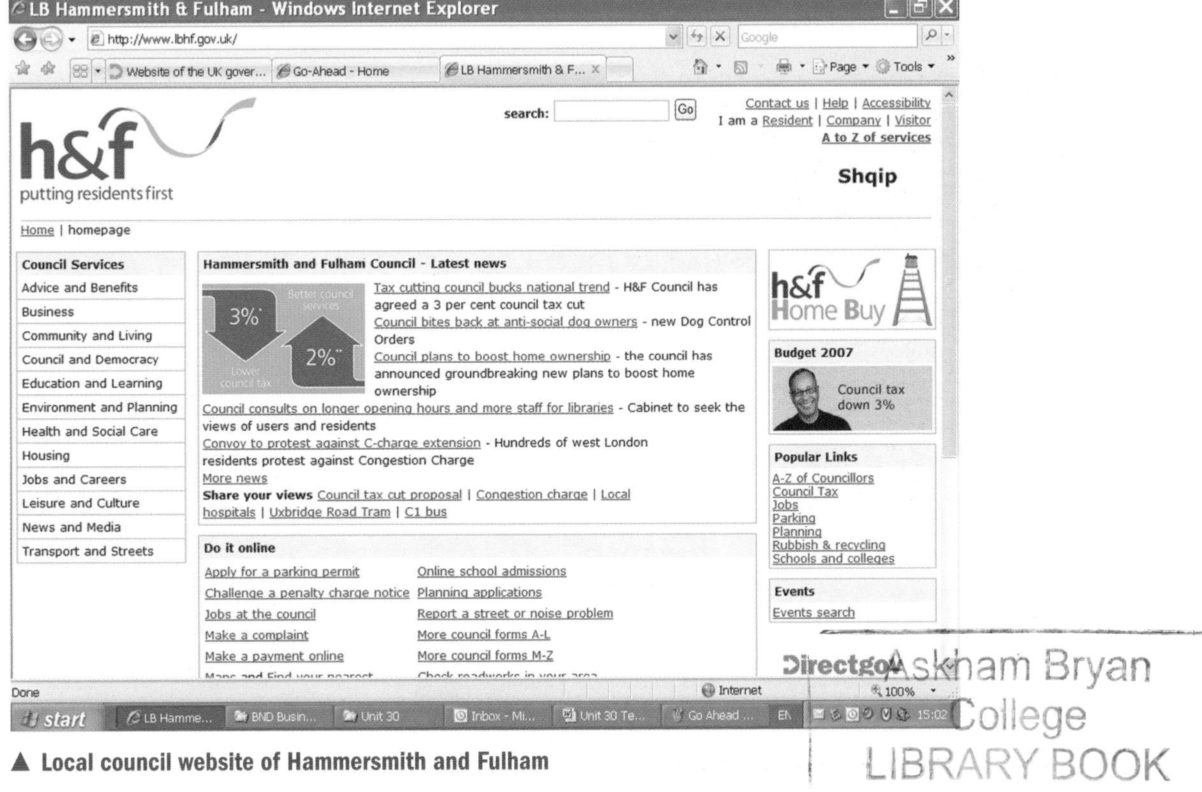

▲ **Local council website of Hammersmith and Fulham**

Askham Bryan College LIBRARY BOOK

One way to give the public access to a broad range of online services is to use a national government **portal**. The national government portal can be found at www.DirectGov.gov.uk, for example.

Key Term

Portal A gateway site that offers many links into other sites related to the same theme.

The national government sites that have been mentioned so far address the needs of both private individuals and businesses. As its name would suggest, the Department of Trade and Industry specialises in offering advice and service to industry.

Remember

The web is capable of being used by private businesses and national and local government to carry information that can either inform or persuade.

Voluntary sector groups

The voluntary sector also uses the web to great effect. Voluntary bodies rely on the public for support for their particular cause. These bodies do not have the pursuit of profit as their main aim. They exist to further a particular cause and hopefully gain public sympathy, whether that cause is to help artistic talent within inner cities or to inform people about the work of the Youth Hostels Association (www.yha.org.uk).

Campaigning groups

Some groups come together to raise a specific issue, by bringing it to the attention of the government and the public. There are many issues that are of national and indeed global importance. Perhaps the most obvious of these are to do with our natural environment. The Greenphase portal shown on page 133 illustrates how well environmental organisations are represented on the web.

▲ The national government portal offers links to many government services

Case study

MySpace: charity joins the revolution

International development charity ActionAid is launching a new website inspired by the success of community site MySpace to offer support to fundraisers. Users can join an online community to publicise upcoming events, collect donations, then blog (to write about experiences, like an online diary) about their experiences.

While collecting money online is well established, the new site allows users to swap tips on successes and disasters. Fundraisers can upload blogs and pictures, swap ideas and discuss their sponsored singalong, marathon run or coffee morning with like-minded people. One area of the site offers users the chance to share tips on getting fit for sponsored runs.

www.myactionaid.org.uk aims to be easy to understand and allows users to create their own colourful fundraising page 'in a matter of minutes'.

Simon Molloy, head of community fundraising at ActionAid, says: 'ActionAid's fundraisers ride bikes across Malawi, kayak through the Brazilian jungle and throw themselves out of planes to help fight poverty. We wanted to create an online community that would give everyone who raises money for ActionAid the chance to show the world what they're planning and make it easy for them to raise as much money as possible.'

Source: Adapted from *The Guardian*, 13 February 2007

1. Why do you think that voluntary sector bodies find using the web useful? ✓
2. What features of the web are being employed by this website? Do you think they will work? ✓✓
3. Study the website mentioned in the article. Evaluate the extent to which you think it will meet the voluntary sector objectives outlined. ✓✓✓

▲ **This site offers links to thirteen other environmental websites**

Apart from the environment, there are many other specific causes that are represented by organised groups.

- Some of these exist to exert *pressure* on the government to change policy (e.g. the campaign for divorced fathers at www.wifesgone.com)
- Others exist to represent the *interests* of a particular group (e.g. www.rcn.org.uk, the body representing nurses).

Remember

The internet carries websites that intend to persuade people to support voluntary causes (such as Fairtrade); it also carries websites from pressure groups such as Greenpeace and interest groups such as trade unions.

Purposes of non-commercial websites

Non-commercial websites are intended to carry information. Is the information meant to persuade, influence or inform, or all of these? Is the website designed to collect data from people and organisations? Website designers, as we will see on pages 139–151, need to spend a great deal of time with the people seeking to go online to discover the purpose(s) of the website. It is vital that these intentions are known. The whole look and feel of a website, perhaps the simplicity of its design, its layout, imagery and content are governed by its basic intention.

Remember

Many websites do not intend to sell anything. They give information designed to influence views and gain support.

Practice point

Investigate two websites – one from a profit-seeking business and another from a non-profit seeking organisation. Create a simple presentation to explain the way each website helps the organisation to achieve its purpose(s).

Marketing concepts

Marketing is the set of professional activities designed to satisfy an organisation's customers, whoever and wherever they are. This applies increasingly to the public sector as well as to the private sector. For example, in creating a website, your local council is trying to improve citizens' views about it and provide a better service.

For the private sector (the sector that first took up marketing in response to global pressures to do so), marketing has evolved into a sophisticated and important function. Private sector businesses want to attract and retain customers.

There are three key marketing concepts:

- targeting
- segmentation
- the marketing mix.

Each of these is assisted by the availability of the internet.

If you think about the word 'marketing' for a moment, you will realise that it contains within it another word – i.e. *market*. We all know that a market is a place where people buy and sell things. In a market, sellers display their goods and buyers come looking for the best deals.

Marketing is, as we have seen, about making sure that goods and services meet customer expectations. To do this properly means that marketers try to make sense of the whole 'market'. Two basic techniques help in this:

- targeting, and
- segmentation.

Targeting and segmentation

Some products (e.g. Mars Bars) could be said to be aimed at everyone who enjoys chocolate – in other words, a *mass* market. However, others are *targeted* at specific groups. An example of **targeting a market** might be a magazine that is clearly aimed at teenagers. Others would be particular razors, cosmetics, jewellery and clothing.

Marketers use various criteria to 'target' a market. They can use age, social class, lifestyle, psychographics and geographic location. Each of these can then be used to isolate particular characteristics and meet their specific needs.

Key Term

Targeting a market Tailoring communications in order to attract sales from a specific group of people.

Associated with targeting is another tool known as 'segmentation'. Here, an entire market is divided into subgroups sharing similar characteristics. A market segment is then available for targeting particular products. Just as an orange has separate segments making up the whole, so a market has many segments. Marketing professionals find out what the segments are, then aim the marketing approach to satisfy that segment.

Remember

A market is where buyers and sellers come together to exchange cash for goods or services. For marketing people, markets can be segmented into smaller groups. These subgroups can be 'targeted' with a specific marketing message.

The marketing mix

Once marketing professionals have discovered their market segments and determined the groups they wish to target, the next set of decisions revolve around the tactics used to meet the needs of the target group. These tactics come from the marketing mix. The marketing mix is often described as the 'four Ps', these days extended to the 'seven Ps':

- product
- price
- place
- promotion
- *people*
- *physical evidence*
- *process.*

Each P word describes the methods that marketers can use to address the needs of a target market. The three Ps in italics were added because of criticism that the original four Ps did not take into account that many businesses today are in **service industries**, and therefore factors other than product, price, place and promotion were important.

The marketing mix can be summarised as follows.

■ Product

The marketing function considers the features of a product offered to a market.

- What is it?
- Who would it be aimed at?
- What does it do?
- What *should* it do?

The product could be a **tangible** thing (e.g. a toothbrush with a manoeuvrable head). Alternatively, it could be an intangible service (e.g. a delivery service).

Key Terms

Service industries Industries not dealing in physical products but offering services such as finance or insurance.

Tangible Something you can touch.

■ Price

The marketing function also considers the price a product should be pitched at.

- What sort of customers will buy at a particular price?
- What is the best price to attract a particular kind of customer?
- What price might get more people to buy?
- What price might create the best image?
- What might be the effect of a change in price?

■ Place

Marketing specialists consider how a product would find its way to consumers to a place where they could make a purchase. This would include physical distribution and merchandising. Physical goods must be transported from manufacturer into storage, through distribution centres to wholesalers, then to the high street retailer. Businesses working in between a manufacturer and a retailer are known as 'intermediaries'.

■ Promotion

Marketing professionals have to consider ways of bringing products to the attention of potential customers. This includes advertising via the various media, as well as other ways of promoting products in the eyes of consumers, such as special offers. These activities, in the physical world, are designed to 'push' products and services into the eyes and ears of potential consumers.

These four Ps are a set of tactical ingredients, to be 'mixed' according to what a firm's marketing strategy is designed to achieve – hence the term 'marketing mix'. The 'extended mix' (i.e. the last three Ps) has been added to deal with *services*.

■ People

Service products are delivered by people. If the bus driver you had on your way to school or college this morning was horrible to you, you would be upset. If people are nice to you, you might return for more business. People make businesses!

■ Physical evidence

If you go somewhere to receive a service (e.g. a meal in a restaurant), you expect it to be in pleasant surroundings. Businesses try to make sure that there is a good physical environment for customers.

■ Process

If you want to use a service, what is the process of getting it? Is it easy? Or is it so complicated you want to run away? Marketers need to consider people's views about this and respond.

The website in the marketing mix

The internet has added to the range of marketing tactics and tricks available to marketing professionals. A business website, depending on what the business does, *can* be its product. In the case of businesses selling other physical products, the website becomes the shop window. In either case, the technology offered by the web lets businesses modify the marketing mix in a number of ways. This is sometimes referred to as the 'marketing remix', as the diagram below shows.

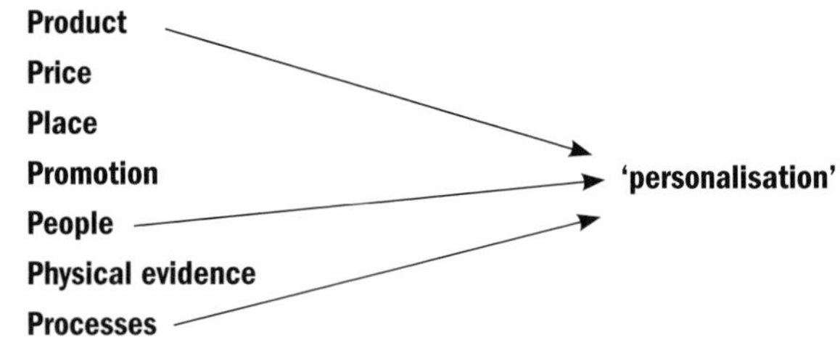

▲ The internet e-marketing remix – the seven Ps

Each element of the internet marketing 'remix' can be affected by a website.

- **Products.** These are displayed and described in detail. Indeed, online the web makes an individual offer because it is a one-to-one relationship when a customer accesses a website. This allows for '*personalisation*'. (As an example, try registering with amazon.co.uk, browsing some particular products and then returning to the site.) The website will offer you recommendations and show you what products you have recently viewed. Products can also be extended by giving additional offers of guarantees or other enhancements. In internet terms, this is known as bundling products together.

- **Prices.** These are visible; they are often lower because costs are lower.
- **Place.** This is affected because people can often download from a website if the products offered are in digital format (e.g. software, music or film). Often there is direct selling. This means that 'middlemen' are cut out of the chain.
- **Promotion.** This can be placed on all websites. Businesses can carry banner adverts and affiliate links to other business sites. They can have strong PR stories on their sites and, of course, they can make special offers. Promotion is very effective online, if used well.
- **People.** These are behind every website. However, online customers do not meet people face to face. If a problem occurs in a transaction there needs to be back-up support staff. Very often this is done through contact centres. A website should inform customers how to make contact. There could be features like FAQs, virtual assistants and auto-responders built into the site. In the case of a website offering a personalised service, there is a one-to-one relationship.
- **Physical evidence.** This is only represented by the look and feel of a website, which in effect becomes the replacement for the environment a service is delivered in. Customers have to feel comfortable in the site and know their way around.
- **Process.** This refers to how easy it is to receive a service or product. If a site visitor decides to take advantage of an available product, how easy is it to get what they want? EasyJet has a famous three-click process for ordering a flight ticket. This can be a major selling point and again can be done on a personalised basis.

Remember

When a business goes online it can design features into the website that add to the marketing impact. The marketing mix is, in fact, remixed with some added ingredients to give customers a positive experience.

Websites in the promotion mix

Modern businesses are using their websites to offer lots of promotional material, both for themselves and, through affiliate programmes, for other businesses. Promotional activities in the marketing mix can take several forms; this is referred to as the promotion mix. Websites can:

- carry advertisements
- have sales promotions
- assist in personal selling
- carry PR materials
- help in direct marketing.

Not only does a website help a business to deliver these promotional strategies very quickly and cost effectively, but also the website assists in targeting the correct audience by using e-mail. A business can customise a message to suit a particular market segment. All of this can help to build better relationships with customers.

Remember

A website can be used to deliver a number of important promotional techniques and these can be more effectively targeted on the internet.

Current and future developments

In the internet world, technological developments seem to happen so quickly that businesses and individuals struggle to keep up. One of these – broadband connection to the web – is extremely fast-growing.

Broadband in homes

Broadband internet connections are much faster and smoother than the now old-fashioned dial-up connection. Movies, music and software downloads are now speedy and relatively easy to achieve on broadband. It is little wonder that more and more households are switching over.

Telephone developments

One of the most important parts of customer service provision is to ensure that telephone calls are handled

Case study

Broadband: its rapid UK growth

New research predicts continued growth in UK broadband coverage over the next two years, with broadband penetration reaching levels of up to 90% in some areas.

Point Topic's forecast uses data from each of the 222,000 Census areas in the UK, allowing them to paint a geographical picture of broadband take-up around the country.

The report predicts that the proportion of homes with broadband will almost double – from 34% at the start of 2006 to 64% at the end of 2008 – when households with broadband installed should number 18.5 million.

The fastest growth in broadband penetration will occur in rural areas, which currently have the lowest levels of broadband use. Meanwhile, the highest take-up is expected to remain in the south-east. It is predicted that 80–90% of households in the south-east will have broadband access by 2009.

Point Topic Chief Analyst Tim Johnson believes his figures show that broadband use has grown beyond previously predicted levels.

Source: Adapted from an article on www.point-topic.com

1. Why do you feel broadband is growing faster than expected?✓
2. What are the current statistics for broadband connections in home users? ✓✓
3. What would you say is the business case for having a broadband connection? ✓✓✓

efficiently and quickly. More than 80% of customer communication is still by voice. The latest software products can automate responses and reroute calls quickly to a member of staff.

VoIP (Voice over Internet Protocol) allows a person to make telephone calls using a computer network over a data network such as the internet. VoIP converts the voice signal from a telephone into a digital signal that travels over the internet, then converts it back at the other end so you can speak to anyone with a normal phone number.

Scalability in planning a website

Typical website development occurs gradually. The key aspect at the initiation of many web design projects is **scalability**. Scalability means that while the website may have certain features and facilities now, in all likelihood there will be additional requirements in the future that are not applicable now.

This is a typical scenario, where companies like the website usability and structure but want to provide for expansion without having to go back from the beginning again, with all the associated implications.

Key Term

Website scalability The capability of a website to grow alongside the growth of the business.

Remember

A website is designed to help a business achieve its aims and objectives. If it succeeds the business may grow and the features of the website will have to grow with it. This means scalability. How capable is a website of further growth?

Practice point

Carry out a search for two contrasting profit-making businesses working online. Make notes about how these businesses are using the web to deliver their marketing mix. Be ready to give a 3-minute verbal explanation to your teacher.

Outcome activity 30.1

Scenario

You work for the local council's Economic Development Unit which is keen to encourage new 'e-business' into the area. You have been asked to do a preliminary investigation and prepare a short presentation about how different businesses can use the internet.

Pass P1

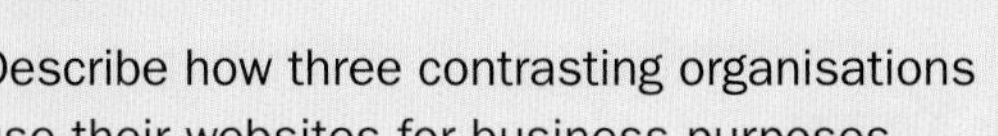

Describe how three contrasting organisations use their websites for business purposes.

Grading tip

Pass P1

To meet the pass criteria, you need first to consider why an organisation has a website. Is it to sell? Offer a service? Inform? Then, look at the features of the websites of the contrasting organisations and describe what they offer users. Say how you think this online presence helps the organisations achieve their goals.

30.2 Web design for usability and visual appeal

The internet has emerged as a key aspect of many modern businesses. When planning and designing a website the intention is not only to *attract* visitors, but also to *retain* their interest. We saw in the previous section that organisations have many diverse functions and purposes. However, there is little point in having a web presence at all if users simply visit your site, then quickly pass through. For this reason, design features relating to usability and **visual appeal** are very important.

Key Term

Visual appeal A pleasant and appropriate look and feel that is appropriate to the organisation.

A website should encourage a visitor to look at the site content, easily find something of value and draw them step by step into the site. The ideal sequence is shown in the diagram below. To achieve this there are several important considerations, as the following sections of text show.

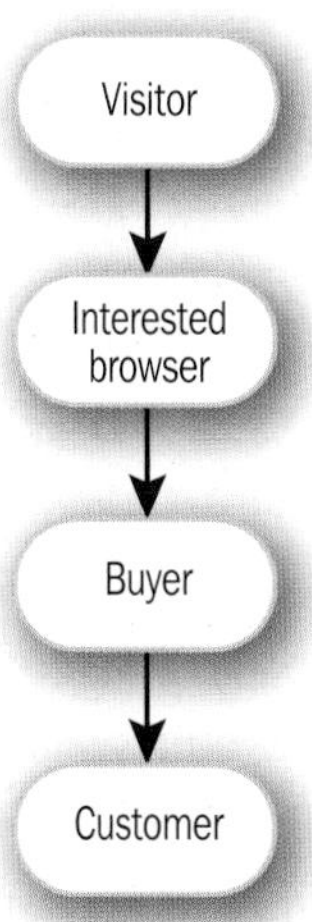

▲ Turning a website visitor into a customer

Usability

How easy is a website to navigate? Have you ever visited a site that was difficult or frustrating to use? There can be many reasons for this, for example:

- links on the site do not work
- the page takes an age to load into your browser
- images do not show properly
- the site does not show in the browser you are using.

For a website to be successful it must do what the user wants. In other words, it must do what it is designed to do. This means it should offer clear and useful information. Links that are intended to take users elsewhere should work, and images within the site should serve a clear purpose and not take ages to load.

Web customers are slow to please and easy to deter. One slip, one faulty link or one confusing page and a user will quickly leave. It is important to recall that 'the door' is merely a click away.

Key Term

Usability The ease with which staff and visitors can use a website.

Retaining customers

Customer retention is a key purpose of usability. It is far cheaper to retain a customer than it is to acquire new ones. Once visitors have entered the site there should be a strong enough proposition for them to stay. The site should have a value to users. They should find it easy to:

- see what they want
- buy what they want.

An initial visit should, ideally, lead the customer painlessly through to a purchase.

Key Term

Customer retention Keeping customers so that they choose to come back to your site to make repeat purchases.

Trust in the website

Web visitors need to be given reassurance when they visit a site that it is trustworthy and secure.

Case study

diy.com: giving confidence to buyers

'You can be totally confident when you shop with www.diy.com! We are so confident about the payment security we offer on our site that we will back every purchase with our security guarantee.

'Our site uses Secure Server software that encrypts your credit or debit card information to ensure your transaction with us is private and protected as it travels over the internet.

'Every payment transaction we process is checked by our fraud control systems to validate the authenticity and validity of the payment cards used, as well as indicators of possible fraudulent use.

'In the unlikely event of fraudulent or unauthorised use of your payment card in online transactions, most banks and card issuers that subscribe to the Banking Code either cover all the charges or may limit your liability to just £50.00. For a list of subscribing banks see www.bankingcode.org.uk/supportlist.htm'.

Source: www.diy.com, the online sales channel for B&Q

1. Why do think feel that online customers feel insecure about paying online? ✓
2. What would you recommend a possible new online business to do about security fears of a website? ✓✓
3. How effective do you feel that website security reassurance is when it is done like diy.com? Will this approach work? Justify your response. ✓✓✓

Factors affecting usability

There are a number of factors that affect the usability of a website.

- **Navigation.** Creating good website navigation is the most important task a web designer has to accomplish in the web design process. Website navigation is the pathway people take to navigate through sites. It must be well constructed, easy to use and intuitive.
- **Language.** Language problems on the web can arise if a website is intended for international use and the only language available for users is English. Software is available to translate languages online. They can also arise if language used on a site is too technical. It is important to remember that web information should be accessible to as many people as possible.
- **Efficiency.** The website should be efficient. This means it should be quick to load and should offer speedy navigation, with all links up to date and working. People online expect things to work.
- **Accuracy.** The information contained on a website should be up to date and accurate. People could leave the site never to return if they have no confidence that the content is correct.
- **Speed of response.** If customers place orders or make enquiries, it is crucial that they receive a prompt response. There should therefore be systems within the business that ensure online queries or orders are dealt with.
- **Respect for privacy.** Online customers value their privacy. If customers entrust an organisation with personal information, they have a right to expect that the information will be kept private unless they have given explicit permission for the data to be given to someone else.

Remember

Usability is one of the most important factors affecting the success of a website.

Each of the key factors influencing a website's usability can be worked on by developers as shown in the following sections.

Navigation

As we saw earlier, website navigation should help users to find their way quickly and easily around a website. There are several design techniques to build navigation into a site. A good website should always provide a set of text only navigation links to enable non-graphical browser users to navigate your site. Other navigation techniques include the following.

- **Mouseover image navigation.** Mouseover images add entertainment value and impact to the user's experience of visiting a site. A mouseover is an image that reacts when users place their mouse over the image, by swapping to another image in exactly the same place and the same size.
- **Rollover image navigation.** This is similar to mouseover, but the image can appear in a different part of the web page and can also be a different size.
- **Drop down menu navigation.** Navigation can be created in layers that allow links to appear and disappear in sections when activated by the user.
- **Navigation images/graphics.** Navigation opportunities can be highlighted to users with images.

These techniques should take account of user types and their needs, e.g. whether the target audience is other businesses or teenagers.

Remember

When developing a website, make it easy for users to find their way around the different pages.

Ability to complete transaction

For most website visitors on sites where buying and selling takes place, the ability to **complete the transaction** is vital. There is no point at all in having all the links, images and navigation options working well if at the end of the process there is no chance of placing an order and making or taking payment. (We saw at the start of the unit that many people abandon their online shopping.) This is completing the transaction – something is exchanged or promised at the time of the visit.

Key Term

Completing the transaction Actually making the sale from the website; funds are transferred with the promise of the product.

Language

The web is purely an information-based medium. Content is therefore everything. Web designers must think carefully about the style and tone associated with website content. The words used on a website must have meaning for typical users. Language problems can be caused by a lack of understanding of English or excessive technical jargon, or they can be caused by inappropriate tone.

So just as in face-to-face interactions, the user of website information can be distracted and lose interest if the words used are not well thought out.

Remember

The words used on a website should be very clear and easy for users to understand.

Legible text

If something is legible, it can be read. If something is illegible, you are not able to read it. (Ever heard a teacher say that your hand writing is illegible?) It is important for web designers to make sure that the text used on a site is legible. Careful selection of font and font size is essential.

Another factor that will be examined later is the question of accessibility for those who have sight problems. Web designers should take note of the law in relation to this.

Efficiency

A business website must be efficient for the user. There should be something online that is of value to the customer, and this should be available quite quickly and easily. EasyJet has, as a selling point, its three-click online booking process to get an airline ticket.

The information and presentation of the navigation options through the site should be economical and time efficient. Users are always impressed if a process is easy.

Speed of response

The internet carries data using a set of protocols. The most significant of these in relation to speed is TCP (Transmission Control Protocol). Data is broken down into packets for transfer, then reassembled at the receiver's end. The rate of transfer is slow if data packets are lost. These days, when more and more consumers and businesses are using the internet, the transfer speed has become a real selling point.

Web developers use several technical tricks to ensure that a user's experience on a website appears to be smooth and easy. One of these is called AJAX. This is JavaScript code that requests only a small portion of data is transferred. An example would be where a user is registering with a website and is asked to choose a username. The user moves on to the next action while in the background AJAX coding has already sent a request to check whether the selected username is available. If it is not, the user quickly receives a polite message suggesting they try another name.

The effect of this coding is, of course, to speed up the process experienced by the user.

When a customer types a URL (web address) into the address bar of the browser, there is a subconscious sense of frustration caused by the fact that it takes even a few seconds for a web page to load. This is made worse if the web page itself takes longer than a few seconds to load. The point is that anything a web designer can do to speed up the process of response will make customers happier.

Web designers in the past have been guilty of incorporating all sorts of images and multimedia features into websites at the expense of speed. Users of websites need to be able to see what the content is for. There should be a logical flow of content, and the text and visual content needs to be attractive and interesting.

Remember

Speed is important in a website. A site should load as quickly as possible.

Remember

Speed of data transfer is affected by the use of visual media or complex graphics. This can be a major frustration for customers.

Respect for privacy

The privacy of personal information is a big concern of many internet users and needs to be considered by web designers.

Businesses trading from a website receive and store certain types of information whenever you interact with them. Many websites use cookies (see pages 144 and 158) and obtain certain types of information when a customer's web browser accesses the website.

Information can be collected and analysed using technology that is not obvious to you, for example:

- the Internet Protocol (IP) address used to connect your computer to the internet
- your login, e-mail address and password
- computer and connection information such as the browser type and version, operating system and platform
- the full Uniform Resource Locators (URL), click streams to, through and from the website, including date and time
- cookie number
- pages viewed or searched for
- your site history and phone number used to make contact.

Case study

Is the internet reaching its capacity?

According to a new report by Deloitte: 'Internet bottlenecks, due to a lack of investment and growth in video traffic, will become noticeable this year.'

The report says that one of the key possibilities for 2007 is that the internet could be approaching its capacity.

'The twin trends causing this are an explosion in demand, largely fuelled by the growth in video traffic and the lack of investment in new, functioning capacity,' said Igal Brightman, global managing partner at Deloitte. 'Bottlenecks are likely to become apparent in some of the internet's backbones, the terabit-capable pipes exchanging traffic between continents.'

Source: www.pcpro.co.uk, 19 January 2007

1. Why do you think that some business websites use video images in their site? Give examples in your response. ✓
2. Analyse why video and images are useful in some business contexts. ✓✓
3. Take one of your examples and evaluate the extent to which video and other visual media contribute to the organisation's objectives. ✓✓✓

Cookies

Cookies are pieces of information that can be transferred to your computer's hard drive through your web browser when you are viewing a website. These pieces of information allow the website to act on information that will make a customer's use of the website more rewarding. Cookies enable a business system to recognise your browser and provide features such as easier login and greater security, and for storing information about you between visits.

Thinking point

Investigate the websites of at least three trading organisations. Can you identify any statements on these sites about **privacy**? How do you feel about the privacy issue? Do you think that businesses should make it clear to web customers that personal information is being collected?

For a business to be successful on the web it is essential that no intrusive or irrelevant requests for information are made from a website. Users frequently want to know why information is needed and to what purposes such information will be used. People have fears about third parties being given their personal details.

For the web designer it is wise to be open and honest about:

- what, if any, information about customers is being collected
- how it is being collected
- the uses to which data will be put.

Remember

Respect for customer privacy can be a selling point for an online business. People have a right to their privacy being respected. They also have a right to be made aware of what information is being collected about them and the ways such information may be used.

Web page design

Remember that the point of web design is to give the user (not the designer!) a satisfying and useful experience while on the site. There are many things to consider in relation to this.

User paths through the site

The most basic difference between reading a web page and reading a page like this in a textbook is that in the case of the web we are looking at **hypertext** and in the book we are reading *linear* text. Linear text is read from left to right in order for us to make sense of what it is saying. Hypertext contains hyperlinks that allow us to jump all over, from page to page and document to document (even from site to site). This has immediate repercussions for web designers. People can skip from one page to another in an instant – and frequently do. Rarely do visitors read text on a web page in a linear fashion. What web visitors do is skim across text, often looking for relevant links. The web designer must try to ensure that links offer clear pathways to relevant pages within a site.

Key Terms

Privacy The level of security of personal information – a crucial factor in a website's status in the eyes of users.

Hypertext Text available on the web that contains hyperlinks to other web pages.

Ranking information

Depending on the site, its purpose and the target audience, a web page should not usually contain large blocks of text (the so-called 'wall of words'). Information on the page should be ranked using

Case study

Gareth Rushgrove: Web designer

Gareth Rushgrove, a Durham University Physics graduate, is a professional web designer dedicated to making the internet work for both businesses and their customers. Working for a rapidly growing Newcastle -Upon-Tyne based new media company called THINK (www.think.eu), Gareth takes a very user-centred view of the design process.

'Web design must be done with users in mind. Often I will consult with senior management in an organisation, and they will carefully outline what *they* expect from a website. Of course, I listen carefully and note their requirements. I go back to the office and produce a 'low fidelity' version of the site, precisely as they believe they want it. Then I go and speak to people in the corridor (staff) and show them the outline site on a laptop. I call this the 'Hallway Test'. This inevitably leads to changes. Next, I will do what I call the 'Tesco Test', often involving people having coffee in Tesco! This leads to even more changes. Gradually, the website evolves to become user friendly.'

The point is that Gareth sees his role as giving the users of a website a satisfying online experience – knowing that by doing this, organisational leaders will discover that their website achieves their objectives. While management may think they know what they want, this is not always what is needed by their own staff or their customers and clients.

1. What do you understand by the term 'user-centred design'? ✓
2. Want do you feel are the advantages and disadvantages of the so-called 'Hallway' and 'Tesco' tests? ✓✓
3. Evaluate the idea that senior managers may not always appreciate the real needs of staff or client users of a website. Can you find any evidence of this in a website you have experienced? ✓✓✓

Thinking point

Investigate the age profile of the UK population. How has this changed over the last 30 years? Considering the changing age profile of our population, what would you recommend the web design community does to help older users make use of a website?

headings in a clear hierarchy. Text should be broken up with headings and bulleted lists. The reader of the web page should be given convenient visual resting points such as a list or an emboldened piece of text.

Visitors to a website could arrive on the site at any page, not just the home page. Designers should make it easy to get back to the home page with easy navigation.

Remember

Always try to break up text on a web page by ranking headings and using bulleted points.

Search engine operation

One of the most vital jobs of good web designers is to bear in mind that search engines automatically search for pages using sophisticated software that is looking at content. A website should be 'search engine friendly'. Google, for instance, reads whole web pages. How is the page 'marked up'? Has the designer used good HTML? Does the H1 tag match the content below?

The days are long gone when designers could simply pack the headers with keywords to draw the search engines onto a site. Today, designers work with copywriters to make sure that web pages hang together in content and HTML tags. If they are done well, the top search engines will rank them highly. As more users visit the site, no doubt because the content is so good, the ranking becomes even more secure.

Other ways to do this are by building links into your site with a view to attracting more visitors.

Remember

Search engine optimisation is a central part of modern web design. A business must ensure that important search engines find its site.

Design for usability and visual appeal

The look and feel of a website are key to attracting visitors and getting them to stay on the site long enough to make a purchase. Ideally, design should not only cause visitors to want to stay on the site (i.e. 'stick around'), but also it should encourage them to return. To achieve this, both usability and visual appeal must be good.

Remember

People are found to judge a website within a 20th of a second on their first visit.

Case study

Good web design makes instant difference

Canadian research suggests that web users make up their minds about the quality of a site or e-commerce store within a 20th of a second!

Dr Lindgaard, who conducted the research, said: 'As websites increasingly jostle for business, companies should take note. Unless the first impression is favourable, visitors will be out of your site before they even know that you might be offering more than your competitors.'

The research does seem to confirm the disappointment that we all get looking at cheap sites or where the design has been homogenised by a committee.

Companies need to spend longer on the design of their websites and to refresh the look of them regularly. Design must be very individual for each site and adapt the offline personality of the brand to the special characteristics of the web.

The use of animation is a controversial aspect of the home pages of many brands and was not covered in the reported research. Some web designers prefer to take the client straight to the front page, meaning it must be beautifully designed. If the researchers are right, a slow animated introduction to a site may not convince visitors, who are already on their way to another site.

Source: Adapted from an article by Jonathon Briggs on www.othermedia.com, 16 January 2006

1. What do you think is meant by the phrase 'adapt the offline personality of the brand to the special characteristics of the web'? ✓
2. What do you think are the important messages from the article for a business commissioning web design? ✓✓
3. What are your views about the claim that people make their mind up within a 20th of a second about a website's worth? Explain your views and justify with reference to a real business website. ✓✓✓

Conflicts between different aspects of usability

Some of the features that make a website appealing to visitors may conflict. There are a number of ways in which this can happen and often a designer may have to compromise.

■ Personalisation versus speed

The web offers businesses a superb opportunity to personalise content. Web pages are capable, if they are designed this way, of remembering a previously registered visitor to a site, then personalising content the next time the user visits. Amazon is a classic case of this technique. If an Amazon customer purchases a book on bee-keeping, the next visit will have related recommendations. However, if this causes the site to slow down, the user may be deterred. Design factors must therefore consider how important personalisation is to the business objectives.

■ Visual appeal versus speed

The temptation to include all sorts of images, font colours and animations is always present for a novice website creator. However, we have already noted that such features can dramatically slow down the load time of a web page. Bearing in mind the case study opposite, perhaps the old saying 'less is more' would be appropriate in many instances. Efficient load up may be more fruitful, rather than flashy images in an attempt to create visual appeal.

■ Visual appeal versus legibility

Visual appeal should not affect the ability of the visitor to actually read the page content. Some websites include colourful backgrounds, but these make it very difficult to read the text.

Remember

Websites always have a purpose beyond visual appeal. It is no use having a great look to a site, if users find the site difficult to use.

Accessibility

The Website Accessibility Initiative (WAI) outlines the international guidelines on accessible web design. The WAI is affiliated with the World Wide Web Consortium (W3C) and works with organisations around the world to increase the accessibility of the web. As part of this work, the WAI published the first version of the Web Content Accessibility Guidelines (WCAG) in 1999. These are accepted as the definitive set of international guidelines used for building accessible websites. All other guidelines and standards are derived from these.

Key Term

Accessibility The ease and comfort with which websites can be used by those with disabilities.

The UK government recommends that web pages must comply with the WCAG guidelines. Web designers and those commissioning web pages therefore have a responsibility to ensure that their website design does not discriminate against disabled visitors to a site.

Remember

Websites must be designed so that they are accessible to people with disabilities.

Disability Discrimination Act (DDA)

The part of the DDA that states websites must be made accessible came into force on 1 October 1999 and the Code of Practice for this section of the Act was published on 27 May 2002. There is now a legal obligation – following the implementation of section 21 of the Disability Discrimination Act (1999) – to make reasonable adjustments to ensure blind and partially sighted people can access a web-based service.

The DDA 1999 expects web designers to make 'reasonable adjustments' to their sites to accommodate and assist those who may have a sight problem.

Remember

The Disability Discrimination Act 1999 expects web designers to make 'reasonable adjustments' to a website to help the visually impaired. This may include things like larger fonts.

Visual appeal

If a website can clearly and efficiently show a potential customer that the company is knowledgeable and up to date in its field of expertise, the customer becomes confident and trusting of the services offered. A website is a multi-functional medium that serves as a communication tool. Thus it plays a central role in improving the impact and image of a brand.

A website is a personal interaction with both current and potential consumers. Yet however gripping a website's content may be, it is the design elements that have a dramatic, if not crucial, impact and contribution to make. There are a few prominent aspects of a website that are greatly influenced by web design.

Whatever the place of a website in the life of a business the visual appeal, commonly referred to as the look and feel of the website, is an important factor when planning the site.

Use of fonts and graphics

The basics of any website include the fonts used for the various levels of text and the graphics used to convey the right impression, or give the right information, to the visitor. The case of Bells, a fish and chip shop (see opposite), illustrates how some of these factors are considered in even the most basic websites.

Advantages and disadvantages of using multimedia

Multimedia elements within web pages allow for video streaming or audio files to be played through a user's browser. There are alternative techniques to design these features into a page. For example, it is possible to have a link to an external media player and only allow for very short clips to be played on the page. Alternatively, the media could be designed to use a fully downloaded media player such as Apple's QuickTime player.

There are advantages for many organisations in building multimedia into a website.

Key Term

Multimedia elements The facility on a web page to show streaming video or sounds to back up the textual information.

Practice point

Consider the following organisations with an online service or product. In your view, which of these would benefit from a multimedia feature available from a website? Copy and complete the table and fully justify your responses with suggestions.

Businesses suitable for multimedia on websites?		
	YES	NO
A fish and chip shop		
An estate agent		
A law firm		
A photographer		
A bus company		
A school or college		
A building firm		

Real lives

Bells fish and chips

▲ **The visual appeal of Bells**

Fish and chip shops would not spring readily to mind when you think of an internet presence. First, it is impossible (so far!) to buy a fish and chip lot over the web. Second, the typical fish shop would appear to have little to gain from being online.

Bells fish and chip shop owner Graham Kennedy decided otherwise.

'I'm not a computer geek by any means and I hardly know how to type,' says Graham. 'I just felt that as a nation we were turning out to be an online economy. If my fish shop didn't have an online existence, it wouldn't be long before others did. In any case, at Bells we do have something to shout about, so why not let people know online?'

Graham Kennedy contacted a local web designer, Scott Oliver. Graham explained to Scott that he wanted a site that would show Bells not only to the local community, but also to the wider world.

'The site would be purely for promotional purposes, but as things changed I wanted to be able to update the content myself.'

Graham consulted Scott Oliver and discussed a number of important things. 'I wanted to know how much it would cost. Scott gave me a figure and I thought it was fair enough. So I then gave him an outline of what I wanted. Within three days Scott had sent me about six alternative "looks" for the website. From these I chose two that I felt were the right image and after discussions with Scott I selected one that we both liked.'

After this agreement there was a process of communications between Graham and Scott as the site developed. For instance, Graham insisted that the font for the Bells wording at the top was changed and he checked out the photographic images.

There were some disagreements: Scott drew the line at animations. 'I thought an animated picture of a union flag on the site might be nice!' says Graham. But Scott would have none of that.

'Now I understand why Scott literally shuddered at my flag idea!' says Graham.

The Bells website offers a crisp, clean image that gives all the essential information and includes good quality images that tell visitors something about the shop.

'I have a content management system as well, meaning I have control over the words on my website. I also have e-mail. I am happy with my online "personality".'

1. Given the type of business that Bells is, which aspects of 'visual appeal' do you feel the owner has tried to achieve? ✓
2. Take a look at www.bellsfishshop.co.uk and, together with the information you have been given above, analyse the visual aspects of the site and comment on the functions, usability and the visual and media design of the site. ✓✓
3. Evaluate the Bells website and one other business site of your own choice. To what extent do you feel the features mentioned above on these websites contribute towards the achievement of the businesses objectives? ✓✓✓

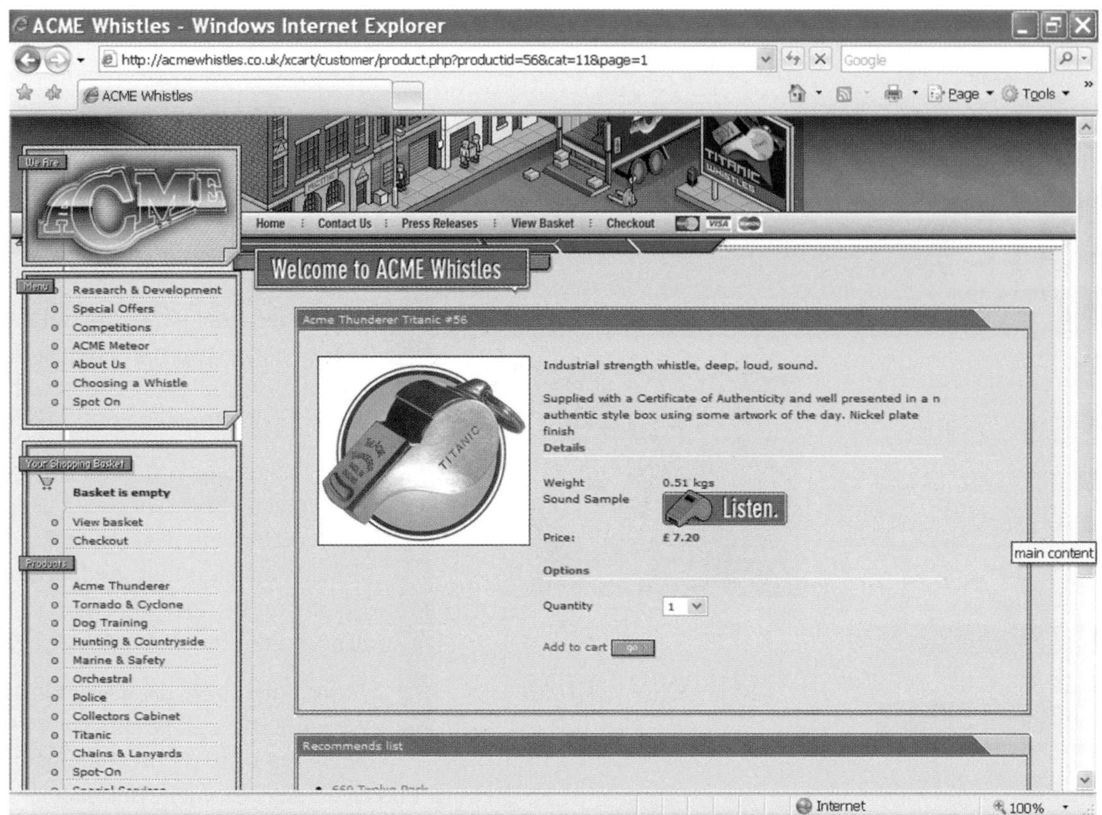

▲ **A website requiring sound effects**

The Acme Whistles website shows a company making use of the web's ability to carry multimedia effects.

Use of white space

White space is the space between the elements on a web page. If there is none or too little white space, a web page will appear disorganised. Web designers should try to make the page look clean, simple, and easy to read and navigate.

Appealing to a target group

It is, of course, possible to design a successful website without a specific target group. However, this does not suggest that the business has an online strategy. Some people have a very clear target audience in mind when designing their websites even without any formal documentation – usually one person start-up businesses that are designing their site according to their own enthusiasms or knowledge of a special interest group.

If someone transfers a 'bricks and mortar' business (i.e. one that operates offline) to the internet, they usually have a pretty good idea who the target audience is – basically the same people as in their established business.

The more an online business knows its target audience, the more it can target a design. This is about the choice between design and practicality. Targeting both form and functionality to a target audience is more likely to ensure web success.

Consistency with brand image

Branding is a centrally important creative activity in a businesses marketing strategy. We all tend instinctively

◀ **The Next online store – a targeted site?**

to know what a 'brand' is. Could you identify, for example, the Tesco brand, the M&S brand or the Ford Motor company 'brand'?

Successful branding means that a business and its products have an instantly recognisable identity. The brand communicates a corporate image.

It is a known marketing fact that strong brands, with their associated values, sell. There are many retailers in the market – e.g. Virgin, M&S, Sainsbury's and Tesco – which have proven that with a strong brand it is possible to diversify from core product offers such as clothing, food and travel, to include new services such as banking and insurance.

Key Term

Brand image The creation of an easy-to-spot identity that consumers get to know well.

Consumer confidence in a strong brand has enabled retailers to sell new ranges that traditionally would not have been considered. Consumers are comfortable with the brand and what it represents, and are confident to purchase additional services.

Consistency in a brand is therefore vital in order to achieve this. For many retailers operating in a market where customers are fickle (e.g. the fashion industry) it is important not only to identify the factors in the core brand, but also to employ them consistently at every point the customer comes into contact with the company. In a competitive market, creating brand loyalty is essential in order to stay ahead.

Customer contact may be in-store, from catalogues or online. In some instances this may also include customer call centres or service departments where the employee may be dealing with customers over the phone. Online, this presents a challenge – conveying the same image that a customer may experience from good service in-store.

Outcome activity 30.2

Scenario

You are employed in the Economic Development Unit of a local city council. One of the key areas of policy of the council is to encourage new businesses into the area, and to help existing businesses to develop and expand. Both of these things will help to encourage economic development in the area.

Your line manager has been given some investigative work to do as part of the background research required to prepare for a series of 'road shows' in which the council will present materials to local business managers. The general topic of the road show is 'the e-economy'. Your manager has delegated the following research tasks to you.

You decide to create a set of well-organised portfolios in the form of notes and handouts.

1. Explain the functions and usability features of the websites of three contrasting organisations. 
2. Explain the use of visual and media design features of the websites of three contrasting organisations. 

Merit

Analyse how the functions, usability features, and visual and media design of a selected website meet the requirements of the target group. m1

Distinction

Evaluate the extent to which the usability features and visual and media design of a selected website contribute to the achievement of the organisation's objectives. d1

Grading tips

Pass 

This involves looking at aspects of websites that are designed to help users. Does the site offer help features? If so, explain why they are there. What functions does the site offer?

Pass 

Why do you feel that these organisations have designed certain features such as multimedia into their sites?

Merit 

To meet this merit criterion you need to identify the attributes of the target group and relate these requirements to the functions, usability features and visual and media design of the website, outlining its advantages and disadvantages.

Distinction 

For this grade you must arrive at a well-explained and justified conclusion about design and usability features of websites and relate this conclusion to the organisation's aims and objectives.

30.3 Issues to be considered when developing an e-business website

Before a company creates an e-business website, there are a number of important factors to consider. We saw from the Real lives study entitled 'Bells fish and chips' (page 149) that even for a small business with little or no potential for sales transactions to be carried on the internet, it is necessary to give some thought to what a website is designed to achieve. This implies an online strategy that places a website within context.

Strategy

Business objectives

All businesses work on the basis of an overarching set of aims and **objectives**. Aims revolve around strategic direction. A small- to medium-sized engineering firm, for example, may set as an 'aim', the desire 'to increase our share of the aerospace components market'. To achieve this there has to be a degree of planning that will specify a series of actions that must be taken. Once these practical actions have been decided, management will set business objectives based on SMART criteria (i.e. specific, measurable, achievable, realistic and time-related). One such SMART objective in the above case may be to increase sales of a particular product by 10% within six months.

There are obvious implications for a website involved in this objective.

- It should include excellent technical information.
- It should include communications and relationship management features.
- It should be well designed with clear information. Potential customers should be made to feel (from the website) that this is a company that sets high standards and will meet all their needs.

Key Term

Objectives Specific and measurable targets that lead to a particular overall goal.

Marketing objectives

Part of the strategy opposite involves establishing marketing objectives.

- What do customers in particular markets want?
- Is there to be a targeted market, or an undifferentiated marketing message?
- How can a website be used to target the market we wish to break into?
- How can we satisfy and exceed customer needs?

The business that is planning a website has to think about the ways in which it is going to promote its activities and products. At the design stage, managers and web designers have to work together, considering the ways in which the website can deliver better service to customers.

A website can be promoted both online and offline. The site can be linked through affiliate promotion on industrial portals or industrial networks. Given that small- to medium-sized businesses enjoy a certain level of 'equality in online presence' on the internet, a good website can be used to raise the company profile in the eyes of possible buyers.

The website should offer a value proposition to potential customers that encourage them to enter the site, stay there for a while and see enough of interest that will cause them to come back. These things are known as **website stickiness**.

Key Term

Website stickiness The capacity of a website to make people stay on the site and eventually make a purchase.

Consumer/customer profile and expectations

In the process of planning to target a particular segment of a market, a business may develop a **customer profile** by collecting information about them. For example, what will be the expectations of young people 18 to 25 years of age? What are their expectations? The characteristics of a young person's lifestyle are taken into account.

The information a business needs to collect depends on the type of business. For example, to sell to individual consumers (b2c) information is needed about:

- their age
- gender
- location
- spending habits
- income.

If selling is to other businesses (b2b) information is needed about:

- what sector they are in
- how big they are
- how much they spend
- what other suppliers they use.

The CIM (Chartered Institute of Marketers) recommends finding out as much as possible about existing customers. This can be done by analysing sales records, talking to customers and, if more information is required, carrying out a survey. A business can build up a database of information about customers. In doing this, it includes as much feedback as possible about how highly customers rate products or services. A business's own records are used to add details of purchasing behaviour, such as:

- the products each customer tends to buy
- when and how the customer buys.

Notice that these information-gathering activities are all helped by being online. The website can be used to capture customer data. By using web analytics, the business can discover how the site works and how customers are responding to it.

Key Term

Customer profile The characteristics of a typical person or business that buys from your website.

Consumer's technical environment and user experience

Another factor to be born in mind when designing a website is the level of customers' technical expertise as well as their experience in using the web. Many more people today are competent in finding their way around websites. However, as we saw earlier in the unit, people are easily deterred if they lack confidence either in themselves or the business they are trying to deal with.

Web designers must think 'ease of use' and 'simplicity' if there is any doubt about customer web experience or confidence.

Analysis of competitor websites

A competitive analysis provides information on a websites' usability, strengths and weaknesses, compared to existing or potential competitors. It can also provide a measure of how a website compares to the overall market.

By examining competitors' offerings (information, architecture, navigation, interaction styles), businesses can identify the features, functionality and design elements of your competitors' sites that work well for customers. Once identified, these elements can be applied to the planned website and often present opportunities for further innovation to stay ahead of the competition. More importantly, a competitive analysis can find out which aspects of your competitor's sites are not usable and help a business involved in website planning to avoid the same pitfalls.

Remember

An online strategy can place a business in a much stronger marketing position if a website is designed with customer needs in mind.

Functions of a website

The following things determine the functions that can be offered to customers from the website.

- The nature of the business.
- The resources available.
- The corporate strategy surrounding a company's decision to go online.

We have seen a number of examples of **website functionality**. Take a look at the example below.

Key Term

Website functionality What the customer can do on the site and the functions the site offers.

Transaction arrangements

Most retail websites offer a shopping basket function allowing customers to select items and place them in the basket. The site calculates the total value of the items in the basket and gives an option of a checkout. At the end of the online shopping process, customers are given payment options involving giving credit/debit card details.

PayPal

PayPal allows any business or consumer with an e-mail address to send and receive payments online. Clearly this is vital if a business is to conduct transactions.

▲ **What other functions does this website offer?**

Case study

Joe's Brew: a business experience

Joe has a small business selling home-made lemonade from a modest shop in a small industrial town. Joe decided he would go online to sell more of his products, but he knew nothing about the internet or computers. However, his nephew – Richard, a bright young lad – did.

Richard was doing a course on web design and created a simple website for his Uncle Joe. Joe bought a domain name for £1.99 and used the services of a low cost web hosting firm to put his site live on the internet. The cost for Joe was only £250 plus £40 per year after that.

Joe felt this was a great way to get more customers and after talking to Richard they spent another few days submitting the site and its keywords to different search engines.

In the first two weeks, Joe received two e-mail enquiries – one from around the corner, the other from Dublin. This was not quite as good as he was hoping for. So he decided to get in touch with the local press, telling them how he was now online and that his business had taken off. They carried a story about him saying that 'local lemonade business is booming'.

The following day, Joe was interviewed by every newspaper and radio station in the region. A few more enquiries came in, but still not as much as Joe had hoped for. Two weeks later a national Sunday newspaper printed a feature on Joe headed 'The online brewer makes it'.

The next day, Joe received about 3,500 e-mails, most of them trying to place orders for lemonade. However, the website was not designed to take money online. There was no facility for customers to pay. Joe asked some people to send cheques or credit card details with their orders.

From having no business online, Joe was now getting between £4,000 and £5,000 worth of orders a day, but because he couldn't keep up with his business, he didn't know about most of them.

To make matters worse, other sites had started to put links to Joe's site and his traffic increased even more. Finally, complaints started to come in from people unable to buy his products.

Joe pulled the plug out of his computer and decided to pretend that his website did not exist. Talk about the internet to Joe now and he changes the subject.

1. For a business attempting to sell bottles of lemonade or packs of lemonade-making ingredients, what functions do you feel the website should offer? ✓
2. For a business like Joe's, who would be the target audience? Justify your response to this. ✓✓
3. Consider the situation that faced Joe and make justified recommendations about the range of functions that a new website of his would need. ✓✓✓

Remember

For a transactional website, there must be payment facilities offered to the customers that are secure and easy to use.

Other background functions

When a business decides to operate an online sales channel it is often assumed that there are adequate background functions and systems that will support the website. A website has to be kept up to date with current information on products. This suggests that there are staff who are able to monitor this and make adjustments when and if they are needed. Many transactional websites depend on background databases to supply the information that is essential to them. These databases might contain:

- product details
- staff details
- prices
- images
- registered customers.

A full e-business today might have an integrated set of digital systems that should be capable of avoiding data duplication.

Personalisation of web experience

When online customers visit a website it is always a one-to-one (personal) experience. Web developers have therefore tried in the last few years to develop sites that can remember customers and tailor a message precisely for them. Amazon, the online bookseller, is the example most often quoted. The site recalls the orders placed by a customer and on the next visit will offer recommendations.

The underpinning thinking behind this is that it benefits both a business and a consumer by establishing a *relationship* between them. Because we are known to the online business, we are automatically given information we really need. Because we feel valued by the business and we always receive the things we want, we are more inclined to go back to that site. In this way, so the argument goes, a relationship is built.

Remember

It costs far more to acquire new customers than retain existing ones.

By 'personalising' user experience on a website, the business hopes to gain customer loyalty and repeat business. Early research into this appeared to show that in b2b contexts, being recognised by the website certainly did help.

Take it further

Investigate two websites: one that is operating within a b2b sector, and another (e.g. amazon.co.uk) operating in b2c. Write a report summarising the benefits for both the businesses and the customers within these contexts. Do you feel that the b2b situation merits personalisation?

However, although web technology allows for personalisation this does not necessarily mean that it is a useful thing to have in all contexts. There are several reasons why some internet advisers may want to argue that personalisation is not suitable.

- **Customers don't want relationships with businesses.** As customers smile at the sound of a store assistant's greeting, they are actually responding to a person, *not* to a corporate message. They don't all want warm personal 'relationships' with the retail businesses they use the most.
- **Personalisation requires data.** Amazon, the master of personalisation, makes the technique successful because book purchases send it a constant stream

of detailed data about individual customers. Most transactions, though, don't provide such easy preference data.

- **Personalisation technology poorly understands consumers.** A recommendation for a needlework book as soon as you order that 'ideal gift' for your favourite aunt makes even the most inexperienced consumers realise that they and an online bookstore aren't that close.
- **Personalisation does work effectively in some cases;** it simply doesn't work in every case.

Remember

Personalisation is a feature of some of the most advanced e-businesses and has been made famous by Amazon. However, it does not have practical use for all customers and may suit b2b contexts better.

There are several tools available to web designers that can assist in customer information-gathering activities.

Cookies

A cookie is a small text file that is sent to your computer via your web browser when you visit some websites. These are used to store information about you for the next time you visit that site – information such as where you went on the site and what you did. Cookie files enable a website to remember you when you next visit.

Resources required

When a business seeks to have a website, not only does the site have to be designed and planned, but also it must be hosted on a web server in order to make it available on the internet. Hosting can involve housing, serving and maintaining files so that visitors are able to view the content of the website.

Hosting a website involves a number of different factors, each of which can have a significant impact on its overall success. These key factors are as follows.

- **The site functions** (discussed on pages 155–157). The range of features offered, the ways in which it presents content to the user, and how the content is kept fresh and updated.
- **Performance.** The speed at which it loads pages and responds to user requests.
- **Reliability.** How high the availability of the site is and how frequently it suffers from down time.

Hosting can be done in-house (within the business) or it can be bought in as a service. There are pros and cons with each approach.

In-house hosting

In-house website hosting is always an option. However, it does require significant resources. Not only will the business need a web server, but also it will need a high-speed connection to the internet. The firm will be directly responsible for its day-to-day operation and 24-hour support. There will also be the cost of software licences to consider.

Advantages of the in-house approach

- There is full control over access to the website.
- The choice of hardware, including the ease and expandability of upgrades, is internal.
- There is full control over the operating environment – the software and systems that run on the web server.
- Web storage space and performance can be effectively managed.
- There are no contractual or legal issues associated with using an internet service provider (ISP).

Disadvantages of the in-house approach

- The cost of purchasing web server hardware, associated software and high speed internet connectivity.
- Technical skills that staff will require in order to develop, maintain and upgrade the website, and to keep up to date with the latest technical developments.

- The need for resources capable of providing round-the-clock support for the website in order to ensure its availability for users.
- The need for specialist security expertise in employing tools and techniques to maintain the security of the website.

The in-house option is probably best suited to larger companies, and/or those with a specialist IT department, as considerable resources are required to handle the ongoing development and support activities. For smaller businesses, external hosting with a content editing system is an option. (See also the Real lives case of Bells fish and chips, page 149.)

Key Term

Hosting A website needs to be held on a server, i.e. 'hosted'. This is a service offered by ISPs or specialist providers.

Using an ISP for hosting

Paying for an internet service provider (ISP) for web hosting is an external hosting solution where the ISP is responsible for providing the business with connection to the internet. ISPs can provide different types of hosting services, as follows.

- **Shared server.** The server is owned by the ISP and is located in its offices. The server is used to host several other websites. This represents a cost-effective approach, but may not be an option if complex technologies are required such as personalising web pages for different users.
- **Dedicated hosting.** A website is the only one that is hosted on a dedicated server. This option is better suited to large websites with high user traffic, or those requiring special software or particularly high levels of security. These approaches offer the most powerful and secure solution, but they are more expensive.

Advantages of using an ISP

- There's no need to invest in your own web server.
- Most ISPs have very fast connections to the internet.
- The ISP's server should offer a very high degree of availability (up time) and reliability.
- The ISP should have a secure operating environment, high quality virus protection and the latest software patches to ensure the security of your site.

Disadvantages of using an ISP

- You need to trust the ISP to maintain the availability and security of the website.
- The website's performance may be compromised if the ISP is hosting too many other sites on a shared server basis.

Remember

Careful choice of an internet service provider will help a business to ensure its website offers the services that customers will need.

Software options

To help with web development at a level that will offer real e-business solutions, there are a number of software applications.

Online shop software

Online shop software allows the web development process to incorporate into a website the many benefits of online shopping. This can include:

- secure 24/7 online ordering and payment collection
- collecting customer information for direct marketing data
- analysis and web analytics.

Online shopping software can build in features that emulate a real-life shopping experience. Customers visit a virtual department, choose their merchandise, go to the check out, choose a shipping option and pay by credit/debit card. The software confirms their purchase and e-mails them a transaction confirmation, along with a businesses customised message.

Use of web authoring tools

Web pages are typically created using Hypertext Markup Language (HTML). It is this, invented by Tim Berners-Lee, which enabled the creation of the World Wide Web of inter-connected documents.

While HTML is a relatively simple code to learn, several companies specialise in developing highly sophisticated authoring software for website creation. These make it possible for even an amateur developer to work within a WYSIWYG (what you see is what you get) environment, to create useful and usable web pages. **Authoring tools** do the HTML automatically.

There are several advantages to using web authoring tools, e.g.:

- speed of creation
- ease of use by non-HTML experts
- ability to create large numbers of consistent pages.

Macromedia Dreamweaver is an industrial standard authoring package. It has been available for several years in different versions. It is both an HTML editor *and* a site management tool. Each version has encompassed new features and improvements.

The typical Dreamweaver working environment shows the main menu bar running along the top of the screen, allowing a website developer to:

- create new files
- modify a page's properties (i.e. set a background colour or image)
- insert several choices (tables, images)
- select font styles or colours.

The 'site' option on the bar allows the developer to view and manage a whole site structure. Most websites contain several pages functioning as an inter-linked group. Dreamweaver maintains and checks the links site-wide and offers a visual reference guide during development.

Dreamweaver, among other visual web development tools, offers a powerful means to create web pages within an environment that could be said to be 'developer friendly'. The effects being sought can be seen immediately. However, these industrial standard authoring packages are relatively expensive to buy and license.

Key Term

Authoring tools Software packages that offer a WYSIWYG user-friendly environment allowing for website design without knowledge of HTML.

Security measures

Websites are gaining in importance as the public face of many businesses. The additional revenues generated by e-commerce systems mean that organisations are becoming ever more reliant on them as significant elements of their business strategy.

▲ The security symbol

With this high level of dependency on the services provided by e-commerce systems, it is essential that they are protected from the threats posed by hackers, viruses, fraud and denial-of-service attacks.

E-commerce systems are based on the web, and this provides open and easy communications on a global basis. However, because the internet is unregulated, unmanaged and uncontrolled, it introduces a wide range of risks and threats.

Remember

Trading on the internet involves an element of security risk and this must be considered in the design process.

A serious e-business should introduce sufficient security controls to reduce risk to its e-commerce systems. The following are typical measures used to protect against attack.

Authentication

There are several techniques used to identify and verify someone seeking to access an e-commerce system. These include the following.

- **A username and password requirement,** where the password can vary in length and include numbers and characters.
- **'Two-factor' authentication** requiring something the user has (e.g. an authentication token) and something the user knows (e.g. a personal identification number).
- **A digital certificate** that enables authentication through the use of an individual's unique signing key.
- **A person's unique physical attribute** (referred to as a biometric). This can range from a fingerprint or iris scan, through to retina or facial-feature recognition.

Key Term

Authentication Proving that you are who you say you are.

Access control

This restricts different types of users to subsets of information and ensures that they can only access data and services for which they have authorisation. These include using:

- network restrictions
- application controls.

Changes to access privileges must be controlled to prevent users retaining them if they transfer between departments or leave the business.

Firewall

This is a hardware or software security device that filters information passing between internal and external networks. It controls access to the internet by internal users, and prevents outside parties from gaining access to systems and information on the internal network.

▲ Firewall software helps to protect vital data

Encryption

This technique scrambles data and is used to protect information that is being either held on a computer or transmitted over a network. It uses technologies such as virtual private networks (VPNs) and secure socket layers (SSLs).

Intrusion detection

Intrusion detection software monitors system and network activity to spot any attempt being made to gain illegal access. If a detection system suspects an attack, it can generate an alarm such as an e-mail alert.

Costs of developing a small website

The costs associated with developing a website depend on the level of sophistication that is built into it. This governs the amount of time and the level of skills that are needed. A number of components go together to determine cost.

Graphics

This includes the page layout and images that are needed to create the look and feel of a site. If a business needs graphic designers to create logos and colour schemes, this can add to the costs.

Photography

This is another cost if the business requires photographs placed on the site. If photos are already held in stock then this brings the cost down.

Coding

This is the actual creation of an interactive site. Web browsers understand the code known as HTML (see page 160). The complexity of the code required governs the time taken and hence the cost.

Content

All websites depend on their content to give them their value to a business and its customers/clients. Website 'copy' refers to the words that are placed within web pages. Copywriting services can be bought and are charged according to the amount of work involved. Often clients requiring a website provide the copy themselves.

Web hosting and domain name

Web hosting has already been covered on page 159. The business adopting a website will pay for the hosting of the site on a web server, sometimes provided by an internet service provider. It will also need to purchase a domain name – a human readable name typed by users into the address bar of the browser. Domain names can be bought quite cheaply from as little as about £8. Ongoing site maintenance and hosting can cost between £90 and £200 for two years.

The answer to the question 'How much?' is therefore not a straightforward one. The easy response is to say that it depends on the kind of site required. For a cheap site that simply acts as an online 'billboard', the cost can be as little as £300. For a small- to medium-sized enterprise looking for a modest, functioning and transactional site, the cost is likely to be about £1,500–£2,000. For the top class sites with all of the functionality available, the costs will go above £5,000. Add to these design costs the cost of hosting and domain name.

Remember

The costs of developing a new website vary according to how big the site is and the functions and features it includes.

Evaluation

One of the most fundamental things overlooked when developing a new e-commerce website is user acceptance testing. Many web developers underestimate what is involved in testing an e-commerce site from the user's perspective. System testing and load balancing are important. If a new site is not user friendly or does not meet the expectation of the target audience, it can cost a new internet business dearly. The following steps need be taken to ensure thorough testing of a new website.

1. Complete all system testing and quality assurance (QA) *before* commencing User Acceptance Testing. This allows the testers to focus on usability issues and not technical defects.
2. Use ordinary online users to test the site. Do not use the development or production team. This ensures people testing the site are new to this online shopping experience. First impressions are important.
3. Write a testing plan explaining in plain English what needs to be tested and how. Construct testing routines for every page in the site, detailing expected results of all the functionality. From these the tester can easily identify the appropriate outcome from every action response.
4. Test on all target platforms and browsers. These should be outlined in the site's technical specification. But make sure they are listed again in the test plan document.

5. A senior project leader rather than the testers should conduct prioritisation of defect fixing. This ensures that change control tasks are allocated to the right people. The project leader should also make sure the development teams change the status of a defect once it is fixed.
6. Conduct at least three rounds of **testing**. This ensures after change control has been completed any 'fixes' do not have an impact on any other functions on the site.
7. After the site is deployed, conduct a final full loop test on the 'live' server (password protected only) with technical and production staff to make sure all defects are corrected and signed off.

Key Term

Testing Trying out the website to make sure it is capable of ease of use by both staff and customers.

Accessibility testing

Given the new regulations outlined earlier in the unit, it is important that new websites are tested to ensure they are available to those with impaired vision. This process should be planned into the testing procedure.

Website launch considerations

After all of the pre-launch planning has been carried out, the day will come when the new website goes 'live' on the web. But even at this stage the site should not be forgotten because there are several considerations that will affect the performance.

Maintenance and updates

It has already been discussed several times in the unit that a website is only as good as its content. 'Content is king' is true as far as the web is concerned. With poor or outdated content, a website is discredited and useless to potential customers. Credibility is essential. Because of this it is well worth making every attempt to ensure that the site is checked, updated and maintained on a regular basis. From a strategic viewpoint, the question is: 'Should content be maintained internally or should an external agency carry this out for us?'

Customer feedback

One of the advantages of the web is the ease with which clients and customers are able to give feedback to the website. This entails building into the site a feedback facility which could be in a form on the site, or a 'contact us' page.

Promotion of a website

A website is a huge potential source of business and goodwill if the online personality and impact is right. Therefore it is well worth extra expenditure to promote the site both offline and online.

Offline promotions can appear on vehicle livery (such as diy.com, Sainsbury and many others), or online promotion can be through affiliate links strategically placed on other sites. Both of these tactics can help to drive traffic through to the new site.

Security of ICT systems

Once the site is launched it is also worth checking on the security measures that have been put in place in response to the concerns described earlier. Security issues change every day and it is unwise for any management to simply assume that security is always tight.

Business continuity plans

A business making big strides online can find itself in difficulty if it becomes dependent on internet technology only to discover that when there is a technical disaster the business is put immediately under threat. This means that the managers would be sensible to have contingency plans based on 'What if …?' scenarios.

- What will they do if something went wrong?
- What will customers do?
- How will orders be dealt with?

Typical costs of a small website

The costs of hosting and maintaining a small website can be anything between £90 and £200 per year.

Outcome activity 30.3

Scenario

You are working for a web development firm and have been given the following brief, with some comments attached from your boss: 'This is a fairly flexible project, but the clients are particularly fussy. Use your imagination and try to come up with something that is appropriate.'

The Copt Hill Preservation Society: background

Copt Hill is a well known local landmark thought to be a pre-historic burial site. It is topped by seven large trees known in the region as the 'Seven Sisters', which can be seen for miles around. Archaeological digs completed in the nineteenth century found evidence of several burials and quite a number of historic artefacts.

The Copt Hill Preservation Society (the client) aims to maintain and improve the Copt Hill site. The society wishes to encourage visitors by informing people about its importance as a site of historic interest. Educational materials are felt to be a good idea and a new membership scheme, the 'Friends of Copt Hill', is envisaged.

It has been decided that a website would be a good way of promoting the activities of the society and reaching a broader audience. Perhaps such a website would encourage many more visitors from abroad.

Your tasks

1. List in your own words the requirements of the Copt Hill Preservation Society.
2. List all desirable design features that would be needed by visitors to the site.
3. Consider the 'target audience' for the site; who will they be?

Your design brief

You have an idea of what the site should do. It is to be largely promotional and raise the status of the Copt Hill landmark. It has to be informational; it has to be educational; it has to encourage membership. The client needs a site that is easy to use and navigate. People must know who to contact to get more information; people should enjoy looking at the site; the site should be accessible through a range of browsers; and it should meet the requirements of the Disability Discrimination regulations on website accessibility.

You have a free hand to design the site as you wish.

Draw up a rough sketch of the structure of the website.

Your test plan

All pages and all links must be tested as the site is developed. If a site is to include advanced features such as JavaScript or other scripts, these will be tested as the site is uploaded onto the web.

The following are the specific tasks you are instructed to carry out.

Pass

Plan and design the website required to meet the specific purpose for the defined target group. 

Draw up plans for the evaluation of the design and the launch of the site. 

Merit

Assess how your own design meets the requirements of the target group and contributes towards the achievement of the organisation's objectives. 

Explain the appropriateness of your plans for the evaluation of the design and the launch of the Copt Hill website. 

Distinction

Make justified recommendations for changes to the website design and launch plans for the Copt Hill website. 

Grading tips

Pass 

This should be an outline plan showing a series of pages that are (at least) produced on paper explaining the design features you envisage for each page. If you have the facilities, implement a functioning site that will serve as a basis for your client to view.

Pass 

This should be a list of the steps you would take in the evaluation process.

Merit 

Explain why certain features you have planned have been included. What is their purpose as far as users are concerned? You need to show an understanding of the organisation's objectives.

Merit 

Think of a 'persona' for the typical user of the Copt Hill Preservation website. What sort of people might they be? Explain why your design should appeal to them.

Distinction 

Consider changes that you would make as a result of consultations with users. Why would you do this?

End of unit test

1. What is the distinction between b2c and b2b transactions?
2. Which of these types of transaction has grown the most?
3. List at least four different kinds of organisation using the web and describe their basic online activities.
4. Why do you think that government bodies use the web? Give examples from your own local council.
5. Select a website that you are familiar with and assess its usability. What features have the designers used that help the user? Could they do more? If so what?
6. What do you understand by 'multimedia' in a website? Select an example to illustrate this and say why you feel it is used in that context.
7. What do you understand by the term 'target group' of a website? See if you can find an example of a website with a particular target audience and explain your choice.
8. Select two different websites to illustrate two contrasting sorts of 'visual appeal'. Explain the different techniques that have been used.
9. Research an example of a website that is designed to meet specific objectives for a private business online. Do you feel that it succeeds?
10. Why do you think it is considered necessary to 'test' a new website?

Books

Chaffey, Mayer, Johnston & Ellis-Chadwick, 2003, *Internet Marketing* (2nd edition)

Goymer, J, 2004, *BTEC National e-Business Book 1*, Heinemann

Websites

www.4projects.com – Project Management processes website

www.acmewhistles.co.uk – An example of a website that uses the web's ability to carry multimedia effects

www.amazon.co.uk – The well-known online retailer

www.bellsfishshop.co.uk – A good example of a website with visual appeal

www.berr.gov.uk – The government department for Business, Enterprise and Regulatory Reform

www.computers.com – Unbiased reviews of the latest computer technology

www.covisint.net – Website of a company that specialises in connecting people and systems across industries

www.eMarketer.com – Market research on e-business and online marketing

www.diy.com – B & Q's online business: a good idea of website functionality

www.wifesgone.com – Website of a pressure group

Grading criteria	Outcome activity	Page number
To achieve a pass grade the evidence shows that the learner is able to:		
P1 Describe how three contrasting organisations use their websites for business purposes	30.1	139
P2 Explain the functions and usability features of the websites of three contrasting organisations	30.2	152
P3 Explain the use of visual and media design features of the websites of three contrasting organisations	30.2	152
P4 Plan and design a website for a specific organisation meeting specified purposes for a defined target group	30.3	164
P5 Draw up plans for evaluation of design and ongoing launch of website for a specific organisation	30.3	164
To achieve a merit grade the evidence shows that, in addition to the pass criteria, the learner is able to:		
M1 Analyse how the functions, usability features and visual and media design of a selected website meet the requirements of the target group	30.2	152
M2 Assess how own website design meets the requirements of the target group and contributes towards achievement of the organisation's objectives	30.3	164
M3 Explain the appropriateness of the plans for the evaluation of the design and launch for a specific organisation	30.3	164
To achieve a distinction grade the evidence must show that, in addition to the pass and merit criteria, the learner is able to:		
D1 Evaluate the extent to which the usability features and visual and media design of a selected website contribute towards the achievement of the organisation's objectives	30.2	152
D2 Make justified recommendations for changes to the website design and launch plans of a website for a specific organisation	30.3	164

Starting a new business

Introduction

For any business to set up and succeed, someone has to be prepared to take a risk. Economists refer to the vital things that firms need to become successful as the 'Factors of production'. Three of these are very obvious and visible.

- Land is the natural resource that the firm uses.
- Labour is the physical and mental skills of the workforce.
- Capital is the manufactured things that firms use such as vehicles, machinery and buildings.

However there is a fourth and less visible factor that is just as important as all the others – enterprise. Enterprise is the ability and willingness of someone to take a risk in order to get the business going and succeed. Without risk there is no business. Some people may need to risk their own money to get the business up and running; others may take a risk by leaving their existing salaried jobs to run the new venture; yet others may simply risk some of their free time to help the business.

Different types of business need different levels of risk, but all businesses need someone who is prepared to take that risk or they will not succeed.

There are many potential pitfalls when starting up a new small business. This unit looks at what's involved and considers strategies to minimise or eliminate the risks. Starting a new company can be an exciting thing to do; good planning can ensure that it is not worrying, too!

What you need to learn

On completion of this unit you should:

1. Be able to present the initial business idea using relevant criteria
2. Understand the skills and development needed to run the business successfully
3. Know the legal and financial aspects that will affect the start-up of the business
4. Be able to produce an outline business start-up proposal.

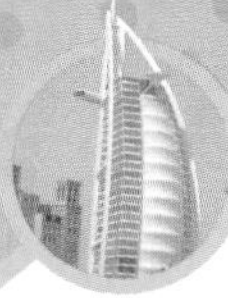

Consider this

There were 3,265 liquidations in England and Wales in the second quarter of 2006 on a seasonally adjusted basis. This was a decrease of 4.9% on the previous quarter and a decrease of 3.3% on the same period a year ago. 0.7% of active companies went into liquidation in the twelve months ended Q2 2006, the same as the previous quarter and the same as the corresponding quarter of 2005.

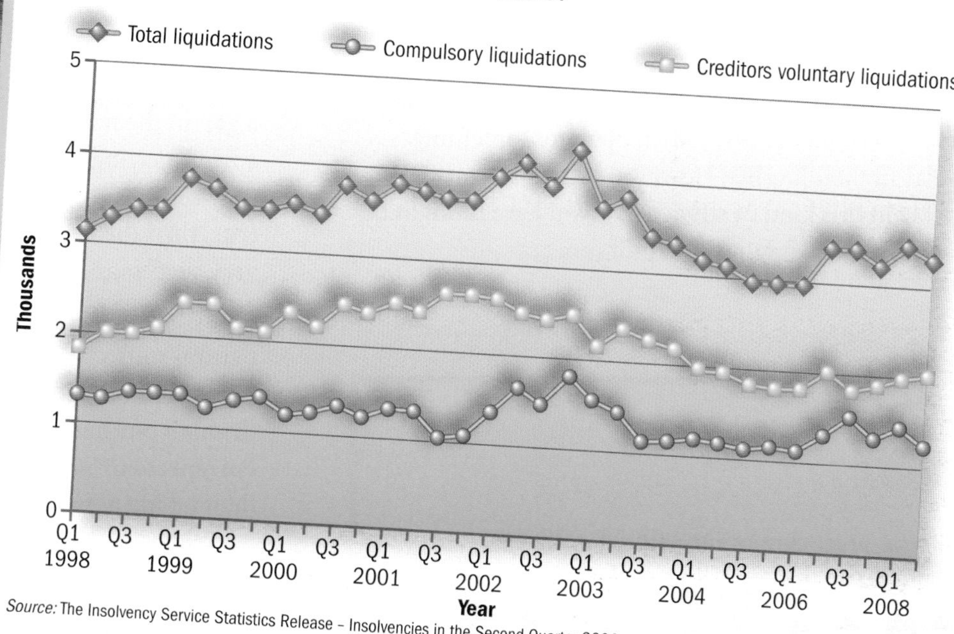

Source: The Insolvency Service Statistics Release – Insolvencies in the Second Quarter 2006

You can see from the above information that a great many businesses fail every year.

- Using the graph, calculate the approximate number of business failures for each of the years 1998 to 2005.
- Which years experienced the highest and lowest levels of business failure?
- What factors do you think might have resulted in more businesses failing in certain years?
- In general terms what do you think might be the main reasons why firms cease trading?
- Discuss the following question with a partner and come up with as many suggestions as possible: If you were starting a new small business what could you do to ensure that you had the best chances of success?

37.1 Presenting an initial business idea

Your first task in this unit is to decide what product or service you intend to produce. To do that you need a business idea, but how do you get a new business idea? These ideas could come from:

- copying something that's already successful
- developing a hobby or interest
- spotting a gap in the market.

Copying successful ideas

For some people it is a case of spotting a business that someone else has made successful elsewhere (perhaps even in another country), then opening something similar in their locality. However, you have to act quickly in this kind of situation; if you have thought of it, someone else might think of it too.

Case study

Local area cleans up with wheelie-bin business

A few years ago someone had the new idea of setting up a wheelie-bin cleaning service in a city suburb. The idea was simple but popular with customers. It was also easy to copy, because it required little capital investment other than a compressor, spray jet, soap, water and some transport. Within weeks banks were being inundated with similar proposals for similar businesses all over the city. Indeed, many of these start-up businesses went on to become successful.

1. What other simple business ideas can you think of that could be set up in a matter of days? ✓
2. Why do you think this business idea became so popular so quickly? ✓✓
3. What are the potential drawbacks to such a business? Evaluate the potential for this type of business. ✓✓✓

Developing a personal interest

For other people the business idea comes from development of a hobby or something they are already interested in. It may be a skill such as woodworking or painting, or maybe even growing plants or vegetables. It may be a service like designing web pages, or acting as a consultant or adviser to clients.

Gaps in the market

Another source of business ideas comes from spotting a gap in the market. You may have heard yourself or a friend saying: 'Someone could make a packet if they only set up a _______ business around here!' If that is true, then the first person to move into the gap may be very successful.

Many business opportunities therefore come from natural sources. They are extensions of what people do or enjoy already, or they are ideas that spring up through our daily lives. One feature of a successful **entrepreneur** is being able to identify opportunities, then taking advantage of them.

Key Term

Entrepreneur A person who sets up and runs a business venture.

Criteria for a new business idea

As part of your assignment for this unit you will need to be able to:

- describe the case for your new business idea
- justify it under various criteria.

On pages 170–180 we will discuss those criteria and what you need to consider for each.

Thinking point

This task will help you to come up with a viable business idea for your assignment.

In small groups, discuss possible business ideas. At this early stage it is best to be as creative as possible in your thinking – some good original ideas may come from some apparently crazy thinking! An unusual idea can be modified and adapted until it becomes a viable proposition. Your group should make a list of 15–20 possible ideas for discussion.

The group should now discuss the merits and problems associated with each of the ideas in order to produce a shortlist of the five best ideas. At this point you need to consider the practicalities of each potential plan too. Proposing to start a night club may sound exciting, but it is a big plan and will take much more work than something simpler than, say, a mobile cleaning service. You also need to think about the potential cost of the project. A night club will require many thousands of pounds to get it up and running; other more modest businesses will not.

Put your five best ideas on flipchart paper and present them to the rest of the class. The class should ask questions at this stage. Finally the class can vote for their favourite ideas. Look carefully through the ideas discussed and either choose or adapt one of them to suit yourself.

Business planning

If we hope to be successful in a new business it is essential to plan ahead. Roughly 40% of new businesses fail within their first three years. Therefore, before embarking on such a venture we must plan carefully to give ourselves the best chance of avoiding the same pitfalls. A well-planned business is much more likely to succeed.

A business plan can never be a guarantee of success, since what we are doing is trying to predict the future. However, it does serve some key purposes.

- It makes you think carefully about the idea to identify possible problems and strategies for overcoming them.
- It forces you to think in detail about what you will need to buy to get the business off the ground and how much this will cost.
- It helps you to identify sales targets that will allow you first to break even, then make a profit.
- It shows a bank manager that you are serious about your ideas and that you have thought them through in detail. Therefore it is more likely that the bank will support your project with some additional finance.

Type of business

Your starting point will be to explain the type of venture you propose to start up. When you decide to start a new venture, there are three basic approaches to choose from. Each has advantages and disadvantages; here is a short summary of each.

Starting a new business

You might want to start a new business from scratch. Perhaps you have a unique idea for it or perhaps you have ideas for adapting something you have seen used by others. Wherever your inspiration comes from, starting with a brand new business idea is the option that will need most work from you. However, it can also be the most satisfying yet most risky option.

Purchase an existing business

An alternative to starting a new business from scratch is to buy an existing business.

Buy-out: advantages

- There will be an existing track record of the firm that you can check.
- The firm has an existing customer base.
- The price you pay will also cover all of the capital items the firm owns, so you will need to buy little additional capital.
- It can be much quicker to get the business running than if you are starting from scratch.
- Agents handle the sales; they will be able to present you with a range of businesses to choose from.
- This method will probably be less risky than a new venture.
- The seller may offer to work with you in the business for a short while to help with the handover period.
- There is no need to find employees, as they are already in place.
- Cashflow and profits start immediately.
- It is easier to raise finance for an existing business than for a new venture.
- You will inherit established suppliers (and possibly credit arrangements).
- Required licences and permits are already in place.

Buy-out: disadvantages

- You need to ask the question: 'Why is this person selling this business if it is so good?' If you can't get a good answer, then beware.
- Will customers stick with you when you take over the firm? Sometimes customers stick with a company just because they like the proprietor.
- You may not be able to find exactly the right business for you.
- It may take a while before you can make changes; you may need to settle in first.
- You may have to pay for **goodwill**, which may or may not be worth anything.
- Current employees may not be up to the job.
- Agents' details will paint the business in as good a light as possible, so let the buyer beware!
- An existing business will normally cost more than starting from scratch.

Key Terms

Goodwill The amount paid by a buyer to the seller of a business that exceeds the value of the assets of the business; it represents the value of the business' reputation, brand, workforce skills and customer base.

Franchise A small business that buys the right to use a larger firms' name, advertising and products.

Remember

When considering buying an existing business always ask yourself why the current owner is keen to sell if the business is so strong.

Franchise

A **franchise** is a business marriage between an existing, proven business and a newcomer. The newcomer (known as the 'franchisee') buys permission to copy the business idea of the established company. Franchisees commit their capital and effort. The franchisor commits the trading name and management experience, and often supplies materials and equipment. Many well-known stores are based on franchising, e.g. McDonald's, KFC, Body Shop, Benetton and Armani.

Franchise: advantages

- Franchisees get the satisfaction of running their own business.
- Still belonging to a large organisation provides security.
- Franchisees get to sell tried-and-trusted products.
- Franchisors provide training for you and your staff.
- Franchisors will often provide uniforms.

Many KFC stores are run as franchises

- Franchisors will help you to find a suitable location and will often help with the costs of fitting out the outlet.
- Franchisees have a guaranteed source of supply of raw materials/products.
- Franchisees benefit from the support of national advertising campaigns designed and paid for by the franchisor.
- It may be possible to get an exclusive dealership arrangement whereby yours is the only outlet for those products in a particular geographical area.
- There are often a number of existing franchisees you could talk to before investing your money.
- The chances of the business failing are minimised.

Franchise: disadvantages

- Franchisees do not have complete control over running the business.
- You have to sell specified products at specified prices.
- You must lay out your store/premises in specified ways and can only use promotions devised by the franchisor.
- A proportion of profits must be given to the franchisor.
- Franchisees have to buy supplies from franchisor, even if there is a cheaper or better alternative available.
- Not all franchises are successful. Newspapers periodically run stories about people who have sunk their life savings into a franchise only to find that the sales projections provided by the franchisor prove to be very optimistic.
- Selling a franchise can be difficult, and it may often only be at the discretion of the franchisor. Either they may insist on vetting new owners or you will have to sell back to the franchisor.
- Bad publicity for the franchisor can have an adverse affect on the franchisee's business.

Thinking point

One of the most important things to do before investing in a franchise is to ask the franchisor as many questions as possible. Look through the information given on pages 172–174, then draw up a list of fifteen questions you think would be essential to ask before investing your money.

Askham Bryan College LIBRARY BOOK

Aims and objectives

Further criteria by which you will need to justify your business choice are your aims and objectives in setting up the business. Business aims and objectives are discussed at length in Unit 1 (Book 1), but here is just a short reminder of what you should consider.

Aims are general broad statements of the purpose of the firm. Domino's Pizza's mission statement, for example, begins with a broad aim: 'Exceptional people on a mission to be the best pizza delivery company in the world.' Objectives state how the firm will achieve its aims by setting targets that are SMART:

- **S**pecific
- **M**easurable
- **A**chievable
- **R**ealistic
- **T**ime-related.

To achieve this, Domino's should set clear objectives for the staff. An objective might be to deliver 99% of pizzas within 30 minutes of an order being received or to ensure that every customer is completely satisfied with their service.

Remember

SMART targets should be set in terms of quality, quantity and time if we are going to be able to monitor them effectively.

The attractiveness of your idea

You will need to make the case that your new service or product is likely to attract interest from potential customers. You could do this by using your USP and demand for new business.

USP

USP stands for Unique Selling Point – what is different about your business and why customers should buy from you rather than elsewhere. It may be that your business is a totally unique idea, or it could be an adaptation of an existing idea that makes your business more attractive, e.g. offering a mobile service or personal designs.

Key Term

USP (Unique Selling Point) The features of a business that make it different from and more attractive than its competitors.

Demand for new business

You will also need to show evidence that there will be demand for your new idea. We will consider how to do this well in the section entitled 'Identifying your **target market**' (see page 177).

Checking profitability

Obviously, a business idea needs to be justified in terms of its potential profitability. This can be done by producing budgets, a **break-even analysis**, **cashflow forecasts** and projected profit and loss accounts. We will examine how to do each of these in the section entitled 'Financial aspects' (see page 198).

Key Terms

Break-even analysis Comparison of a firm's revenue and its costs to identify the minimum sales level needed to break even.

Cashflow forecast A technique for estimating the future bank balance of a company and anticipating overdraft requirements.

Target market A group of consumers, sometimes called a segment, to which an organisation offers its products.

Business trends and external influences

Business is a constantly changing world. These changes present opportunities to companies, but they also present problems that have to be overcome. You will also need to justify your business idea in terms of the trends and changes that are taking place around us.

Businesses face numerous changes such as:
- changes in society
- economic changes
- new political ideas
- new and redundant technologies
- environmental thinking and the law.

Some of these change on a purely local level while others are national or even international trends. All of these pose challenges to the company and many also offer opportunities.

We would normally analyse these influences on a business by performing a **PESTLE analysis** (see the table below), which involves looking at each of those factors separately and identifying which of them pose challenges and which suggest opportunities.

PESTLE analysis is a management technique that helps you to understand the external environment in which the organisation operates. There is a further examination of this topic in Unit 3 (Book 1).

When we conduct a PESTLE analysis it is usual to list the six headings in a table (as below) and write down as many relevant ideas as we can identify under each.

Having identified these factors, you should then examine how they will affect a company. In doing this you should consider the effect on each of the following:
- customers
- staff
- technology used by the business
- the industry as a whole
- competitors.

Key Term

PESTLE analysis An analysis of the environment in which the business operates, looking at Political, Economic, Social, Technological, Legal and Environmental influences.

PESTLE analysis
Political influences: This section might discuss such things as the stability of the government, whether the country is likely to go to war, tax policies and international trade relations.
Economic influences: This section might discuss such things as interest rates, levels of employment and unemployment, consumer confidence, economic growth, inflation, retail sales trends, income levels among customers and the availability of credit.
Social influences: This section might discuss such things as lifestyle changes, population changes, levels of education and crime levels.
Technological influences: This section might discuss such things as the speed of technological change in the industry, economies that could be gained through new machinery and the application of ICT to the business.
Legal influences: This section might discuss such things as new employment laws, health and safety regulations, competition policy and the influence of EU directives and laws.
Environmental influences: This section might discuss such things as pollution laws, pressure groups, arrangements for waste disposal and the local community's views on the business's activities.

To do an effective PESTLE analysis we need good, reliable sources of information. Here are some of the best ones.

- *Glasgow University* has produced an excellent web page (www.lib.gla.ac.uk/Depts/MOPS/Stats/UKStats.shtml) that directs you to a wide variety of statistical sources in the UK.
- *National Statistics* is the organisation set up by the government to provide it and the general public with accurate statistical information about the economy, business and society in the UK. There is a great deal of information about business and economic trends contained in this site. Visit www.statistics.gov.uk and look first at the 'UK Snapshot' section.
- *The Bank of England* publishes a variety of statistical information useful for businesses. Visit www.bankofengland.co.uk/statistics/index.htm for the range it has to offer.

Practice point

Visit a number of the statistical sources given above and draw up a detailed PESTLE analysis for a new company (you choose what product or service they plan to offer), identifying the main opportunities arising for UK companies and also any key threats you can spot.

Seasonal business trends

Some changes take place on a regular basis, every year, every month, every week or even every day. This is known as a **cyclical trend** because, like going round in a circle, we keep coming back and starting again.

Some businesses such as the tourist industry find that sales are higher in certain months. Chocolate manufacturer Thorntons, for example, makes approximately 20% of its annual sales in the weeks just before Christmas. Knowing this trend, the company has to plan in order to meet the demand. Cyclical changes may come about due to the weather, religious festivals, holiday periods or even cycles in the economy. Whatever the reason they need to be anticipated so that the company does not disappoint customers.

Key Term

Cyclical trend A change that recurs on a regular basis.

Thinking point

The following table shows the index for retail sales of non-food items in the UK from May 2004 to May 2006.

2004 May	113.6
2004 June	113.6
2004 July	116.6
2004 August	112.4
2004 September	113.7
2004 October	120.4
2004 November	137.9
2004 December	172.1
2005 January	106.3
2005 February	102.6
2005 March	108.9
2005 April	109.5
2005 May	110.6

2005 June	112.6
2005 July	114.6
2005 August	110.9
2005 September	111.3
2005 October	118.7
2005 November	137.1
2005 December	177.7
2006 January	105.9
2006 February	102.8
2006 March	106.9
2006 April	114.2
2006 May	114.8

Source: www.statistics.gov.uk

- Draw a line graph of this data.
- What is the overall trend in sales?
- Identify any seasonal changes in the data. What reasons can you give for each of the changes?
- What do you think companies in the UK need to do as a result of these seasonal changes? Answer this for:
  - manufacturers
  - importers
  - retailers.
- Looking at the trend and extrapolating it into the future, what do you think sales will be in December 06 and January 07?
- Visit the National Statistics website (www.statistics.gov.uk) to check if your predictions are accurate.

Self-esteem

You may choose to justify your business idea in terms of the pleasure and development opportunities that it brings to you personally. There are many reasons why people choose to become self-employed, e.g.:

- they have independence and can be their own boss instead of someone else making the rules
- they are in total control of the direction their business takes
- they might be looking for, and enjoy, this kind of challenge
- they may gain a great sense of personal achievement through their business successes
- they can escape the bureaucracy of working for a large company
- they have an opportunity to be creative
- they may be able to work from home
- they may enjoy the sense of power to be gained from running their own business
- they may pay less income tax, as some of the expenses they incur as a self-employed person can be used to reduce the amount they might normally pay.

Balancing personal/business needs

There is a great deal of satisfaction to be gained from running your own business well. However, it is also very time consuming. Entrepreneurs need to be very dedicated as, certainly at the beginning of a new business, they may find themselves working many hours. Many people who run their own small businesses find themselves working all day providing their product or service to their customers, then working during the evenings catching up on paperwork, planning, chasing debtors and performing other essential business functions. These demands need to be balanced against all of the positive aspects listed earlier. In fact, many new business people find their social lives severely altered and constrained – and this is a pressure that needs to be considered before a new business venture is started.

Identifying your target market

If you are to make a successful case for your business, you will need to have good evidence that the product or service will sell. This is best achieved by marketing research. At this point you would do well to refer back to Unit 10 (Book 1), as all of these topics are covered in detail there. Meanwhile, here is a summary to remind you.

Remember

Your target market is not always obvious, as the customer (the person who buys the product) is not always the consumer (the one who uses it). For example, much men's underwear is bought by women for their partners, so you might be right to think of the target market for men's underpants as being female. This will almost certainly affect your approach to designing and marketing the product.

The marketing research process is as follows.

- *Define objectives* – decide exactly what information you wish to gain.
- *Write a research brief and proposal* outlining possible methods you could use.
- *Plan* – choose which primary and secondary methods and the sampling technique you will use.
- *Collect the data.*
- *Analyse and evaluate the data* – extract the key messages for the information collected.

Primary research

There is a range of possible methods you could use.

- *Observation* – watching customer behaviour.
- *Surveys* – posing set questions to respondents (this can be done face to face, by post, e-mail or telephone).

- *Focus groups or panels* – in-depth discussions with a group of respondents.
- *Field trials* – testing the product with real customers.

It is up to you which methods you choose to use. Remember, however, that a range of methods is always likely to return more reliable results than using just one method.

Secondary/published research

As we are considering a new business there are no internal sources to use. However, there are a number of external published sources that could be consulted:

- the internet
- government statistics (www.statistics.gov.uk)
- libraries
- university researchers
- company reports and accounts
- specialist research agencies such as Mintel, Datastream and Dun & Bradstreet
- **trade journals**.

These sources should be particularly useful in determining industry and market trends which should inform your planning.

Key Term

Trade journals Regularly published magazines which contain the latest thinking from people who work in specific industries.

Sales forecasts and market trends

A major part of your new business will be the prospect of sales of the product or service. Therefore it is useful to try to estimate potential sales at an early stage. Well-designed questions in your primary research will help with this. You should aim to determine factors such as:

- whether respondents are likely to consider buying from your new business
- how frequently they would buy such a product or service
- how much they would typically be prepared to pay
- whether their buying patterns are likely to change at different times of the year.

The answers to your questions should enable you to come up with some estimates of sales forecasts, although these will be educated guesses at best. You would be right to assume that sales will start slowly, so err on the lower side of your estimates at first. You can build up these figures in later months, assuming your reputation increases.

An understanding of trends in the market is also going to lend weight to your new business proposals. You may have some knowledge of your own from experience or observation of the market that you are planning to enter, but even if you have you should back this up using your primary research questions.

Questions about customers' history of buying the product along with their ideas of how the product should be developed in the future should prove valuable. You may need to ask a fairly open question about this to elicit a wide range of responses and gain valuable insight.

Secondary research may also be able to help with these predictions, depending on what information you can find. If you are moving into an established market, figures of overall market size and recent sales trends could be helpful in estimating your possible sales.

Since you are planning a small business this would be more useful if you can find local sales and trend figures, but these are often difficult to obtain. If you can establish total market sales, you could assume that your business will take a modest percentage of these. This should help you to arrive at a possible sales figure.

Your potential success in breaking into the market will also be influenced by the number and strength of competitors in the market, so you should bear this in mind too (see 'Competition', page 179).

Forecasting sales is notoriously difficult, especially before a business has started up. Once the business has been in existence for some time, historic trends can be extended into the future – and this will give a much more realistic and reliable prediction of sales.

Customers' actions and choices, and their effect on businesses

Understanding customer behaviour is a very complex area and even with extensive experience it is still a very inexact science. Unfortunately buyers are relatively hard to predict and often act on impulse rather than considered thought. Therefore anticipating what they will do is always going to be tough. There have been a lot of writers who have tried to make sense of consumer behaviour, but all of them admit that the topic is extremely complex.

In his book *Marketing Management: Analysis, Planning, Implementation and Control*, Philip Kotler identified a range of stimuli (inputs) that generate the range of customer responses (outputs).

As a small business owner, all you can hope to do is cover the input areas in your primary research questions. Try to elicit from your respondents the sort of reactions you would get to different decisions under each of the areas. This should then inform your decisions about your product offering.

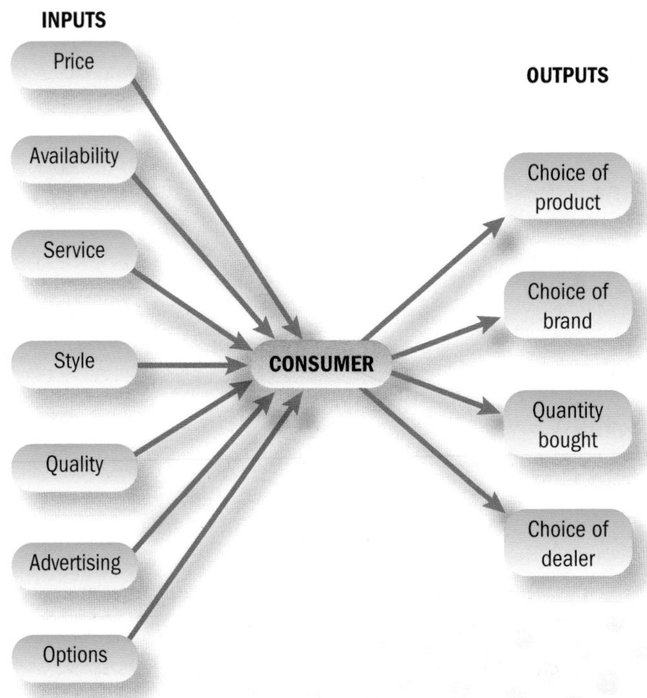

▲ Kotler's black box model

Thinking point

Think about the last item that you bought. Draw up a black box model based on Kotler's model to examine the inputs and outputs surrounding that buying decision. If you were marketing that product, what conclusions could you draw from the model you have constructed?

Competition

Your planning should be influenced by the level of competition in the market you hope to operate in.

First, determine your competitors – both direct and indirect. This will almost certainly require you to visit the locality in which your business will be situated to see what businesses are around there. It might also involve you looking through publications such as *Yellow Pages* to identify others.

Once you have made a list of your competitors you should consider the following questions.

- How many competitors are there?
- How strong are the competitors?
- How aggressively do they market their products or services?
- How might they react to a new competitor?
- What will you do to ensure that you are able to gain a reasonable market share?

Strengths and weaknesses

In business we talk about doing a **SWOT analysis**, and this is very relevant to our thoughts about a new business venture. SWOT stands for:

- Strengths
- Weaknesses
- Opportunities
- Threats.

The idea here is to look at the internal and external situations and influences that may affect our success. Strengths and Weaknesses look internally at the company, while Opportunities and Threats look externally from the company. It is common to show this type of analysis in a table such as the one below. This is a simple completed SWOT analysis for a new takeaway food outlet. A fully detailed SWOT analysis may end up considerably longer than this example. The entrepreneur will then use the findings to draw up plans for exploiting the Strengths and Opportunities while working on eliminating Weaknesses and countering the Threats.

Strengths	Weaknesses
* Young and energetic new entrepreneur. * Some experience in the prepared food trade. * Unique product (home made and designed meals). * Large potential market.	* Little entrepreneurial experience yet. * Shortage of investment capital may limit expansion. * No established reputation.
Opportunities	**Threats**
* No similar local competition. * The 'time poor' public increasingly like food to be made for them, as they do not have the time to do it for themselves. * Increasing disposable income means that people are better able to pay for such a service today. * These days, people like a varied diet. * Opportunity later to diversify into a wider range of products.	* There are a number of national well-established fast food chains that may remain the first choice for customers. * Any future downturn in the economy or increased taxes could leave people unwilling to spend on luxuries. * This is currently a growth area, so additional competitors could be attracted into the market.

Key Term

SWOT analysis Analysis of a business to find its strengths and weaknesses, and to identify the opportunities and threats facing it.

Environmental issues

It is also necessary to understand the business environment that you are operating in. Refer back to the section on PESTLE analysis on pages 175–176.

Practice point

Imagine that you are considering setting up a business as a mobile ironing service.

- Draw up a SWOT analysis for setting up such a business in the vicinity of your school or college.
- Outline the steps that you would take to eliminate the weaknesses and counter the threats that you have identified.

Outcome activity 37.1

The assignment for this unit requires you to prepare and present a business plan for a new business of your choice. The assignment is split into four parts – one part at the end of each section.

Pass

P1

1. Present the initial business idea using relevant criteria and describe how to identify the target market for your new business idea. You will need to identify a potential business venture for self-employment. The best way to do this is to brainstorm ideas along with some of your colleagues. (You will find a good activity to help you do this on page 171. You should do that activity now to help you decide on a suitable venture.)

2. Now prepare a presentation to be delivered to your lecturer covering:
   - a description of your idea
   - a justification of your plan using the criteria discussed so far in this unit
   - the steps you will take to identify your target market.

Merit

M1

Explain and justify the methods you have chosen to use to identify the target market for the proposed business. First, you will need to complete the marketing research process begun in P1 and P2 above. To do this you will do the last two stages:
- collect the data
- analyse and evaluate the data.

Second, you will write notes explaining and justifying each of the methods you have used.

Grading tips

Pass 

There is a range of criteria that you must use to make a detailed justification of your plan (listed below). Ensure you cover them all.

- Your chosen business type.
- Your aims and objectives.
- Your unique selling point and the competitive edge you will have.
- Potential demand for your new business.
- How you will balance your personal and business needs.
- Potential profitability.
- Business trends.
- PESTLE analysis.
- Your self-esteem.
- How business planning will help you to ensure your success.

Pass 

To identify your target market you should follow the marketing research process discussed earlier. You should cover the following in your presentation.

- Define your objectives.
- Write a research brief.
- Write a market research proposal.
- Plan your use of primary and secondary methods.
- Identify an appropriate sampling technique for your research.

Merit 

Explaining will require you to take each research method you have used, give full details of what it is used for and how it is used. Justifying means giving reasons to support your use of the techniques – in other words, you should explain exactly why each technique was appropriate to your research objectives. You should refer to the results that you gained from your research and explain how the methods you used allowed you to find out the key pieces of research information. You should also explain your choice of sampling technique, what it means and why it is appropriate in your circumstances.

37.2 Skills and development needed to run a business

While the example opposite is somewhat extreme it does make an important point. Being self-employed can be exciting and challenging, but it is also a huge commitment – not one to be entered into lightly. Serious consideration needs to be made before embarking on such a project, and you must be prepared to give it maximum commitment.

However, commitment also needs to be linked to good business skills. Therefore in this section we consider what skills and abilities you will need to be a successful business owner.

WANTED

New Business Entrepreneurs

Essential qualities:

- ☑ *Must have little or no social life*
- ☑ *Must be willing to lose the money they invest*
- ☑ *Must be able to do all of the functions of a business*
- ☑ *Must not be hoping to go on holiday in the foreseeable future*
- ☑ *Must have someone who can step in for them if they are sick*
- ☑ *Must enjoy a challenge*

Terms:

Hours – 24/7

Salary – The sky's the limit!

Only serious applicants need apply – no time-wasters

Skills for running a small business

Do you think you have what it takes to run your own business? Many people think so but not all of them make it. Here we consider the abilities and personal qualities you will need if you decide to set out on your own.

Your own contribution

Clearly you will have an important role to play in providing the skills required to make the business succeed. Undoubtedly this will mean you developing new skills as well as utilising those that you already have. Later you will perform a skills audit to identify what skills are needed for your business and what you already possess. Sometimes it is not possible for one person to possess all of the required skills. In this case you may need to consider either taking on a partner or employing someone to fill the gaps.

Technical and operational skills

This is a rundown of the most important skills you will require within your business. However, it is by no means an exhaustive list. Each business requires a unique blend of skills. So you will need to consider which of the following you will need for your venture and what special skills might also be required that are not listed.

Skills relating to products/services

Some products or services require specialist skills to produce. Hand-made jewellery or greetings cards, for example, require someone with particular skills to make the required items. Even if the products can be bought in from manufacturers, those people within your business dealing directly with customers still need to have detailed product knowledge in order to give the best service. The level of product/service knowledge required varies from business to business, depending on the complexity of what the firm is delivering.

Thinking point

Consider the following businesses. Make notes about the degree of product knowledge required to deliver first rate service in each of them. Make lists of the things would you need to know to serve customers effectively.

- A car dealership.
- Gregg's bakers.
- Phones 4 U.
- PC World.

Management

In his article 'Skills of an effective administrator' (*Harvard Business Review*), Robert Katz identified three key components to being a skilled manager.

- *Technical skills* – the ability to get the product made using a detailed knowledge of the processes and procedures required.
- *Human skills* – the ability to interact well with people (both employees and clients), and to influence and lead groups effectively.
- *Conceptual skills* – coming up with new ideas, being able to solve problems well and make effective decisions.

Since this business is to be run principally by you, you will need to display these skills. However, Katz does go on to say that many of these skills can be taught – so don't worry if you don't have them all now!

Recording and checking performance of business

A key role of the business owner is to monitor how well the business is doing so that corrective measures can be taken if things are not looking good. The process for this is as follows.

Step 1 *Performance standards should be set.* These should relate back to the aims and objectives set for the business. It is important that the targets are SMART (involving levels of quality, quantity and time) or it will make step 2 very difficult.

Step 2 *Actual performance is measured.* Information should be collated about:

- how much production has taken place
- how many sales were made
- the quantity of returned items
- financial matters such as the amount of money left in the bank and any changes to the costs of raw materials.

Step 3 *Actual performance is compared to the standards set.* As long as SMART targets are being met, no further action is required.

Step 4 *Corrective action is taken when required.* The root reason why SMART targets are not being met needs to be established (this will not always be obvious) and action taken to ensure it does not re-occur.

Thinking point

In order for performance to be checked, a good system needs to be implemented to record what is happening in the business. Imagine that you are running a new small business dedicated to producing and selling hand-made knitted garments. With a partner you should discuss some practical methods for recording information to help monitor your firm's performance. You might like to do some internet searching or look in some business textbooks to help you think this through. You should identify practical methods for recording performance in the following areas:

- costs (e.g. set budgets for buyers)
- customer satisfaction (e.g. monitor number of returned items)
- quality (e.g. monitor percentage of faulty products produced).

Personal selling

If your product does not 'sell itself', then you may need to employ some personal selling skills to encourage potential customers to buy. Personal selling skills are discussed in Unit 41 (pages 331–35). Meanwhile, here are some of the key skills needed.

- Effective meeting and greeting of customers.
- Identifying product needs in the customer.
- Persuasive presentation of the product.
- Good product knowledge and the ability to communicate this effectively to people with differing levels of prior knowledge.
- Good listening skills.
- The ability to counter objections to the sale from the customer.
- An awareness of the buying signals that customers display when they are interested.
- The ability to effectively close a sale.

Once again these are not skills that always come naturally but they can be learnt and, with practice, most business people will be able to sell effectively.

▲ Personal selling skills are vital to many businesses

Administration

Even if our sales skills are good, poor administration after the sale can let us and our businesses down. It is essential that all details are recorded swiftly and accurately if we are not to disappoint the customer and lose the benefit of our hard work in selling the item.

Administration skills are vital to any business. Without good administrative back-up we may run out of stock, forget to dispatch orders or even forget to collect payment from the customer!

To be good at administration you need to have a logical approach, be well-organised, pay careful attention to detail and have good communication skills. Administration involves a multitude of jobs:

- accurate organisation of customer files
- letter writing and producing other business correspondence
- preparation and dispatch of invoices, and reminders for payment
- managing company budgets
- detailed and accurate research.

Previous experience

This could consist of having already worked in a similar or related business. Alternatively, if you are basing your business idea on a hobby or interest, it could simply be that you have done this particular thing for some time and have built up expertise in the area.

Previous relevant experience is always a useful skill to offer to a new business. It may go some way to ensuring your success, as you may already have witnessed some potential problems that you work to avoid.

Strengths and weaknesses

No one is good at everything. Therefore, we need to be honest about what we can and cannot do. We all have strengths and weaknesses; the important thing is to be aware of them. Strengths that will benefit the business should be built around those things we are good at. Weaknesses should not be ignored. Once we are aware of them, it is important to implement a strategy to either eliminate them or prevent them from undermining the business.

The best way to approach this is to perform a skills audit on yourself. The next section (pages 186–89) explains how to do this.

Real lives

Mark Shaw: Les Stables

Mark Shaw left school aged sixteen with no qualifications but a keen interest in sport. He wanted to work in the sports industry, but he knew he would probably need further qualifications to achieve this. So for three years he went to a college specialising in sports studies.

During that time, one of his lecturers spotted his enthusiasm and motivation, and offered Mark the chance to run a gymnasium – Mark's first real break in the industry.

Working at the gym brought him into contact with lots of people from the sports industry. One person in particular was a retired athlete who was running sporting events as a business. Mark soon started to help out on these events – initially at a very low level, but gradually getting more involved. At this point he decided that if he was to be taken seriously in the industry he would need a degree. So he went to university to study sports science, and continued setting up events in his spare time.

▲ Mark's philosophy is one of risk with security

After he graduated, Mark spent some time working in Australia setting up sporting events for TV company Channel 10. A year later he was back in the UK working for Sport for Television, a big sports promotion company. He worked with them and Sheffield City Council for a number of years building up experience and contacts within the industry.

The recession in the early 1990s meant there was not much work in the sports industry. So Mark went into full-time teaching for a while as a secure profession. However, by 1996 he was keen to get back into event management.

Having attended and taken part in a number of events in the UK, he looked at the way they were organised and thought: 'I know I could do better than that.' This spurred him on to start his own company running triathlon events. The company is known as Transition Sport.

Although Mark knew he could run events well, he also knew it would be beneficial to work with someone who had additional contacts in the industry. So he decided to set up in partnership with someone who could complement his skills.

In the first year they set up events catering for about 800 contestants. These days, they deal with more than 7,000 entries a year, working with three or four major promoters.

One of the overriding themes in Mark's entrepreneurial life as director of Transition Sport has been his willingness to take on risk, but only those risks he is confident he can turn into successes. Mark's philosophy is one of risk with security. For example, many sports event organisers rely on sponsorship income for their profit. This is dangerous, however, as a major sponsor pulling out can jeopardise a whole event, or even the whole company.

Mark and his partner Ian always ensure they can make profits on the entry fees alone; the sponsorships they gain are then a bonus. To achieve this clearly takes some wily financial management, and that is what Mark sees as one of his strengths.

Today Mark is running a new venture – one associated with his current business but that takes him into a whole new area. Over the years, Mark has been on many training camps, but once again he thought: 'I could do this better.' In summer 2007 he opened a training camp for triathletes, cyclists, runners and swimmers in France, known as 'Les Stables' (www.les-stables.com).

Mark intends to differentiate his new business from the competitors by deliberately staying small, offering a personal service to regular customers, who also bring their families to enjoy the sunshine of France. Mark openly admits that five years ago he could not have taken this step, as the risk (especially financial) would have been too large. He has also had to learn a lot, such as French building regulations and how to fit roofing tiles. But with his experience and the success of Transition Sport, he is ready for the new challenge.

Mark believes there are a number of important attributes to any successful entrepreneur:

- the ability to take risks
- the ability to anticipate and overcome problems
- not taking too many big steps too quickly (it is better to take small steps over a long period than to leap into to something too big to handle)
- the ability to identify where others go wrong and avoid the same mistakes
- belief in yourself (you have got to know that you can do it better)
- the willingness to work hard for long hours, and to make personal sacrifices to ensure your business succeeds
- good inter-personal and communication skills (you have to be able to strike up positive relationships with new people very quickly)
- you need to be objective and honest about your own abilities (you need to learn from others and also be prepared to enlist the help of specialists when you know something is too complex for you to handle)
- you have to have qualifications to convince other business people of your professionalism
- you have got to enjoy working for yourself.

1. What do you think were the main factors that have helped Mark to be successful as an entrepreneur? ✓
2. To what extent could he have been successful without qualifications? How important do you consider qualifications to be to a successful entrepreneur? ✓
3. Mark has always taken partners in his business ventures. What do you see as the advantages and potential problems with doing this? ✓✓
4. 'Les Stables' is a very different venture for Mark. What do you see as the major obstacles in the way of his success, and how should he overcome them? ✓✓✓

Take it further

Before you embark on a business venture you must be totally sure you have the personality, skills and attributes to make it a success. Visit the website http://youngentrepreneur.com and see what they suggest as being the most useful skills you will need. What ideas can you add to Mark's list on page 185?

Developing your skills

Identify skills gaps/shortages

You should perform an objective and accurate assessment of your own suitability to run the business you have chosen. This will involve you appraising your own skills honestly and identifying gaps in your abilities. Refer back to pages 182–84, where you looked at the skills and qualities needed to be an effective business person. This might give you some idea of the skills you have and those you lack.

Practice point

In order to analyse your personal development needs you should copy and complete the table on page 187. It is very important that you are completely honest when preparing such an appraisal, because if you are over-confident the appraisal will not be accurate and will be of no use to you. Begin by completing sections 1 to 4.

What you complete on page 187 is a **skills audit**. It is important that you recognise you will not be good at everything and plan to either gain the required skills or find someone else who has them. Having identified the areas where support is required you can then plan to plug those gaps.

Key Term

Skills audit An identification of the skills required and held by the entrepeneur and his/her employees.

Remember

Although as an entrepreneur it is your job to ensure that skills gaps are filled, you do not have to fill them all yourself. In many instances, it makes sense to use someone else's skills – perhaps those of a partner, employee or fellow professional.

Professional help

There are those who can offer professional support to small business people. However, the cost of such help is likely to be expensive, so you should always have in mind how much you can afford and agree what you want to pay before you begin.

Business consultants

There are firms of business consultants that employ experienced business people who are willing to share their experience for a fee. They are able to help with:

- practical advice
- ideas for keeping costs down
- how to develop and expand
- any other general business problems.

Accountants

Someone running a small business will certainly need an accountant to advise them on financial matters during set-up and also to prepare their annual accounting records. Although their fees can be quite expensive, a good accountant will make sure you pay only the necessary income tax so they are worth using.

Solicitors

Solicitors will advise you on any legal matters with regard to your business. Their fees can also be very high, so you would be advised to discuss this with them at an early stage.

Business Link

Business Link is an organisation set up by the Department for Trade and Industry to give advice and support to new businesses. It offers a wide range of

Analysing personal development needs

1 **Personal qualities**
List here all the important skills a business person needs, which you identified earlier. You should also add any further skills that are necessary for your specific business. Next to each of them, comment on whether you have that quality yourself and give some evidence to support your claims.

Skills	Do I have them?

2 **My personal strengths**

....

....

3 **My personal weaknesses**

....

....

4 **Skills and abilities I do not have**

....

....

5 **How I will compensate for those weaknesses (including timescales)**

....

....

6 **What I will do about each of those missing skills and abilities (including timescales)**

....

....

services not dissimilar to those provided by business consultants, but because it is government funded the costs to your business are kept to a minimum. However, the few Business Link advisers there are have large caseloads, so they would not be as readily available as the other professionals mentioned would.

Thinking point

Visit the Business Link website (www.businesslink.gov.uk) and summarise the services available to new businesses. Now search the internet for some business consultants and visit their websites. Compare the services offered by them to those offered by Business Link.

Training

A number of the skills gaps that you identified could be filled by enrolling on training courses. These could be taken at local colleges or might be provided by business consultants. Local colleges will undoubtedly be the cheaper option, so you should explore this possibility first. However, consultants may be more flexible about when they can deliver the training, so this should be considered. If you need to plug a gap urgently and the local college cannot help you until the start of the new academic year, that could be a problem.

Partners

One of the best reasons for taking on a partner is because that person may complement the skills you have. A carefully selected partner might have most of the skills you lack. In this way there will be no expense to you or the business. However, you must be prepared to live with the problems that partnerships can bring (see pages 190–91).

Networking

Networking is a support mechanism for entrepreneurs. It involves visiting events that attract other business people, talking to them, making friends, useful contacts and people who can offer advice, as well as possible sales leads. The idea is to mix business with pleasure, attend an enjoyable event and do some business or gain some support at the same time.

▲ Conferences are excellent opportunities to network and build up valuable business contacts

Networking can take place at trade fairs, conferences, speeches and local events set up by like-minded people. Here are some sources of good networking opportunities.

- *Business Link.* Your local adviser will have contacts with lots of business people in your area.
- *Chamber of Commerce.* Visit the Chamber of Commerce website (www.chamberonline.co.uk) to find out about your local organisation.
- *Federation of Small Businesses.* Visit the FSB website (www.fsb.org.uk) to find out how to join.
- *Trade associations.* Visit the Trade Association Forum website (www.taforum.org) to find out about associations relevant to your business.

Employees

If you are reluctant to take on a partner, you could always advertise for an employee with particular skills. If you would be employing someone anyway, then this need not be considered an extra expense to the business. That said, it is likely that an employee hired for specific skills may well command a higher salary.

Planning and timescales

Now you know the options open to you it is possible to draw up a personalised plan to plug those skills gaps. It is important to identify both *how* you are going to do it and *when*. Some needs will be more urgent and pressing than others, and clearly they should be prioritised. It is essential to set timescales, as this will help you to monitor your own development to check it stays on schedule.

Practice point

Revisit your skills audit (see page 187) and, using the ideas on pages 186–89, complete sections 5 and 6.

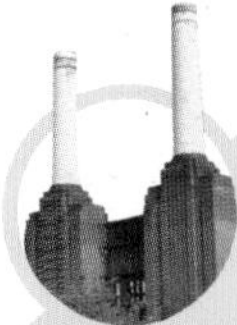

Outcome activity 37.2

This activity continues the business plan begun in Outcome Activity 37.1 (see page 180).

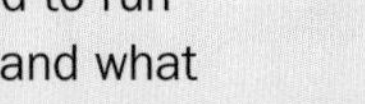

Pass

Describe the skills that you will need to run your chosen business successfully and what skill areas will require further development.

Merit

Analyse the skills development needed to run your selected business successfully.

Grading tips

Pass 

You can achieve this criteria by completing a detailed skills audit using the method outlined in this chapter. Be honest when performing this activity. You will not be required to actually perform the action plan you draw up for filling your skills gaps, but your lecturer will grade you on how realistic you are in your analysis.

Merit 

Analysing requires you to break down the situation and look in detail at all aspects. In this case you should take each skill or ability you lack in turn. For each you should:

- explain in detail why it is necessary to the success of your chosen business
- explain and justify the timescales you have set for addressing this skill need
- explain clearly how the action plan you have drawn up will address this gap
- outline how gaining this skill will improve the performance of your business
- state how you would check to ensure that the skills gap has been successfully filled.

Legal aspects

There are many laws and regulations surrounding the conduct of new businesses. This section runs through the most important areas that the new business owner needs to be aware of.

Legal status

If you decide that you wish to start a new business from scratch, the first task is to decide on your legal status. The text that follows covers the available options.

Sole trader

A sole trader is a business owned by just one person.

Advantages

- There are few legal restrictions on forming such a business.
- It allows you to offer a personal service to your customers.
- Decision-making and implementation of change is fast.
- Profits don't need to be shared.
- Financial information is kept private.

Disadvantages

- Growth is limited to the amount of capital one person can raise.
- You will have unlimited liability for the debts of the firm (see page 191).
- It is difficult to take holidays.
- Ill health can cause long-term problems for the business.
- Working hours are often long.
- A sole trader may lack some important skills needed to make the business succeed.
- If you have problems, it can feel very lonely.

Partnership

A partnership is a business owned by at least two partners who share the responsibility for running and financing the business.

Advantages

- A partner can introduce additional capital to the firm.
- A partner can increase the level of expertise available to the firm.
- The decision-making process can be shared.
- Decision making is still fast, as there are few people to consult.
- It is still possible to offer a personal service.
- There is someone available to cover for sickness and holidays.

Disadvantages

- Growth is still restricted to the amount of capital the partners can raise.
- Problems can arise if partners disagree or fall out.
- If one partner decides to leave, the partnership has to be dissolved.
- Partners still have unlimited liability, unless they form a limited partnership. Often they will each have joint and several liability, meaning that all partners are liable for all of the debts.
- Profits have to be shared.

Limited company

A **limited company** is owned by its shareholders.

Advantages

- It allows further capital to be introduced to the business, thus helping growth.
- Shareholders benefit from limited liability for the debts of the firm (see page 191).
- The company will continue even if a shareholder dies or sells his or her shares.

Disadvantages

- Financial details of the firm must be disclosed to a limited extent.
- A proportion of profits must be distributed to shareholders.
- Decision making is considerably slower.
- Legal formalities for setting up are more complex, although today you can buy a new company set-up pack for around £100–£150.

Key Term

Limited company A business that is owned by shareholders, all of whom have limited liability for the firm's debts

Co-operative

A **co-operative** is a less common form of business enterprise. It is owned by and operated for the benefit of those using its services. These people are known as members. They might be the employees, customers, managers or a combination of all three. Profits are shared among the members. Each member can vote at meetings and the company is run by directors elected by the members.

Advantages

- The business is partly owned by employees. Therefore they are likely to work hard to make it succeed.
- Members receive equal shares in business profits.
- Conditions of work for employees are normally good.
- Decision making is very democratic.

Disadvantages

- Members have very limited voting power, so it is difficult to influence business decisions.
- All members, which may include customers, share an equal liability for company losses.
- Managers are subject to the wishes of the members.

Key Term

Co-operative A business owned by and operated for the benefit of those using its services.

Franchise

These were discussed at the start of this unit (see pages 172–73).

Legal liabilities

Different business owners face different situations if the business fails owing money. If the firm is a sole trader or partnership, the owner(s) have **unlimited liability** for the firm's debts. However, the owners of limited companies and the members of co-operatives benefit from **limited liability**.

Unlimited liability

This is a situation where the business owner(s) are personally responsible for all the debts of the firm. If the business fails and money is owed to **creditors**, the personal assets of the owners can be used by the courts to pay off these debts. The owners' houses, savings, cars and other valuable possessions can be taken to offset against the debts if the firm becomes insolvent.

Limited liability

In this situation the liability of the shareholders or members is limited to the amount of money they invested in the business. In the case of shareholders, this is limited to the amount they paid for the shares they own. If these monies are insufficient to clear the debts of the insolvent firm then none of the shareholders' or members' personal assets can be taken to clear the debts.

Key Terms

Creditor A business or person the firm owes money to.

Limited liability Shareholders lose no more than the value of their shares if the business should fail.

Unlimited liability Business owners are personally responsible for all the debts of the firm and their personal possessions can be seized to clear company debts.

Trading terms and conditions

When you sell a product or service it makes good sense to make very clear the terms on which you are selling to avoid disputes arising later. The terms you set are intended to protect your company from unreasonable claims from customers, so they should always include details of price, payment terms (such as immediate cash payment or an agreed period of credit) and arrangements for the delivery of the product or service. Whenever possible, you should state these terms in writing and make sure that the customer agrees to them (also in writing if possible) before the deal is struck, as this will make the terms much more legally binding.

When you buy in goods and services it is also important to be clear about the terms on which you are buying, so that you know whether they will be acceptable to you.

Trading standards

Trading standards protect consumers from unscrupulous business traders. You have probably seen TV or newspaper reports about innocent customers duped by disreputable businesses – garages who wind back the milometer on second-hand cars to make it look like they have not done many miles; products being sold with prestige brand names that turn out to be forgeries; and the family that arrives at their holiday destination only to find that the time-share villa they bought does not exist. Clearly all of these types of activity are illegal and laws are in place to try to protect consumers from such dodgy deals.

It is important that you become aware at an early stage what your responsibilities are to customers and also what rights you have when buying from suppliers. Check through Unit 21 of this book, which takes a look at the legal aspects of business. Additionally, the government-run Trading Standards Institute (TSI) provides help and advice on a variety of related issues. Its website (www.tradingstandards.gov.uk) has lots of information for new businesses setting up. Its guidance leaflets cover important areas such as:

- *consumers' rights* – standards your customers can expect from you
- *fair trading* – advice on correct labelling, describing and pricing of products and services
- *food laws* – there are a lot of regulations surrounding the supply of food
- *safety* – ensuring that the products you sell meet legal safety requirements
- *weights and measures* – your obligations to supply correct quantities of products to customers
- *animal health and welfare* – if your business involves the use of animals there are further laws that must be followed.

Licences

Many types of business require licences to operate. Some (such as public houses, nursing homes and nightclubs) are obvious. However, many other ventures (such as child-minding services, mobile shops, cinemas, bars, theatres, taxis, tattoo parlours, pet shops and hairdressers) also need to be licensed. You need to find out if your new venture needs a licence and, if so, where that licence can be obtained. Some are from local government departments, while some are granted on a national basis.

Practice point

Visit www.tradingstandards.gov.uk, click on the 'Business' link, then the link to 'Guidance Leaflets for Business'. Using the information on the site choose one of the businesses below and make notes on the regulations you need to be aware of when setting up such a venture.

- Selling hot dogs from a mobile van.
- Buying garments and selling them at car boot sales on a regular basis.
- Running a small café.
- Buying and selling goods over the internet.

Practice point

Think of a business that you are familiar with. This could be one that you work for, a family business or a local shop that you regularly visit. Your task is to determine the licences the business should have in place.

Visit the Business Link website (www.businesslink.gov.uk). Click on the 'Licences' link on the right of the page. Then, imagining the business that you have chosen, complete the questions that follow on the next few pages. Print out the final list of licences that the business will need.

Record keeping

Records of the firm's financial (and other) affairs are very useful for keeping track of the firm's progress. By law, certain financial records must be retained for at least six years. The following are documents that must be kept by all firms.

▲ Record keeping is an important part of running a business

Cash book

This is a record of all of the money coming into and going out of the business. Although it is entitled 'Cash book', it should also contain details of cheque deposits and payments along with credit and debit card transactions – in other words, all deposits and withdrawals from the firm's bank account should be included.

Sales and purchase ledgers

A sales ledger is a record of all sales made by the firm and monies received for those sales. A purchase ledger is a record of all purchases made by the business.

Wages and petty cash books

Records of all wages and salaries paid by the firm must be kept, as must records of small items of expenditure made with cash.

Accident records

The Reporting of Injuries, Diseases and Dangerous Occurrences Regulations 1995 (RIDDOR) requires that records be kept of accidents and injuries sustained on the firm's premises. This information is generally kept in an 'accident book', which must be retained for a minimum of three years.

Stock records

Records should be kept of the firm's stocks of raw materials and finished goods, so that fresh orders can be made promptly to avoid the company running out of important stock items.

Minutes of meetings

Records should also be kept of meetings that take place in the company. These records are normally kept indefinitely and are referred to regularly to check and clarify decisions taken.

Thinking point

- Why do you think it is necessary to keep the financial records described above? What are these records likely to be used for?
- Why do you think it is necessary to keep records of accidents? Who benefits from such records being kept?

Resolving problems

Good communication and positive relationships between managers/owners and staff can avoid most potential problems. However, it is important to have measures in place to cater for problems that do arise.

- The staff should have a *collective voice* such as a **trade union** or a staff association, and regular consultations and meetings with these representatives should enable most problems to be eliminated.
- The law requires that a sound *grievance procedure* should be put in place to aid staff who feel they have not been dealt with fairly by the company managers/owners. This procedure must be communicated in writing to all staff members.
- The law also states that clear *disciplinary procedures* should be in place. This, too, must be communicated in writing to all staff members. This procedure should outline the standards expected of employees and what types of behaviour will be regarded as gross

misconduct. This is particularly important, as an employee found guilty of gross misconduct can be dismissed immediately and without notice.

Key Term

Trade union A group of workers who join together to negotiate pay and working conditions – for example, the National Union of Teachers.

Practice point

The Employment Act 2002 is a wide-ranging act that established many new regulations to strengthen the rights of employees in the UK. Among other things, it lays down minimum standards for disciplinary and grievance procedures. Using textbooks and the internet, you should research these minimum standards. Draw up a set of procedures that meet these minimum standards.

National/local laws

As a new entrepreneur it is important to recognise that you have a number of legal obligations. Therefore, you should identify which laws affect your business and take steps to understand what you must do to comply with them. Some of these are described below.

Insurance

Some insurances are compulsory for businesses, while others are optional. Compulsory insurance includes the following.

- *Employer's liability insurance.* If you employ any staff, you must have this insurance. If an employee sustains an injury while working for you, this protects you from any legal damages claims and court costs claimed against you or your company. Sole traders who employ no one do not need this cover.
- *Motor insurance.* If you run a company vehicle, it must be insured and the policy must cover all people who will drive it.

Non-compulsory insurance is optional, but you should give it serious thought as it could be very helpful.

- *Buildings insurance.* If your premises burn down, explode or are otherwise damaged, this insurance will rebuild them for you.
- *Contents insurance.* The contents of your premises, including stock, fixtures and machinery can be insured against theft or damage.
- *Keyman insurance.* If your business is highly dependent on the work of a particular person or persons, you can insure them so that the company can claim if they are off work through sickness or injury for an extended period.
- *Owner's liability insurance.* If someone enters your premises and gets injured they could sue you for damages. This insurance protects against such claims.
- *Product liability insurance.* If you make a product and it injures someone, this will insure you against damages claims.
- *Public liability insurance.* If you or a member of your staff causes injury to a person or damage to property during the course of your business, this will insure you against damages claims.

Legal responsibilities as an employer: contracts, duties and responsibilities

There are many legal responsibilities for any employer – far more than can be listed in this book. However, here is a summary of the major areas of concern. All of these areas are discussed in more depth in the Business Link website (www.businesslink.gov.uk).

Contracts of employment

Within two months of starting work employers must provide employees with a written statement of the main terms of the contract. This should include:

- the names of employer and employee
- job title or job description
- date employment commenced, the place of work and the address of the employer
- the amount of pay and how often payments will be made
- hours of work
- holiday pay entitlement

- sick pay arrangements
- pension arrangements
- notice periods
- for temporary jobs, the date employment will cease
- grievance and appeal arrangements
- disciplinary rules, although these are now covered by the Employment Act 2002, and all firms should abide by this.

Practice point

Drawing up contracts of employment can be tricky. You have to satisfy the needs of:

- the company, which requires maximum effort from the employee
- the employee, who wants to get maximum benefit from working for the firm.

You should perform this activity in groups of eight students – four of whom will role-play the company workers and four the company managers. Assume that you all work for a small manufacturing company making PCs. The two halves of the group (workers and managers) should sit separately. Each should draw up a contract they feel would be acceptable to them in their roles. The workers and managers should then come back together to negotiate a final contract that is acceptable to both of them. Your teacher will act as arbitrator in case the discussions become a little heated!

Paying employees

The law requires employers to:

- supply employees with itemised pay slips
- comply with the national minimum wage legislation: £5.35 per hour for workers aged 22 or over; £4.45 for those aged 18–21; and £3.30 per hour for those aged 16 and 17 (**Note**: by the time you read this book the rates may have changed, so check for the latest information)
- make statutory payments including maternity, paternity, adoption, sick and guarantee pay.

You should also set yourself up as an employer with the Inland Revenue so that you can make income tax and **National Insurance** payments for your employees.

Key Term

National insurance A tax paid according to the size of a person's income; it goes towards paying for the NHS, social security and state pensions.

Hours of work

The Working Time Regulations state that workers aged 18 and over are entitled to:

- four weeks' holiday a year
- work *no more than* six days out of every seven
- a 20-minute break every six hours
- work *no more than* an average of 48 hours a week.

Discrimination

Employers must take reasonable steps to ensure that disabled people are not prevented from working effectively on their premises.

You must also be aware that it is unlawful to discriminate on the grounds of someone's gender, sexual orientation, marital status, race, colour, nationality, ethnic origin, religion, beliefs, age, or because of pregnancy or childbirth. Part-time workers must also be given the same rights and conditions as full-time workers.

VAT (value added tax)

You only need to register for VAT if you sell more than £61,000 of products or services each year. If you do fall into this category then you must account carefully for VAT in your sales and purchases. A business will pay VAT on its purchases and charge VAT on its sales. If it pays more than it receives, then it can claim this back. However, if it receives more than it pays, this must be remitted to **HM Revenue and Customs**.

Key Term

HM Revenue and Customs
The government department responsible for collecting taxes as well as paying tax credits and child benefits.

■ Other laws

Below is a list of laws that your new business must be aware of. You might also want to revisit Unit 21, which covers various aspects of business law.

- *Trade Descriptions Acts 1968 and 1972.* It is a criminal offence to give a false or misleading description of goods, services, accommodation and facilities. Businesses may be prosecuted for not abiding by this. With regard to sale prices, if you quote a higher price from which the goods have been reduced, the Act insists that goods must have been sold at the higher price for at least 28 consecutive days during the previous six months if they are to be labelled as sale items.
- *The Sale of Goods Act 1979.* This Act implies five key conditions:
  - the seller must have the right to sell the goods, e.g. they were not stolen by the seller
  - the goods will correspond with any description given when selling them (the seller does not have to describe goods for sale, but if a description is given the goods delivered must fit that description)
  - the goods should be of satisfactory quality
  - the goods should be fit for the buyer's purpose (so a new piece of furniture should not break when used)
  - where goods are sold by sample, the bulk delivered must correspond with the sample.

There are various remedies open to customers who feel that they have not been treated fairly, including claims for damages.

- *Supply of Goods and Services Act 1982.* This implies three terms when services are supplied.
  1. The supplier will carry out the service with reasonable care and skill.
  2. The service will be performed within a reasonable time.
  3. A reasonable price will be charged.
- *Weights and Measures Act 1985.* It is an offence for traders to give short weights of items bought or short measure on fluids. Inspectors will check shops, restaurants and garages to ensure that the dispensers, scales or pumps used are accurate.
- *Consumer Protection Act 1987.* This covers safety regulations for potentially dangerous products such as flammable items and potentially poisonous products such as chemicals and bleach. Warnings should be placed on such items and damages can be claimed against manufacturers of defective products which cause death or injury.

▲ What does this symbol warn the consumer of?

- *Environmental Protection Act 1990.* This controls pollution, noise and waste disposal where this might damage the environment.
- *Food Safety Act 1990.* This requires those businesses that handle food to take all reasonable precautions when manufacturing, transporting, storing, preparing and selling food items to ensure that food sold is perfectly safe. In early 1999 the UK government announced the launch of the Food Standards Agency to monitor such processes and to give the consumer confidence when buying such products. This followed some high profile news items suggesting that food items were not safe, e.g. the BSE beef crisis and outbreaks of E-coli poisoning.
- *Sunday Trading Act 1994.* This Act was to regulate the activities of shops opening on Sundays. Large businesses can open for six hours only between 10am and 6pm. However, small businesses may ignore these rules, as may chemists, service stations and petrol stations.

Health and safety

All business owners are responsible for the safety of their employees and people who visit their premises, e.g. customers. The Management of Health and Safety at Work Regulations require owners to undertake a risk assessment to check how to make their premises as safe as possible. The firm should also have a written Health and Safety Policy that sets out the systems and procedures for ensuring the health and safety of staff, visitors and customers.

Practice point

Visit the Business Link website (www.businesslink.gov.uk). Then, using the links listed below, draw up a policy for a new business idea that you might plan.

- Health, safety, premises
- Managing health, safety and environment
- Create and operate a health, safety and environment policy

By-laws

By-laws are local laws drawn up by local government and approved by central government. Company managers should check with their local council to see what local laws might affect them.

Regulations

There are numerous regulations firms need to abide by. Below are some of the more common ones.

- *COSHH regulations.* The Control of Substances Hazardous to Health regulations set rules about the use and disposal of dangerous chemicals, including paints and cleaning materials as well as more obvious dangerous substances. Owners should assess the specific dangers in their firms and take adequate precautions. These processes should be monitored regularly, and employees should be fully informed of risks and how to prevent them.
- *Data protection.* Firms that store information about customers must comply with the Data Protection Act 1998, which strictly regulates how such information may be collected and used.
- *Distance selling regulations.* These cover purchases made over the internet, by telephone and via mail order. The regulations require the selling firm to provide written details of orders to customers and gives them a 'cooling-off' period of seven days during which such orders can be cancelled.
- *E-commerce regulations.* Companies that sell or advertise over the internet will need to abide by these regulations. Customers should be able to print out and store copies of contracts created online.
- *Fire regulations.* Fire risk assessments should be undertaken and steps implemented to prevent hazards identified. Adequate escape routes and equipment should be employed and all staff need good training in fire safety in the firm's premises.
- *Planning permission and building regulations.* Firms wanting to build or extend premises, or who wish to change the use of a building, will need to seek permission from their local authority.
- *Telephone marketing regulations.* The Privacy and Electronic Communications Regulations 2003 restrict firms' direct marketing activities over the telephone. Individuals can opt-out of such approaches by registering with the Telephone Preference Service. The TPS register must be consulted by firms engaged in telephone marketing.
- *WEEE regulations.* The Waste Electrical and Electronic Equipment regulations affect firms manufacturing or selling electrical items and introduce strict rules about the recycling of such items. Producers must now finance this at the end of the useful life of the product.

Practice point

Choose a business with which you are familiar. (It could be one that you work for, or one you buy from or visit regularly.) Make notes on the regulations and laws that you feel this business must comply with. Explain why you feel each of these laws and regulations is necessary.

Take it further

To what extent do you think these laws and regulations will help or hinder the firm's activities? Consider each of them in turn and explain your reasons for your answers.

Regulatory bodies

A number of bodies have been set up by the UK government and UK industries to monitor standards in various industries. They set standards that must be adhered to. Here are some of the high profile ones.

- *Financial Services Authority.* Regulates the financial services industry including all banks, building societies and insurance companies.
- *Food Standards Agency.* Sets standards of food preparation and delivery to protect the public's health.
- *Gambling Commission.* Regulates the activities of casinos, bingo companies, lottery companies and other forms of gambling.
- *Medicines and Healthcare Products Regulatory Agency.* Ensures the safety of medicines and medical devices
- *Office of Fair Trading (OFT).* Protects customer interests by monitoring business activity to ensure that business is competitive and fair to consumers.

Sources of advice

Running a business on your own can feel very lonely if things are not going smoothly. This is why it is important to build up networks of people you can go to for advice and support through organisations such as the British Chamber of Commerce, the Federation of Small Businesses, Business Link and Trade Associations (see 'Networking', page 188). There are one or two other advice sources that you could consider.

■ DTI

The Department for Trade and Industry (www.dti.gov.uk) is a UK government department that provides a range of start-up support, advice and information for developing your business.

■ Local Enterprise Agencies

These organisations are contracted through Business Link (www.businesslink.gov.uk). They are partnerships between private sector businesses and local authorities. They provide training and consultancy services to local businesses. Visit www.nfea.com to find out more about their activities.

■ Websites

Many websites offer support to business owners, although some are better than others. Be careful of those run to serve the USA, as their laws and regulations will be different to those in the UK. Try to limit your search to sites based in the UK, e.g.:

- www.better-business.co.uk
- www.smallbusinessadvice.org.uk

Financial aspects

Managing your company's finances is every bit as important as complying with the law. Poor financial planning is likely to condemn a business to failure. Paying good attention to those aspects early on in your new business will give you a better chance of success.

One of the new business owner's key initial considerations may be to keep start-up costs as low as possible, and so he or she may choose to rent or lease rather than buy capital assets. There is a trade-off here however. A rented or leased asset never becomes part of the asset value of the business. Instead it becomes a permanent financial commitment as the owner has to continue to pay for it indefinitely. While buying an asset may cause some initial pain financially, it does add to the value of the company. This is just one of the financial aspects of running a business that needs to be considered, and there are a number of others.

Personal survival budget

One of the biggest changes to your life when starting a new business is likely to be your income. You will now need to ensure that your business brings in sufficient income to keep you personally solvent. This requires some planning and is often done by means of a personal survival budget. There are various methods for doing this, but here is one of the easiest (see page 199).

The empty rows are to insert items of income or expenditure that are peculiar to you and are not included in the headings listed. Once the tables are completed, the total for 'Estimated other income' should be deducted from the total for estimated 'Annual expenditure'. The result is the amount of money you will need to take from the business to survive.

Estimated annual expenditure	£s
Mortgage/Rent	
Council tax	
Utilities	
Food	
Clothing	
Savings/Pension	
Motor expenses	
Loan repayments	
Telephone	
Entertainment	
Total (£)	

Estimated other income	£s
Other earned income	
Partner's income	
Benefits received	
Total (£)	

▲ Planning your personal survival budget

This gives you a target to aim for in your new venture. When compared with your cashflow forecast (see pages 202–209), this should show if the business activity will be sufficient for you.

Key Term

Mortgage A large loan for an extended period, normally given for the purchase of property.

Practice point

Complete a personal survival budget for yourself. How much would you need to take out of your business each week to survive?

Cost of premises

Choosing appropriate premises is clearly crucial to the success of your business, so it is not a decision to be taken lightly. You will need to investigate potential sites by visiting commercial estate agents and picking up written details. These days, however, many estate agents are on the internet. So you might begin your search in this way.

When trying to choose an appropriate site, you should consider the following questions.

- Is the site located near potential customers?
- Where is the competition in relation to your site, and how strong are they?
- Is the location accessible by pedestrians and/or near public transport?
- Economically, is the area growing or declining?
- Is there adequate parking for employees, customers and delivery vehicles?
- Is the rent/purchase price affordable?
- Is there room for expansion at a later stage?
- Are there adequate storage facilities on site?
- Will people be able to find you?
- Does the building or location have the amenities you need?

Bear in mind that the more a property meets these criteria, the more expensive it is likely to be – especially if you decide to base yourself in a city centre. Therefore you need to balance these business requirements with the cost of the premises to come up with the best solution for your business.

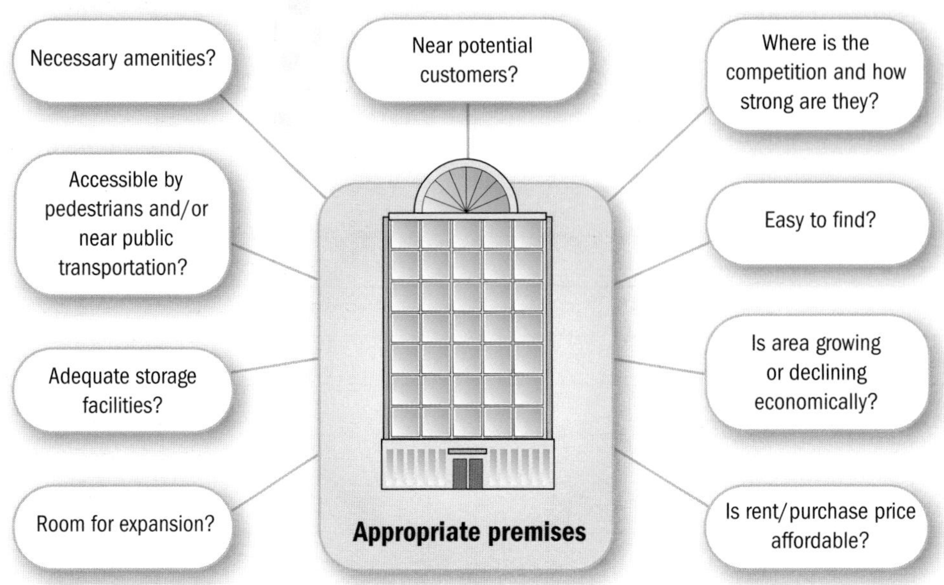

▲ There are many factors to consider when choosing premises for a business

Equipment

Something you need to consider at an early stage is the equipment required to operate the business. In fact, you must decide this before you can begin your cashflow forecast, as these items will be a substantial initial cost to your business. You should therefore produce a capital needs breakdown, which should look something like the one below. Start by listing all the items you will need, then proceed to research prices for each item.

Suppliers

You will also need to decide on appropriate suppliers for any raw materials or products that you will sell. These can often be found on the internet. Obviously, you should search for the suppliers that offer the best range and prices.

Employing staff

Employing staff will be a major expense for your business. Indeed, for many companies it is their largest single expense.

▼ Capital needs breakdown

Shop fittings	£10,000	
Equipment	£1,500	
Total	**£11,500**	
Comprising:	**Shop fittings***	**Equipment****
	Storage & shelf space £4,250	Tills £500
	Seating £750	Lighting £575
	Cupboards £1,500	Scanning equipment £425
	Signage £1,500	
	Counter £2,000	
Totals	**£10,000**	**£1,500**

- First, you will need to pay these people, and this must comply with the current minimum wage legislation (see page 195).
- In addition, you will need to make national insurance payments on behalf of each of your staff.
- Some employers choose to contribute to the pension schemes of their employees, but this is not a legal requirement.

Running costs

There are many other running costs involved in running a business. We will consider these further when we examine the cashflow forecast later in this section (pages 202–209).

Pricing policy

Correctly pricing your products or services is very important to the success of your business. There are a number of methods you can use to determine a satisfactory price.

Cost-plus pricing

This involves calculating the cost of making the item you are selling and adding a percentage for profit. For example, if you calculate that the cost of raw materials plus labour for making a product is £10 and you decide to add a 25% mark-up for profit, the price will be £10 + £2.50 = £12.50. This method seems simple and acceptable. However, it does raise one or two questions.

- It is often hard to calculate the exact cost of making something. How do you allocate costs such as advertising and rent, for example, to the production cost?
- How do you calculate the cost of providing a service?
- If something is very cheap to make, should you necessarily charge a very low price and miss out on the chance to make additional profit?

Demand-orientated pricing

Often firms are keen to maximise profits and therefore decide to use this method. It fixes a price on the level of demand rather than on the cost of production. In other words, the opportunity is taken to charge a price well in excess of the costs of production because of the demand. Here are some examples of this method.

- *Penetration pricing.* This method is used when launching a new product or service, when the company is unsure how popular the new product is likely to be. If it is felt that some effort will be needed to build the market share for the product, a low price may be set for the product initially. This is intended to encourage prospective customers to try the product and to build market share quickly. Once market share has been established the price can be increased to a level at which decent profits can be made. Care has to be taken at this stage, as customers may only be buying the product because it is cheap and the increased price may put them off continuing to buy.
- *Skimming.* This is the opposite of penetration pricing. If a firm is confident that a product will sell very well when it is launched, there is a chance to charge a high price at the outset to maximise profits. When the initial demand starts to fall, the price may be lowered to attract further customers. This technique was used very successfully with Sony's PlayStation2, which launched at £299 in the UK and was selling for less than half that two years later.
- *Promotional pricing.* When a product or service has been on the market for some time and demand is beginning to fall, reducing the price temporarily may stimulate renewed interest in it.
- *Competition pricing.* This is used in very competitive markets where a slightly higher price than a competitor's can result in a business losing customers. In this case prices are set to match those of competitors and firms closely monitor the pricing of competitor companies so that they can match any changes.

Remember

A business rarely uses the same pricing strategy all the time and will often change this more than once during the life cycle of a particular product or service, so your strategy might include more than one method.

Thinking point

Identify the pricing strategy you would choose in each of the following situations. Give reasons for your decisions.

- You are launching a new CD produced by a local band that are, as yet, virtually unknown to the general public.
- Your firm is launching a new type of high capacity MP3 player. Your market research suggests that initial demand will be very high.
- You are opening a new sandwich shop in your town. There are a number of competitors reasonably close by.
- You are selling a unique service offering custom-made jewellery to a select income-rich market.

Cashflow forecasting

More small businesses fail as a result of bad cash planning than any other reason. Therefore, it is vital that a new entrepreneur gets to grips with this important topic at an early stage. It is a known fact that a number of businesses with full order books fail simply because they do not properly manage their cashflow.

Case study

Mick the mechanic

Mick was a car mechanic who was very good at his job and had many regular customers. However, he was not very good at getting his customers to pay. Unfortunately he was not getting cash into his business quickly enough (he had a tendency to allow too much credit to his regular customers and friends). Nor did he chase people who owed him money. Ultimately this slack financial management cost him his business, because he reached a stage where he could not pay his bills. What he had failed to appreciate was the importance of cash to his success in business. He felt that because he had a long list of customers he would survive. That said, he failed to recognise that without good cash balances he would be unable to:

- pay his employees
- keep up with the lease on his premises
- continue to make repayments on his bank loan
- make payments to his suppliers.

Ultimately it was a combination of these factors that forced him out of business. Ironically, his business was making good profits. However, profits do not pay bills. Cash pays bills, and if you cannot pay your bills promptly, you will fail.

1. Identify the key mistakes Mick made. What circumstances might have caused him to make such errors? ✓
2. Explain methods that Mick could have used to avoid these problems. ✓✓
3. What lessons should a new entrepeneur draw from Mick's experiences? ✓✓✓

Mick was approached at one point by a major local car dealer to do some work for them. The arrangements were that he would not be salaried but would need to invoice the company for the work that he completed on a monthly basis after completion of jobs. Mick believed that this could be his salvation.

- Mick's friends thought he would be a fool not to take the deal. What do you think?
- What problems can you foresee from this new arrangement?

Thinking point

The following cashflow cycle shows seasonal fluctuations, but the bank and entrepreneur would be concerned about this trend. Why? What do you think the business owner should be doing in a situation such as this?

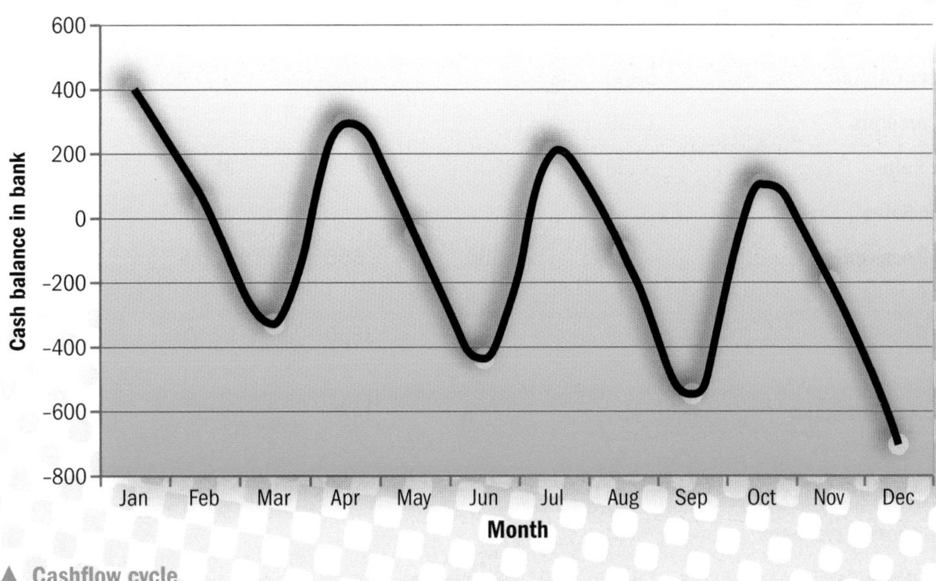

▲ Cashflow cycle

If an entrepreneur is aware of the cashflow situation that is developing, then it is often possible to put in place strategies to avert crises. It is possible to plan ahead by preparing a cashflow forecast. This should highlight periods when problems may appear. The cashflow forecast lists all of the cash receipts and payments month by month and keeps a track of the monthly bank balance.

Cashflow forecasts were discussed at length in Unit 5 (Book 1), so you should look there for a detailed discussion of this topic. Meanwhile, on page 204 is a reminder of what such a forecast should look like when completed. The cashflow forecast on page 204 is for Piotr Grudzinski, who plans to set up a shop selling second-hand CDs and DVDs. The forecast is for the months January to April.

Profit and loss budgets/accounts

Once a cashflow forecast has been constructed it is possible to use this document to produce a forecasted profit and loss account and balance sheet for the company to show projected levels of profits. You may have seen how to construct these documents in Unit 5 (Book 1). Here we see how to produce the statements beginning with a cashflow forecast.

On page 205 there is the full cashflow forecast for Piotr Grudzinski.

This is the opening balance in the bank at the start of the year

Balance B/F is the same figure as the Balance C/F for the previous month

The Totals column summarises all of the months shown on the forecast

The balance B/F figure at the start of the forecast

	January £	February £	March £	April £	Totals £
Balance B/F	0	-361	-180	52	0
Income					
Owners Capital	5000				5000
Total receipts	1500				1500
Cash Sales	3000	3500	3000	3500	13,000
Credit Sales				1000	1000
Rent Received	650	650	650	650	2600
Total Receipts	**10,150**	**4150**	**3650**	**5150**	**23,100**
Total Cash Available	**10,150**	**3789**	**3470**	**5202**	**23,100**
Expenses					
Initial Stock Purchases	3000				3000
Cash Purchases	650	950	400	500	2500
Credit Purchases				400	400
Gas and Electricity	123	123	123	123	492
Fixtures and Fittings	1450				1450
Equipment	2150				2150
Drawings	1400	1400	1400	1400	5600
Advertising	300	55	55	55	465
Insurance	93	93	93	93	372
Rent and Rates	740	740	740	740	2960
Wages	550	550	550	550	2200
Overdraft Interest	0	3	2	0	5
Loan Repayments	55	55	55	55	220
Total Payments	**10,511**	**3969**	**3418**	**3916**	**21,813**
Balance C/F	**-361**	**-180**	**52**	**1286**	**1286**

Total Receipts is all the Income items added together

Total Cash Available is Balance B/F plus Total Receipts

Balance C/F is Total Cash Available minus Total Payments

Total Payments is all the Expense items added together

These two figures should be the same. This shows that your forecast balances

▲ Cashflow forecast January – April

	Jan £	Feb £	Mar £	April £	May £	June £	July £	Aug £	Sept £	Oct £	Nov £	Dec £	Totals £	
Balance B/F	**0**	**-361**	**-180**	**52**	**1286**	**2520**	**3754**	**4988**	**6222**	**8076**	**10,315**	**12,554**	**0**	
Income														
Owners Capital	5000												5000	**M**
Bank Loan	1500												1500	**L**
Cash Sales	3000	3500	3000	4500	4500	4500	4500	4500	5500	6250	6250	6250	56,250	**A**
Rent Received	650	650	650	650	650	650	650	650	650	650	650	650	7800	**D**
Total Receipts	**10,150**	**4150**	**3650**	**5150**	**5150**	**5150**	**5150**	**5150**	**6150**	**6900**	**6900**	**6900**	**70,550**	
Total Cash Available	**10,150**	**3789**	**3470**	**5202**	**6436**	**7670**	**8904**	**10,139**	**12,372**	**14,976**	**17,215**	**19,454**	**70,550**	
Expenses														
Initial Stock Purchases	3000												3000	**B**
Cash Purchases	650	950	400	900	900	900	900	900	1280	1300	1300	1300	11,680	**C**
Gas and Electricity	123	123	123	123	123	123	123	123	123	123	123	123	1476	**J**
Fixtures and Fittings	1450												1450	
Equipment	2150												2150	
Drawings	1400	1400	1400	1400	1400	1400	1400	1400	1400	1400	1400	1400	16,800	**N**
Advertising	300	55	55	55	55	55	55	55	55	200	200	200	1340	**I**
Insurance	93	93	93	93	93	93	93	93	93	93	93	93	1116	**H**
Rent and Rates	740	740	740	740	740	740	740	740	740	740	740	740	8880	**E**
Wages	550	550	550	550	550	550	550	550	550	750	750	750	7200	**F**
Overdraft Interest	0	3	2	0	0	0	0	0	0	0	0	0	5	**G**
Loan Repayments	55	55	55	55	55	55	55	55	55	55	55	55	660	**G**
Total Payments	**10,511**	**3969**	**3418**	**3916**	**3916**	**3916**	**3916**	**3916**	**4296**	**4661**	**4661**	**4661**	**55,757**	
Balance C/F	**-361**	**-180**	**52**	**1286**	**2520**	**3754**	**4988**	**6222**	**8076**	**10,315**	**12,554**	**14,793**	**14,793**	**K**

▲ Full cashflow forecast for Piotr Grudzinski

We need a little additional information to complete a profit and loss and balance sheet for Piotr as follows.

1. Piotr expects to finish the year with stocks of £3,250. (This must be a rough estimate, as this is twelve months into the future.)
2. He will depreciate his equipment at 15% per year based on original cost and his fixtures and fittings at 20% per year.

We can now construct his profit and loss account using the figures in the Totals column of his forecast.

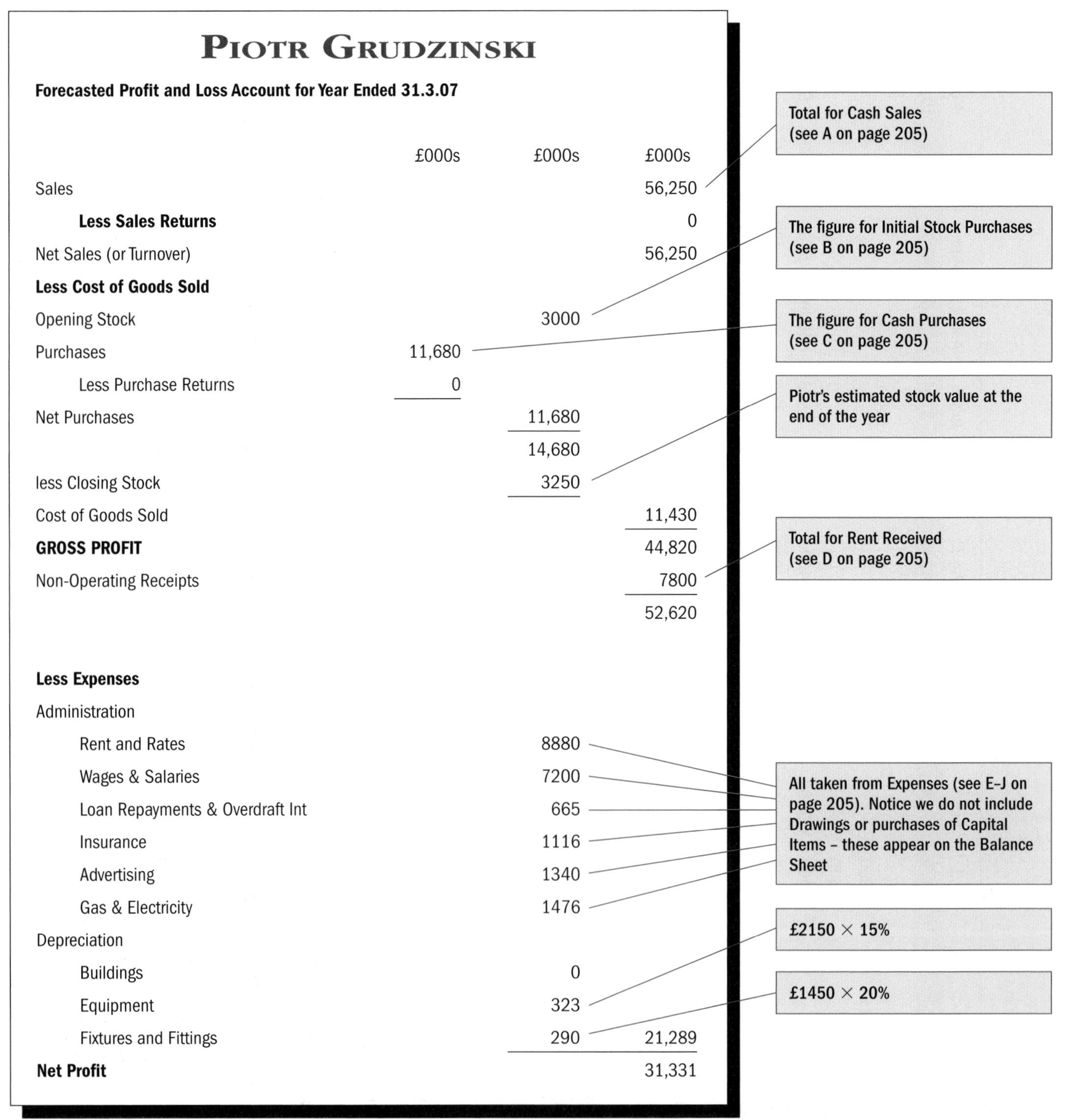

PIOTR GRUDZINSKI

Forecasted Profit and Loss Account for Year Ended 31.3.07

	£000s	£000s	£000s
Sales			56,250
Less Sales Returns			0
Net Sales (or Turnover)			56,250
Less Cost of Goods Sold			
Opening Stock		3000	
Purchases	11,680		
Less Purchase Returns	0		
Net Purchases		11,680	
		14,680	
less Closing Stock		3250	
Cost of Goods Sold			11,430
GROSS PROFIT			44,820
Non-Operating Receipts			7800
			52,620
Less Expenses			
Administration			
Rent and Rates		8880	
Wages & Salaries		7200	
Loan Repayments & Overdraft Int		665	
Insurance		1116	
Advertising		1340	
Gas & Electricity		1476	
Depreciation			
Buildings		0	
Equipment		323	
Fixtures and Fittings		290	21,289
Net Profit			31,331

▲ Forecasted accounts for Piotr Grudzinski

Carrying the net profit forward, we can now produce a forecasted balance sheet for Piotr.

PIOTR GRUDZINSKI

Forecasted Balance Sheet as at 31.3.07

	Cost	Accumulated Depreciation	Net Book Value
	£	£	£
Fixed Assets			
Buildings	0	0	0
Equipment	2150	323	1828
Fixtures and Fittings	1450	290	1160
	3600	613	2988
Current Assets			
Stock		3250	
Debtors		0	
Bank		14,793	
Cash		0	
		18,043	
Less Current Liabilities			
Creditors	0		
Overdraft	0		
		0	
Working Capital			18,043
			21,031
Less Long-Term Liabilities			
Bank Loan			1500
NET ASSETS			19,531
FINANCED BY			
Capital			
Opening Capital			5000
Add Net Profit			31,331
			36,331
Less Drawings			16,800
			19,531

Piotr's estimated stock value at the end of the year

The final balance C/F (see K on page 205)

See L on page 205

See M on page 205

This comes from the bottom of the Profit and Loss account

This is the amount the owner pays him or herself (see N on page 205)

▲ Forecasted balance sheet for Piotr Grudzinski

Askham Bryan College LIBRARY BOOK

Practice point

Using the following information you should create a cashflow forecast, profit and loss account and balance sheet for Salma Rashid. Salma is planning to open a new business offering a personal jewellery design service. Customers will have a consultation, view samples of hand-made jewellery and she will make pieces to order. She plans to run the business through craft fairs in her local area. She has done extensive research and has ascertained the following.

- Initial stock purchases will be £500.
- Hiring stalls at craft fairs will cost £150 per month.
- Salma will require £2,500-worth of equipment.
- She has decided to pay herself £1,500 per month. This will appear as 'Drawings' on the forecast.
- Advertising will cost a regular £25 per month.
- Insurances total £24 per month.
- Wages will be £1,000 per month.
- Salma has agreed to borrow £3,000 from the bank. Repayments on this will be £55 per month. She is also putting £2,500 of her own savings into the venture.
- Overdraft interest will be charged at a rate of 10% per year. This will be paid each month following an overdrawn end of month balance.
- Sales and purchases for the first twelve months will be as shown in the table opposite.

Salma Rashid's sales and purchases for the first twelve months of business

	Sales	Purchases
January	3,000	300
February	3,000	300
March	3,000	300
April	3,000	300
May	3,000	300
June	3,000	300
July	3,000	300
August	3,000	300
September	3,000	300
October	4,000	400
November	4,000	400
December	4,000	400

Additional information

- Salma expects to finish the year with stocks of £600.
- She will depreciate her equipment at 15% per year based on original cost.

Compile a full cashflow forecast, profit and loss account and balance sheet for the first year of a new business using these details.

Break even

The cashflow forecast can also be used to calculate the break-even point (BEP) of the business. This is a particularly helpful exercise for a new business venture, as it will indicate at an early stage the level of sales that the business will need in order to stay afloat. Break-even analysis was discussed in detail in Unit 2 (Book 1), so you might like to review that now. Here is a brief reminder of the method.

The break-even point can be worked out as follows.

$$\text{BEP} = \frac{\text{Total fixed costs}}{\text{Unit contribution (selling price – variable cost per unit)}}$$

To complete this, therefore, you will need to classify the expenses of your business on the cashflow forecast as either fixed or variable costs (variable costs are those that change as more products are sold). The totals for each of the fixed costs on the cashflow can be added up to get the total fixed costs. The other costs must be variable. They need to be added together, then divided by the number of products sold to calculate the variable cost per unit.

For example, assume that for a particular business:
Total fixed costs for the year = £12,000
Total variable costs for the year = £10,000
Sales for the year = 2500 products
Selling price for each product = £10

$$\text{BEP} = \frac{\pounds 12{,}000}{\pounds 10 - (\pounds 10{,}000 / 2500)}$$

$$\text{BEP} = \frac{\pounds 12{,}000}{\pounds 10 - \pounds 4}$$

$$\text{BEP} = \frac{\pounds 12{,}000}{\pounds 6} = 2000 \text{ sales}$$

This tells us the firm must make 2000 sales in the year to break even. We can then divide this by 12 to get a monthly target (167 sales per month) or by 52 to get a weekly target (39 sales per week).

Practice point

Joe runs a café, and he has predicted the following figures:

Total fixed costs for the year = £11,250

Total variable costs for the year = £12,000

Sales for the year = 8,000 meals

Average selling price for each meal = £4

Calculate Joe's weekly breakeven number of meals served.

Take it further

What would you conclude if Joe's total fixed costs for the year were actually £22,500?

Sources of finance

All new business ventures require some form of finance, whether you are starting a new airline and need billions of pounds or you are launching a cleaning service and simply need to buy some buckets, cloths and sponges! So whatever you plan, money will make it happen, but where can you raise money from? There are several sources that you can consider. Some of them will represent a debt to the business and have to be repaid, while others will not. First, we consider the sources that do not become creditors for the firm.

Own savings

This is a great source of finance, and probably an essential one if you hope to persuade anyone else to help finance the plan. The beauty of using your own savings is that it does not cost you anything to use the money, other than the loss of the interest that you would have earned had you put it into the bank. You are also unlikely to turn yourself down, so it is a safe bet you will be able to get the money!

Your own financial stake in the business will also persuade others, such as banks, to lend you more. Unlike loans for consumer goods where you can often borrow the full amount of the purchase price, banks may not lend you more than you have put in yourself when setting up a new business venture. Banks want to be convinced that they will get their money back. They feel that if you have an equal stake in the venture, then you are more likely to work hard to make it succeed.

Gifts from friends and relatives

This is another source of finance that involves no repayment and no interest.

Grants and sponsorship

Grants are non-repayable sums of money to aid new businesses. Although they are not available to all new entrepreneurs there are some sources that might be considered.

Regional Selective Assistance

RSA is a system of grants offered by the UK government to provide help on new business projects with fixed capital expenditure over £500,000. The government recognises that certain areas of the UK need more assistance in creating jobs, so they have appointed a number of Assisted Areas, and RSA is only available in these areas.

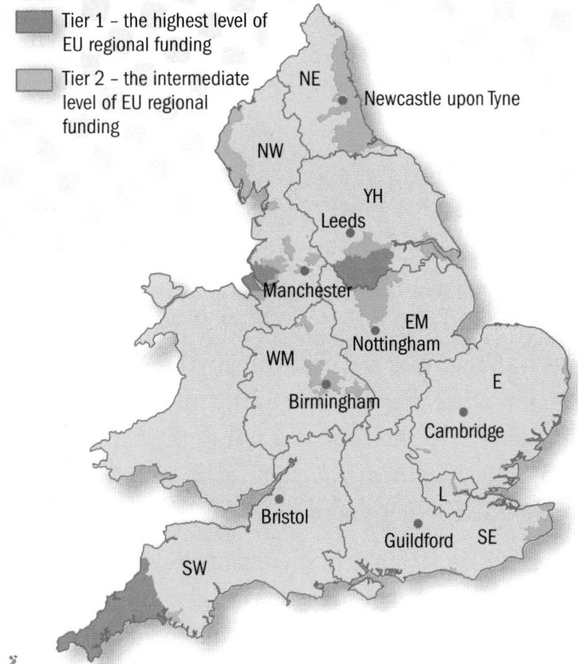

▲ Regional selective assistance map

Source: www.berr.gov.uk

Note that this map is currently being redrawn as decisions are taken about how RSA will be allocated from 2007 to 2013. Once the new map is completed it will be available on the Department for Business, Enterprise and Regulatory Reform's Regional Economic Development page (www.berr.gov.uk).

Limited companies, partnerships or sole traders are all eligible for RSA grants, but they are not available simply to transfer jobs from one part of the country to another. RSA is available for:

- establishing a new business
- expanding or modernising an existing business
- setting up research and development facilities.

EU convergence region funding

The EU makes money available to support projects that will increase economic growth and create jobs in disadvantaged regions. Areas of the UK that qualify are Cornwall, the Isles of Scilly and large areas of Wales. For more details on this policy see Unit 39.

The Prince's Trust

The Prince's Trust is aimed particularly at young people who have found school difficult, or who have been in care, in trouble with the law or are long-term unemployed. The aim is to offer practical support that may include sponsoring, training, mentoring and financial assistance for 14–30 year olds.

For young people who wish to start up in business but have failed to raise financial support from other sources, the Prince's Trust offers some hope. The Trust is able to offer:

- low interest loans of up to £5,000
- grants of up to £1,500 in certain circumstances
- a grant of up to £250 for test marketing
- marketing support and specialist advice
- regular advice from a volunteer business mentor.

Visit www.princes-trust.org.uk to find out more.

Loans and borrowing

Let's now consider the sources of business finance that require some form of repayment.

Bank loans

Loan amounts available range from a few thousand pounds up to hundreds of thousands of pounds, depending on the project proposed and the amount of security available to back the loan. They are normally granted for an extended period for the purchase of capital items.

Practice point

Research a number of financial institutions that offer business loans. You should compare the deals offered by copying and completing the following table. You may find some information on the internet. Alternatively, you may need to visit some branches to get further details. You should now decide which of them is currently offering the best deal. Explain your reasons for your choice.

Name of lender	Amounts offered	Interest rate	Periods available	Fees or charges	Special features

Overdrafts

Overdrafts are not used for purchasing capital items. Instead, they are used to ease temporary cashflow problems. Perhaps the business is owed some money shortly but has a bill to pay immediately and there is not enough cash in the bank to meet the payment. In these circumstances an overdraft is the best type of finance.

Overdrafts are only to be used on a short-term basis as the interest rates are normally significantly higher than those for a bank loan. Therefore, taking out an overdraft for an extended period will prove costly.

Overdraft facilities are normally granted for a period of time, e.g. one year. It would be available for use on any number of occasions during that year. As long as it is used responsibly, the bank is likely to renew the facility for further years, for a small fee. Once again, the best advice would be to shop around for the best deals.

Mortgages

A mortgage is a large loan, normally given for the purchase of property. A typical mortgage will last 25 years. It is always secured on the property that is being purchased.

Practice point

Research a number of financial institutions that offer business overdrafts. You should compare the deals offered by copying and completing the following table. You may find some information on the internet. Alternatively, you may need to visit some branches to get further details. You should now decide which of them is currently offering the best deal. Explain your reasons for your choice.

Name of lender	Amounts offered	Interest rate	Periods available	Fees or charges	Special features

Leasing

Leasing is an alternative to buying capital assets. To buy equipment such as computers or machinery can be very expensive, particularly for a new business. Leasing offers a way to avoid this initial expenditure, so it can be a significant help to a new firm's cashflow situation. There are two basic types of leasing arrangement available.

- *Direct lease.* With this method the firm chooses an asset it would like to acquire, then arranges for the leasing company to buy it on its behalf. The leasing company rents it to the firm for an extended period. The asset remains the property of the leasing company. Once the lease ends it must be returned to the leasing company. Sometimes, at the end of a lease, the leasing company may allow the firm to buy the asset from it for a minimal cost.
- *Leaseback.* An asset already owned by the company can be sold to the leasing firm. The company then leases it back. As with a direct lease, the asset remains the property of the leasing company.

Venture capital

Venture capitalists are groups of investors who specialise in supporting new ventures that may be considered risky by traditional lenders such as banks. They will interview the managers of new businesses that are looking for financial support, and those that present the most promising plans will be supported.

Venture capitalists are different from other sources of finance in that they will normally invest by purchasing shares in the business rather than simply loaning money. Consequently the venture capitalists actually have a stake in helping the company to succeed and grow, since they will ultimately make their profit by selling the shares. Venture capitalists will often take seats on the board of directors of the firm so that they can provide technical and expert help and advice to the firm. In this way the business benefits from their experience and is more likely to succeed as a result.

Key Term

Leasing Renting a capital item such as a car or machinery.

Venture capital Venture capitalists invest money into new businesses that are high risk.

Record keeping

It is important that careful financial records of the business operations are kept. Ultimately the business owner will have to answer to HM Revenue and Customs (aka 'the taxman') for profits earned and VAT collected, so meticulous records are very important. Employing a good accountant will help with this, but all staff should be aware of the need for keeping thorough records of all financial transactions.

Outcome activity 37.3

This activity continues the business plan begun in Outcome activity 37.1.

Pass 

Write notes describing the legal and financial aspects that will affect the start-up of the business.

Merit 

Write notes that assess the implications of the legal and financial aspects that will affect the start-up of your chosen business.

Grading tips

Pass 

There is a lot to cover for this criteria. Therefore you should go through the preceding section of this unit (pages 190–212) and ensure that you have considered all the legal and financial aspects discussed. Pick out those that are relevant to your business and describe them. You should describe the implications of your choice of legal status, and all laws and regulations that will affect your business. You should also show your awareness of the necessity for a personal survival budget, the sources of finance that will be available to you, the potential costs of equipment, supplies and employing staff, along with the necessity for producing financial statements such as pricing policy, break even, cashflow forecast, and profit and loss account and balance sheet. At this stage you do not need to produce the financial documents; simply describe them and what they are used for.

Merit 

You will now revisit the legal and financial aspects you described in P4 above, and will assess the impact that each of them will have on your business idea. In order to do this it will be necessary to describe the systems that will need to be in place to ensure that each financial and legal requirement is met. For example, you may need to describe the recording systems that will be required for your tax and VAT liabilities.

37.4 Producing an outline start-up proposal

This section presents you with a checklist of areas that you must cover in your business planning. Following this list should give you the best chance of being successful. You will be preparing a business plan for the assignment for this unit, so you should follow this list to ensure that you have covered all of the necessary areas. All of these areas have been discussed previously in this and other units.

Business proposal

Most commercial banks produce model business plans that could be used to get you started on your proposal. However, bear in mind that they will not avoid you having to do your own thinking and research. They merely provide a framework for your thoughts.

As we have discussed previously, business planning is an opportunity to review your ideas, gather information to inform your planning and to review those ideas in the light of research conducted. It should also enable you to set realistic targets and goals for the new business along with a list of tasks that must be performed to give the business the best chance of success.

Some of the commercially available business plan models are better than others, so make sure if you use one that it fully covers the areas listed below.

Your plan will need to include the following components.

Section 1: Type of business

This should include the following.

- A description of the business.
- The aims and objectives of the business.
- Its USP and how a competitive edge will be maintained.
- Expected levels of demand.
- A PESTLE analysis for the business.
- Your motivations in setting up the business.

Section 2: Target market

This should include the following.

- Your market research objectives.
- The research brief and proposal.
- The research plan – including details of primary and secondary methods used.
- A summary of the data collected.
- An analysis and evaluation of the data – including details of sales forecasts, market trends, customer buyer behaviour, competition analysis and a SWOT analysis of the plan.

Section 3: Human resource plan

This should include the following.

- A skills gap analysis.
- Details of methods you will adopt for filling the skills gaps identified.
- An action plan with defined timescales for filling the gaps with approximate costs.
- Details of your requirements for additional staff/partners for the business.
- Details of the contracts of employment you will use.
- Your plans for paying your employees and complying with minimum wage legislation.
- The hours of work you will require from your employees and how you intend to comply with the working time regulations.
- Your policy on discrimination.

Section 4: Legal and physical resource plans

This should include the following.

- Your chosen legal status with reasons for choice.
- Your legal liability position.
- The trading terms and conditions you will use.
- Your responsibilities for trading standards with your chosen business.
- Licences required and where they will be obtained from.
- Details of records you will need to keep.
- Policies you will use for resolving grievances and other problems in the business.
- Details of the main national and local laws you will need to abide by.

- Details of the main regulations and bylaws you will need to abide by.
- Your health and safety policy.
- Details of how you will comply with fire regulations.
- Your insurance requirements to cover your legal liabilities.
- The premises you will use along with any planning permissions you will need to obtain.
- Details of any other laws peculiar to your business.

Section 5: Financial resources plan

This should include the following.

- Your personal survival budget.
- Details of costs of chosen premises.
- Your capital needs budget.
- Your choice of suppliers, with reasons for your choices.
- Details of your main running costs for the business.
- Your pricing policy with justification of your choice along with sample prices.
- A twelve-month cashflow forecast.
- A forecast profit and loss account and balance sheet.
- A break-even analysis for the business.
- Details of the sources of finance chosen for the business.

Section 6: Growth and development plan

This should include details of how you see the business developing in the long term. What scope is there for expansion and what form(s) do you see that taking?

Section 7: Financial contingency plans

It is important that the business has some finances to fall back on in times of difficulty. These could be provided by the owners of the business through their savings or assets. Alternatively, the contingency plan could be to borrow from a bank or other source of finance. Whatever you choose, your plan should detail what assets or lending you could draw on if the need arises. To do this you might look back at the Sources of finance section (pages 209–11) to see what other possible avenues could be pursued.

Outcome activity 37.4

This activity continues the business plan begun in Outcome activity 37.1.

Pass **p5**

Produce a written outline proposal for starting up your new small business following an acceptable business model. To complete this task you will first need to produce a written business plan. This could be done using a commercially available business plan template such as those supplied by most high street banks. Second, your teacher will arrange for you to present your plan to a bank manager, who may provide funding for your venture. This will take the form of an interview, and the manager has asked you to present your proposals in the form of a short presentation.

Distinction **d1**

Present a comprehensive business proposal that addresses all relevant aspects of business start-up.

Grading tips

Pass 

Ensure that you have covered all of the key business plan areas: type of business, target market, human resources plan, legal plan, physical resources plan, financial resources plan, growth and development plan and your financial contingency plan. You should prepare a short presentation using visual aids and handout notes which explains your plan, is persuasive and gives arguments to support your decisions. You should conclude your presentation with the opportunity for the bank manager to ask you questions.

Distinction 

You will need to draw all your evidence together into a comprehensive business proposal that addresses all relevant aspects of your business start up. To do this you are strongly recommended to go through the checklist in the final section of this unit (pages 213–14) and ensure that all of the areas listed are covered. The previous pass and merit criteria tasks that you have done in the earlier Outcome activities will already have covered a lot of the evidence you will need. However, for distinction you will need to present all of the evidence in a professional-looking and fluent proposal. You should seek guidance on the preparation of your proposal from your tutor and/or a business mentor if possible. You should make improvements and revisions to your plan in the light of their comments before presenting your final version.

End of unit test

1 What factors might persuade you to buy an existing business rather than setting one up from scratch?

2. You are considering opening a new mobile phone shop. Prepare a SWOT analysis for such a venture.

3. What factors might persuade you to start a franchised business rather than setting one up from scratch?

4. Choose three new products that you have seen launched in the last few months. Identify the USP for each.

5. Give three reasons why it is crucial for a new business to have a clear idea of its target market.

6. State what you consider to be the three most critical personal skills a new business owner will need. Explain why you feel they are so important.

7. Many sole traders prefer to stay sole traders even when given the opportunity to become a partnership or limited company. List the reasons why this might be so.

8. Give three reasons why it is not a good idea to put all of your savings into a new business venture.

9. What are the potential problems associated with poor record keeping for a business owner?

10. What are the main benefits of doing a cashflow forecast?

11. 'Demand-orientated pricing strategies simply rip off customers.' As a business owner, what would be your reaction to this statement?

12. Identifying the range of regulations, bylaws, licensing laws and standards that a new company must abide by is not easy. Where might a new business owner go to gain help in this area?

13. Why do you think the law requires that within two months of starting work, an employer must provide employees with a written statement of the main terms of their contract of employment?

14. What is the purpose of a personal survival budget and why is it important for a new business owner?

15. What are the main benefits of doing a forecast profit and loss account and balance sheet?

Books

Barrow, C, 2002, *Financial Management for the Small Business, 5th Edition,* Kogan Page Ltd

Barrow, C, 2002, *The Complete Small Business Guide, 7th Edition,* Capstone Publishing Ltd

Butler, D, 2000, *Business Planning; A Guide to Small Business Start-Up* , Butterworth-Heinemann

Covello, JA and Hazelgren, BJ, 1994, *The Complete Book of Business Plans,* Sourcebooks, Inc

McMullan, D, 2002, *Be Your Own Boss,* Kogan Page

Stone, P, 2002, *The Ultimate Business Plan,* How To Books

Websites

www.berr.gov.uk – The Department for Business, Enterprise and Regulatory Reform offers a wide range of advice to business owners

www.better-business.co.uk – Help for business people

www.businesslink.gov.uk – Business Link is a government-sponsored organisation that gives detailed advice to business people

www.lib.gla.ac.uk/Depts/MOPS/Stats/UKStats.shtml – Glasgow University portal to UK statistics

www.nfea.com – The National Federation of Enterprise Agencies

www.princes-trust.org.uk – Charity set up by Prince Charles to help disadvantaged young people to start in business

www.smallbusinessadvice.org.uk – More help for business people

www.statistics.gov.uk – The government site for statistics, including those on economy

www.tradingstandards.gov.uk – The office responsible for upholding consumer interests in the UK

www.young-enterprise.org.uk – Young Enterprise is a charity that encourages new young business people

http://youngentrepreneur.com – Advice for young business owners

Grading criteria	Outcome activity	Page number
To achieve a pass grade the evidence shows that the learner is able to:		
P1 Present the initial business idea using relevant criteria	37.1	180
P2 Describe how to identify the target market	37.1	180
P3 Describe the skills needed to run the business successfully and what areas require further development	37.2	189
P4 Describe the legal and financial aspects that will affect the start-up of the business	37.3	212
P5 Produce a written outline proposal for starting up a new small business following an acceptable business model	37.4	214
To achieve a merit grade the evidence shows that, in addition to the pass criteria, the learner is able to:		
M1 Explain and justify methods used to identify the target market for the proposed business	37.1	180
M2 Analyse the skills development needed to run the business successfully	37.2	189
M3 Assess the implications of legal and financial aspects that will affect the start-up of the business	37.3	212
To achieve a distinction grade the evidence must show that, in addition to the pass and merit criteria, the learner is able to:		
D1 Present a comprehensive business proposal that addresses all relevant aspects of business start-up	37.4	214

38 Understanding business ethics

Introduction

The word 'ethics' comes from the Greek word 'ethikos', meaning 'character'. One way to think about business ethics is to consider the ethics of people you might know. For instance, if you were asked about people who live in your area, you might describe someone who is funny, someone well known for doing good things (being nice), someone it might be better to stay away from (a 'dodgy' character), etc. Individuals have different standards of ethics and so do businesses. Ethical behaviour is good behaviour; it measures up to standards and no one suffers from it.

What you need to learn

On completion of this unit you should:

1. Understand the meaning and importance of ethics in the business world
2. Understand the implications of businesses operating ethically
3. Know the social implications of business ethics
4. Understand the ethical concerns facing different communities.

Consider this

A farmer growing bananas gets only a penny of the 30 pence we pay for each one in the supermarket. A garment maker in China gets 16 pence per hour for working long hours making the fashionable clothes you could be wearing. Should we, as consumers, be interested in these things? You might think not.

How about this then? If we pump carbon dioxide into our atmosphere at the present rate (from burning oil and petrol for instance), we will change the planet forever. Sea levels will rise, coastal areas will disappear, large areas of London will flood, and we will suffer increasingly from extreme weather. Perhaps we should all be interested in this?

38.1 The meaning and importance of ethics in the business world

Operational activities

'Business operations' refers to what a business actually does. So, a factory making clothing contains machines and has people running them; it makes and receives deliveries; materials are moved about; people travel to and from the factory. 'Operational management' is about controlling how a business works, so that it achieves the aims and objectives set by strategic management. Wherever a business operates, there are effects – some good, some not so good.

What is business ethics?

An organisation works to achieve corporate aims. These are dictated by the kind of organisation we are speaking about. A public service organisation, for instance, must deliver government services such as social services; a private business seeks profit for the benefit of its owners. Business managers in these organisations are paid to make decisions that will help the business to achieve its aims and objectives. These decisions can be related to staff, financial investment, marketing strategy, products or location.

Operational activities refer to anything a business does in order to achieve its aims. Marks & Spencer, Asda, Tesco and Sainsbury have retail outlets all over the UK. This is an aspect of these businesses operating in order to sell. Their other operational activities include buying, storing, delivering, advertising and so on.

Issues connected to ethics in business arise because some businesses make poor decisions. These can hurt local people, staff or the customer. Other businesses make mistakes. Sometimes, individuals within businesses act selfishly or incompetently. Whatever the reasons, business ethics is now a vital part of management.

Thinking point

Consider at least two businesses that you have investigated as part of your course. Describe their activities. What does the business do? (Buy and sell? Deliver? Manufacture? Provide a service?)

When a business has a strategic direction, it knows what it is trying to achieve. Managers then take operational decisions.

Remember

Operational activities are the day-to-day actions taken by a firm to achieve its primary purpose.

Definitions of business ethics

Ethics are to do with what's 'right' and 'wrong'. When a particular business seeks to achieve its aims, is it right that it might do so by paying low wages? Is it right that our planet is damaged through business activities? Ethics plays an increasingly important role in business today. A business is part of society and, just as society requires a certain standard of behaviour from individuals, it also expects businesses to abide by similar standards.

Business ethics is therefore the application of **ethical values** to business behaviour. It applies to any and all aspects of business conduct – from boardroom strategies and how companies treat their suppliers to sales techniques and accounting practices. Ethics goes beyond the legal requirements for a company and is therefore a matter of choice. Business ethics applies to the conduct both of individuals and to the organisation as a whole. It is about how a company does its business and how its activities affect all of its 'stakeholders' (see pages 232–35).

Ethical behaviour from a particular business is different from an ethical business. An ethical business sets out from the beginning to work ethically. Ethics for such a business form a part of its strategic aims. Two well-known businesses that work like this are The Body Shop and the Co-Operative Bank.

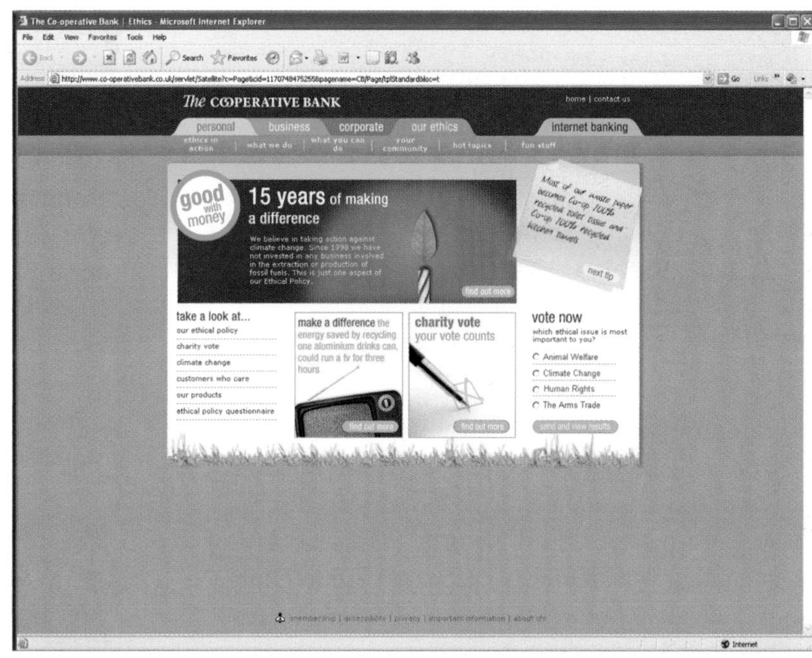

▲ Co-Operative Bank: ethical banking

Key Term

Ethical values The standards that are set by a business or individuals that control their behaviour.

Ethical activities

An ethical business has a broad agenda and focuses on making a positive contribution to the community. An ethical bank such as the Co-Operative Bank, states that it seeks to make the world a better place by taking a different approach to banking. In the case of this type of business, ethics becomes at least as high a priority as profitability.

Business values

The Body Shop presents a very clear and identifiable corporate culture. This culture is based on five core 'values'. The Body Shop corporate culture comes from the philosophy of the founder of the business, Dame Anita Roddick.

AGAINST ANIMAL TESTING We consider testing products or ingredients on animals to be morally and scientifically indefensible and should be banned. So we don't test our cosmetic products or ingredients on animals, nor do we commission others to do so on our behalf. We never have and we never will.

SUPPORT COMMUNITY TRADE A fair price for a fantastic product or ingredient, from a disadvantaged or small-scale supplier. When we purchased our first Community Trade product we became a pioneer of fair trade in the cosmetics industry. That was in 1987; now we have 15,000 people, in 31 communities, across 24 countries supplying ingredients for over 1,000 of our products.

ACTIVATE SELF ESTEEM We promise only to create products that do exactly what they say on the label and communicate honestly and clearly, without confusing jargon and misleading product claims. So you can make your own mind up. Our motto? Know your mind, love your body.

DEFEND HUMAN RIGHTS We strive to ensure that we have rigorous systems in place so that we only source from suppliers that commit to our ethical trade standards where working conditions are safe and hygienic, child labour is not used, living wages are paid, working hours are not excessive and no discrimination is practised.

PROTECT THE PLANET We promote the use of renewable resources and sustainable raw ingredients, supporting sustainable wood through the use of the Forest Stewardship Council certified wood products. We actively strive to minimise waste and the unnecessary use of excess packaging on our products. We use renewable energy and have committed to becoming carbon neutral by 2010.

◄ The Body Shop logo and core values

Businesses have the power to do good. That's why the mission statement of The Body Shop opens with the overriding commitment: 'To dedicate our business to the pursuit of social and environmental change.' We use our stores and our products to help communicate human rights and environmental issues.

Source: www.AnitaRoddick.com

So what is meant by 'values'? Individuals' values can come from religion or from culture. In mathematics, a value is a number, a quantity. In economics, a value is a measure of what something is worth. (The school or college building you are in has a monetary value.) But personal values are not written down anywhere because they are in fact a state of mind.

Parents and carers might try to ensure children are brought up with a good set of personal values. This might mean, for example, the children will feel instinctively that they should care for others and try to behave in a certain manner. The things they will hold to be important – their personal values – will consciously or unconsciously determine how they behave.

Remember

Personal values affect the way people behave, both at work and in their private life. In a business context too, the values held by certain key individuals are often translated into specific corporate behaviour – as we saw in the example of Anita Roddick of The Body Shop (page 221).

Remember

Some businesses work on an ethical basis in everything they do. These are ethical businesses such as The Body Shop.

What is professional ethics?

Professional ethics relates to how people behave in relation to their chosen careers. Doctors, lawyers, accountants, engineers and other professionals are expected to behave in certain ways or follow specific codes of conduct. This helps to guard against their actions bringing their profession into disrepute. Living up to professional ethics can lead to dilemmas in the workplace. An example might be where a professional duty to 'whistleblow' (see page 255) conflicts with a sense of loyalty to a company.

Case study

ICA: ethical statement

The following statement is from The Institute of Chartered Accountants.

Ethics is principally concerned with human character and conduct. Ethical behaviour goes beyond obeying laws, rules and regulations. It is a commitment to do what is right, as well as merely what is allowable. A distinguishing mark of the accountancy profession is the acceptance of the commitment to act ethically and in the public interest. Members working in business may find themselves in situations where values are in conflict with one another, due to responsibilities to employers, clients, the Institute and the public.

Source: The Institute of Chartered Accountants, www.icaew.co.uk

1. An Accountant is asked by a client to hide some income because otherwise it will be liable to taxation. Is this an ethical dilemma? Explain your response. ✓
2. Based on the above ethical principal given by the Institute, which values of an accountant might be in conflict? ✓
3. Why is it important to the Accountancy profession that professional ethics are maintained? ✓ ✓

Remember

Professionals such as accountants, doctors and lawyers are governed by the rules of conduct laid down by their own professional institutes. Failing to comply with these can result in these professionals losing the right to practise.

Individual ethical behaviour

Once a business grows beyond a particular individual (i.e. sole trader – see Unit 37, page 190) it becomes a corporation with a legal personality all of its own. This gives the business a corporate identity. However, even large corporations consist of individual personalities. No matter what ethical principles a corporation might claim to possess, if individuals within the business take unethical decisions, these may have negative effects.

We will see in the following pages that many corporations take a firm ethical stance on many issues. It is the responsibility of managers to make sure that individual members of staff act in an ethical manner.

Thinking point

If you were the manager of a medium-sized building firm, what stance would you take if you received a call one day accusing one of your drivers of dumping building rubble near a public park? How would you ensure that all staff acted in an ethically correct way?

Ethical issues

Corporate governance

When a business corporation is brought into existence, there arises the question: 'Who makes decisions?' A limited company consists of a board of directors who are responsible for overarching strategic direction (hence the term 'directors'). Answerable to the board are usually a number of operational managers at various levels.

Case study

Tesco and Dairy Crest

Below are **Corporate Governances** from a national supermarket and a national food producer.

We are committed to the highest standards of Corporate Governance. We recognise that good governance helps the business to deliver our strategy and safeguard shareholders' long-term interests. We believe that the revised Combined Code provides a useful guide from which to review Corporate Governance within the group. This statement describes the board's approach to Corporate Governance.

Source: Tesco, www.tesco.com

The company's Corporate Governance procedures have met the requirements of section 1 of the Combined Code on Corporate Governance ('the Code'), with the one exception that no meetings were requested or held between shareholders and the Chairman and the senior independent non-executive director during the year. However, the Board considers that arrangements are in place to ensure a balanced understanding of the issues and concerns of major shareholders.

Source: Dairy Crest, www.dairycrest.co.uk

1. Investigate www.fsa.gov.uk, the website of the Financial Services Authority. With a partner, draft a statement that summarises section 1 of the Combined Code on Corporate Governance. Why is this important to businesses like Tesco and Dairy Crest? ✓
2. Explain what is meant by 'corporate governance'. ✓✓
3. 'Anyone can be unethical in a business. Governance is not relevant'. Do you agree? Justify your response. ✓✓✓

The 'governance' of a medium to large business is important. How do directors know what managers are doing? In the case of public limited companies (PLCs), how are shareholders consulted about policy, performance and decisions? Of course, there are rules about shareholders' rights. Nevertheless, the specific means by which individual businesses consult and control the various decision makers within the corporation are crucial.

Key Term

Corporate governance The people and procedures for taking the major decisions within a business.

Corporate social responsibility (CSR)

At the start of the unit we suggested that you can compare the ethical position of a business to that of a human being. Some people care about others; some people are very selfish. **Corporate social responsibility** refers to the extent that a business considers what it does in relation to the wider world.

Read the following passage from the government.

> The government sees CSR as the business contribution to our sustainable development goals. Essentially it is about how a business takes account of its economic, social and environmental impacts in the way it operates – maximising the benefits and minimising the downsides. Specifically, we see CSR as the voluntary actions that business can take, over and above compliance with minimum legal requirements, to address both its own competitive interests and the interests of wider society.

Source: The government's gateway website on CSR, www.csr.gov.uk/whatiscsr.shtml

The UK government wishes to encourage CSR. All businesses are expected to think about what they do.

Real lives

Ryanair: corporate social responsibility

Ryanair boss Michael O'Leary rejected criticism from a government minister, arguing that his airline was 'the greenest in Europe'.

Minister Ian Pearson had said that budget airline Ryanair was the 'irresponsible face of capitalism'. O'Leary said Pearson 'hadn't a clue what he is talking about'.

In an interview Pearson said: 'When it comes to climate change, Ryanair is not just the unacceptable face of capitalism, it is also the irresponsible face of capitalism.' He also attacked British Airways, saying it was 'only just playing ball' on environmental regulations.

O'Leary defended his company and the industry as a whole, saying: 'What he should be attacking is the power generation stations and the road transport industry, who between them account for over 50% of emissions.'

1. What is the ethical issue Ryanair faces in this case? Why is it an ethical issue? ✓
2. Do you think that Ryanair shows a lack of CSR in the case above? Justify your answer. ✓✓
3. What do you think of the debate about budget airlines? Do you think cheap flights should be restricted? ✓✓✓

Key Term

Corporate social responsibility (CSR) The policy of a business towards all stakeholders that takes their interests into account.

Remember

Corporate social responsibility (CSR) is when a firm establishes its own policies regarding its standards of behaviour and its relationships with stakeholders.

The emissions of carbon dioxide into the Earth's atmosphere – caused by petrol engines, oil burning and coal burning among other industrial activities – have caused a 'greenhouse effect' that effectively warms the Earth's surface. The gas forms a barrier that prevents the Sun's rays from bouncing back away from the Earth and out into the atmosphere. The danger is, we are now slowly starting to 'cook'.

Environment

The Ryanair case study on page 224 is, of course, an environmental and therefore an ethical issue, because the emissions coming from aircraft are believed to have a bad effect on the Earth's atmosphere, leading to **global warming**, which affects us all.

It is now widely felt that most of the global warming that has taken place over the last 50 years has been caused by human activity.

▲ What is the size of your carbon footprint?

Some reasons for global warming

- Since the start of the twentieth century, the Earth's average surface temperature has increased by 0.6°C (1.1°F).
- The twentieth century saw temperature increases greater than in the previous 400 to 600 years.
- Seven of the warmest years in the twentieth century were in the 1990s.

Some effects of global warming

- Mountain glaciers all over the world are receding (melting).
- The Arctic ice pack has lost about 40% of its thickness in the last 40 years.
- Global sea levels have risen three times faster over the last 100 years than over the previous 3,000 years.
- Plants and animals are changing their range of behaviours in response to climate change.
- The climate is changing and we don't understand how.

▲ The Antarctic ice pack is receding as a result of global warming

Source: www.GreenFacts.org

Remember

Business activity creates wealth, but it also has an effect on the planet we all depend on.

Key Term

Global warming The gradual warming of the planet's surface caused by carbon dioxide build-up in our atmosphere. It has the effect of changing the climate in the long term.

Sustainability

While there is no universal agreement on this, the evidence is strong that our planet cannot sustain (keep up) for too long increasing levels of industrial development – particularly development that uses carbon dioxide-producing technology (e.g. engines and oil burning). This is the 'sustainability' question – something that affects us all.

Human rights

When we talk about business ethics we are considering the actions taken on behalf of organisations and asking

Case study

The Go-Ahead Group: an environmentally responsible company?

The Go-Ahead Group of transport companies recognises that its activities impact on the environment. It acknowledges that it should take reasonable measures to look after the environment for both the present and future generations.

The Go-Ahead Group aims to minimise the bad effects of its activities within its financial, technical and operational constraints to ensure ongoing improvement in environmental performance, in addition to compliance with all statutory duties and regulatory requirements.

The Group Environment Manager will provide assistance and advice to operating companies where appropriate and particular attention should be given to the following areas recognised as being the primary environmental issues relating to our activities.

- *Pollution of air, water and land*. Actual and potential sources of pollution should be identified and all appropriate measures taken to reduce or prevent pollution. Particular regard should be given to vehicle exhaust emissions with purchasing, maintenance, operational and technical solutions evaluated within the decision making process.
- *Generation and disposal of waste*. All feasible waste minimisation and recycling initiatives to reduce the amount of waste generated should be established and implemented.
- *The use of natural resources*. The most environmentally sensitive resources used should be identified. Environmental considerations should be incorporated within the purchasing processes for these materials, and the use of such materials monitored with appropriate measures implemented to ensure efficiency.
- *Nuisance*. A degree of nuisance, particularly noise, is an inevitable consequence of the group's activities. However, it must be ensured that nuisance caused by operations is kept to a minimum and any complaints received are dealt with promptly and sympathetically within the operational constraints that apply.

Source: Adapted from Go-Ahead PLC's 'Environment Report', www.go-ahead.com

1. How does the Go-Ahead policy outlined here show concern for 'sustainability?' ✓
2. What other ethical issues are shown in the statement? ✓
3. Why does a PLC like the Go Ahead Group consider CSR to be important? ✓✓
4. It is impossible for a bus operator to be 'environmentally friendly'. Do you agree? Explain your response ✓✓✓

the general question: 'Is this for good or bad?' In other words, are the actions of business hurting us collectively and/or individually?

Many of the questions that we deal with in business ethics relate to major questions affecting us all (the environment is one). However, there are some issues that relate to fundamental human rights that we all have as individuals. Later in this unit (pages 235–42) we will see that this is a worldwide concern.

Human rights revolve around some very important questions. Some of these are to do with discrimination. For instance, it is illegal in the UK to treat people differently on the grounds of race, gender, religion, sexual orientation or disability. This is a human right and it is basic. Other human rights are also built into our legal system. We are entitled to a contract of employment, to work part time, to be able to join a union and to have a hearing against wrongful dismissal.

Thinking point

Access www.yourrights.org.uk and list as many 'rights' of employees as you can find. Of these, select at least three issues and describe how they can become ethical issues for employers.

Corruption

Corruption can be a major public concern. It arises in many forms. A person or a business corporation is 'corrupt' if they use influence or unfair means to gain business or personal advantage. Local councils may employ a lot of building companies to carry out construction work in their areas (e.g. to build roads, bridges, houses and offices). There is a lot of money to be made from local council contracts and it is only fair that when a local council has a building project

Case study

The Office of Fair Trading (OFT) at work

A door supplier has been stopped by the OFT from supplying and installing poor quality goods.

The owner of a specialist door company has given written undertakings under the Stop Now Regulations that he will stop breaching the Supply of Goods and Services Act 1982. Assurances were also provided by Mr X under the provisions of Part III of the Fair Trading Act 1973.

The OFT received a number of complaints from consumers that the company:

- supplied doors and fittings that were unsatisfactory in quality
- supplied doors not fit for their purpose
- supplied goods that did not match their description
- failed to deliver and/or fit goods within the agreed time or at all
- fitted goods without reasonable care and skill.

John Vickers, director general of Fair Trading, said: 'Consumers have a basic right to goods of satisfactory quality that are fit for their purpose, match their description and are installed properly. The OFT and trading standards services will act against suppliers who breach these rights.'

1. Why was this door company 'trading unfairly?' ✓
2. Was it in the businesses interests to do so? ✓
3. Do you think it is necessary for the government to step in and protect consumers like this? Justify your answer. ✓✓
4. What might be the implications if the government were to abolish the OFT? ✓✓

to complete, the contract is openly and fairly made available to all firms. Competition should be based on price, quality, ability to do the job and so on. However, what if one of the officers or councillors were related to a builder and this builder were given the job? What if one particular builder paid cash to an officer or a councillor to secure the work? These are examples of serious corruption. A process that is meant to guarantee fairness has been corrupted.

Key Term

Corruption Not following fair and equal procedures to make decisions; attempting to persuade by using cash or opportunity.

Remember

Ethical issues can be of worldwide concern or they can be about the relationship between a customer and a business.

Trading fairly

Fair trade is where:

- business is carried on in an open manner
- competition takes place on grounds that are equal for all parties
- consumers can feel secure that the goods and services they are buying are going to be of satisfactory quality.

The Office of Fair Trading (www.oft.gov.uk) exists 'to make markets work well for consumers. Markets work well when there is vigorous competition between fair-dealing businesses. When markets work well, good businesses flourish.'

Legal and regulatory compliance

There are several areas of law that businesses must follow. These are designed to protect a business's consumers, its employees and others in the wider environment.

Consumer law

When a consumer makes a decision to buy something there is an element of trust and of risk involved. An unethical trader could potentially give a false description of something or overcharge for a product. Businesses are therefore subject to the law.

It is illegal to give a false description of something, or to mislead consumers. This body of law is known as 'consumer protection' law. Consumers have rights, and businesses must respect these. The well-known Acts of Parliament in this area are:

- the Consumer Protection Act 1987
- the Sale of Goods Act 1979
- the Trades Description Act 1968.

These Acts give ministers the right to make future regulations that further control what businesses can do. At a local level, all businesses must comply with trading standards. Trading Standards officers exist to ensure consumers are given protection against **rogue traders**, whether they are selling goods or offering services.

Key Term

Rogue traders A trader operating as a legitimate business without the necessary skills and abilities to do the job.

Take it further

Visit the Trading Standards website at www.tradingstandards.gov.uk. This offers a useful list of government laws applying in England and Wales. Summarise the issues covered in the list of government laws and create a summary of those Acts that try to protect the consumer.

Protecting employees

Just as a consumer accepts an element of risk when buying, an employee places trust in an employer. Government has taken steps to establish laws that protect people employed by business. This area of law is known as employment law. Businesses are required by law to treat employees fairly and without discrimination. The Sex Discrimination Act (1975), the Equal Pay Act (1970) and the Employment Protection Act (1975) all place businesses under an obligation to deal with staff in a fair and open way.

Employees are also offered protection under health and safety laws and regulations. Employers have a duty of care to monitor the health and safety of their staff. This is to ensure that they do not carry out jobs that have too much risk or danger.

All of these Acts of Parliament are capable of being enforced by the courts or by government agencies. Regulations are made as a result of each Act, and these control what businesses can lawfully do. The effect of the law, therefore, is to regulate (modify or moderate) business activity.

Remember

The way an employer looks after its staff is an important ethical question.

The wider environment

An unethical business could, if left unregulated, cause immense damage to the environment around it. We saw on page 224 that the budget airline Ryanair appears in conflict with government ministers about cheap flights that add to air pollution.

At the local level businesses are held responsible for what they do. It is unlawful for a business to:

- dump rubbish
- pollute waterways
- build without authority from planners.

The government has an agency called the Environment Agency (see www.environment-agency.gov.uk), which is responsible for enforcing environment regulations.

▲ **Polluting the atmosphere is now a major ethical question**

Case study

Air pollution prevention

An international company was fined £35,500 for four offences of breaching Pollution Prevention and Control (PPC) regulations. The company was also ordered to pay £30,000 costs to the Environment Agency.

When a plant was built, an automatic process shutdown system was not installed – even though it was stipulated as a condition in the pollution control regulations in the permit. This would automatically have shut down the plant in the event of equipment failure. The abatement plant was put in place to reduce potentially harmful substances such as oxides of nitrogen (NOx) to safe levels.

Because there were no such safety measures, the permitted level of emissions were grossly exceeded over several months. There is no evidence to suggest that environmental harm or harm to human health occurred as a result of the incident. However, there was potential for environmental harm and harm to nearby residents if such releases were allowed to continue for a prolonged period.

Apart from excessive releases caused by the failure to install an automatic shutdown system, there was a failure of the oven seals in another part of the same process. This caused the escape of oven gases resulting in elevated levels of NOx within the perimeter of the company premises.

The company failed to notify the Environment Agency that there had been a detection of escaped NOx that could have caused pollution. Nor did it notify the Environment Agency that there had been a malfunction, breakdown or failure of the plant or techniques that either caused or could have caused pollution.

A local Environment Agency officer said: 'In each of the failures by the defendant to comply with the terms of the permit, its conduct fell way below the standards required of it and expected of a company of this size and experience working in this industry.'

Source: Adapted from an article on www.environment-agency.gov.uk

1. Based on the story, what do you feel were 'the standards required' of the business concerned? ✓
2. Who were these 'standards' designed to protect? ✓
3. Analyse the overall work of the Environment Agency. In your view, in what ways does it affect the ethical behaviour of businesses? ✓✓

Business practices

The law covers the main ethical issues that can affect many key stakeholders in a business (consumers, staff and the immediate neighborhood). But there is still a potential for actual business practices to fall short of legal requirements. If this were not the case, perhaps there would be no need for regulations. Why does this happen?

Businesses exist to achieve their aims and objectives. Every business manager has a degree of pressure to meet targets (see pages 232–35 covering stakeholders). Managers themselves are employees; they have senior management as well as (in some cases) shareholders (see page 232) to consider. These pressures can sometimes result in neglect or **malpractice**. A business manager may neglect to fully comply with health and safety regulations, because to do so would cause delay. An accident caused as a result of this will have serious consequences for the business.

Things can become more serious and sinister when a business uses malpractice to achieve objectives. This could be through corruption or illegal activity. Perhaps the most famous example in recent times is the case of Enron (see Take it further opposite).

Key Term

Malpractice This refers to any occasion when someone does not follow accepted normal practice (usually to gain advantage).

LIBRARY BOOK

Take it further

To illustrate the difference between an ethical issue caused through a mistake and one caused through malpractice, investigate the following cases. Then prepare a presentation on both of them for the benefit of your class.

- Enron (Enron executives bribed tax officials in order to fabricate accounts)
- Cadbury's (Cadbury's withdrew a million chocolate bars which may have been contaminated with a rare strain of salmonella).

Working conditions

When people start working for a business organisation, they are entitled to a set of minimum working conditions. These conditions are not just about wages and salaries. They also cover aspects of work such as hours, holiday entitlement, privacy, harassment and discrimination. It is up to employers to create working conditions that are fair, just and open. Trade unions have the traditional role of defending worker rights against bad employers.

Individual ethical responsibilities

At the start of the unit we saw that individuals, as well as businesses, have ethical responsibilities. Individual ethics determine our basic values and standards of behaviour. Management is responsible for staff working in a business. The human resources function tries to employ the right people who will carry out their job roles well. It is up to HR specialists, as well as line managers across a business, to make sure that staff follow the ethical guidelines of a firm. However, it is up to individuals to follow their own ethical principles at all times.

Remember

Ethical business behaviour is promoted by company policies, governmental policies and public concern about things affecting us all.

Outcome activity 38.1

Pass 

Describe the general ethical issues a particular business needs to consider in its operational activities.

Merit

Assess how a selected business could improve its operations ethically.

Grading tips

Pass 

You could take a local firm and, after investigating its basic operations, outline at least three ethical concerns. Note: this does *not* mean that the business should be doing something wrong, just that these things are 'concerns' for it.

Merit 

This requires careful consideration. Think about the issues you have described for the pass grade and assess how/if the business could deal with them better.

Askham Bryan College LIBRARY BOOK

38.2 Implications of businesses operating ethically

Stakeholders

All businesses have a number of **stakeholder** groups, each with different interests in what the business does. Business owners – perhaps the key stakeholders – want good financial performance from their investments. Business managers know it is their first responsibility to deliver good financial results.

However, while it was always acknowledged that businesses exist in a diverse social, economic and political environment, today it is also accepted that a business should be managed with the interests of *all* stakeholders (including shareholders) in mind. It has become a fashionable thing for business to try to be the friend of all stakeholders. The text that follows looks at the different types of stakeholders.

Key Term

Stakeholder Individual or group with any sort of interest in the activities of a business.

Shareholders

Shares in UK businesses might be held by private individuals or institutions holding blocks of company shares as investments for pension funds or mortgage endowments. If a business is performing very well, then it is likely that the share value – and therefore the value of the business – will rise. The big question is, what decisions will help the business to prosper? Those that sacrifice short-term profit for long-term security?

Practice point

You are employed by a large pub/restaurant chain. You are considering implementing a 'No Smoking' policy in all public bars and restaurants of the chain.

- How might you convince shareholders that such a policy might be for the best in the long term?
- Consider the stakeholders in the situation. Who might be the 'winners' and 'losers'?

Employees

As ordinary citizens, we benefit from business activity because we provide a labour force for business leaders to create wealth. One of the basic tensions and difficulties involved in our kind of economy is that labour is a major cost of business. In the past in the UK, owners of firms could be ruthless – even employing children to work in mines and factories. Workers could be exploited and made to work long hours, then be 'laid off' (sacked) when they were no longer needed.

Nowadays it is expected that employers will provide satisfactory working conditions and that workers – who, after all, are the ones directly adding value to provide products or services – will be kept safe from danger. It is illegal to employ children and there is a minimum wage.

In modern business, the needs and fears of employees are expected to be taken into account by managers. Some modern businesses try to treat staff not just with 'fairness'; they give them first-class working conditions and benefits so that they are a world-class employer (see Royal Bank of Scotland on page 236).

Customers, suppliers and competitors

If you have a favourite takeaway near you it becomes quite an important issue if the business is suddenly sold. If we are regular customers of any business it can be assumed that we are satisfied with the service received. We are naturally stakeholders because we hope that we can continue to be satisfied. The business is serving our needs.

In many industrial markets this relationship between customers, suppliers and competitors can be very important. The existence of some businesses can be affected by the success or performance of another. If one significant firm fails or takes dramatic decisions about strategy, there can be a whole network of other related firms, especially suppliers, that are affected. In each market there can be a chain of businesses relating to each other. The decisions of one can have a major impact on the others, even if they are competitors.

Real lives

Competition inquiry could force a giant supermarket land sale

Supermarkets could be forced to sell land and alter their relationships with suppliers after the Competition Commission reports its first findings on Britain's grocery market today.

The commission is investigating whether Britain has become a 'supermarket state', with thousands of local specialist stores being killed off by big supermarkets moving into the convenience store sector. Critics believe this could eventually limit choice and push up prices for customers.

An 'emerging thinking' report today will give the first indications of whether the commission will attempt to break the power of the 'Big Four' supermarkets (Tesco, Sainsbury's, Asda and Morrison) by outlawing 'bully boy' tactics and promoting fairer pricing.

'It is an absolute certainty that the report will discuss land ownership and the relationship between supermarkets and their suppliers,' said Jonathan Pritchard, a retail analyst at Oriel Securities.

The 'Big Four' are believed to have spent tens of millions of pounds on lawyers and consultants to fight accusations that their dominance is hurting consumers.

Tesco has even set up a special website to try to refute some of the claims made by suppliers, MPs and members of the public in written responses to the Competition Commission inquiry.

Tesco is the focus of concerns about supermarket power, because it takes £1 in every £8 spent in the high street. Critics say it has gained an effective monopoly in a number of communities, and it is opening small convenience outlets at the rate of two a week.

The investigation is also looking at the expansion of Asda, Sainsbury's and Morrisons. If it believes that there is a problem, the commission has the power to impose planning restrictions on all four supermarkets, and could force them to sell land they have earmarked for new stores. It could also outlaw the practice of 'price flexing', where supermarkets sell staple items such as bread, baked beans and bananas at below cost-price in certain areas of the country to entice customers away from rivals.

In submissions to the Competition Commission, an independent body, some food suppliers and farmers said they were afraid of the supermarkets, which use their power to drive prices down to unsustainable levels. The National Farmers' Union complained of a 'climate of fear and oppression' for some suppliers and of an abuse of power by supermarkets.

Mark Tinsley, a farmer who supplies major supermarkets, said vegetable packers and processors will not pay extra for British produce in times of shortage because they are afraid of the supermarkets, resulting in supermarkets paying half the price of imported products for UK vegetables.

Consumer groups have also complained about the supermarket practice of holding areas of land for development, supposedly to prevent rival supermarkets from building near their existing stores. Tesco denies that it is sitting on a vast land bank.

The 'emerging thinking' report will outline the progress that has been made by the commission. The next stage is a provisional findings report that is due in June.

Source: Article from www.telegraph.co.uk, 25 January 2007

1. According to the article, what ethical concerns face local communities as a result of the big supermarkets? ✓
2. Why are these ethical concerns? Do you feel they are justified concerns? ✓✓
3. What CSR measures would you suggest for the big supermarkets to adopt? ✓✓✓
4. Carry out a search in which you investigate the question of supermarkets and land acquisition. What are the justifications for companies like Tesco, in relation to buying up land in and around towns and cities? ✓✓✓

Practice point

Research the 2005 collapse of car manufacturer Rover at Longbridge. Write a clear set of notes describing the ways in which various stakeholder groups were affected. Pay particular attention to the question of suppliers and distributors.

Citizens

Business activity occurs within a community. So it is important that the local population is considered in major business decisions. Many firms adopt a specific company mission to do 'good work' in the community. (e.g. Proctor & Gamble). This is in part why public relations is such a key feature of business.

Many businesses have national importance and their activities are very significance to members of communities. Tesco, for instance, is a powerful presence in any community. It can have a considerable impact on traffic, new buildings, employment and established businesses.

Sometimes a business or a governmental agency takes a particular strategic decision that will have an effect on the natural environment. For example, a business park is developed. Some derelict land might be used beneficially, jobs created and building firms get work. These are good things for those who benefit – winners.

However, in the background there are other consequences: green land is lost, wildlife loses its habitat and some plant species are lost. The natural environment – plants, trees, wildlife – can suffer as soon as human beings intervene – losers.

Finally, it is important to remember that the whole world is a global community. We all have a 'stake' in the health and well-being of our planet. When natural disasters such as the 2004 Indian Ocean tsunami or the 2005 hurricanes *Katrina* and *Rita* devastated the US gulf coast, business concerns are placed in perspective. The world seems – temporarily at least – to come together as one. We can quickly realise through a 'wake up call' how much we all have in common.

Remember

When businesses behave ethically, the staff are well looked after in terms of their individual needs; customers are given good service and the wider community is kept informed through an open CSR policy.

Bankers, stock markets and financial commentators

Public companies are listed on the Stock Exchange and attract investment from wealthy individuals and professional investors such as insurance companies or pension funds. These groups and individuals constantly monitor the performance of companies and entire markets. They will sell shares in companies that are expected to do less well (because their value might fall) and buy shares in companies that are expected to do better (because their value will go up).

Financial commentators can have a big influence on what people or investment professionals will do. Expert opinion of the banks, markets and commentators can sway the stock markets one way or another.

Key Term

Stock Exchange The market place where company shares are bought and sold.

Take it further

Access www.bloomberg.co.uk, then write a concise description of this web service. What kind of market data or commentary is provided? In what ways, if any, do you feel that business investors might be influenced? What other media influences are there on business?

Conflicts of interest between stakeholder groups

Businesses today have to balance the sometimes conflicting aims of a number of stakeholders. This is sometimes difficult because the interests of stakeholder groups can conflict with each other.

There are a number of issues where important stakeholder interests conflict. For example, shareholders have a financial interest in a business. It is in their interest that the shares in the business increase in value, so that their investments also increase. Environmentalists are people or groups that actively campaign on issues to do with protecting the natural environment.

Take it further

Consider the following stakeholder groups. Which ones might be in conflict with each other? How might this happen?

- Employees
- Managers
- Customers
- Suppliers
- Citizens
- Shareholders
- Government agencies

If a business successfully launches a new product and all is going well, the shareholders will be very pleased that their cash investment looks like returning a healthy profit. If, however, an environmental group mounts a big campaign to prevent this business operating in the way it does, these two stakeholders are in conflict. Success for environmentalists may mean a loss for shareholders. That said, others may argue that, in the longer term, all businesses gain by protecting our environment.

Implications of operating ethically

Adapting business behaviour

We live in a world that is increasingly inter-connected. Communication is instantaneous. When an incident happens on the other side of the world, we hear about it within minutes. Is it any wonder, then, that business leaders now fear the consequences of unethical actions by their staff or being accused of an unethical practice?

Most large-scale businesses today take their ethical responsibilities very seriously. They are therefore prepared to adapt their behaviour to avoid accusations of doing wrong, as the following statements show.

- *The Go-Ahead Group PLC*: 'Every person in the UK is a stakeholder in the public transport industry. The Go-Ahead Group is acutely aware of this, and of our resulting social and environmental responsibilities to the local environments and the people who live in areas where we operate.'
- *Marks & Spencer*: 'As almost all of our products are made just for us, we can ensure they are produced carefully, in ways that help to protect the environment, the people who make them and our customers.'
- *Unilever*: 'We are committed to managing our social and environmental impacts responsibly, to working in partnership with our stakeholders, to addressing social and environmental challenges and to contributing to sustainable development.'

Real lives

Global suppliers feel ethical pressure

Europe's largest oil and gas companies are planning to quiz their suppliers to establish for the first time a global database on supplier corporate social responsibility policies. The survey, understood to be initially piloted by BP, Shell, Statoil and Norsk Hydro, will be sent to suppliers in September and follows a similar exercise by 45 British utility companies last month.

'The message they are trying to give is that your attitudes to corporate responsibility are important to us and also to every player down the supply chain,' said an oil company executive.

The surveys will be self-assessed, but it is expected that the oil companies will audit the information to build up an accurate ranking of suppliers across the world.

If successful, the pilot could be extended to 52 other oil and gas companies that use Achilles to help manage their supply chains. More than 1,000 of the 5,000 suppliers surveyed by UK-based utility companies have already responded.

It is known there is a diverse supplier attitude to social responsibility. Suppliers would not be immediately blacklisted for failing to complete the survey.

The moves mark an escalation of individual attempts by large companies to put pressure on their suppliers to adopt ethical and socially responsible policies that echo their own in order to reduce the risk of damage to the reputation of their own brands.

Clothes manufacturers such as Nike and Gap, plus other retailers, have taken a close interest in the employment practices of their suppliers for some time, with UK retailers setting up the Suppliers Ethical Data Exchange 18 months ago to share the results of supplier audits.

The government has repeatedly tried to encourage large companies to use their buying power to ensure that suppliers meet certain health and safety, employment, environmental and wider social standards. The government has used the Company Bill to require directors to operate their businesses 'with regard' to impact on the environment and local community.

On Monday, the Royal Bank of Scotland launched its latest corporate responsibility report, setting out initiatives for customers, employees, the environment and local communities. The bank spends more than £5 billion a year with suppliers around the world. A spokesperson said that to become one of its main suppliers, businesses have to sign up to its Group Ethical Code for Suppliers, which covers labour rights, the environment, and bribery and corruption.

The government has committed to becoming a leader in so-called sustainable procurement in Europe by 2009. In June, Environment Secretary David Miliband pledged to improve the way it buys its goods and services after a critical report by the Sustainable Procurement Task Force, a business-led group.

And in May, Achilles won a contract from the UN Environmental Programme to develop an online supplier management service for a group of IT and telecoms firms in an initiative chaired by BT.

Source: Adapted from the *Daily Telegraph*, 20 July 2006

1. In your own words, summarise the efforts identified in the article to encourage CSR policies. ✓
2. What are the ethical issues for the suppliers of large scale oil companies mentioned in the article? ✓✓
3. Do you feel that this kind of pressure upon suppliers to adopt CSR policies is likely to work? Why? ✓✓✓

Practice point

In pairs, investigate the corporate social responsibility (CRS) policies of at least three businesses. Prepare a short presentation outlining how this represents an illustration of businesses 'adapting' their normal behaviour.

Responding to ethical pressures

The CSR programmes of businesses are a response to the growing pressures placed on managements to take account of ethical concerns. The Real lives study on page 236 shows that several very large companies operating in some significant industries are beginning to exert pressure on their own trading partners to follow socially responsible policies.

Implementing ethical practices

Some household names have begun to implement an ethical stance on issues that affect us all. Take the case study from Walkers crisps (below). This is hard evidence that one of the UK's major snack manufacturers is working with consumer health in mind. There are other clear indications of this too. McDonald's fast food chains increasingly work to offer healthy options.

Influence of stakeholders and pressure groups

Many businesses in pursuit of their primary goals cause damage to the planet. The stakeholders in this, of course, are all of us. Environmental issues are the focus of several well-known pressure groups. **Pressure groups** are not elected by anyone. They form to raise awareness of an issue, or several issues. Examples of environmental pressure groups include:

- Greenpeace
- ENCAMS (environmental campaigns)
- National Pure Water Association
- Friends of the Earth.

The influence of pressure groups' activity is significant. Their work attracts much media attention and government always takes into account the voice of public opinion. For the modern business, public opinion is vital. The market orientated company must take care of its public image. Although businesses do not seek votes and they are relatively free (within the law) to pursue unpopular policies and tactics, they do fear public disapproval for commercial reasons. This is one of the reasons why so many CSR policies are so clearly outlined.

Key Term

Pressure groups Voluntary organisations that exist to create a case that will be listened to by decision makers everywhere. This includes business leaders and politicians.

Case study

Walkers crisps: reduces saturated fat by 70%

The text below outlines Walkers' ethical approach.

'A standard bag of Walkers crisps now contains less than a gram of saturated fat. That's just 5% of your guideline daily amount and less saturated fat than half a chocolate digestive! And it's all because we're now cooking our crisps in sunseed oil, one of the healthiest oils there is.

'Our crisps now contain just 8% of your guideline daily amount of salt. We have reduced the salt in our crisps so that a standard bag now only contains 0.5g of salt; that's 8% of your guideline daily amount and the same as a slice of bread!

Source: Walkers, http://walkers.corpex.com

1. Why do you think Walkers have taken this step? ✓
2. Which ethical issues would you say are related to this measure? ✓✓
3. In what ways do you feel Walkers will gain (if at all) from this? ✓✓✓

Practice point

Investigate www.labourbehindthelabel.org – a pressure group (Labour behind the Label) concentrating on the fashion industry. Prepare a report outlining the concerns of this group. Conclude by giving your opinions as to whether you feel they can change things in the fashion industry.

Take it further

Examine the ethical questions that face the food and drinks industry. Create a presentation outlining any evidence you can find that the industry is taking ethical issues seriously.

Remember

Corporate social responsibility is partly a response to external stakeholder pressure, partly a response to pressure group campaigns and partly recognition that public disapproval could lead to commercial disaster.

Impact on competitiveness, reputation and public image

The following Real lives case is about Timberland, a clothing and footwear company. It illustrates perfectly the way in which businesses can use global ethical concerns to boost competitiveness within their market.

Case study

Ethics debate booted about

In the lobby of Timberland's New Hampshire headquarters are collections of the company's iconic yellow boots redesigned by children.

A board behind the boots reads: 'Deep within our heritage there's an equally important ingredient to our success — our beliefs. Humanity, humility, integrity and excellence.' The company's mission statement is: 'To equip people to make a difference in their world.'

If it all sounds like a holier-than-thou pitch to the UN rather than a sales drive in the shopping malls of the mid-west, there's one man to blame: Jeff Swartz, the third generation of the Swartz family to run the outdoor clothing and footwear firm and one of the most outspoken chief executives in America.

Timberland is in trouble. 'Authentic youth', as Timberland calls the category formerly known as 'urban', are kicking off their boots in favour of less cumbersome footwear. Sales are down and a once-solidly performing company is reviewing its future.

Valued at nearly US$2 billion (£1 billion), it has reportedly hired financial company Goldman Sachs for advice. However, no deal is possible without Swartz family approval, because they control 70% of voting shares.

Swartz won't comment directly, but said his options are open. If Timberland can't reverse the sales decline, it could be sold. In the meantime, he is determined to reposition it as the leading voice in a new debate on social responsibility in corporate America.

If they seem like unrelated objectives then, as far as Swartz is concerned, you've missed the point. And he is determined that you get it. He believes corporations more than governments have to take the lead on social responsibility. He acknowledges many of his customers may not care how or where his products are made, but believes they will and sees it as his responsibility to start that debate.

Just as organic food sells at a premium, getting the eco-message out there should also help Timberland underpin its higher margins while doing some good, said Swartz. 'I want people to believe in the power of the marketplace to make things better,' he said.

Timberland and Swartz have long been seriously interested in corporate social responsibility. His workers are given 40 hours' paid leave a year for volunteer work and can take six-month sabbaticals to non-profit organisations.

The company runs a variety of eco-friendly projects. For example, it will plant a tree for every pair of boots bought at its Regent Street store in London.

Now he believes it is time to push the debate harder. 'This year, 30 million people will buy something from our brand,' he said.

The Green Index will tell shoppers how eco-friendly Timberland's shoes are and the answer will not always be good. Graded from nought (the best) to 10 (worst). The yellow boot is a 6 and Timberland has yet to produce a nought.

Swartz said he was inspired by Marks & Spencer and its 'Look behind the label' campaign that details the British retailer's ethical standards for manufacturing.

But for all the ethical talk, Swartz acknowledges he has one big problem: China. Some 40% of Timberland's goods are made in China, where workers have no political freedom and conditions can be appalling.

Financially, Timberland has to be in China, said Swartz. 'But if I could not manufacture in China, I wouldn't. If you ask me to justify being in China, I cannot,' he said.

In an attempt to square the circle, Timberland has a code of conduct its factories must adhere to. Last year it pulled out of one factory after repeated infractions (infringements of the law). It has also imposed a maximum 60-hour week on workers at its Chinese factories.

After imposing the cap, Swartz said he was left with another dilemma. Workers at Timberland's factories complain that their hours are capped when they could be earning more at plants run by rivals like Skechers.

Companies have a duty to do what they can and be open about it, said Swartz. But they also have a duty to do the best they can for their shareholders.

This year Swartz has not been holding up his end of that deal. Timberland's shares have fallen as the stock market has soared. The company expects full-year earnings per share to decline 30% this year.

Swartz said the decline was mainly 'a fashion problem', but he doesn't expect a quick solution. 'Go to Europe right now and it's like summer. The weather is dreadful for Timberland,' he said.

As well as weak boot sales, Timberland faces rising wage pressures and anti-dumping duties in Europe on products shipped from China and Vietnam, a decision he said was '100% politics and 0% logic'.

Unlike most chief executives, Swartz can afford to ride out the storm, thanks to his family's support. But it is clear that all options are being explored and he talked openly about other 'ethically minded' brands that had sold out to larger corporations.

Swartz said he would 'give up control for more power'. What he seems more wary of is the 'Ben & Jerry syndrome'. Critics charge that the famously leftist ice cream company lost its soul after selling out to consumer-goods giant Unilever. 'They sold the company and went home,' said Swartz. Swartz would have to be carried out with his boots on.

Source: Adapted from www.Timesonline.co.uk, 3 December 2006

1. Read the article on Timberland and, working with a partner, list and describe the ethical issues that are mentioned. ✓
2. To what extent do you feel that Timberland is adopting an ethical stance in order to improve its own 'competitiveness'? Justify and explain your response. ✓✓
3. Evaluate the ethical position of Timberland as you understand it. Do you feel that the business will gain from this? Fully explain your response. ✓✓✓

Ethical trade

The Real lives study on Timberland's position in relation to trade with China also shows how a well-established business is prepared to take into account the implications of trading with factories that employ labour in appalling conditions. Ethical trade is a way of doing business that takes into account the conditions and practices that occur throughout a supply chain.

Ethical trade became a growing issue during the 1990s because companies with global supply chains – in particular those in the clothing and food sectors – were coming under increasing pressure to ensure decent working conditions for the people who produce the goods they sell.

Remember

Ethical trade is where big companies take account of ethical questions all along their supply chain so that they buy from businesses that treat workers fairly and give them a fair price for their products.

Value added

A study undertaken by the Institute of Business Ethics showed clearly that in the years 1997–2001, those with an explicit commitment to doing business ethically produced profit/turnover ratios that were 18% higher than those without a similar commitment. The conclusion was made that businesses which had set up their own codes of ethics were adding significant value to their business.

Key Term

Value added Where value is added to something through work and application of skills and understanding.

Complying with relevant legislation and codes of practice

We have already seen that, in the UK, businesses must comply with a large range of legislative (legal) regulations (see pages 228–31) such as those relating to:

- health and safety
- employment
- planning
- environmental and pollution.

European Union (EU) laws

In 2007, the European Union is a political and economic union of 27 nation-states that encompass more than 490 million people. Countries as diverse as Britain and Romania, Cyprus and Slovenia are now part of this Union. It is natural that ethical issues that affect us all are the subject of EU law. This law covers common issues such as employment and environmental pollution. (What use is controlling atmospheric pollution in Britain, if France was polluting?)

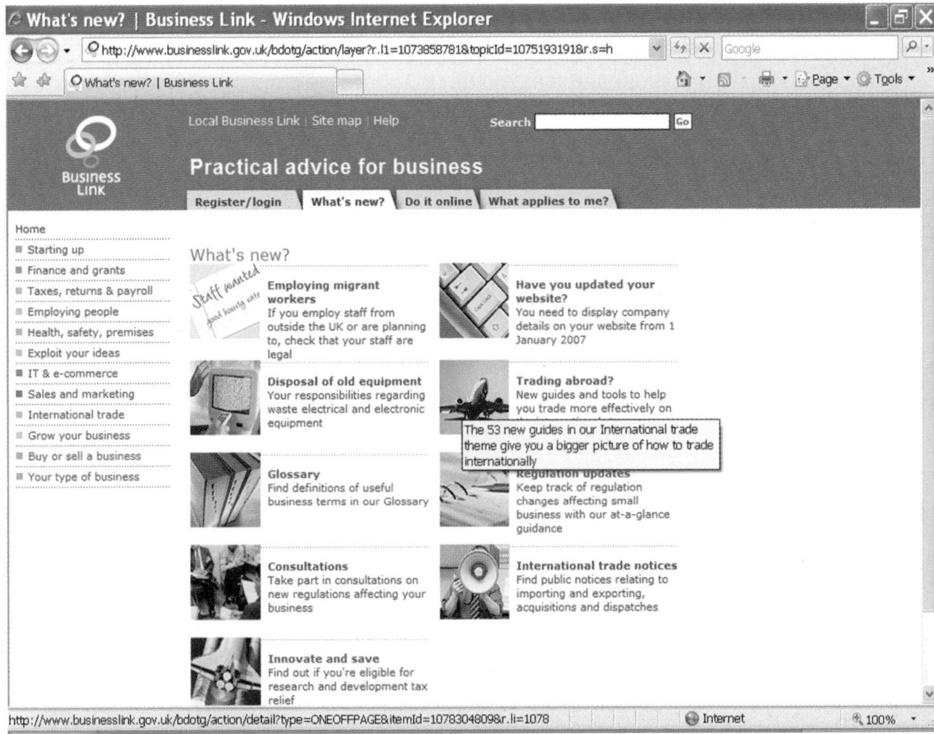

▲ The Business Link service gives advice on codes and legal requirements

Employment law is an illustration of EU influence in working conditions.

- An *EU Directive* tells a member state that it must implement law in a particular area. The 1993 Directive 93/104/EC lays down provisions for a maximum 48-hour working week (including overtime), plus rest periods and breaks, and a minimum of four weeks' paid leave per year for employees.
- The *Working Time Directive (WTD)* was introduced because of the clear link between long working hours and health and safety. Working long hours leads to tiredness, and tiredness leads to accidents.

However, the UK government negotiated an 'opt-out' from the WTD on the following conditions.

- The worker can agree to do more than 48 hours.
- No worker should be disadvantaged by deciding not to opt out.
- The employer must keep records of all workers who carry out such work.
- Records must be kept available for authorities.

In 2005, the EU voted to stop this opt-out from the Working Time Directive.

Despite the WTD, the UK is the only member state in which working time has actually increased over the last decade.

Remember

The European Union tries to set standards that apply across all member states.

UN Declaration of Human Rights

The United Nations Declaration of Human Rights was first produced in 1948, soon after World War II. At that time, there was an intense desire to create a better world, based on fairness and justice. Part of the Declaration covered the question of paid employment.

◀ The United Nations logo

Article 23 of UN Declaration of Human Rights

- Everyone has the right to work, to free choice of employment, to just and favourable conditions of work, and to protection against unemployment.
- Everyone, without any discrimination, has the right to equal pay for equal work.
- Everyone who works has the right to just and favourable remuneration (pay), ensuring for themselves and their families an existence worthy of human dignity, and supplemented (added to), if necessary, by other means of social protection.
- Everyone has the right to form and join trade unions for the protection of his interests.

UN Global Compact

On 31 January 1999, the then United Nations Secretary General Kofi Annan called on the world's leading business people to initiate a Global Compact of shared values and principles, 'which will give a human face to the global market' (see www.unglobalcompact.org).

Early in 1999, the World Economic Forum meeting in Davos (Switzerland) took as its focus the need to underpin the free market system with a stable and just society. Kofi Annan challenged business to 'embrace, support and enact a set of core values in the areas of human rights, labour standards and environmental practices'.

Economic activity

The UN made its Global Compact steps in order to take an overview of the global economy. In a world where so many newly emerging industrialising countries (e.g. China and India) are opening up their economies and beginning to develop into so many markets, the fear remains that such operations will carry on practices that cause immense damage both to people and to our planet. The question is, how does a global authority exert influence over these economies?

Take it further

Re-visit the Timberland case study (pages 238–39). How does that example serve to illustrate the need for a Global Compact? Do you feel that these measures can succeed?

Outcome activity 38.2

Pass 

Explain the implications for the business and stakeholders of a business operating ethically.

Distinction 

Evaluate the impact of a selected business's ethical behaviour on stakeholders and the business.

Grading tips

Pass 

Consider the benefits of ethical behaviour by businesses. Who wins? Staff? People in developing nations? The environment? Are products any better? How do consumers benefit?

Distinction 

This should focus on *one* business and cover as many stakeholders as possible. Look also at the remaining issues in the unit to add to your perspective. Remember, these are your views, but they should be backed up by clearly researched evidence.

38.3 Social implications of business ethics

Social implications refer to those actions of business that have an effect on society as a whole. These issues relate to a number of areas of activity.

Areas of activity

Ethics in finance

The average debt of the typical UK family today is so high that about a quarter of families have debts they cannot afford to repay. Businesses in the financial sector that offer loans which are expensive to repay (resulting in even worse debt for the borrower), are increasingly subject to scrutiny. Financial advice given several years ago caused many people to invest in endowment schemes that have failed to result in expected returns. For these reasons, financial advice services have been increasingly regulated.

In business matters, finance is always an area with a great deal of scope for unethical behaviour. The primary purpose of **free enterprise** is to generate profit. Anything standing in the way of this goal can be a target for financial malpractice. There are a number of areas in financial affairs where unethical behaviour arises, as the following text shows.

Key Term

Free enterprise An economic system in which people are free to offer goods and services to meet demand.

Remember

In financial dealing and payments, there is scope for several kinds of unethical behaviour. Regulations and voluntary codes try to make sure that ethical practices are observed.

Bribery

This is the straightforward use of financial muscle to gain unfair advantage over others. The word 'corruption' was dealt with earlier in the unit (see page 227). Bribery is a form of corruption. An example would be attempting to gain planning permission by giving money to a planning official or councillor. Another would be gaining the award of a contract by giving cash to a decision maker in a business or government department.

Executive pay

One problem that will not go away is excessive pay for top executives. However, US companies now have to include in their annual reports a single figure for the total pay of their executives including salary, perks and pensions.

This at least tells shareholders exactly what their top executives are earning. It is a response to public concern about pay rises that are unrelated to effort, plus a number of high-profile cases of failed executives getting pay-offs of up to US$100 million and others having stock options backdated to give them a share of earlier capital gains.

Insider trading

Insider trading refers to illegal use of privileged information in dealing on a stock exchange. For example, when a company takeover bid is imminent, shares are rapidly bought up then sold at a big profit. Insider trading is, in theory, detected by the Securities and Exchange Commission (SEC) in America, and by the Securities and Investment Board (SIB) in the UK. Neither agency has any legal powers other than public disclosure. Nor can they bring prosecutions themselves.

Lobbying

Lobbying politicians can be a source of corruption. To 'lobby' means to approach an MP or minister with requests for actions or information. The intention is to persuade politicians to adopt a particular cause or issue, in order to benefit it. In business, if a particular company was under pressure to take certain actions, they could informally 'lobby' an important minister in an attempt to gain influence over policies.

Ethics in human resource management

The law is used to ensure that when jobs are advertised, there is no discrimination. People are entitled to feel that job selections are made on the basis of merit rather than on the basis of race, nationality, gender or other unfair grounds. This is why HR professionals are trained to avoid discrimination of all kinds.

Worker surveillance can be an important question in some organisations. The question is, to what extent is it reasonable for a member of staff to be watched, to have their e-mails checked, to have calls listened in to? There are important questions of privacy involved. We will look at 'whistleblowing' (on page 255), a question that is directly relevant to worker surveillance. How safe can staff feel if their management 'snoop' on them?

Ethics in production

The production of goods can also lead to ethical problems for business, e.g. in animal testing. More than 2.7 million live animal experiments were authorised in Britain in 2002. This number has halved in the last 30 years. Around the world, animals are used to help in the development of products ranging from shampoo to new cancer drugs.

▲ Would you buy a product if it had been tested on animals?

British law requires that any new drug must be tested on at least two different species of live mammal. One must be a large non-rodent. UK regulations are considered some of the most rigorous in the world. The Animals Act 1986 insists that no non-medical animal experiments should be conducted if there is a realistic alternative.

Almost every medical treatment used on humans has been tested on animals. Animals were used to develop anaesthetics to prevent human pain and suffering during surgery. The ethical questions revolve around the general value of human life in relation to animals. There are also questions about the extent to which animals suffer during testing.

Planned obsolescence

A free market economy means that business produces goods and services that people need or want so that they will pay for them. Businesses try to convince people, partly through advertising and promotions, that they 'need' products. There is nothing unethical in this. However, it is not in the interests of business to produce goods that last for ever. To avoid this, 'planned obsolescence' is the deliberate development of products that will need replacing after a time.

Ethics in sales and marketing

Sometimes businesses employ unethical means to try to generate sales. They can do this in a number of ways.

- *Spamming.* This refers to sending e-mails to thousands of users – similar to a chain letter. E-mail spamming may be combined with e-mail spoofing (see below), which makes it very difficult to determine the originating e-mail address of the sender. Some e-mail systems have the ability to block incoming mail from a specific address. However, because these individuals regularly change their e-mail address, it is difficult to prevent some spam from reaching an e-mail inbox.
- *Spoofing.* This refers to e-mails that appear to have been originated from one source when they were actually sent from another. Individuals sending junk e-mail or spam typically want the e-mail to appear as though it is from an address that may not exist. This way the e-mail cannot be traced back to the originator.
- *Raising their own status.* This happens when businesses place false recommendations or blogs onto a website. These recommendations either come from paid individuals employed by marketing companies or are employees of the business pretending to be satisfied customers. People engaged in this type of activity are known as 'shills'. Online consumers are being conned into believing that legitimate consumers are recommending a product.

Marketing involves a good deal of public relations. Press releases and positive news stories all serve to raise a company profile and improve it in the eyes of consumers. However, in an age where we are all becoming more concerned about our environment, some businesses engage in crude 'greenwashing' – they try to appear 'greener' than they really are.

Ethics in intellectual property

Intellectual property law allows people to own their creative work in the same way that they can own physical property. The owner of intellectual property can control and be rewarded for its use. This encourages further innovation and creativity to the benefit of everyone. The four main types of IP are as follows.

- *Patents* for inventions – new and improved products and processes that are capable of industrial application.
- *Trade marks* for brand identity – of goods and services allowing distinctions to be made between different traders.
- *Designs* for product appearance – a product's appearance is designed by someone with special skills and this is an asset that can be protected by copyright.
- *Copyright* for material – literary and artistic material, music, films, sound recordings and broadcasts, including software and multimedia.

This means that those individuals or business organisations that have invested their time, resources and talents to create something useful or enjoyable for others, have rights to protect it from being stolen. This applies to computer software as well as to music records.

▲ **Free music downloads – an ethical question**

Real lives

Slump in record industry caused by illegal file sharing

Illegal peer-to-peer file sharing, which allows users of software such as Kazaa, Grokster and eDonkey to swap pirated tracks over the internet, has been blamed by the record industry for contributing to a 25% slump in global sales since 1999, worth around £1.3 billion a year.

The record industry has pursued a 'carrot and stick' approach, taking legal action against the worst offenders while encouraging the use of legal download sites such as Napster and iTunes.

Sylvia Price (53), of Cheltenham (Gloucestershire), was forced to pay £2,500 compensation for around 1,400 songs downloaded by her daughter, Emily (14), on the family's home computer. In March, 23 file sharers agreed to pay £2,200 each in compensation for uploading their music libraries onto the internet for others to copy.

Source: Article in *The Guardian*, 22 August 2005

1. What do you feel are the main issues involved in peer-to-peer music file sharing? Do you agree that it is unethical? Why? ✓
2. What do you feel are the implications for the music industry if file sharing were left to continue without restriction? ✓✓

Environmental implications

Could you imagine a world where individuals and businesses were allowed to do exactly what they wanted? The implications for everyone, if businesses were left to carry on without any restrictions at all, would be very serious.

Case study

China: facing environment 'crisis'

In 2004 a Chinese official said that the country's environmental problems had reached crisis levels.

The official said China's industrial development was unsustainable because its environment and resources could not cope. Problems such as pollution, acid rain and contaminated rivers had become key policy issues for China.

In 2007, is China failing to meet new targets on energy efficiency and pollution? The government has set targets to reduce the environmental impact of the country's rapid economic growth. But in pursuit of these targets only Beijing and five other areas have managed to improve efficiency by at least 4% and cut emissions by at least 2% in the first half of 2006.

Chinese officials have not revealed the extent of the failure to reach the targets. The targets, part of the 2006–10 Five Year Plan, call for energy consumption per unit of GDP (gross domestic product) to be cut by 20%, and emissions of pollutants to fall by 10%.

Many Chinese factories ignore the law, and pump toxic waste into rivers and lakes. And with the country still focused on fast economic growth, there is little sign that standards are going to improve in the short term.

1. What do you understand by the statement that China's economic development has become 'unsustainable'? ✓
2. What do you consider are the major implications of inaction in environmental matters by the Chinese government? ✓✓
3. Evaluate the actions that have been taken on a global scale to combat environmental damage from developing economies like China. Do you feel enough has been done? ✓✓✓

The environment

We saw earlier in the unit (page 225) that, on a global scale, the natural environment is already under threat. It is no exaggeration to say that perhaps the most serious threat facing us all in current times comes from climatic changes caused to the planet by human activity. One of the major problems today is that economic activity is growing quickly in different areas of the world.

Corporate implications

The desire of an intelligent business leadership to take account of ethical concerns is now an accepted part of good management. When managers establish corporate social responsibility (CSR) policies, they are responding to the need to take account of stakeholder concerns. Every one of us is a stakeholder in business activities. Business managers are required to comply with the law in many areas, including:

- staffing (discrimination, data protection, health and safety and others)
- consumer protection (sale of goods, trades descriptions, consumer credit)
- the environment (planning, waste management, noise and light pollution, etc.).

Each area creates internal policies, practices, rules and procedures. Without these, businesses can easily fall foul of the law and be fined or suffer worse penalties.

An example is the Age Discrimination Regulations 2006. Since October 2006, it has been unlawful to discriminate on grounds of age against those in or seeking employment and vocational training.

> The Regulations apply to employment and vocational training. They prohibit unjustified direct and indirect age discrimination, and all harassment and victimisation on grounds of age, of people of any age, young or old.

Any business employing staff has to consider this regulation in its selection process.

Remember

Social implications of ethical behaviour affect everyone by ensuring more open, fair and just behaviour.

Outcome activity 38.3

Pass

Describe the social implications of business ethics facing a selected business in its different areas of activity.

Merit

Assess the social implications of business ethics facing a selected business in its different areas of activity.

Grading tips

Pass 

Consider those ethical issues that you think affect society as a whole. Describe what these issues are and why they are of concern. Relate your thinking on this to a business you know of.

Merit 

After giving your full description, to what extent do you feel that these social issues are a real problem in the case of the particular business you are looking at? Consider what the consequences are for different stakeholders.

38.4 Ethical concerns facing different communities

The communities

We speak of a community to refer to:

- the localities we live in (local communities)
- regional and national areas
- the whole of Europe (the European Union) and beyond (globally).

In today's inter-connected world, we increasingly think as one large community.

Local communities

Many businesses are of national importance and their activities have a crucial significance to local communities. Tesco, for instance, is a powerful presence in any community and can have an influence in many different ways (see pages 233–35).

For more than 150 years, the British coalfields offered mining work to the communities around them. But these communities were scarred for generations because of them.

Mining communities suffered a lot of environmental damage, with ugly slag heaps and, in some coalfields, serious coastal damage. Miners suffered long-term health problems too; today many former coal miners still suffer from illnesses caused directly by their job.

Even today, modern businesses leave their mark in many different ways on communities. Despite the environmental

Case study

Buncefield fuel depot: Europe's biggest fire

▲ **Buncefield Depot, dramatic local effects of an industrial accident**

More than 300 tonnes of petrol gushed unnoticed for 40 minutes from the top of a storage tank at the Buncefield oil depot before the spill triggered Europe's biggest fire since World War II, an official report into the 11 December 2005 blaze has concluded. A faulty gauge allowed thousands of gallons of unleaded petrol to be pumped into the already full tank at the site near Hemel Hempstead, Hertfordshire. Emergency safety systems failed to stop the tank over spilling. The resulting vapour cloud ignited, injuring 43 people (two of them seriously).

The resulting explosion destroyed 20 similar tanks and sent up columns of black smoke that drifted across southern England. Firefighters took almost three days to extinguish the blaze and used more than 55,000 gallons of foam, which contained a potentially toxic chemical, perfluorooctane sulphonate.

The Environment Agency said that groundwater at the Hertfordshire site had been contaminated. It plans to dig more boreholes to monitor the situation. Spilled fuel and contaminated firewater have passed into the 'underlying water table' and it could take months or years for the full effects to be known.

Some 12 million litres of contaminated water left over from efforts to put out the fire are sitting in tanks at a sewage treatment works near Rickmansworth, while experts decide what to do.

1. This was, of course, an accident. Are there ethical concerns? What other concerns might the local community have near the Buncefield depot? ✓
2. What steps could be taken to improve the corporate responsibility of Buncefield? ✓✓
3. What arguments could you give, despite the accident, to suggest that the Buncefield depot is a good thing to have in an area? ✓✓✓

and other negative effects, local authorities still welcome new businesses. They bring jobs and cash to areas.

When businesses of any size operate within a locality, there are always ethical concerns. These concerns become highlighted whenever people's worst fears come true – as the Buncefield case study (above) shows.

Regional and national communities

The accident at Buncefield, Hemel Hemstead, shows that while local people can be in immediate danger from a catastrophic event such as an explosion, an entire region is affected when an industry faces ethical questions. Environmental issues do not stop at local, national or international boundaries.

However, specific regions tend to contain particular industries. In the UK, the Midlands contained the heart of the British motor industry. Yorkshire, the north-east, Wales, Scotland, Kent and Nottingham held the bulk of the UK coal mining industry.

When entire industries go through difficulties, there are regional, and often national, effects. The UK car industry suffered from poor planning, inefficiency and bad industrial relations. The coal industry was also troubled by strikes and a national move away from coal as a standard fuel, towards alternatives.

Thinking point

Read the following extract. What do you think? Are the multi-nationals a good thing for a *local* population?

> Multi-national corporations setting up in low wage economies pay wages on average twice that of local businesses. If the multi-nationals are American, the wages are even higher. If this is exploitation, then the problem in our world is that the poor countries are not sufficiently exploited.

Source: Jonathan Dingel, 2004

Pressure groups

Environmental pressure groups consistently do exactly what their name suggests. They force issues into the public's attention and therefore pressurise both governments and business leaders into action. The two best known pressure groups are Greenpeace and Friends of the Earth.

▲ Greenpeace works to stop climate change

Greenpeace is committed to halting climate change caused by burning oil, coal and gas. The group investigates, exposes and confronts those who promote dirty sources of energy, including nuclear power. Greenpeace promotes a clean energy future. It supports decentralised energy systems including renewable technologies and energy efficiency.

Friends of the Earth

▲ Friends of the Earth works locally and globally

Friends of the Earth (FOE) seeks to influence policy and practice through what it describes as 'an honest, accurate and open approach'. It does this in the following ways.

- *Working local to global.* From 200-plus local groups to 70-plus Friends of the Earth International groups, FOE is the only local–global environmental campaign group.
- *Solutions-based research.* FOE tries to find credible alternatives to problems.
- *Enabling campaigning.* FOE provides information and tools to help people act.

The impact of overseeing bodies

It is increasingly recognised that many of the ethical questions that concern us cannot be dealt with just within national boundaries. This means that national, continental and international bodies are taking actions to oversee the activities of business all over the world. Generally, these actions have been based on voluntary measures.

UK Government

The UK government has tried to pass laws or create regulations, codes and practices for as many areas of ethics as possible. The government effectively oversees professional practices, as well as selling, trading, employment, health and safety and pollution or waste management. The UK government is also aware of the wider concerns about global warming and has been a supporter of collective efforts to reduce carbon emissions under the Kyoto Protocol.

There are several regulatory bodies that exist in order to protect the ongoing interests of UK stakeholder groups. These include:

- Financial Services Authority (www.fsa.gov.uk)
- Food Standards Agency (www.food.gov.uk)
- Advertising Standards Authority (www.asa.org.uk).

Practice point

Investigate each of the bodies listed above. Then write a concise report stating what they try to do.

Take it further

Research the Business Link website by going to www.businesslink.gov.uk and enter the word 'Environment' into the search box on the home page. Create a presentation informing others in your class about the variety of areas the government tries to monitor.

United Nations (UN)

The United Nations is based in New York – although the land it uses is international, *not* American, territory. The UN (as it is usually called) is made up of 191 countries from around the world. It was set up in 1945 (after World War II) as a way of bringing people together to avoid war. In fact, the UN logo shows the world held together in the 'olive branches of peace' (see page 241).

On page 241, we saw that in 1948 the UN issued its Declaration of Human Rights. This sets out the basic expectations that anyone, wherever they are, should be entitled to expect from employment. These days, the UN is trying once again to influence the global business community in order to protect vulnerable people from exploitation by multi-national businesses. There is a UN Global Compact that calls on businesses to issue regular reports to stakeholders about social and ethical responsibilities. It also makes a commitment that a business will follow ethical policies.

European Union (EU)

As we saw on page 240, the EU now covers almost half a million people in 27 nations. The EU can issue directives to member states, effectively instructing them to implement law.

World Trade Organization (WTO)

The World Trade Organization is an international body whose purpose is to promote free trade by persuading countries to abolish import taxes and other barriers. As such, it has become closely associated with globalisation. The WTO is the only international agency overseeing the rules of international trade.

World Health Organization (WHO)

The World Health Organization is a branch of the UN that promotes physical, mental and social well-being across the world. It funds international health research, co-ordinates inter-governmental health policies and monitors standards of health globally.

Case study

Scrapped cars: EU encourages recycling

There are 30 million motor vehicles on Britain's roads and around two million are scrapped each year. Previously, car owners paid about £50 to have their vehicles scrapped, which encouraged some people to dump cars illegally. But under new EU laws, all this is about to change.

The End of Life Vehicles Directive (which forces member states to legislate) intends to reduce pollution and waste by encouraging more recycling of materials from scrapped cars. Manufacturers will cover the cost. As a result, the government and environmentalists hope fewer cars will be dumped.

The European legislation sets a target of 80% of the materials in old vehicles to be reused or recycled, rising to 85% in 2015. The change was brought in despite protests from car manufacturers, who said when the law was proposed it would bankrupt them.

Two companies, Autogreen and Cartakeback, will handle the UK's scrapped vehicles. They will issue certificates of destruction to the owners, so that the vehicles can be deregistered from the government's DVLA (Driver and Vehicle Licensing Agency) database.

1. Why do you feel that the scrapping of old motor vehicles should be a concern to the European Union? ✓
2. What other ethical issues does the EU appear to become involved in? ✓✓
3. What arguments, if any, could you put forward to say that it is important the EU acts on these issues? ✓✓✓

Ethical issues facing communities

The consequence of business activity across the world is having a dramatic effect on many local communities. Some of these communities are primitive tribal peoples whose entire way of existence is threatened by business corporations seeking more profit. Many others are agricultural/rural communities.

The South American Amazon Basin is a vast area, the majority of which is in Brazil. The area used to contain more than two million square miles of rainforest. Over the last 30 years the Brazilian government has allowed deforestation to permit industrialisation and the creation of a network of roadways. This has had a serious impact on the scattered communities living there, as well as on the forest itself.

The same process has occurred in Africa, where commercial logging, mining, drilling and clearing for living space have all led to large areas of deforestation.

In the Philippines, mining companies are not only granted mineral mining rights, they are also granted a logging concession allowing them to chop down trees to supply timber for its pit props and sluices.

The problems associated with deforestation and mining are dramatic for local populations.

- Tribal groups suffer loss of land.
- There is huge disruption to their local ways of survival.
- This can result in loss of cultures.
- There is damage to the health of those living in these communities, not least because of pollution of the local water supplies.

Some globally known corporations work hard to involve the local populations in their corporate activities. Levi Strauss, the jeans manufacturer, has a training and education programme involving over 12,000 employees worldwide. The Levi Strauss Foundation engages in local charitable causes and offers matched funding to help local people.

▲ The Amazon Rainforest is of global significance

Real lives

Shell and the Ogoni People of Nigeria

On 6 June 2001, the Shell Oil pipeline, which passes through the Baraale community (home to the Ogoni people of Nigeria), ruptured and started spilling crude oil into nearby forests, farmlands and houses. Aseme Mbani, chief of the community, was in his farm when the pipeline ruptured.

'I was working when I saw crude oil rushing into my cassava farm. Then I went to the pipeline and I saw where it was leaking. It flowed into my house and flooded my entire home with crude oil.' He had to abandon the house.

The chief took steps to ensure that Shell repaired the ruptured pipeline. 'I reported the matter to the Shell contractors in charge of the pipeline and also to the police. After that, we wrote Shell a "Save Our Soul" letter. When there was no response I went to Shell to report the matter at a section they call "Ogoni Re-entry". They told me they had seen the letter I wrote. They said we should suffer the spillage because we caused it. They said we had been cutting pipelines and we should reap what we sow.'

Chief Mbani said the oil continued to leak and he kept 'repeating and repeating' his visits to Shell to urge them to act fast before the situation worsened. But Shell never responded.

Source: ERA Field Report No. 89 'Shells Oil Spillage'

1. In what ways, if any, do you think the local people in the Ogoni community of Nigeria benefit from Shell Oil activities on their land? ✓
2. Explain why multi-nationals like Shell should have a responsibility to people like the Ogoni. ✓✓
3. How might Shell benefit from addressing issues like this? ✓✓✓

Globalisation

The world at the start of the twenty-first century has become inter-connected. Business markets now extend around the globe and it is modern communication systems that have made this possible.

- The British service sector (banks, IT services, etc.) is able to deal with customers from a call centre in India.
- A sportswear manufacturer can design its products in Europe, make them in south-east Asia and sell them in North America.

Making use of employees or production facilities abroad is called 'outsourcing'. And this is where the anti-globalisation arguments really begin. If these practices replace domestic economic activity with an economy that is heavily influenced or controlled from another country or continent, then the process of globalisation can also be seen as a surrender of power to the big corporations, or a means of keeping poorer nations in their place.

For some of its critics, **globalisation** has come to be symbolised by:

- low-paid sweatshop workers
- genetically modified seeds forced on developing world farmers
- the selling-off of state-owned industry to qualify for International Monetary Fund (IMF) and World Bank loans
- increasing dominance of US and European corporate cultures across the globe.

Not everyone agrees that globalisation is necessarily evil, or that globalised corporations are running the lives of individuals, or are more powerful than nations. Some say that the spread of globalisation, free markets and free trade into the developing world is the best way to beat poverty there.

Key Term

Globalisation Where the economies of the world are becoming more dominated by a few multi-national businesses

Remember

Globalisation means that the world is developing into one huge inter-dependent economy. The problem is that this economy is controlled by multi-national business, not democratically elected people.

Cultural imperialism

Culture governs every aspect of our lives:

- our dress sense
- our manners
- our outlook and opinions
- our art and architecture
- our education
- our lifestyle.

To govern culture, it seems, is to govern the world. But what is **cultural imperialism**?

Imperialism means dominating another country to achieve your own aims. (Britain was an imperialist nation for many years when it had an overseas empire.) Cultural imperialism is a very divisive topic. In other words, it can cause a great deal of disagreement. Some people argue that countries with dominating cultures (e.g. the USA, the UK) are forcing their own culture on others through unfair trade practices. Others argue that nobody can be forced to accept cultural imports.

However, some complaints are not easy to dismiss – particularly those surrounding companies rather than countries. Look at the accusations that follow.

- Western media companies have been using large budgets and aggressive 'monopoly-like' practices to steadily push their smaller, less aggressive, competitors onto the sidelines, both at home and abroad.

- While demanding increased access to markets, Western producers and distributors have been very protective of their domestic front. They keep their home audiences largely oblivious to the existence of other products and use their dominant market positions to make it difficult for smaller distributors to bring products into the Western market.
- Western producers and distributors have been protecting their domestic markets by releasing only selected products themselves, or only releasing products after they have been 'adapted' or 're-branded' to meet Western cultural norms.

Remember

Cultural imperialism refers to the tendency for Western business corporations to impose Western ways of life on other cultures around the world.

Key Term

Cultural imperialism Where local ways of life are being influenced and altered through the effects of Western values and practices spreading all over the world.

Ecology concerns

Just as there are concerns about global (Western-dominated) businesses imposing their own cultural assumptions on local cultures around the world, so there are concerns that economic developments are wiping out local wildlife and bio-systems. An ecological system links plants and animals which exist naturally and in harmony in an area. Any interruption to this delicate balance can result in both plants and animals dying out.

Fair trade

▲ Look for this Mark on Fairtrade products (www.fairtrade.org.uk)

Fairtrade is not only about trading fairly, it is also about development. With Fairtrade, producers receive an agreed and stable price that covers the cost of sustainable production. In addition, producer organisations receive an extra payment, known as the Fairtrade social premium, to invest in social, environmental or economic development projects.

The Fairtrade Foundation was established in 1992 as an independent certification body that licenses the FAIRTRADE Mark to products that meet international standards which are set by Fairtrade Labelling Organisations International (FLO). Certified producer organisations and registered traders must comply with these standards to ensure better terms of trade and decent working conditions.

In addition, producers must institute process requirements to encourage their organisations to continually:

- improve working conditions for workers and product quality
- increase the environmental stability of their activities
- invest in the development of their organisations and the welfare of their producers.

Fairtrade trading standards stipulate that traders must:

- pay a price to producers that covers the costs of sustainable production and living
- pay a premium that producers can invest in development
- make partial advance payments when requested by producers
- sign contracts that allow for long-term planning and sustainable production practices.

Child labour

UNICEF (the United Nations Children's Emergency Fund) has said that globally:

- 352 million children aged between five and seventeen years are engaged in some kind of employment
- 97% of all working children employed in developing countries (many in enforced labour), work in extremely bad conditions.

Children continue to be forced into labour because:

- they do not cost very much to employ
- in some cases, the money they earn can mean the difference between survival or starvation for their family.

Child exploitation is therefore largely caused by poverty.

- In the 43 countries with an average family income of US$500 or less per person, child labour runs at 30%–60%.
- Where average income is between US$500 and US$1,000, the figure falls to between 10% –30% of all children.

Whistleblowing

Sometimes in a workplace (whether it is a private business or a public service organisation), corruption can occur. An example would be where a manager gives a close relative confidential information so that they win a money-making contract. What happens if another member of staff finds out about this and feels that something should be done about it?

The Public Interest Disclosures Act 1998 made it an offence to discipline anyone who made a disclosure about something believed to be in the 'public interest'. This is '**whistleblowing**', i.e. alerting everyone to something that is wrong.

Key Term

Whistleblowing Informing managers or other authorities about unethical practices going on within an organisation.

Outcome activity 38.4

Pass

Describe the ethical concerns facing the communities in which a selected business operates.

Merit

Explain ethical concerns facing the communities in which a selected business operates and suggest measures that could be taken to improve corporate responsibility.

Grading tips

Pass

Select a particular business or industry, then describe the ethical concerns that are generated by its activities. These concerns are likely to be local ones. Example: a forest or woodland is being lost; a local ecological system is disrupted.

Merit

Give a full explanation of why there are concerns about the activities of the business. What steps, if any, could the management of the business take to minimise the concerns?

Askham Bryan College LIBRARY BOOK

End of unit test

1. In your own words, write an explanation of what is meant by 'business ethics'.
2. What is the distinction between an 'ethical business' and a business that tries to act ethically?
3. Explain what is meant by 'sustainability'.
4. What is 'corruption'?
5. Who are the 'stakeholders' in a business?
6. How would you distinguish 'stakeholders' from 'shareholders'?
7. Why might there be a conflict of interest between different stakeholders in a business?
8. What is meant by 'ethical pressures'?
9. How can pressure groups influence ethical questions?
10. What are the main areas of legislation in the UK that influence the ethical behaviour of businesses?
11. What are the distinctive features of ethics in relation to human resource management?
12. What is 'planned obsolescence'? Why is it an ethical concern?
13. Why should we be concerned with global warming? What has this got to do with business?
14. Give a brief outline of an ethical issue that affects each of the following:
    - the local community
    - the regional community
    - the national and international community.
15. What is meant by corporate social responsibility? Is it important and why?
16. What is 'globalisation'? Is it important?
17. Select an ethical issue and prepare a presentation about it for the rest of your class. Explain why it is an 'issue' at all.

Books

Gillespie, A, 2002, *Business in Action*, Hodder Arnold, 2002

Websites

http://anitaroddick.com/aboutanita.php – explains Anita Roddick's ethical stance

www.bbc.co.uk/news – BBC news website

www.berr.gov.uk – website for Department for Business, Enterprise and Regulatory Reform

www.business-ethics.com – deals with a range of business ethics questions

www.co-operativebank.co.uk – website of an ethical business

www.csreurope.org/aboutus – deals with corporate social responsibility

www.dti.gov.uk – website for Department for Trade and Industry

www.ethicalconsumer.org – campaigning website on behalf of ethically-minded consumers

www.foe.co.uk – site of pressure group Friends of the Earth

www.greenpeace.org.uk – Greenpeace information

www.hse.gov.uk – Health and Safety Executive website

www.hse.gov.uk/workers/whistleblowing.htm – about whistleblowing at work

www.ibe.org.uk – Institute of Business Ethics website

www.telegraph.co.uk – Daily Telegraph website

www.thebodyshop.com – Body Shop's site

www.tuc.org.uk – the Trade Union Congress website

Grading criteria	Outcome activity	Page number
To achieve a pass grade the evidence shows that the learner is able to:		
p1 Describe the ethical issues a business needs to consider in its operational activities	38.1	231
p2 Explain the implications for the business and stakeholders of a business operating ethically	38.2	242
p3 Describe the social implications of business ethics facing a selected business in its different areas of activity	38.3	247
p4 Describe the ethical concerns facing the communities in which a selected business operates	38.4	255
To achieve a merit grade the evidence shows that, in addition to the pass criteria, the learner is able to:		
m1 Assess how a selected business could improve its operations ethically	38.1	231
m2 Assess the social implications of business ethics facing a selected business in its different areas of activity	38.3	247
m3 Explain the ethical concerns facing the communities in which a selected business operates and suggest measures that could be taken to improve corporate responsibility	38.4	255
To achieve a distinction grade the evidence must show that, in addition to the pass and merit criteria, the learner is able to:		
d1 Evaluate the impact of a selected business's ethical behaviour on stakeholders and the business	38.2	242

Exploring business and the economic environment

Introduction

Business people are not always masters of their own destiny. It is possible to plan extensively only to find those well laid plans disrupted by external influences over which a company has no control. One of the biggest influences is that of government. Many government actions have effects on businesses – some positive and some negative. Each action needs to be considered and reacted to positively by business leaders. Also, as business becomes more global, international factors become increasingly influential on the success of businesses. This unit examines economic change and how it impacts on companies. It is important to understand these influences so we are better prepared to exploit opportunities that arise and meet economic challenges positively.

What you need to learn

On completion of this unit you should:

1. Understand the impact on businesses of changes in the economic environment
2. Know how government spending impacts on businesses
3. Understand fiscal and monetary policies and the effects on spending
4. Know how the global economy affects UK businesses and competition.

Consider this

Airport tax puts airlines and passengers in a spin

From 1 February 2007 the UK government has decided to increase air passenger duty (commonly known as airport tax) from £5 per passenger for short haul economy flights to £40 for long haul business class flights. The government has said that the money raised will be used for improving public transport and environmental projects.

This has left airlines with a dilemma. Many passengers had already paid for their flights – often several months before the new tax was announced. However, the Treasury insists that the new duty should be paid. British Airways has decided it will not ask its passengers to pay any more if they have already booked flights, and it has agreed to pay the extra tax out of its profits. The budget airlines, though, are finding things much more difficult. Easyjet and Ryanair have been quoted as saying that their profit on each seat sold is so low they cannot afford to absorb the extra costs. They are therefore planning to contact all their customers to ask them to pay the extra duty. If customers do not pay before they fly, they will not be allowed to board the plane.

Passengers were left bewildered and angry that the government could increase tax on a service they had already paid for. Many were dubious about Gordon Brown's claims that the money would be used to help the environment. 'It's just another way of stealing money from my wallet,' said one.

- Who is Gordon Brown?
- What does his job entail?
- What is the likely impact of the above events on:
  - the airlines
  - airline passengers
  - the UK government.
- Why do you think the government needs to raise tax?
- This additional duty is intended to be 'used for improving public transport and environmental projects'. What are the justifications for taxing flights to pay for such projects?
- This is an example of an indirect tax, which means a tax added to the price of goods and services that we buy. It has been estimated that a typical British household will pay more than £200,000 in indirect taxes such as VAT and other duties over its lifetime, and a further £400,000 in direct taxes such as income tax.
  - What is your reaction to these figures?
  - Why do you think the government chooses to raise tax by adding it to the cost of things we buy?
  - What would you like to see happen to the tax you pay?

39.1 Impact on business of changes in the economic environment

Business cycles

The economies of the world are constantly changing. Sometimes they are doing well; sometimes the picture is more bleak. In the UK, for example, the economy has improved in recent years. However, back in the early 1990s the picture was very different.

Between 1990 and 1992 the UK experienced a period of recession (i.e. a period when economic outlook is very poor).

- Many firms struggled to survive.
- Many people lost their jobs; several others were afraid they were about to lose theirs.
- Living standards fell.
- There was a great deal of uncertainty about the future.

Since then prospects have improved considerably. Indeed, the UK is now going through one of the longest periods of growth (an improving economy) on record.

If we look back over UK economic history we can see that this pattern is a repeating one. Periods of economic prosperity inevitably seem to be followed by periods of economic downturn, but eventually the good times return again. We describe this as a 'cycle' – something that goes around and around. Look at the diagram of the **business cycle**, below.

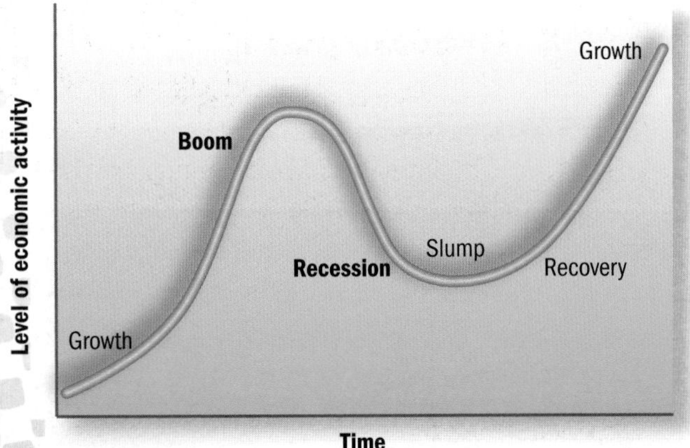

▲ The business cycle

Key Term

Business cycle Changes in the levels of economic activity in a country, normally featuring alternating periods of growth and slump.

The period of time covered on the graph is several years – possibly as long as 15 to 20 years. That said, economic cycles do not all last similar periods of time and some are much longer or shorter than others. The different points on the graph mean the following.

- ***Growth*** – a period of improving economic circumstances. Business profits are improving, consumer confidence is improving, jobs are being created, wealth is being earned and the government is able to provide good levels of public services.
- ***Slump*** – the opposite of growth. Business profits begin to fall, firms stop hiring new staff and start to shed surplus workers, less wealth is being earned and since tax revenues begin to fall it is harder for the government to provide additional public services.
- ***Recovery*** – the first signs of growth. Businesses see orders starting to improve and profits begin to pick up. Employment prospects will start to improve but not immediately as firms wait to make sure that improvements in trading are lasting ones.

Key Terms

Growth A period of improving economic circumstances.

Slump A period of declining economic circumstances.

There are two other points marked on the chart: 'boom' and 'recession'. These appear in bold to indicate that they are extremes of economic activity or inactivity and do not occur in every business cycle.

Boom

A **boom** period is how we describe growth that is very rapid. During a boom period:

- wealth quickly increases
- business profits leap upwards
- living standards across the economy make rapid improvements.

The UK experienced a boom during the mid- to late 1980s. China is currently experiencing a very rapid boom period as its economy improves at a fast rate. Indeed, many Chinese people are experiencing greater wealth than ever before.

Recession

Boom periods are very exciting times but they do not last forever and eventually a slump will set in. Sometimes the economy climbs so far that when the slump comes it is a very deep and rapid one.

When the slump began in the UK back in the late 1980s the economy declined very rapidly. The slump was quick and ultimately very deep.

- Businesses found life extremely difficult.
- Many people lost their jobs.
- Because they had lost their jobs and weren't earning money, many people also lost their homes.

A very deep slump is known as a **recession**. This is a painful time for both citizens and businesses in the country concerned.

If we were to redraw the graph on page 260 over a longer period of time we would hope to see a pattern of improving growth (above right).

Although the pattern of growth-slump-recovery-growth (with occasional booms and recessions) is regularly repeated, the overall trend is an improving one. Each slump is slightly less deep than the previous one and each period of growth goes slightly higher than the last one: overall the economy is an improving one.

In recent years, the UK government has tried to even out the highs and lows so that the growth rate is more steady and predictable. This policy has met with some success during the late 1990s and the first half of the 2000s.

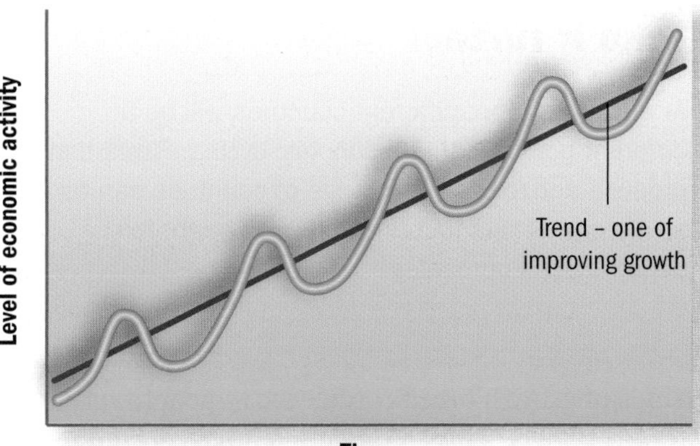

▲ The long-term business cycle

Key Terms

Boom A period of very rapidly improving economic circumstances.

Recession Officially two consecutive quarters of negative growth. This is a period of rapidly declining economic circumstances.

Remember

Although we regularly experience growth, slump and recovery during business cycles, boom and recession are not inevitable. With astute economic management they can often be avoided and therefore do not appear in every cycle.

Thinking point

What do you think are the main implications for both businesses and individuals of periods of growth and slump? Copy and complete the following table with your thoughts.

	Growth	Slump
Impact on businesses		
Impact on individuals		

Take it further

At any given time, different countries will be at different points in their economic cycles. Firms that produce and/or sell in a range of countries can take advantage of this fact. In what ways might this benefit such companies?

Periods of growth breed confidence in people and business leaders. This confidence tends to encourage more spending, which creates more optimism. Consequently, we experience an upward cycle of economic growth and improvement. If this upward cycle moves quickly, a boom could result. Visit http://money.howstuffworks.com/recession5.htm for an excellent pictorial example of this effect.

This upward spiral will generally continue until there is a major shock to the economy. Perhaps the government may need to raise interest rates sharply; perhaps share prices begin to tumble; or maybe the country goes to war with another one. Once the upward spiral stops, uncertainty creeps into the thoughts of the people in the country. They begin to spend less and save more 'just in case'. The reduced demand for business products means that firms cannot employ as many people. This, in turn, further reduces consumer confidence. The slump becomes a downward spiral which, if not checked, could lead to a full recession. Visit http://money.howstuffworks.com/recession6.htm to see how this effect works.

Indicators of economic change

There will always be changes and fluctuations in the level of economic activity within an economy since levels of spending, production and employment do not remain constant. Hence, we get regular ups and downs in economic activity, which creates the business cycle.

What would prove helpful is if you could predict when the country is about to enter a different stage in the cycle. Good business decision making is bound to be helped by such knowledge. Although this is a very imprecise activity, there are a number of indicators that can help with economic predictions. These are described below.

Changes in Gross Domestic Product (GDP) and economic growth rates

Gross Domestic Product (or GDP) is the value of all the goods and services produced in a country over the period of a year. For example, according to the Office for National Statistics (www.statistics.gov.uk), the GDP for the UK in 2005 (at market prices) was £1,224,461,000,000 (that's 1.224 trillion pounds!).

Economic growth occurs when a country increases its ability to produce goods and services. Economic growth is important, as it provides a measurement of how standards of living in the country are changing. Steady growth leads to substantial improvements in standards of living. Increased growth provides additional earned income, improved employment prospects, additional business profits, further government spending on vital services and therefore improvements in standards of living for all citizens.

Economic growth is measured by calculating the percentage changes in GDP from one year to the next. We always describe economic growth in terms of percentages, and growth rates of 4% or 5% are very good. If they can be maintained for several years they can lead to substantial rises in living standards for a country.

Key Terms

Gross Domestic Product (GDP): The total market value of all the goods and services produced by a country in one year.

Economic growth: Increases in GDP that lead to improvements in standards of living for the country's citizens.

Typically, over the last 40 years in the UK we have achieved between 2% and 3% per year. This is respectable, but not nearly as great as the rises experienced by some of our trading partners such as Germany and Japan, which have regularly achieved growth rates in excess of 4%.

While these differences may not seem great, taken over a period of years they can lead to widening gaps in standards of living – gaps that are very difficult to reduce.

Changes in growth rates are good indicators of how the economy is progressing through the business cycle. Increases in levels of GDP indicate that the country is moving into a period of growth. Rapid growth rates suggest that a boom is beginning. Falling levels of economic growth suggest that the country is entering a period of slump. If they fall very low this could result in recession.

The official government definition of recession is two consecutive quarters of negative growth – in other words, where growth is actually negative (falling GDP) for a six-month period. Keeping an eye on trends in GDP should, therefore, give indications of impending changes in the business cycle.

Rates of inflation

Inflation is a general increase in prices for goods and services in an economy. The UK government uses a number of measures to monitor levels of inflation. The most frequently used is the Consumer Price Index, or CPI.

The CPI measures inflation by assessing the price of buying a range of goods and services. The price is compared with the price of buying the same goods and services at the same time the previous year. The difference is the effect of inflation. We normally refer to inflation in percentage terms. The UK government has set itself a target of keeping inflation down to 2% per year. Rapid rises in inflation are generally bad news for an economy.

- Inflation makes it difficult for businesses to predict the cost of materials, which makes it harder to plan for growth.

Practice point

The table below shows GDP figures (in millions) for the UK for each quarter from 1978 to 1983.

1978 Q1	£154,409
1978 Q2	£155,849
1978 Q3	£157,492
1978 Q4	£158,632
1979 Q1	£157,255
1979 Q2	£163,976
1979 Q3	£160,082
1979 Q4	£161,730
1980 Q1	£160,164
1980 Q2	£157,277
1980 Q3	£156,955
1980 Q4	£155,163
1981 Q1	£153,980
1981 Q2	£154,174
1981 Q3	£156,149
1981 Q4	£156,029
1982 Q1	£156,464
1982 Q2	£158,359
1982 Q3	£158,253
1982 Q4	£158,976
1983 Q1	£161,274
1983 Q2	£162,451
1983 Q3	£164,321
1983 Q4	£166,221

Source: www.statistics.gov.uk

- Draw a line graph of the data above. Make sure you label the graph well.
- Identify the periods of growth, boom, slump, recession and recovery on your graph.
- Describe the levels of consumer and business confidence you would expect in 1978 Q3, 1979 Q2, 1980 Q3, 1981 Q3 and 1983 Q4.
- What are the dangers for businesses and consumers of boom periods in an economy?

- Business costs may also rise further as workers demand wage rises to compensate for rising shop prices.
- Price increases make it harder for consumers to buy products, so demand falls. This makes it harder for firms to survive.
- Consumers on fixed incomes (e.g. pensioners) find their standard of living falling because they cannot buy as much as they used to.
- Price rises make it harder for firms to sell abroad, so exports fall.

Inflation therefore hastens a country's movement into periods of slump and possibly recession. So monitoring levels of inflation can also be an indicator of changes in the business cycle.

Key Term

Inflation An increase in the general price levels in a country. This is generally regarded as problematic for a country's economy.

Practice point

Visit www.statistics.gov.uk – the Office for National Statistics website.

- What are the latest figures for inflation in the UK?
- What has been the trend over the last three years?
- What does this tell you about our prospects in the business cycle in the near future?

Take it further

- Using www.statistics.gov.uk again, find the CPI figures for 1989 to the present day. Outline the trends you identify. Identify the times when the figures would give you concern and comfort. Explain your answers.
- Why do you think the UK government does not target 0% inflation?

Employment rates

Employment rates are often regarded as an indicator of economic events. However, they are not generally very useful in predicting trends. This is because employment is what economists refer to as a 'lagging indicator'. This means something that reacts slowly to changes in economic conditions and 'lags behind' events.

Jobs tend to be lost during periods of slump, although they are not generally lost until the slump has begun. They *react* to the slump rather than *predict* it is about to happen. Similarly, jobs are created during periods of growth. However, it is not until growth has been happening for a little while that firms have the confidence to take on new employees. Consequently, although employment levels do change during the business cycle they are of little predictive value.

Trade surpluses/deficits and the balance of payments

The **balance of payments** is, in its simplest terms, an account showing the difference between the total exports and the total imports for a country. Exports are those goods we sell abroad. Imports are those we buy from abroad. Any individual or business will wish to ensure it has more income than outgoings. Countries are no different, except we say they hope to encourage more exports than imports and thereby earn wealth for the country.

A situation where we sell more abroad than we buy from abroad is known as a **trade surplus** situation. This is what governments regard as a sound balance of payments situation. If the value of imports exceeds the value of exports money is leaving the country. This is known as a **trade deficit** situation.

Export sales are very significant to the UK economy. In 2005 the UK exported £32.3 billion goods and services. Therefore, changes in this market are likely to affect our growth prospects significantly. Any event that reduces our ability to sell abroad could severely reduce our GDP and therefore help to move our business cycle into a period of slump. Equally, any improvement in our prospects of selling to other countries could help to move us towards growth.

Key Terms

Balance of payments The difference between the level of exports from a country and the level of imports into that country.

Trade deficit A period where imports exceed exports.

Trade surplus A period where exports exceed imports.

Leading indicators of recovery

The Office for National Statistics (ONS) has identified a number of indicators that suggest a country is about to enter periods of recovery and growth. It breaks these down into Longer and Shorter Leading Indicators.

Longer Leading Indicators

These usually pre-date general economic recovery by about 12 months.

- Housebuilding picks up – the construction industry is particularly sensitive to the business cycle.
- Companies begin to declare financial surpluses (profits).
- There are improvements in the general price of shares (which may be monitored by using indices such as the FTSE 100 Index).
- Short-term interest rates fall.
- Business optimism improves. The Confederation for Business Industry (CBI) does regular surveys to monitor levels of optimism among business leaders, and this is the indicator that is usually used.
- There are rises in GDP. The ONS gathers this information and uses trend analysis to predict how the GDP might change in future months.
- There is a stable money supply. This is the amount of spending power in the economy. Fast rises in the money supply can lead to inflation, which could be harmful to growth.

Shorter Leading Indicators

These indicators will normally give immediate warning of recovery.

- There is growth in levels of credit taken out by consumers.
- The number of new car registrations increase.
- New orders taken by UK firms increase. Once again, the CBI surveys these statistics and publishes them regularly.

Leading indicators of recession

The same economic indicators that tend to predict growth can also be used to predict slump and recessionary periods. For example, housebuilding is normally one of the first industries to be affected when recession is about to take place. So a fall in housebuilding can indicate that a slump is imminent.

Remember

It is important to look for patterns when we are looking for indicators. One of the above factors could suggest an imminent change in the cycle. But it could equally have been caused by another event. However, if two or three of the indicators appear, it is a much clearer sign of possible change.

Practice point

Use the internet to research details about the current state of the leading indicators listed above. What are your predictions for the business cycle in the near future? Visit www.statistics.gov.uk. Some further searching should reveal other useful sites. You might also visit www.bbc.co.uk/news – the BBC news site.

'Ripple effects' of downturns in particular industries

A downturn in one industry generally has a knock-on effect on others. This tends to magnify the overall negative effect on the economy. For example, when a business such as construction sees a downturn, this has negative 'ripple' effects for a number of industries. The flowchart below illustrates several of these effects. Note the number of industries that see falls in demand. The resulting job losses all have further ripple effects. The fact that people are losing their jobs means there are even fewer people in a position to buy a new property. This exacerbates the downturn in all the industries named (see arrow Z) as the process starts all over again.

Thinking point

A downturn may be caused by an unexpected event, often referred to as a 'trigger'. For example, it could be argued that the recession in the UK in the early 1990s was triggered by the large increases in interest rates that took place between May 1988 and October 1989 when the interest rate rose from 7.38% in May 1988 to 14.88% in October 1989 (source: www.bankofengland.co.uk). This caused severe problems for:

- businesses that had borrowed money
- individuals with mortgages and other forms of borrowing.

You should work with a partner on this task. Make notes about how individuals and businesses would have been affected by these events and the ripple effects this might have had which led to slump and recession in the early 1990s. Produce a flowchart like the one below to show how these ripple effects would have happened.

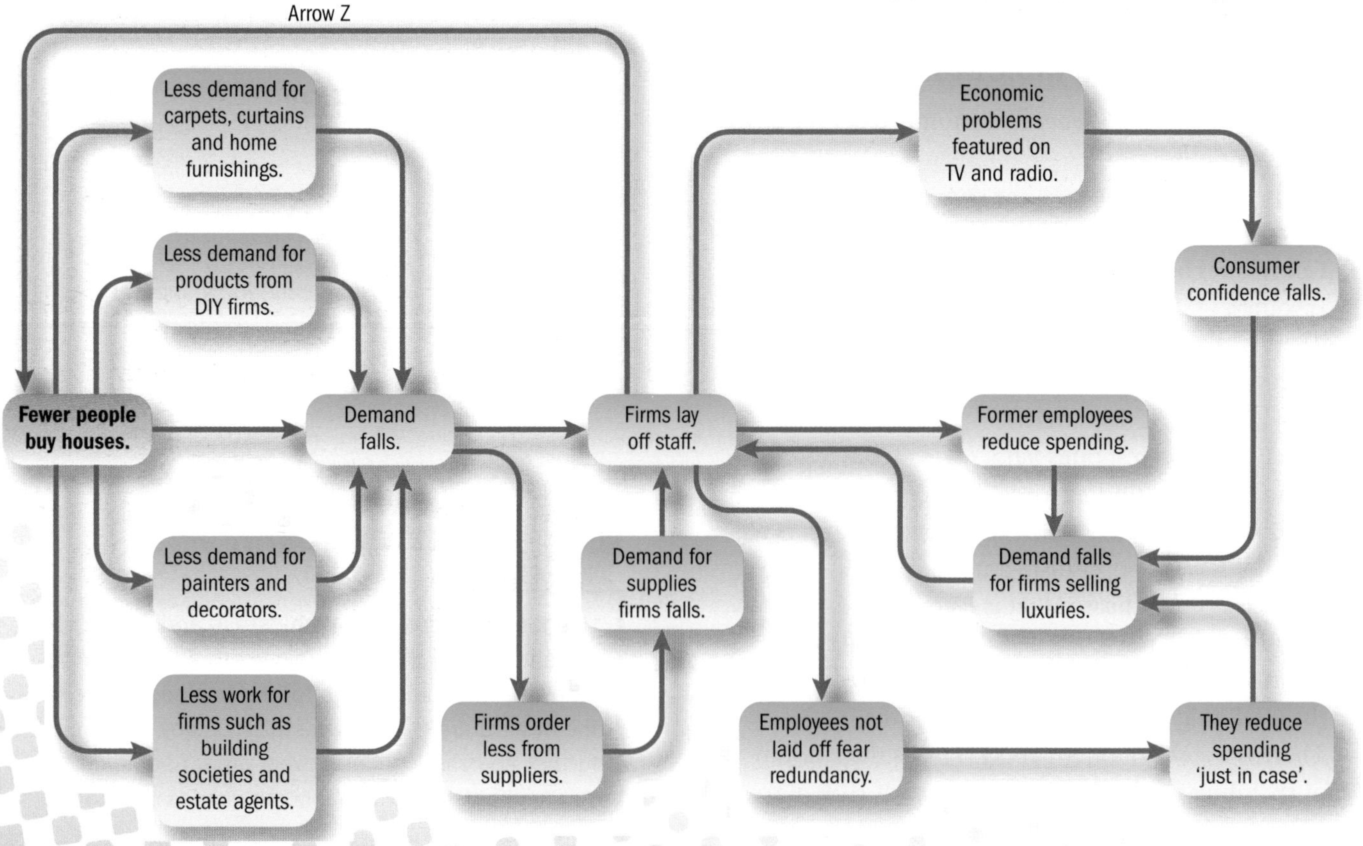

Arrow Z

Fewer people buy houses.

Less demand for carpets, curtains and home furnishings.

Less demand for products from DIY firms.

Less demand for painters and decorators.

Less work for firms such as building societies and estate agents.

Demand falls.

Firms order less from suppliers.

Demand for supplies firms falls.

Firms lay off staff.

Economic problems featured on TV and radio.

Consumer confidence falls.

Former employees reduce spending.

Demand falls for firms selling luxuries.

Employees not laid off fear redundancy.

They reduce spending 'just in case'.

▲ **Ripple effects of a downturn in the construction industry**

Take it further

Not all triggers come from economic events. Some have political or social roots. The USA entered a recessionary period in late 2001 and early 2002. This was made far worse by the terrorist attack on the World Trade Center on 11 September 2001. This attack was the trigger for a steep slump in business activity in the USA.

Draw a flowchart (use page 266 as an example) showing how this event might have caused a downturn in the USA's business cycle. Try this on your own, but visit http://money.howstuffworks.com/recession7.htm if you run out of ideas.

- The terrorist attacks in the USA also had a downward effect on the UK's business cycle. Why do you think this might have happened?
- How inter-related do you think the business cycles of different nations are? Give examples to support your answer.

Outcome activity 39.1

The assignment for this unit requires you to consider the effects of a changing economy on a selected business. You will base your answer around a particular UK company, Balfour Beatty. You would be well advised to find out more about what Balfour Beatty do before you go any further. Visit www.balfourbeatty.com to read about them in detail.

Pass

Describe the likely effects on Balfour Beatty of variations in the economic environment.

Grading tips

Pass P1

For a thorough answer you should ensure that you cover the following.

- A description of the business cycle, including explanations of the nature of each stage of the cycle.
- Details of how you think Balfour Beatty will be affected by each stage of the business cycle. In particular you should focus on:
  – the changing levels of demand across the cycle
  – ripple effects during slump or recession
  – the indicators of recovery that the managers of the company should look out for during slump or recession
  – how the changing employment levels at each stage will affect the firm.
- You should also discuss the probable impacts of periods of high and low inflation in the UK economy on Balfour Beatty.

How government spending impacts on business

Case study

Pre-Budget report provides major boost for building firms

In his Pre-Budget Report in December 2006, the Chancellor announced that an additional £2.85 billion will be spent between 2007 and 2011 on building new schools and improving existing school buildings, bringing total spending on school buildings over the period to £27.9 billion.

The building programme is to be funded by a combination of government money and private finance initiatives. A number of construction companies are expected to benefit from the announcement, including Carillion and Balfour Beatty, who both saw their share prices rise following the announcement. Both of these companies have strong portfolios of publicly funded projects.

Source: *The Daily Reporter*, 8 December 2006

1. Explain why this announcement was such good news for Balfour Beatty and Carillion. ✓
2. Explain the phrase 'The building programme is to be funded by a combination of government money and private finance initiatives'. You may need to do some research to answer this question. ✓✓
3. What are the dangers of having 'strong portfolios of publicly funded projects'? What might happen in the future and what could be the effects on these companies? ✓✓✓

The UK government, both national and local, has a lot of influence on UK businesses because government is the biggest spender of money in the economy. Many of the products and services the government spends money on are provided by private companies. Indeed, for some companies the government is their major customer. Consequently, changes in levels of government spending can have significant effects on the success of certain businesses.

▼ UK government spending by area

Spending area	Planned spending 2006/7
Social Security (includes state pensions, Jobseekers Allowance, Child Tax Credits and other benefits such as Incapacity Benefit).	£151 billion
Health (finances the National Health Service paying for medicines, surgery and hospital buildings and health professionals).	£96 billion
Education (covers the funding of schools, further and higher education).	£73 billion
Law and order (including both the police and court system).	£32 billion
Defence (pays for military personnel and hardware).	£29 billion
Debt interest (interest payable to banks for money borrowed by the government in previous years).	£27 billion
Personal Social Services (includes services such as home helps, child protection and residential care).	£26 billion
Transport (public transport services and maintenance of roads).	£21 billion
Industry, agriculture and employment (money to help businesses, create jobs and support farmers).	£21 billion
Housing and environment (public housing and environmental services).	£19 billion
Other	£57 billion
Total	£552 billion

Source: The Guardian, 23 March 2006

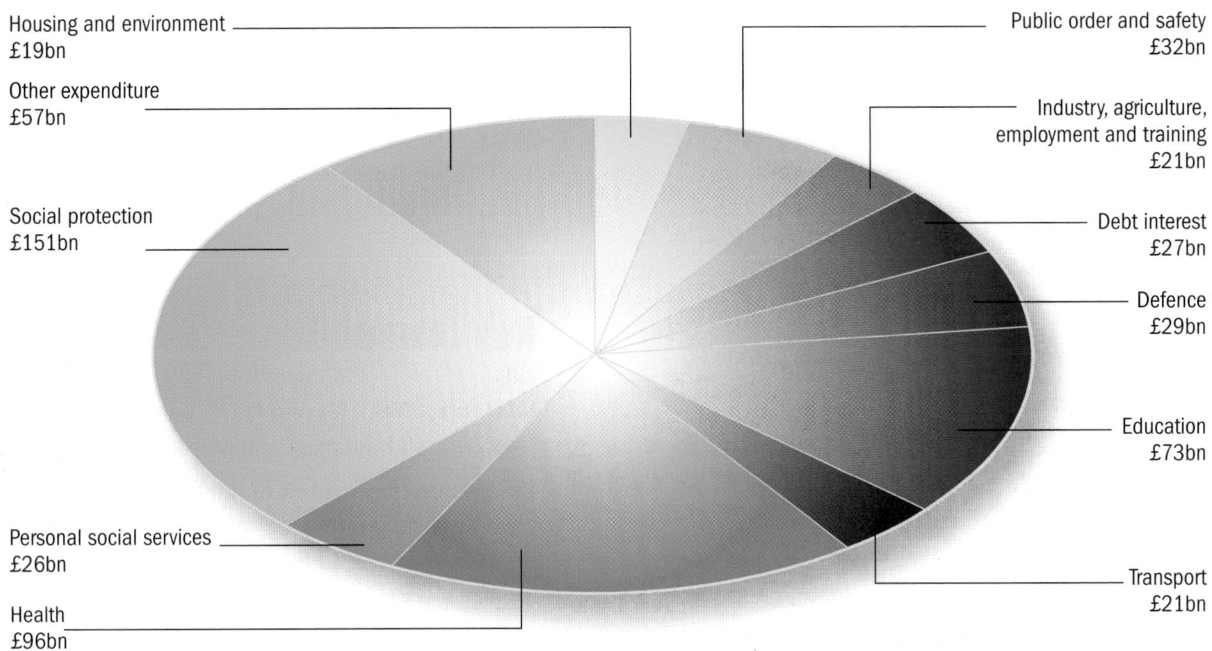

▲ **How taxpayers' money is spent**

UK government spending occurs in many different areas. Much is spent on public services through government agencies. But high amounts are also spent on services provided by private business organisations. The table on page 268 gives a breakdown of the UK government's planned expenditure as announced in the Budget, March 2006.

A number of these areas involve payments to organisations owned and controlled by the government. However, much of the money finds its way into the hands of private businesses. Money spent on health, for example, will go to hospitals. But some of the services provided within the hospitals (such as cleaning and meals) may well be undertaken by private firms. This means that a large amount of public spending will result in additional income for privately owned firms.

When money is spent on large capital projects such as new buildings or roads, private construction companies will do the actual building so more government spending boosts their revenues. Similarly, if future governments decided to reduce spending, these firms would find life much more difficult as their revenues would be reduced.

Thinking point

- Obtain details of the latest Budget. You should be able to find this information by visiting the Treasury website at www.hm-treasury.gov.uk or by visiting newspaper websites.
- Consider the latest spending announcements. Identify examples of firms that are likely to benefit from these announcements and explain the ways in which they might benefit.
- Are there any firms that might suffer as a result of the Budget? Explain your answers.

Government spending and the multiplier mechanism

Economists use the **multiplier** to assess the effect of proposed changes in government spending on the economy as a whole. Experience shows that a relatively small increase in government spending can have a much larger effect in total income in an economy. This is because new money is spent several times over. For example, if the UK government injects new money into an Assisted Area to encourage new businesses to open in that area, new jobs are created. As a result:

- employees have more money to spend
- they spend it in the local shops, restaurants, etc.
- the owners of these businesses have more profit and more money to spend, so they may expand and perhaps employ further employees
- they then have more money to spend … and so on.

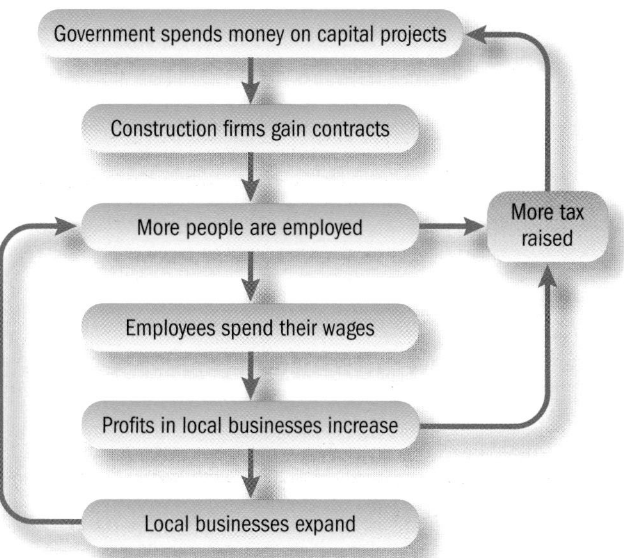

▲ **The multiplier mechanism**

In theory the money could be continually spent forever, except that there are **leakages** from this Circular Flow of Income. For example, people and businesses will choose to save some of this extra income. The size of the multiplier can be assessed using the following formula:

$$\text{Multiplier} = \frac{1}{1 - \text{proportion of extra income spent}}$$

For example, if people generally save 10% of extra income (their marginal propensity to save) and spend 90% (their marginal propensity to consume) the multiplier would be:

$$\text{Multiplier} = \frac{1}{1 - 0.9} = \frac{1}{0.1} = 10$$

In these circumstances if the government injected an extra £25 million of spending, the multiplier effect would mean that the actual increase in incomes in the country would be £25 million x 10 = £250 million. Note that this method ignores additional leakages – principally taxes and the purchase of imports.

Key Terms

Leakages: Savings and taxes paid. These reduce the effect of the Multiplier.

Multiplier The number of times that additional government spending on the economy is re-spent and the resulting overall increase in spending.

Practice point

- The UK government decides to invest an additional £125 million into the tourist industry in the UK, supporting companies building new hotels and tourist attractions. Assuming there is a marginal propensity to consume of 75%, how much extra income will be generated in total?
- List and explain all the potential knock-on effects of this additional spending for UK incomes.

Government spending, therefore, is very important to the health of an economy, to the extent that governments may often engage in additional spending even when their tax revenues cannot support it in order to keep the economy buoyant.

Deficit funding

The money to pay for the government's spending plans comes from various sources. The table on the next page shows the anticipated revenue for 2006/7 in the UK. Definitions of the income areas are given on page 274.

▼ **Anticipated government revenue for 2006/7**

Income area	Expected revenues 2006/7
Income tax	£144 billion
National insurance	£90 billion
Value added tax (VAT)	£76 billion
Corporation tax	£49 billion
Excise duties	£40 billion
Council tax	£22 billion
Business rates	£21 billion
Other	£74 billion
Total	£516 billion

Source: The Guardian, 23 March 2006

If you compare the table above to the one on page 268 detailing the government's spending plans for the same period, you will see a discrepancy in the totals. Projected spending totals are £552 billion, while projected revenue totals reach just £516 billion. This leaves a shortfall in revenue of £36 billion, which will need to be borrowed (see details on PSNB on page 277).

You might argue that this is imprudent financial management on the government's behalf and that it should not be spending what it has not got. Sometimes, however, governments believe this is necessary to improve public services and/or avoid any downturn in economic activity.

This overspending tends to take place fairly regularly. From 1998 to 2002 the UK government actually raised more revenue than it spent, which meant it was able to repay some of the debt accumulated in previous years. However, before and since that period borrowing has been necessary.

The money to fund a budget **deficit** will come from the banking system. Short-term money can be raised using Treasury Bills usually bought by the banks. Longer-term financing can come from government bonds which are sold to banks, pension funds and individuals. National Savings are also a valuable source of revenue for the government when financing deficits. A final source would be borrowing from the Bank of England.

Of course, interest must be paid on all of these sources of finance and the capital must ultimately be repaid, although some government borrowing is over very long periods. For example, in December 2006 the UK government finally made the last instalment on loans taken out after the Second World War to help rebuild UK infrastructure and industry.

Key Term

Deficit funding Finding the money to pay for an overspend by the government.

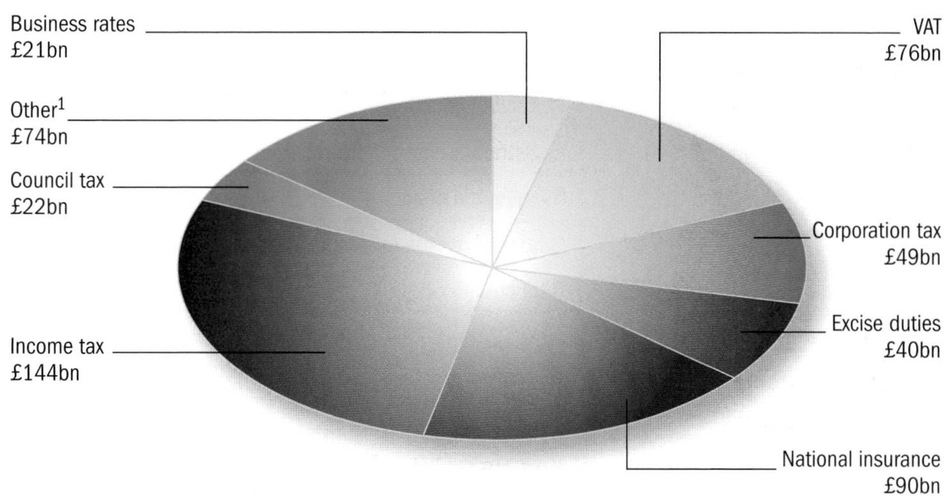

[1] Other includes capital taxes, stamp duties, vehicle excise duties, and non-tax receipt (e.g. interest and dividends).
Source: HM Treasury 2006-07 projections. Figures may not sum due to rounding.

◀ **Where taxes come from**

Thinking point

Funding deficits may be desirable to keep an economy upbeat, but there are disadvantages to this activity. What are they? Explain your answer.

Local impacts

Although we have considered government spending on a national scale, the local effect of the activities of local government are equally, if not more, important to many businesses. Local government provides a wide range of services paid for through council tax, business rates and central government grants, much of which will provide work for local companies. The table opposite gives an example – the expenditure budget for Nottinghamshire County Council 2006/7.

Thinking point

Consider Nottinghamshire County Council's budget, shown opposite. Which areas of local council expenditure do you consider could be provided by private firms? Which would be best provided by staff employed by the local council? Explain your reasons.

Take it further

Interview a senior member of staff from your school or college.

- Which services are provided to the school/college from private industry?
- What are the advantages to the school/college of using private industry to supply these services rather than employing their own staff?

Service provided	£ millions
Services for young people	
Schools	385.2
Other education services	35.6
School transport and passes	10.9
Care for children and families	48.5
Youth work	8.2
Youth justice	2.7
Services for adults	
Care for people with disabilities	62.9
Other adult care	12.6
Adult and other education	1.8
Services for the elderly	
Care for elderly people	76.7
Concessionary fares	1.1
Tackling environmental issues	
Road maintenance and traffic management	29.7
Waste disposal and recycling	21.1
Public transport	8.5
Approval of planning applications	1.4
Countryside and conservation	3.9
Working with the community	
Libraries	14.2
Community safety and development	5.7
Tourism, country parks, sports and arts	4.8
Developing the local economy and jobs	4.3
Protecting consumers	3.3
Registrars, welfare rights, coroners, etc.	3.2
Running the council	7.1
Loan repayments and interest, etc.	32.7
Total cost	786.1

Source: 'Your 2006/07 Council Tax' brochure, published by Nottinghamshire County Council

Clearly, local council spending is also crucial to many firms. Increases in council budgets and increased council spending leads to increased business opportunities. But cutbacks in local council spending could be very bad news for some firms.

Outcome activity 39.2

This activity continues the study on Balfour Beatty begun in Outcome Activity 39.1.

Pass

Identify and describe the impact of government spending on Balfour Beatty. 

Merit

Analyse the implications of government policies on Balfour Beatty. 

Grading tips

Pass 

For a thorough answer you should ensure that you cover:

- a description and examples of the type of work Balfour Beatty does that is funded by government spending
- a description of how general government spending might affect Balfour Beatty
- an explanation of PFI work and how the PFI policy has affected Balfour Beatty
- an assessment of how important government spending is to Balfour Beatty and the knock-on effects of changes in government spending levels.

Merit m1

Analysing requires you to break the situation down and look in detail at all aspects. In this case you should look in detail at the following.

- A thorough discussion of how changes in the levels and priorities of government spending might affect Balfour Beatty. You should also outline how the managers of Balfour Beatty might react to such changes.
- An explanation of the multiplier mechanism, how changes in government spending affect it and how this in turn could affect Balfour Beatty. You should also outline how the managers of Balfour Beatty might react to such changes.
- Effects on the firm's possible expansion plans.

39.3 Fiscal and monetary policies and their effects on spending

Government has two key weapons when controlling the economy. These are:

- **fiscal policy**
- **monetary policy**.

Both tactics may be used to regulate levels of demand in the economy. Both can therefore also be used either to stimulate the economy to help businesses and jobs or slow it down to reduce inflation.

Key Terms

Fiscal policy Refers to changing government spending and taxation levels.

Monetary policy Refers to changes in money supply and levels of interest rates.

Fiscal policy

Fiscal policy aims to alter levels of demand by using taxation and government spending changes.

Taxes can be split into two major types:

- **direct taxes**, which are paid according to a person's income or wealth
- **indirect taxes**, which are added to the price of goods and services sold.

While you do not need to know how each of these works in detail, you should know a little about each.

Direct taxation

The following are types of direct taxation.

- *Income tax* – charged on earned income. The more you earn the more you pay. This is known as a progressive tax.
- *Corporation tax* – tax on business profits. This is proportional to the size of those profits and is therefore another example of a progressive tax.
- *National insurance* (NI) – a direct tax deducted from wages to contribute towards the NHS, social security and state pensions. Firms also make NI contributions on behalf of their staff. The rate firms pay is slightly higher than the amount their employees pay. This has led some business owners to condemn NI as a 'tax on employing people'.
- *Capital gains tax* – tax on investments that have gained in value. However, you only pay this tax when you sell or realise the assets.
- *Inheritance tax* – paid on large inheritances.
- *Council tax and business rates* – paid to local government to pay for local services. The amount paid is relative to the value of the property. The higher the value, the more you pay. In theory this is also a progressive tax aimed at charging those with greater wealth more. However, some older people have found themselves in houses that have grown substantially in value and have ended up facing high council tax bills, even though their incomes are relatively low.
- *Stamp duty* – a tax paid when buying a property. The amount paid varies according to the value of the property.

Indirect taxation

These are as follows.

- *Value added tax (VAT)* – charged on goods bought. The tax is added to the price paid. At the moment, VAT is charged at 17.5% on most items, although some such as food and drugs are zero-rated. VAT is known as a regressive tax, meaning that you will pay the same amount however much you earn. So if someone buys a new camera, they will pay the same VAT amount whether they earn £20 a week or £20,000 a week.
- *Excise duty* – additional sales tax levied on certain goods such as alcohol, cigarettes and fuel. This is also a regressive tax.
- *Customs duties* – all goods imported from outside the EU are subject to this tax.
- *Air passenger duty (airport tax)* – a tax that is added to all flights. The rate charged varies with the class of ticket purchased.
- *Insurance tax* – all motor and home insurance premiums attract an additional tax payment built into the premium (the monthly payment).
- *Landfill tax* – tax paid by firms disposing of waste at landfill sites. The amount paid varies according to the amount of waste.

Other types of tax

Other types of tax include licence duties such as:

- TV licences
- driving licences
- dog licences.

These are a set fee and are therefore regressive taxes.

Key Terms

Direct taxes Taxes paid according to a person's income or wealth.

Indirect taxes Taxes added to the prices of goods and services sold.

Impact of changes in taxation on costs

Changes in tax levels can have significant effects on the costs incurred by a business, which in turn can affect its profitability.

Thinking point

Consider each of the taxes listed on page 274. Assume that the UK government decides to increase the rate of all taxes in the country. Make a list of the tax increases that will affect business costs. Explain how each will affect a business.

Impact of changes in taxation on aggregate demand

Government can alter demand levels in the economy by manipulating tax rates. Tax changes alter the level of **aggregate demand** in the country. Aggregate demand is the total of all demand in the economy, i.e. the sum of all the consumer spending on goods and services, as well as business spending and government spending. The diagram below shows how it works.

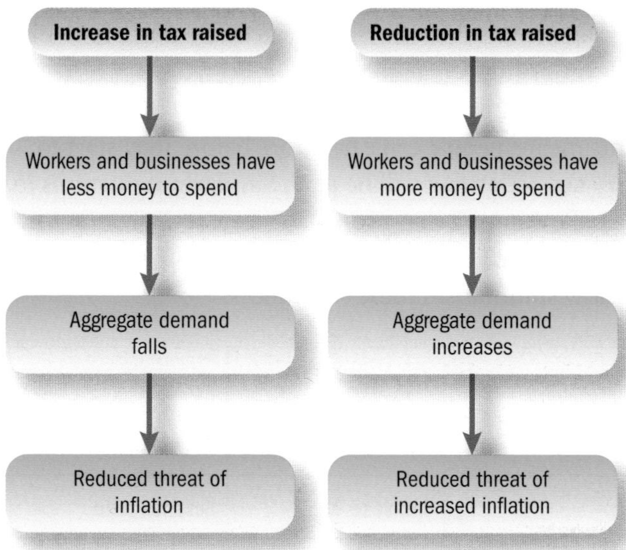

▲ **The impact of changes in taxation on aggregate demand**

Since government is the major spender in the economy, it is in a unique position to influence levels of demand. Government spends on a multitude of areas such as:

- health
- education
- road building
- social security
- defence
- regional policy
- the arts.

If it increases spending in these areas this will automatically create demand, which in turn should aid business profits and jobs. However, if it reduces spending, business profit earning is threatened and firms may have to cut costs, possibly shedding jobs.

Key Term

Aggregate demand The total amount of demand for goods and services in an economy.

Thinking point

Consider each of the taxes listed on page 274. Assume that the UK government decides to reduce the rate of all taxes in the country. Give examples of how each change might affect aggregate demand in the economy.

Impact of changes in tax-free allowances

The effect of changes in tax rates is generally well understood, but the concept of tax allowances can sometimes cause confusion. The rates of income tax in the UK for 2006/7 are shown in the following table.

Income tax allowances	2007/8
Personal allowance	£5,225
Personal allowance for people aged 65–74	£7,550
Personal allowance for people aged 75 and over	£7,690
Income limit for age-related allowances	£20,900
Married couple's allowance aged under 75 and born before 6 April 1935	£6,285
Married couple's allowance aged 75 and over	£6,365
Minimum amount of married couple's allowance	£2,440
Blind person's allowance	£1,730
Taxable bands 2006/7	
Starting rate 10%	£0–2,150
Basic rate 22%	£2,151–33,300
Higher rate 40%	More than £33,300

Source: www.inlandrevenue.gov.uk/rates/it.htm. Rates correct as at December 2006

As you can see there are three income tax bands. Currently we are charged 10% on the first £2,150 we earn each year, 22% on anything we earn between £2,151 and £33,300 and 40% on anything we earn over £33,300.

Note The Chancellor announced in his 2007 Budget that this system will be changing from April 2008. From this time there will be two tax bands: the Basic Rate band, which will be charged at just 20%, and the Higher Rate band, which will continue to be charged at 40%.

However, in addition to this, each person has a **tax allowance**, which is an amount that can be earned before any tax is paid. As you can see, this is £5,225 per year for many people. However, it may change if you marry or when you reach retirement age.

Tax is therefore paid in slices on your income.

- The first slice is nothing.
- The second slice 10%.
- The third slice 22%.
- If you are a high wage earner, the top slice is 40%.

You could visualise it something like the diagram opposite.

It is important to remember that if you get a pay rise and move into a higher income tax slice, it does not mean you pay extra tax on *all* your income. You only pay it on that portion of your income that is above the next tax rate threshold. For example, if you were earning £5,000 you would not pay any tax. If you had a £50 pay rise you would then move into the starting rate tax slice, but you would only pay tax on the £15 you were earning over the threshold of £5,035. In this case you would pay £15 x 10%, or £1.50 tax for the year.

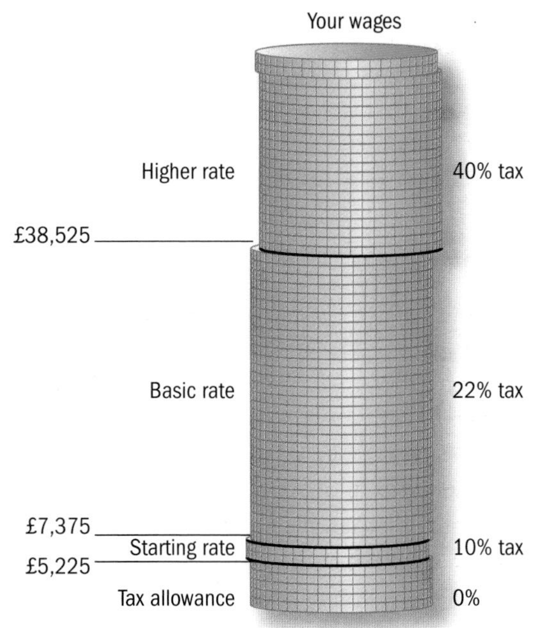

▲ **Tax rates and allowances**

Tax allowances can therefore also be used to manipulate the levels of tax paid, but they work in the opposite way to tax rates. If the government increases tax allowances, this means people can earn more before they start to pay tax, so less tax will be paid. Similarly, reductions in tax allowances mean people will start to pay tax at lower levels of earnings. Therefore, more tax is paid. The table below summarises these allowances.

Tax rates	Increase =	more tax paid
	Decrease =	less tax paid
Tax allowances	Increase =	less tax paid
	Decrease =	more tax paid

Practice point

Visit the Inland Revenue website (www.inlandrevenue.gov.uk/rates/it.htm).

Check the latest rates of tax and allowances. Assess the effects of the changes that have taken place since this textbook was published. Look at this from the point of view of a business in the UK.

Key Term

Tax allowance An amount of money a person can earn without paying income tax.

The Budget

Fiscal decisions are made annually in the Budget by the Chancellor of the Exchequer. So it is likely that tax rates will change every year to some extent. The Budget is delivered each March or April, although it has become traditional for the Chancellor to make a pre-Budget announcement shortly before Christmas to outline the measures he intends to change in the official Budget in the coming year. This enables him to gauge public reaction to those changes before final decisions are made.

The budget is a statement of the estimated revenue and expenditure of the government for the coming year. It states how the money will be spent and how it will be raised, including any changes to tax rates or allowances. The Budget has two aims:

- to regulate the economy by manipulating levels of demand through fiscal measures
- to redistribute income and wealth fairly across the country.

Thinking point

Using an internet-based news source (for example www.bbc.co.uk/news) obtain the details of the latest Budget or pre-Budget announcements. With a partner, assess the potential effects of these changes on businesses in the UK.

Public finances and public sector borrowing

Sometimes planned government expenditure will exceed the revenue that is likely to be raised. If this is the case, the government will have to borrow money to finance the gap. This gap is known as the **Public Sector Net Borrowing**, or PSNB. An example of this is shown below.

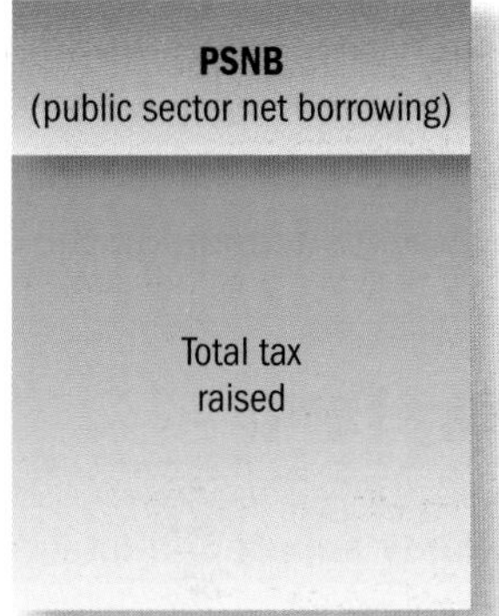

▲ Public Sector Net Borrowing (PSNB)

The borrowing will be in the form of issues of gilt-edged stocks, Treasury bills and National Savings. In difficult economic times the government will frequently run up large PSNB totals. However, this is often justified as the government may be attempting to inject life into an ailing economy or keep it going under difficult circumstances. In better times the government expects to achieve a 'balanced budget', where no borrowing is required. Better still, it aims to achieve a surplus, so that borrowing from previous years can be repaid or money put aside to finance future government spending.

Key Term

Public Sector Net Borrowing (PSNB) The amount the government has spent above the level of tax raised.

Monetary policy

Monetary policies have been used extensively in the UK since 1979 when Margaret Thatcher became prime minister. She decided a new approach was required. The methods she adopted were very successful at controlling inflation, so much so that they are still used extensively today.

Aggregate demand and trading conditions

Monetarist policies are based on the assumption that the economy can be regulated by measuring and manipulating the levels of **money supply** in the economy. The money supply is the total amount of money available for spending within a country. You might like to think of it as being the total amount of purchasing power within the country. Monetary policy is the government's main tool for controlling inflation in the UK. It assumes that inflation is created by excess aggregate demand in the economy.

Key Term

Money supply The total purchasing power in the economy.

Monetarist theory

If resources are being used efficiently in the economy, this may lead to increases in demand in the country. Excessive demand, over and above our ability to expand production, can lead to prices rising. This is known as demand-pull inflation. An example is shown below.

This explanation of the roots of inflation has become increasingly important as the government's strategy for controlling inflation for the last 25 years has been largely based on tackling this cause.

The monetarist theory on inflation assumes there is a direct link between bank lending, the money supply and ultimately inflation. The flowchart below shows how it works.

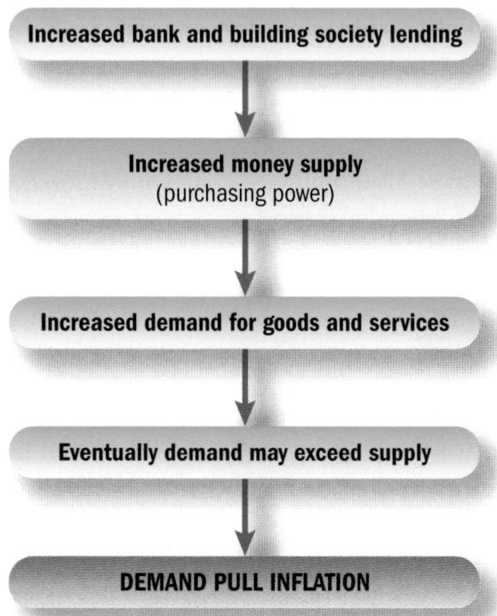

▲ The link between money supply and inflation

This theory, therefore, draws a direct link between bank lending and the rate of inflation.

- If there is a causal relationship between these two,

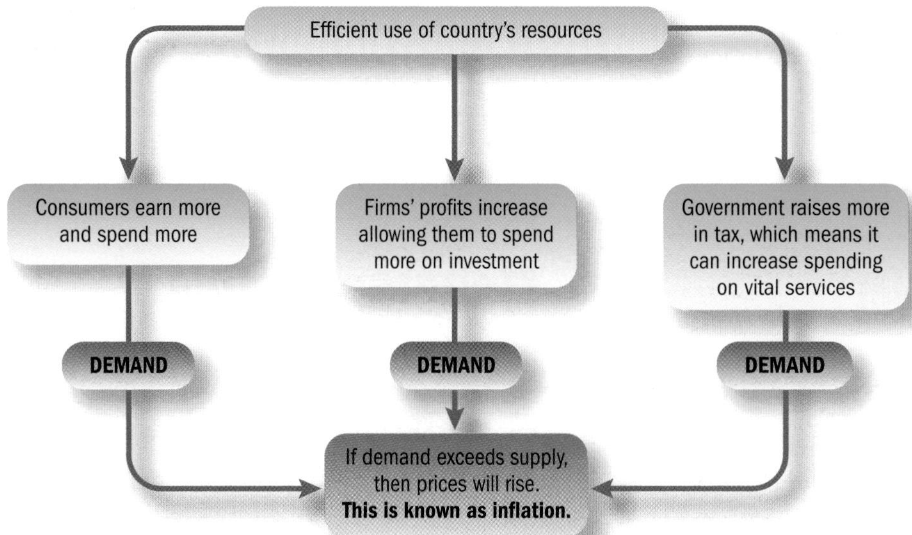

◀ Demand-pull inflation

then controlling bank lending should control levels of inflation.

- If we reduce bank lending, this should reduce purchasing power (money supply).
- This, in turn, should reduce demand and that will reduce or eliminate demand-pull inflation.

Monetarists assume that the key factor determining the amount of bank lending taking place is the rate of interest charged.

- High rates discourage lending (as the repayments are so high).
- Low rates mean lending is likely to increase. The government can therefore regulate the economy by altering interest rates to suit their objectives at the time.

Interest rate policy can be used in two main ways:

- to reduce inflation
- to stimulate the economy.

The flowcharts below explain this process. The two policies may be used at different times when priorities change.

In the 1980s, when the main priority was to reduce inflation, interest rates were increased in order to reduce inflation. This tactic had the desired effect. However, there is a price to pay for this success. Inflation is reduced in this way by suppressing demand in the economy.

Unfortunately, industry needs demand to enable it to develop, so a regime of high interest rates can be very difficult for industry. Not only is business borrowing more expensive, increasing operating costs and preventing expansion, but also demand is low. High costs and low demand is a bad recipe for business. Not surprising, then, that many businesses found it difficult to survive under high interest rates. However, it did achieve its objective and inflation did fall dramatically.

As we attempted to come out of the deep recession of the early 1990s, the government was aware that industry needed help to get it moving again. This was provided by using interest rate policy in the opposite way – to stimulate the economy.

Interest rates were reduced, thus reducing business costs and stimulating demand – a fine recipe for business success. This was one of the key factors that helped the UK out of the recessionary problems of the early 1990s.

There could have been a price to pay, however, as increased demand might have led to further inflation. So the government treads cautiously when changing interest rates, often choosing to change rates by small amounts of 0.25% or 0.5%. The government is treading a tightrope all the time, wanting interest rates to be high enough to discourage inflation, but low enough to stimulate industry – a tricky task!

Remember

Monetary policy will only be effective if people and businesses are 'interest rate sensitive'. In other words, they must be affected by the changes in interest rate and this must affect their behaviour, or the policy simply will not work. Our experience since 1980 suggests that the UK economy is interest rate sensitive, although some economists worry that this will not always be the case.

Using interest rates to reduce inflation:

Using interest rates to stimulate the economy and create employment:

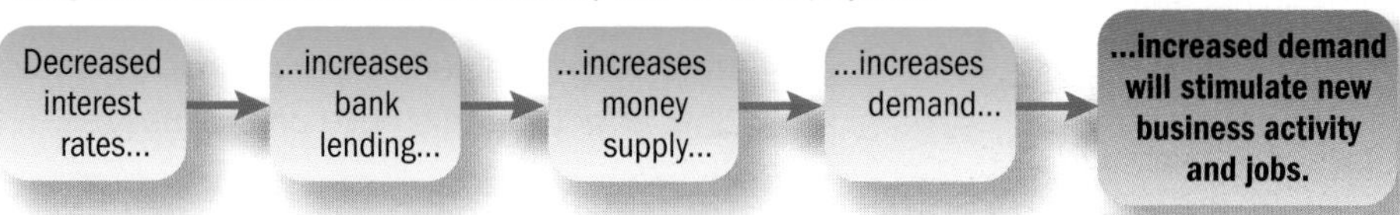

◄ Interest rate policy

The Monetary Policy Committee

Until May 1997 all UK monetary policy decisions were taken by the UK government through the Chancellor of the Exchequer, who made decisions and announced any changes.

In May 1997 the new Labour government decided to alter this. There had been accusations that some interest rate changes were made at times that suited the government best rather than the economy. So interest rates might have been reduced just before a general election to make the government more popular and give it a greater chance of re-election.

To avoid this possibility of bias in the future, the Chancellor of the Exchequer, Gordon Brown, announced that all interest rate decisions would be made by the Bank of England. He appointed a Monetary Policy Committee, chaired by the Governor of the Bank of England, and instructed it to meet monthly to decide on interest rates for the next month. The specific objective was to achieve the government's underlying inflation target of no higher than 2.5%. At the time of writing, this had been reduced to 2%.

Thinking point

- Visit the Bank of England website (www.bankofengland.co.uk/monetarypolicy/decisions.htm) and check the latest decisions on interest rate changes that have taken place. What do you think were the reasons behind the latest decisions taken by the MPC?
- What effects will those decisions have had on the following groups:
  - mortgage payers
  - businesses
  - exporters
  - investors
  - companies looking to expand
  - consumers.

While the Chancellor retained the right to overrule the Committee's decisions in 'extreme economic circumstances', the Committee is now free to independently make decisions they believe are right for the country, without fear of bias. The process has been operating for some time now and appears to be working smoothly. Although not everyone agrees with all of the decisions taken, we can be sure that they were made without the influence of political pressures.

The Bank of England website (www.bankofengland.co.uk/monetarypolicy/overview.htm) gives more details on the role of the MPC.

Investment decisions

Monetary policy has a significant impact on decisions about company investment. Whenever managers are considering whether to expand a business, one of the main forms of finance for this will be bank lending.

- Repayments on loans will be high if interest rates are high. This is likely to deter managers from borrowing. In these circumstances they may put off investment decisions until interest rates fall.
- Repayments on loans will be low if interest rates are low. This is likely to encourage firms considering new borrowing and expansion.

Thinking point

The government's interest rate policy has significant effects on businesses in a number of ways.

- Assume that the country is experiencing a period of high interest rates. Consider how this will affect the following groups in the country and how each will affect businesses in the UK.
  - Consumers who might need to borrow money in order to buy products.
  - Firms considering expansion.
  - Consumers who have mortgages.
  - Consumers who have large amounts of savings in the bank.
- How do you feel consumer confidence will be affected by this period of high interest rates? What effect will this have on businesses in the UK?

Impact of anticipated changes in interest rates

Consumers are affected by actual interest rate changes but their buying behaviour is also affected by anticipated changes. The press regularly speculates over what it thinks will happen each month when the MPC meets. It also tries to predict longer-term changes. All this speculation does have an effect on demand in the economy.

- Speculation about rising interest rates can deter people from borrowing and spending.
- Speculation about lower interest rates encourages more borrowing and spending.

Of course, the speculation is not always correct so sometimes buyers change their spending despite the fact that nothing has changed.

Outcome activity 39.3

This activity continues the study on Balfour Beatty begun in Outcome Activity 39.1.

Pass

Outline how both fiscal and monetary policy decisions have affected Balfour Beatty. 

Merit

Analyse the effects of fiscal and monetary policies on Balfour Beatty in terms of the market in which it operates. 

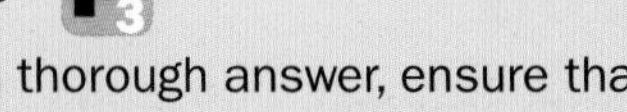

Grading tips

Pass p3

For a thorough answer, ensure that you do the following.

- Explain the meanings of the terms 'fiscal policy' and 'monetary policy'.
- Using the internet, research recent fiscal and monetary policy decisions made by the UK government. Visit these websites to help you with this:
  – www.bankofengland.co.uk/monetarypolicy/decisions.htm (identify the interest rate changes that have taken place in the last year)
  – http://news.bbc.co.uk (in the Search box, key in the words 'Budget 2007' to get the latest details; change the year as necessary).
- Go through each of the key changes you have identified and discuss their possible effects on Balfour Beatty.

Merit 

Analysing requires you to break down the situation and look in detail at all aspects. In this case you should look in detail at the following.

- A clear description of the market in which Balfour Beatty operates.
- The effects of the changes in fiscal and monetary policy that you have identified on demand for Balfour Beatty's services.
- The effects of the changes on Balfour Beatty's business costs.
- Effects on the firm's possible expansion plans and how Balfour Beatty's managers might need to react to such changes.

39.4 How the global economy affects UK businesses and competition

Global issues

International events, both economic and political, can have significant effects on the activities of businesses in the UK and worldwide. These events are completely out of the control of individual businesses. Yet they can have profound effects on their success.

On 11 September 2001 (or 9/11 as it is commonly referred to) the terrorist attacks on the World Trade Center in New York, USA, sent shock waves around the world. Not only was there terrible loss of life on that day, but also the events contributed to significant economic changes, some of which have had lasting effects on businesses in the USA and abroad.

In the immediate economic aftermath of 9/11, it has been estimated that:

- nearly 18,000 businesses in and around the World Trade Center were disrupted or destroyed
- approximately 130,000 workers lost their jobs.

These effects led to large losses in tax revenues for the US government. When the **stock markets** reopened a week later, nervous investors were selling shares. This led rapidly to the **Dow Jones Index** falling by more than 14% – its largest one-week drop in history – wiping almost £1.2 trillion off the value of US companies.

Key Terms

Dow Jones Index An index that records changes in the value of share prices on the US Stock Exchange.

Stock market The market where stocks and shares are bought and sold.

There were huge falls in tourism in New York City leading to roughly 3,000 people losing their jobs in that industry alone. This effect was felt across the USA and throughout the world. People became very nervous about travelling and flying in particular. Hoteliers in America and across the world reported major falls in room occupancy in the weeks following the 9/11 attacks.

The decline in air traffic caused significant problems for an airline industry that was already struggling. The huge insurance claims involved put insurance companies under considerable financial strain.

Over the longer period many businesses worldwide are now experiencing higher costs as a result of 9/11 due to increased spending on security and higher insurance premiums. Resources that firms might have used to boost their productivity have since been redirected towards providing better security, which must have limited the growth rates of many companies.

It is difficult to be precise about the actual economic effects we can attribute to the events of 9/11. The airline industry, for example, was already in deep trouble before it happened and many economists believe that 9/11 only contributed to, rather than caused, these difficulties. But it cannot be denied that many firms were adversely affected by what happened.

What this does illustrate is that there is a range of economic and political events that can heavily influence the success of companies, some of which happen on a global scale. Some global changes are specific to certain industries, such as the threat of avian 'flu to the poultry industry. Many of them may affect a wide range of businesses. The text that follows considers some of the major influences of modern times.

Stock market fluctuations

The prices of shares are moving all the time as people buy and sell them.

- When a company is doing well investors tend to *buy* its shares. This increase in demand tends to force up the price and value of those shares.
- If a firm is performing poorly, shareholders tend to *sell* their shares. As a result the price of such shares will fall.

The price of shares is therefore occasionally treated as a measurement of the performance of the firm. But there are various other reasons why share prices may change.

As we have seen already, the events of 9/11 caused major changes in the value of a wide range of company shares. This was caused by nervousness among investors who were worried about the financial future and decided to sell their shares at a reasonably high value before they lost money. This clearly had nothing to do with the companies themselves. It was all down to the terrorist events.

Sometimes share prices move because of rumours about a firm. Some good news is passed around about a company, so investors start to buy its shares and share prices rise. This news may ultimately prove to have been unfounded.

■ A company's shares

On a day-to-day basis small changes in the value of a firm's shares do not have any effect on the firm's operations. However, when the changes are larger and more long lasting this can affect the company. Let us look at the effects of a falling share price on a firm.

- Issuing shares is a very popular way for firms to raise finance. However, a falling share price makes this harder because many investors will worry about losing the value of their investment and will be reluctant to buy such shares. This can seriously hamper the firm's ability to expand, develop new product ideas or take over other firms.
- The directors of such a firm may come under pressure from the shareholders to boost the share value by increasing the profit performance of the firm. This might be achieved by cost cutting, which is often done by shedding staff. So some staff may find their jobs at risk if the shares in their firm continue to fall.

General movements in share prices also influence firms because much of the wealth of the nation is tied up in shares, as the next section explains.

■ An individual's shares

These days, many individuals are share owners and their wealth is affected by changes in the value of these shares. When share prices fall they have less money to draw on for spending, so demand in general for company products falls.

Even people who do not actually hold shares are likely to be affected by share prices. All those who have money invested in pension schemes, company share option schemes, endowment policies and various other forms of investment will be affected because the fund managers of these products invest in shares to provide returns for their clients. This has been one factor contributing to the disappointing performance of endowment policies over the past few years: large amounts of endowment fund monies were reinvested in shares, so when share values fell so did the value of endowment policies. A falling share market undermines wealth and spending throughout the economy.

The opposite is true, of course, of a market that experiences rising share values. This breeds confidence and spending, and all businesses benefit from the increases in sales that result.

Corporate failures

Firms are interdependent. This means that, to some extent, one firm may be dependent for its success on the performance of other companies. In 2006, for example, Dell Computers had to recall 4.1 million laptops after several of its machines had overheated and caught fire. It turned out to be the biggest electrical product recall ever. The problem was the batteries, which had been supplied by Sony. Dell was forced to take a considerable financial hit (loss of money) and a lot of bad press as a result of defective parts from one of its suppliers. This is a good example of how the performance of one firm, Dell, was significantly affected by one of its suppliers, Sony.

While both Dell and Sony suffered some damage, they were each strong enough to survive the events. When a firm goes out of business, however, it can have a serious effect on a number of other businesses that are dependent on that firm.

In April 2005, following years of difficult trading, MG Rover finally **went into administration**. The firm closed, putting almost 6,000 Rover employees out of work. What's more, the closure affected several other

Case study

PS3 delay hits share prices

In September 2006, Sony announced a major delay in the launch of the PlayStation 3. It was originally due to be available for Christmas 2006, but a number of technical problems resulted in the launch in Europe being delayed until at least March 2007 – even though it was available in Japan and the USA by November 2006.

The stock market reacted badly to the news, with Sony shares falling by 2.38% on the day of the announcement. Stock market analysts Goldman Sachs downgraded Sony's rating from 'buy' to 'neutral' following the launch confusion.

The bad news also affected other firms. The share price of videogame publisher Electronic Arts (EA), which had a number of products lined up for the new console, fell by 2.3%. Meanwhile, shares of its rival Activision fell by 1.7%. Shares in games retailer Game Group fell by almost 5%.

1. Using the internet, find out what has happened to the share prices of the companies quoted in the case study since these events. A good site is http://uk.finance.yahoo.com/. Have the falls in share price persisted? ✓
2. Explain the reasons for the falls in share prices described in the case study. ✓
3. Explain the phrase: 'Stock market analysts Goldman Sachs downgraded Sony's rating from "buy" to "neutral".' What is the potential effect of this on Sony? ✓✓
4. If the falls in share prices were to persist, what might be the long-term effects on each of the companies? ✓✓✓

businesses that relied on the success of MG Rover for their own success. 'Real lives' (opposite) illustrates the problems of corporate failure for interdependent firms.

Key Term

Go into administration A step taken before a company becomes completely bankrupt. The firm is taken over by a team of administrators, possibly accountants, who try to save the business by finding a buyer or sell off bits of the firm to raise money on behalf of the creditors.

Sometimes the collapse of a major firm in one country can have significant effects on the business activities of firms in other countries. The collapse of the industrial giants Enron and Worldcom in 2001, for example, had ripple effects on the activities of dependent firms across the world. The events even touched firms that had no direct connection with these companies, as most countries have had to introduce more rigorous financial checks and controls as a result of these scandals.

War and political instability

The problems of global interdependence become magnified when one of the countries concerned has a period of political instability or even war. The Middle East has seen extensive political upheaval for many years. Any firm relying on companies in these countries for supplies or as customers is, at times, likely to experience major disruptions to their business activity. However, sometimes unexpected problems break out with countries that have been perfectly stable in the past.

War has dramatic economic effects for the countries concerned.

- It is very expensive, so resources are directed towards fighting rather than buying and selling.
- Trade links become severely disrupted and war also tends to increase inflation, so people can buy less.
- Governments at war may also raise taxes to finance the war effort, which reduces domestic demand.

Real lives

Fight for survival in Rover ghost town

▲ Rover car and the Longbridge factory

At the parade of shops in Parsonage Green, things are looking grim. Sitting in the shadow of the MG Rover Longbridge plant, almost every one of the small businesses has been affected with varying degrees of severity by the shutdown of the factory nine weeks ago. The Colton Cafe has closed, the shelves of Annand newsagents are thinly stocked and the post office has had to diversify into selling flowers to stay afloat. Even the hairdresser is reporting a drop in business.

It is a depressingly similar story for shops scattered around this vast plant, which not so much dominated Longbridge but was Longbridge. Barely a household or business did not have a Rover connection. Generations of families had worked there. With no other major employer around, the small businesses lost 5,000 potential customers overnight.

'It's been dreadful,' said Theresa Bond, who owns the post office and general store. 'Our mainstay has always been the sandwiches, pies and pasties for the Rover workers, and that has gone down the tubes. Look around; there's nobody here. The cafe shut down almost straight away. We've had to look at ways of diversifying to survive and selling flowers is doing OK. Not enough to stay afloat, not enough when you've got two children to feed, but it's OK. We will survive but it is now a question of trying to appeal to a wider audience and get some passing trade.'

It is lunchtime and half a mile away at Longbridge Fish and Chips, Lyndsey Edwards would, in the past, be rushed off her feet. Yesterday the place was empty. 'It's bad, really bad,' she said. 'We'd be mobbed at busy times of the day but it's really quiet now. I don't know how long we can put up with it. But it's still going to get worse when people have to sell their houses and when the redundancy money runs out and they haven't got another job. It's bad now but I reckon it's the tip of the iceberg.'

Sandra Whitby, who runs The Salon hairdressers in Longbridge, said: 'I have lost around eight to ten of my regular men, along with any passing trade. It wasn't just Rover workers, it was the lorry drivers, the sales people, the printers. What we need is a decision to be made and for something to be done with the plant to bring people back. We can't go on umming and erring for the next five years.'

As well as the Rover workforce, most of the company's suppliers, based around the country, have been hit. One of the worst affected, the car panel firm Stadco, has made 230 people redundant at its Holbrooks plant in Coventry and a further 50 at Harlescott in Shrewsbury. By summer next year the Holbrooks site will be closed completely, leading to a further 200 job losses. Martin Haynes, a spokesman, said: 'The collapse of MG Rover has hit us very hard. We have had to lay off 230 workers there. We were hoping to keep the remaining 200 staff members on but it is not proving viable.'

Source: Adapted from *The Telegraph*, 17 May 2005

1. Why has the collapse of Rover been so significant to the Longbridge area? What examples of the interdependence of businesses are given in the case study? ✓
2. What have been the major financial costs to the businesses and people of Longbridge following the collapse of Rover? ✓✓
3. What have been the major social costs to the businesses and people of Longbridge following the collapse of Rover? ✓✓
4. Use the internet to find what aid the UK government has given to the area. What more do you think the government could have done? ✓✓✓

All of this means that any firm relying on such a country as either customer or supplier will see their business severely disrupted. The people in that country are likely to have little money available to buy your products. Alternatively, their companies that produced your raw materials will no longer be able to supply to you. All of this can be a severe blow to a firm and could lead to lasting damage to the company.

Of course, after the conflict, construction companies may see an opportunity for extra business as the towns and other infrastructure are rebuilt.

Terrorism

The cost of terrorism to UK business is difficult to estimate. Since Britain appears to be on the list of possible terrorist targets, there has undoubtedly been significant impact in recent years. In August 2006, there was a major security alert at all UK airports following the discovery of a plot to blow up planes leaving Britain. This led to a large number of flights being cancelled and lengthy delays following the introduction of much tighter security procedures in the airports. In November 2006, British Airways announced a fall of £100 million in profits for the year. It claimed that the events in the summer had led to many lost bookings and disruption to flights.

Thinking point

On 7 July 2005 four suicide bombers struck in central London, killing 52 people and injuring more than 770. The attacks hit the transport system towards the end of the morning rush hour. Two bombs went off on underground trains outside the Liverpool Street and Edgware Road stations. Another bomb exploded on a train travelling between King's Cross and Russell Square. The final explosion was about an hour later on a double-decker bus in Tavistock Square.

- As well as the tragic loss of life, these events caused major disruption to businesses. What do you think would be the major effects of these events for businesses?
- What do you think are the long-term implications for UK business of these events?

Individual terrorist acts (or the threat of them) therefore cause significant disruption to business activity and subsequent loss of profits.

- Just knowing that terrorism exists costs extra, because many firms introduce tighter security measures to deal with potential threats.
- Large-scale terrorist acts tend to lead to:
  - drops in levels of tourism
  - increases in insurance premiums
  - reduced revenues for transport and entertainment companies.
- Trade sanctions imposed by governments in response to terrorism could also adversely affect businesses – in particular those that have trade relations with the country in question.

Organization of the Petroleum Exporting Countries (OPEC)

Oil is one of the most important resources for modern businesses. Indeed, oil and petrol are used extensively by most firms in the world.

- Transport firms use large amounts of petrol, diesel and oil.
- Some factories may rely on these products for running their machinery.
- Oil is used in the production of:
  - medicines
  - detergents
  - plastics
  - synthetic rubber used in car tyres and footwear.
- Service businesses use oil for delivering products or fuelling company cars.

The *uses* of oil are endless. Unfortunately, the *supply* of oil is not. In fact, it is strictly limited. The supply of oil is concentrated in a number of nations, many of which are in the Middle East (e.g. Saudi Arabia, Kuwait, Iran and Iraq). In 1960 these countries set up an organisation to meet their needs as oil exporters, to co-ordinate their policies about the supply and price of oil to safeguard their interests. This is OPEC – **Organization of the Petroleum Exporting Countries.**

OPEC countries account for more than half the oil exports of the world – making them a powerful group.

When they set quotas for production they significantly influence the price of oil. Since so much industry is dependent on oil, OPEC has a huge impact on business costs and profitability. This is clearly illustrated by the price of crude oil.

- In 1970 it was less than US$3 (£1.50) a barrel.
- By mid-2006 it was selling for US$75 (£38) per barrel.

It would be wrong to think that OPEC was solely responsible for this increase in price. Rapid and increasing demand – particularly from China, with its massive increase in wealth and industry – is also responsible. That said, there is no doubt that OPEC quota policies have been a big influence.

Thinking point

Using the BBC website (www.bbc.co.uk) find the current price of crude oil and what has been happening to it over the last few months. What do you think are the effects of these changes on UK businesses?

Key Term

Organization of the Petroleum Exporting Countries (OPEC) The group of countries that produces the majority of oil exports for the world.

Environmental concerns

Many people and governments are increasingly concerned about the effects that modern life and industry are having on the world's environment. The problems being caused are numerous.

- *Depletion of natural resources and destruction of the environment.* 'The Living Planet' report by the World Wide Fund for Nature published in October 1998 estimated that a third of the Earth's natural resources had been lost in the previous 25 years.
- *Pollution.* This includes water and air quality pollution as well as dust, noise and increasing levels of ozone in the lower atmosphere.
- *Depletion of the ozone layer.* Modern chemicals are breaking down the ozone layer in the stratosphere that protects us from harmful radiation from the sun.
- *The greenhouse effect.* Our use of coal, oil and natural gas have led to large emissions of carbon dioxide that are gradually increasing global temperatures, which could lead to catastrophic rises in sea levels as polar ice melts.
- *Waste.* Both consumers and industry create a phenomenal amount of waste that needs to be disposed of safely. This waste includes:
  - chemical by-products from production
  - non-biodegradable plastics
  - waste paper
  - highly toxic nuclear waste from nuclear power generation.

Did you know that every day across the world people throw away about 8 million disposable nappies, most of which are very poor at biodegrading and therefore will sit in landfill sites for hundreds of years?

Little wonder therefore that people around the world are taking steps to reduce this problem. On a global scale the countries of the world have tried to agree measures to reduce emissions and other environmentally damaging effects. In 1997, for example, the United Nations (UN) agreed the Kyoto Protocols. These protocols set targets for the reduction of greenhouse gases by all nations that signed the agreement (including the UK).

The signatories to the agreement meet periodically to review their progress. The November 2006 meeting, for example, was attended by representatives from 180 countries. The Rio Earth Summit in 1992 was also hosted by the UN with the objective of helping governments to rethink their economic development plans and find ways of avoiding mass destruction of natural resources.

While these initiatives are clearly very important to our future, they do impose restrictions on what businesses can do. In some cases they *increase* business costs because the environmentally friendly way of doing something is often more expensive than non-friendly ways.

Another environmental concern is genetically modified (GM) products. GM food crops are ones that have had genes altered by scientists who hope to develop strains of food that are resistant to disease or that yield greater crops. Some people are concerned that GM crop testing may contaminate the environment and affect natural crops, causing unexpected side effects.

Case study

The EU and emissions trading

The EU is trying to limit environmental damage is emissions trading.

1. Use the internet to find out what emissions trading is. ✓
2. What do you think are the main advantages to such a system? What problems can you foresee from such a scheme? ✓✓
3. What do you see as the main effects on business of the EU emissions trading scheme? ✓✓
4. On balance, how effective do you expect such a system to be? Give reasons to support your judgement. ✓✓✓

International trade agreements: trading blocs

Countries that have strong economic and trading ties occasionally decide there would be mutual benefits if they were to strengthen those links by creating a trading bloc.

Countries in a bloc will normally share some common cultural background and will be located close together. The bloc is simply an agreement that enables its members to co-ordinate their foreign trade policies for the benefit of all bloc members.

Although there are a great many trading blocs around the world, there are three major trading blocs.

- The North American bloc comprises the USA, Canada and Mexico. It is known as NAFTA: the North American Free Trade Agreement (see below).
- The European bloc contains most of Western Europe with leading roles played by Germany, Britain and France.
- The Asian bloc includes Japan, Korea, Taiwan, Hong Kong, Malaysia, and others.

Maastricht Treaty

This is an agreement among the EU nations signed in 1992. It was designed to form a more economically and politically integrated European economy, including the reduction or elimination of tariffs and non-tariff barriers and the creation of a single monetary unit (the euro).

NAFTA

The North American Free Trade Agreement (NAFTA) is a treaty between the USA, Canada and Mexico. It was launched in 1994, probably in response to the threat posed by the Maastricht Treaty two years earlier. It also eliminates trade barriers between member nations, including the reduction or elimination of many tariff and non-tariff barriers.

The USA is currently engaged in negotiations for a new bloc to be called Free Trade for the Americas (FTAA). This will cover both North and South America and include more than 30 countries.

Non-trading blocs

Although trading blocs eliminate tariffs between members, tariffs may be, and often are, imposed on imports coming from outside the bloc. In the EU, for example, we use the Common External Tariff (CET) which imposes tariffs on goods and services entering the EU from non-EU countries. This has the effect of encouraging trade within the bloc and hampering potential imports from elsewhere.

New trading blocs

In the last ten years there have been a large number of new blocs created. Today about 43% of all trade in the world takes place within these blocs. Therefore, **trading blocs** have significant influence over world trade and the way firms do business. In the UK, for example, it is much easier to trade with our European partners than with Mexico because of the different trading blocs that we are part of and the use of common external tariffs.

Key Term

Trading bloc An agreement between countries that are often geographically close. It enables its members to co-ordinate their foreign trade policies for the benefit of all bloc members.

Thinking point

What do you think are the main advantages of forming a trading bloc?
Are there any potential problems with such agreements?

Outsourcing

Outsourcing is the process of taking certain functions of the business (e.g. data input or call centre operations) and paying another firm to do them on your behalf. The main objective of outsourcing is to save business costs by reducing staff costs. That said, firms have also experienced benefits in terms of improved flexibility.

Outsourcing is not a new idea but it has become much more popular in recent years as business has become more global. Many developing nations can offer significant advantages when it comes to staffing costs, which has proved very attractive to many existing firms. This has led to firms such as Raleigh Bicycles relocating its manufacturing to India, Dyson relocating to Malaysia, HSBC Bank using call centres based in India, and even Tesco, the UK's most successful supermarket chain, outsourcing a range of business support jobs to India. A recent report estimated that India could be earning up to US$60 billion (£30 billion) per year from outsourcing by 2010.

However, there is a potential downside to outsourcing. Some economic analysts are warning that transferring so many jobs away from British workers will significantly reduce the amount of spending possible in the UK, which could hit demand for British firms.

Key Term

Outsourcing Paying another firm to take on some of the functions of your business in order to reduce costs and increase company flexibility.

European developments

Growth of the European Union (EU)

In recent years the European Union (EU) has experienced its biggest growth.

- Ten countries (Cyprus, the Czech Republic, Estonia, Hungary, Latvia, Lithuania, Malta, Poland, the Slovak Republic and Slovenia) joined on 1 May 2004.
- Bulgaria and Romania became members in January 2007.
- Turkey and Croatia have applied for membership. Talks are currently being held, but it is likely to be some time before these countries actually join.

The EU has gradually evolved since its creation in 1951. It has already successfully been enlarged successfully on four occasions. In 1957, the Treaty of Rome was signed, establishing the European Economic Community (EEC). This was drawn up by the six original founding members:

- Belgium
- France
- Germany
- Italy
- Luxembourg
- Netherlands.

Enlargement has happened as follows.
1973: Denmark, Ireland and the UK.
1981: Greece.
1986: Portugal and Spain.
1995: Austria, Finland and Sweden.

The 2004 enlargement was the biggest in terms of the number of countries involved (ten), the geographical area (an increase of 34%) and population (an increase of 105 million).

In order to become members, each of the countries has had to supply evidence that it can fulfil the economic and political conditions known as the Copenhagen Criteria. These state that each new member must:

- be a stable democracy, respecting human rights, the rule of law and the protection of minorities
- have a functioning market economy
- adopt the common rules, standards and policies that make up the body of EU law.

The impact of these recent enlargements has been significant for both new and existing members of the EU, as the table below shows.

Confectionery giant Cadbury has set up a manufacturing plant in Poland, Ready Mixed Concrete (RMS) and other building companies such as Costain have set up joint ventures in the former East Germany, Poland and elsewhere. Oil giant Shell is building new pipelines for the transportation of gas and oil in some of these countries.

The benefits of the enlargement should be greater for new members, since they are currently less economically developed. But there are benefits to the existing members, too – particularly in terms of new markets to sell to.

A 1997 study by the Centre for Economic Policy Research estimated that the enlargement would bring an economic gain for existing members of €10 billion,

	Existing EU members	New EU members
Benefits	• A wider zone of peace, stability and prosperity in Europe. • Strengthens the EU's position in world affairs (the more people the EU represents, the more influential it becomes in areas of global policy). • New markets to sell to. • Additional sales should create new jobs. • Opportunities to set up production/branches in developing economies. • Developing nations look to replace existing capital goods with newer technologies. This creates export opportunities for existing members (see below). • New source of raw materials and food.	• A wider zone of peace, stability and prosperity in Europe. • New members benefit from being part of an influential world group. • Should help to boost economic growth. • Improved standards of living for citizens. • Reduced barriers to trade means new markets to sell to. • Additional sales should create new jobs. • Financial support from EU to help them develop industry. • Common Agricultural Policy (CAP) means they should receive better prices for their products and access to the CAP support mechanisms. • CAP will support their rural development policies.
Drawbacks	• Lots of new countries have free access to the markets of EU countries. • Potential influx of cheap products. • Threats to domestic industry of cheap imports. • Possible job losses due to cheap imports from the new member countries. • Open borders could lead to widespread migration of workforce into existing EU countries. • Open borders could make smuggling, illegal immigration and trafficking more prevalent. • EU funding that supports developing industries and deprived regions will be taken away from existing member countries and given to new member states that are poorer and therefore deemed to be more needy.	• Strong EU economies have free access to the markets of the new members. • Threats to the domestic industry of new member countries due to high quality imports from existing members. • Increased imports from the existing member countries could adversely affect balance of payments. • Possible job losses due to increased imports. • Difficulties meeting EU quality standards with ageing machinery and capital goods. • Increased political and economic interference from European Parliament and Commission.

▲ The impact of recent enlargements of the EU

and for new members of €23 billion. This was backed up by a further study in 2001 by the European Commission, which estimated that enlargement could increase the growth of GDP of the new members by between 1.3% and 2.1% annually, and for the existing members by 0.7%.

Thinking point

In two groups, debate the advantages and disadvantages of allowing Turkey accession to the EU in the near future.

- Each group should research the recent economic performance of Turkey.
- Each group should bear in mind the political significance of allowing entry of the first predominantly Muslim nation into the EU 'club'.

Performance of EU economies

The economies of EU countries are quite varied. The amount and types of industry vary greatly, as do the wealth and standards of living of the citizens. The table below gives a snapshot of the performance of the UK economy.

Practice point

With at least two partners, research the economic profiles of other EU nations. Use the web addresses listed in the sources for the table below. Compare and contrast the performances of each of the countries.

▼ Snapshot of the UK economy

GDP	$1.818 trillion (2005 estimate)	This has seen steady increases in recent years. The UK is still the sixth-biggest economy in the world in terms of GDP.
Growth	1.9% (2005 estimate)	The UK has experienced steady growth for most of the last decade.
Inflation	2.7% (Nov 2006)	Although this has been rising recently, the UK is currently going through its longest period of low inflation on record.
GDP per capita	$30,100	This shows the level of output per person in the economy and is a good estimate of efficiency. The UK is in the top 25 countries in the world.
Unemployment	4.7% (2005 estimate)	Considering the world average is about 14%, the UK has been performing well in this area – certainly better than a number of its competitors such as the USA and most of the EU.
Exports	$372.7 billion	Although the UK sells a lot abroad (it is the sixth-biggest exporter in the world) it consistently buys more in (it is the fourth-biggest importer).
Imports	$483.7 billion	
Main export partners	USA (15.1%) Germany (10.5%) France (8.9%) Ireland (7.3%) Netherlands (5.5%)	
Main import partners	Germany (12.8%) USA (8.7%) France (7.1%) Netherlands (6.6%) China (5%)	

Source: www.statistics.gov.uk

The euro

Early in its history, the EU talked about creating a monetary union between the members. It was decided that individual currencies such as the franc (France), the mark (German) and the lira (Italy) would, in effect, cease to exist. They would be replaced by a single currency, known as the **euro**.

On 1 January 1999, eleven of the EU countries (excluding the UK, Sweden, Greece and Denmark) started the **Eurozone**. On that day, the exchange rates of all their currencies were irrevocably fixed and the euro was officially introduced as legal currency. In January 2002, euro coins and bank notes were introduced. Six months later, national currencies disappeared.

The UK, Sweden and Denmark decided to stay outside the Eurozone. Greece did not join initially because it failed to meet the **convergence criteria**. However, on 1 January 2001, having fulfilled the criteria, it became the twelfth country to adopt the common currency.

■ Convergence criteria

Each member state must satisfy four criteria in order to participate in monetary union and join the euro. These criteria are listed below.

1 *Price stability.* Prices must not be rising too quickly. The **inflation rate** of the country must not be more than 1½% higher than that of the three best-performing member states during the previous year.
2 *Government finances.* The government of the country should not be over-spending. In practice this means:
   - the amount over-spent by the government (the annual government deficit) must not be more than 3% of last year's GDP
   - total government borrowing (government debt) must not be more than 60% of last year's GDP.
3 *Exchange rates.* The country must have taken part in the EU exchange-rate mechanism without any break during the two previous years without severe tensions. In addition, it must not have devalued its currency on its own initiative during the same period.
4 *Long-term interest rates.* The long-term interest rate in the country must not be more than 2% higher than that of the three countries in the EU with the best inflation records.

Key Terms

Convergence criteria The conditions a member needs to meet before being allowed to join the Eurozone.

Euro The single currency now being used by many of the countries that are members of the EU.

Eurozone The group of countries using the Euro.

Of the ten new member states that joined in 2002, Estonia, Lithuania and Slovenia have already entered the 'waiting room' for the common currency. The other seven countries have yet to meet the related criteria.

The UK remains outside of the euro for the foreseeable future and opinion about our prospects for joining are sharply divided. Some economists and politicians are strongly in favour; others feel it would be a big mistake. Below are some of the main arguments for and against.

■ Arguments for the euro

- A fixed exchange rate will end currency instability in Europe. Buying and selling with different EU members will be just like buying and selling within your own country.
- It will make it much easier for firms to trade across Europe, opening up new markets for UK firms.

- It will be substantially easier for travellers from the UK to Europe. There would be no need to exchange currencies prior to travelling.
- Firms would avoid the costs of exchanging currencies when buying and selling with Europe. This could encourage additional trade.
- The exchange risk would be eliminated. Sometimes a firm agrees a deal, but by the time payment for the sale is made the exchange rate changes, making the deal much less profitable. This danger would be eliminated under the euro and therefore more trade should take place.
- Exchange risk is one of the main deterrents to trade with Europe.
- It will create price transparency, i.e. it will be simple to compare prices for the same products from different countries. This should increase competition and improve prices for consumers.
- Joining would mean that the UK would adopt the same interest rate as the rest of Europe. This lower rate would reduce mortgage and loan prices, encouraging more borrowing and growth in sales.
- Low interest rates and a fixed exchange rate will encourage more progressive and long-term government domestic policies, and boost trade and investment.
- The euro should be strong enough to compete against the dollar and the yen on world markets, making the EU a more powerful and influential trading bloc.
- The extra trade encouraged by the euro should create new jobs in the UK as more workers are required to meet the extra demand.
- It will improve relationships with the rest of Europe.
- It might encourage more inward investment into the UK from other EU countries and also international firms looking for a European base for production.

Arguments against the euro

- National governments will have less control over monetary policy. Effectively, the UK would lose the ability to alter interest rates to affect monetary policy to the benefit of the UK economy. It has taken 25 years of tight monetary policy to deliver a UK economy with low inflation and steady growth. Do we really want to lose the control that has been instrumental in delivering those sound economic conditions?
- The European Central Bank would set an interest rate to cover the whole of Europe. It is difficult to imagine a rate that would deliver the right economic conditions for the variety of different economies in the EU. What might be right for Germany could be a major problem for Greece. Ireland has discovered this very problem. Since joining the euro, its inflation has risen but it is powerless to control this using interest rates. This problem would be exacerbated if some of the new members eventually join the euro.

Practice point

Byfields plc produces lighting equipment. Recently, the company has agreed to a deal with a German buyer to deliver a large shipment of ceiling lamps. It has agreed a price of 250,000 euros. The current exchange rate is currently 1.49 euros to the pound. The directors have calculated that this deal should give them a profit of £30,000. It has been agreed that payment will be made to Byfields in euros in one month.

- How much sterling can Byfields expect to receive in one month when it exchanges the euros at its bank?
- How would Byfields' profit change if the exchange rate changes to 1.25 euros to the pound during the month?
- How would Byfields' profit change if the exchange rate changes to 1.85 euros to the pound during the month?
- How would this situation be different if the UK were a member of the Eurozone?
- What practical steps could Byfields take to minimise the exchange rate dangers inherent in this sort of deal?
- If the exchange rate were to stay at 1.25 euros to the pound for an extended period, what effect might that have on UK exports? Explain your answer.

- Losing the pound is a loss of heritage for the UK.
- If we join when the exchange rate for the pound is high, we will be locked into a situation of expensive exports and cheap imports. It would take a long period of cost reductions to make up for such a trap.
- The cost of converting computer systems and cash registers is enormous. This cost would have to be born by industry. Marks & Spencer estimate the cost for this to be more than £100 million for its company alone.
- Unemployment could increase, at least in the short term, if a government comes under pressure to cut public expenditure owing to restrictions relating to the requirement to limit its deficit.
- Critics fear that the German central bank (the Bundesbank) will dominate proceedings.
- The European Monetary Institute and European Central Bank might not look beyond the issue of price stability, and might ignore the knock-on social and political effects of monetary policy.

Remember

The UK is not a member of the Eurozone and the UK government has said we will have a referendum before we ever join. No date has yet been set, so it is likely that we will stay outside the Eurozone for some time to come.

Mobility of labour

The EU is committed to ensuring equal opportunities for all its citizens in all of the member countries, and this is the basis behind the EU policy to mobility of labour. The Regulation on the Free Movement of Workers within the Community was completed in 1968. It states that:

- any citizen of a member state is entitled to take up work in the territory of another member state without restriction
- those migrant workers must be treated the same as any of that country's national workers
- such workers have the same rights to training, social benefits, trade union rights and tax benefits as national workers.

So effectively any citizen of the UK (including you!) could take up a job in any other EU country without restriction.

This regulation has caused some concern in the UK in recent times. Prior to the accession of the new EU states in 2004 it was anticipated that there would be some movement of workers from some of the poorer new member states to the UK, where wages were higher. Initially this was generally looked on as a positive move, particularly when many of the workers coming to the UK filled jobs in construction where the UK was in urgent need of additional skilled workers.

The UK has now become the favourite destination for migrant workers from the new member states.

- In May 2004 it was estimated that 15,000 would come from these countries to the UK seeking work.
- By September 2006 the actual figure was 510,000.

Some UK nationals believe we may be accepting too many additional citizens. There are further concerns that numbers will increase following the accession of Bulgaria and Romania in 2007.

Thinking point

Do some research of news sites on the internet – www.bbc.co.uk/news is a great place to start. To what extent have workers come from Bulgaria and Romania since their accession to the EU? How is this being portrayed in the press? Positively or negatively? Do you agree with the views expressed?

Take it further

What do you consider to be the main advantages and disadvantages of free movement of labour within the EU?

European trade policy

The EU operates a single European market. This means that member nations should be able to trade with each other without restriction. In theory, a UK firm should find it no more difficult to trade with a firm in Munich than it does with a firm in Manchester. The individual governments believe that:

- all citizens and states of the EU will benefit from allowing trade to take place without restriction between members
- increased trade between the nations will result in a greater ability to generate wealth and improved standards of living in all of the member countries.

The EU has therefore taken a number of steps to promote trade between the member nations.

Step 1: the single market

Established in 1993, the single market removed all **tariffs**, **quotas** and other artificial trade barriers between member nations.

Free trade brings multiple advantages to nations, but it also brings problems. Much manufacturing industry in the UK has found it very difficult to survive in the face of fierce foreign competition. Many companies have disappeared as a result. Those that have survived have only done so thanks to severe cost cutting or redesigning of products. Consequently governments around the world are lobbied by representatives of industry to protect their livelihoods by reducing the quantity of imports allowed in. Sometimes governments have sympathy with these lobbies. In these cases, governments may resort to protectionist measures – steps to reduce the volume of imports. These can take a number of forms. Below are some of the most popular methods.

- *Tariffs.* Taxes are placed on all goods entering the country. These have the effect of increasing the selling price of these items when in the shops and making home-produced products more competitive. Thus sales of home-produced products rise (because they are now relatively cheaper) and import sales fall.
- *Quotas.* A limit to the number of imported items is set. Once this is reached, no more are allowed to enter the country.
- ***Subsidies.*** The government gives money to the home producer so that they can make the products more cheaply and therefore be more competitive.
- *Administrative barriers.* These are sneaky. The government does not prohibit imports at all, but does insist that imports must meet very stringent quality standards or makes the paperwork required very onerous. The hope is that importers will not be able to reach these standards, so imports are reduced.

All of the above methods prevent free trade. Therefore, they distort world markets. All of them potentially hinder growth prospects for the world economy, so all are frowned upon by EU governments. As a result, all EU governments have outlawed the use of these methods. The hope is that by removing these barriers more trade will take place, which will boost the economies of all the EU countries.

Key Terms

Quota A limit to the number of imports allowed.

Subsidy Non-repayable money paid by the government to a company.

Tariff A tax on imports.

Step 2: common standards

Many laws have been standardised across the EU, meaning that all the countries follow exactly the same rules. For example, standards for the safety of products have been made the same across all EU countries.

Before this was introduced each country had its own standards. Therefore, a product that would be acceptable according to UK law might not be acceptable in France.

This meant that exporting firms needed to adapt their products to meet the legal requirements of all the countries they were selling to. In some cases this led to multiple different versions of the same product.

Not only was this process time consuming, but also it was costly for manufacturers. Therefore it had the tendency to reduce the amount of trade that took place.

Having common standards means that a product acceptable in the UK can be exported to any other EU country. This makes trade much easier and more feasible.

Thinking point

The EU tends to refer to common standards as 'harmonised rules'. Using the internet, find details about five harmonised rules that have been recently introduced. You might begin your research at the official EU site (http://europa.eu/index_en.htm).

Take it further

Outline the potential effects of the harmonised rules you have identified on the UK businesses involved.

■ Step 3: the euro

One of the main benefits of the introduction of the euro is to encourage trade. Removing the uncertainty of exchange rate fluctuations should encourage more firms to trade abroad. For more details, see pages 292–94.

Thinking point

The UK is not currently a member of the Eurozone. Bearing in mind that the euro is designed to promote trade between Eurozone members, how might this be affecting UK businesses hoping to sell into the Eurozone?

Take it further

What practical steps can you suggest to overcome the problems you have identified in the previous question?

■ Step 4: integrated transport policy

One of the main problems associated with trade is that of transporting the goods thousands of miles through multiple countries. The EU has attempted to make this process easier and quicker by:

- removing border controls between member nations so that delivery lorries do not have to stop and show papers before crossing from one country to the next
- allowing hauliers to operate in countries other than their own (in the past they often returned empty following a delivery to another country because of the restrictions placed on where the firms could trade)
- the liberalisation of air travel, which has made freight transport cheaper with more flights to more places
- making money available to improve transport links in individual countries.

Thinking point

Although trade restrictions have been removed between member nations, the same is not true for non-EU members wishing to sell goods or services into the EU. They are faced instead with a tariff called the Common External Tariff (CET).

- Using the internet or textbooks find the details of the CET.
- Why do you think the CET exists?
- What do you think are the benefits and problems associated with operating the CET?

Take it further

The EU is an example of a trading bloc. Find details of other trading blocs in the world.

- Why do you think trading blocs exist?
- How many of them operate Common External Tariffs?

Common Agricultural Policy (CAP)

The main purpose of the Common Agricultural Policy has been to guarantee future supplies of food in Europe and to support the farming communities of the EU. CAP was adopted by the Community in the 1960s. The main objectives of the policy were to:

- keep people working in agriculture
- keep such a vital sector of industry viable
- prevent the decline of rural areas in the EU
- provide decent incomes for farmers so that they could afford to continue their work
- modernise the agricultural sector across the EU and to improve its efficiency.

To greatly simplify the explanation, the policy was intended to work basically on the two-fold principle of:
1. subsidising farmers
2. protecting the price of their produce within the common market from directly competitive exposure to lower 'world prices', such as those maintained outside the Common Market.

The CAP enabled farmers to keep the price of their produce in the single market artificially higher than the price outside (i.e. the flat price paid in the rest of the world – the 'world price'). This was achieved by placing an import tax on all cheaper foodstuffs entering the Common Market. This created a 'threshold price'. The import tax effectively raises the price of cheaper imports up to the same level as that of the Common Market (and often higher).

The farmers have been subsidised by EU citizens/consumers who pay an artificially high price for their food products. They are also subsidised by the member states, which pay large sums of money to the Community budget so that the EU can guarantee a market for their produce.

CAP has come in for severe criticism because it has led to the massive over-production of some agricultural products. Journalists have regularly reported about 'grain and butter mountains' and 'wine lakes' – huge surplus stocks that have arisen because of the subsidies on these items. Not surprisingly, farmers have concentrated production on those products with guaranteed prices, leading to higher quantities of products than could ever be consumed in the EU. The other major problem has been the huge cost. By 1999, CAP made up 50% of all EU spending.

Reform of the CAP

As a result of the problems outlined above, many people felt that CAP has been ready for reform for some time. In 1997, Agenda 2000 was presented by the European Commission. This included proposals for reforming CAP, bearing in mind past experiences, international trends, enlargement of the EU and the budgetary controls affecting member states. Agenda 2000 was basically the farm and financial reforms needed to prepare for the EU enlargement.

The emphasis of the policy is now shifting somewhat, so that rural development is becoming a major priority in order to achieve sustainable agriculture and preserve the environment. CAP no longer aims just to support farmers financially. It now focuses on food quality, preserving the environment and animal welfare, landscapes, cultural heritage and social balance and fairness.

Reform of CAP began in 1992. Since then guaranteed prices of beef, dairy and cereals have been cut and, by 2006, the cost of supporting arable crops, beef and dairy production have fallen from €34 billion in 2000 to just €14 billion. The 'mountains' of surplus products that brought CAP into such disrepute have become much less of a problem. Meanwhile, imports from developing countries have been substantially increased. Export subsidies have also been severely reduced.

European Structural Funds

The EU also concerns itself with job creation and the economic development of those poorer areas of the EU. Under EU Regional Policy, areas of great need have been identified so that they may be targeted with financial aid. Between 2000 and 2006 these regions were known as Objective 1 Regions (those of greatest need) and Objective 2 Regions (those with intermediate levels of need) and different funds of money were available to support these areas. A new policy was introduced in 2007, which is known as the EU Cohesion Policy. This will run until 2013.

Maps have been drawn up covering all of the EU and identifying those areas of greatest economic need. Page 299 shows a map for the whole of the EU.

Case study

Common Agricultural Policy (CAP)

In June 2003 European agriculture ministers finally agreed reforms to the CAP that would guarantee farmers subsidies until at least 2013, as long as they work to produce better food quality and provide greater environmental care.

This means that farmers no longer qualify for subsidies according to the quantity of food that they produce, and Margaret Beckett, the Agriculture Secretary, said she would decouple all English farmers' subsidies from January 2004.

The agreement requires farmers to keep their land in 'agricultural order', for which they will be paid a fixed, single farm payment no matter how much or how little food they produce.

Farms that continue to produce food have to meet eighteen 'cross-compliance' requirements on environmental, animal welfare and food quality standards to receive their payment. Mrs Beckett said that by removing the link between farm subsidies and quantity of food production, farmers would be able to 'produce for the market, not the subsidy'. The new agreement should also satisfy the World Trade Organization as it has demanded that the EU end its trade-distorting subsidies.

Countries are be able to retain 25% of cereal production subsidies and the new agreement also gives some limited control over subsidies for the production of cattle and sheep. Up to 10% of CAP payments will also be used to encourage farming in less favoured areas.

Not everyone has been happy about the new agreement, though. French farmers, the largest beneficiaries of CAP payments, are very concerned about their futures.

1. Explain the phrase: 'farmers would be able to "produce for the market, not the subsidy".' ✓
2. Explain the sentence: 'The new agreement should also satisfy the World Trade Organization as it has demanded that the EU end its trade-distorting subsidies.' ✓✓
3. What do you think is the logic behind subsidising farms that no longer produce food? ✓✓✓

The Convergence Regions are those of highest need. €308 billion has been allocated to be spent on Regional Policy between 2007 and 2013, 82% of which will go to the Convergence Regions to support projects that will increase economic growth and create jobs in those regions. You will notice that most of the UK does not have Convergence Region status. However, Cornwall, the Isles of Scilly and large areas of Wales do qualify.

A further 16% of the money will be available to the other EU areas and will be used to support innovation, sustainable development, better accessibility and training projects. This is known as the Regional Competitiveness and Employment Objective. The remainder of the money will be used for cross-border, transnational and interregional co-operation. This is known as the European Territorial Co-operation Objective.

To support the policies there are three basic funds of money available.

1 *The European Regional Development Fund (ERDF).* This fund is available for projects based on research, innovation, environmental protection, risk prevention and infrastructure.

2 *The European Social Fund (ESF).* This fund is available for projects designed to enhance quality and productivity at work, improving the adaptability of workers, increasing social inclusion by fighting discrimination and improving access to work for disadvantaged people.

3 *The Cohesion Fund.* This is available for aiding environmental projects and trans-European transport networks across the poorer EU nations.

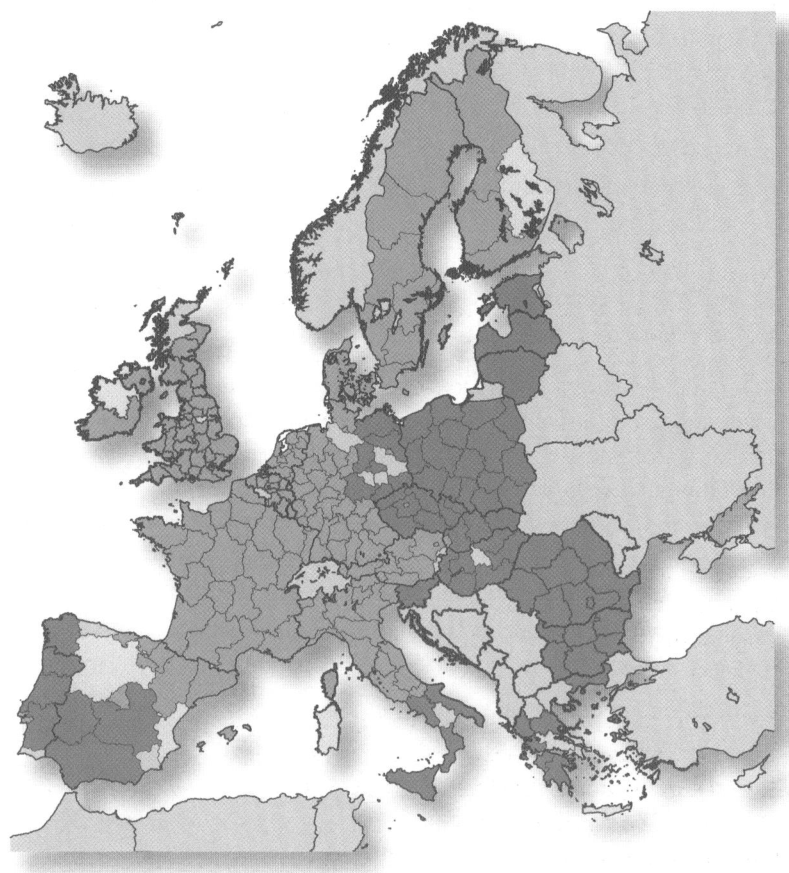

Objective

Convergence Regions

Phasing-out Regions

Phasing-in Regions

Competitiveness and Employment Regions

▲ **The EU structural funding map**

Outcome activity 39.4

This activity continues the study on Balfour Beatty begun in Outcome Activity 39.1.

Pass

Describe the impact on Balfour Beatty of developments in the global and European economies. **P4**

Merit

Assess the impact of changes in the global and European business environment on Balfour Beatty. **M3**

Distinction

Evaluate the impact of changes in the economic environment on Balfour Beatty. 

Grading tips

Pass **P4**

For a thorough answer you should ensure that you consider the following areas. For each, you should briefly describe any major events that have taken place and then make a brief assessment of the effect of the changes on Balfour Beatty. Discuss the changes that you intend to include with your lecturer, as it is possible that some of the following effects may not have been influential at the time you are writing this assignment and therefore may be safely omitted from your answer. You will need to do some research into recent economic developments to answer this task, you should consult newspapers, their websites or www.bbc.co.uk.

- Stock market fluctuations.

- Any major corporate failures.
- War and political instabilities.
- Terrorism.
- Actions of OPEC.
- Environmental concerns and actions.
- Outsourcing.
- International trade agreements.
- Any industry specific developments.
- The influence of the EU, also highlighting the impact of any recent changes in the operation of the EU.

Merit 

For a thorough answer you should revisit each of the changes that you outlined in your answer to P4. For each of them you should do a detailed discussion of the impact of the changes on Balfour Beatty. Your assessment should analyse the potential impact on a range of areas, such as:

- levels of demand for Balfour Beatty's services including the firm's prospects for international sales
- the effects on the firm's costs
- effects on the firm's possible expansion plans
- how Balfour Beatty's management may need to react to these changes.

Distinction 

Evaluation is about considering in detail the positives and negatives of something, and coming to conclusions as a result of this analysis.

To answer this task you will need to review all of your answers for P1, P2, P3, P4, M1, M2 and M3, then draw on the information and ideas that you have covered in them. This answer will therefore discuss changes in the business cycle, government spending, fiscal policy, monetary policy, global developments and the impact of the European Union.

To evaluate this case you should outline the key positive changes that have taken place in the economic environment and compare them with the most significant negative changes that you have identified, from the point of view of Balfour Beatty.

You might also look at possible economic changes that are on the horizon to see how Balfour Beatty might prepare itself for these changes. You should be able to identify these possible changes by reviewing recent articles in the press.

Finally you should come up with a judgment about how positively or negatively Balfour Beatty has been and may be affected by recent and possible future changes.

End of unit test

1. Describe the business cycle and its main stages.
2. What is a recession? What are the main features of a recession?
3. How do we measure economic growth?
4. What are the main problems for businesses associated with a period of inflation?
5. Name four of the key leading indicators of recovery.
6. What are the three biggest areas of government spending?
7. Explain the multiplier mechanism. Why is it so important to industry?
8. What is deficit funding and where does the money come from?
9. Explain the meaning of fiscal policy. What is it used for?
10. Explain the meaning of monetary policy. What is it used for?
11. Explain the difference between direct and indirect taxes. Which do you believe is fairer?
12. Explain the link between bank lending and inflation.
13. In what ways can a fall in the firm's share price affect that company?
14. What are the key advantages and disadvantages of the recent expansions in EU membership?
15. How is EU trade policy helping UK industry?

Books

Anderton, A, 2001, *Economics* 3rd Edition, Causeway Press Ltd
Grant, SJ, 2000, S*tanlake's Introductory Economics* 7th Edition, Longman
Marcouse, I, Gillespie, Martin, B, Surridge, M, Wall, N, 2003, *Business Studies* 2nd Edition, Hodder and Stoughton
Mercado, S, Welford R, Prescott, K, 2001, *European Business* 4th Edition, Prentice Hall
Parking, M, Powell, M, Matthews, K, 2003, *Economics* 5th Edition, Pearson Education

Websites

www.bankofengland.co.uk – The Bank of England is instrumental in effecting UK monetary policy and its website gives much insight into this subject
www.bbc.co.uk – One of the most reliable sources for news information
www.cia.gov/cia/publications/factbook/index.html – The CIA World Factbook has detailed social, political and economic information about every country in the world
http://europa.eu/index_en.htm – The official site of the European Union
www.hm-treasury.gov.uk – The Treasury controls public finances in the UK; its website is a good source of fiscal information
www.inlandrevenue.gov.uk – Comprehensive details about taxes in the UK
www.intute.ac.uk/socialsciences/economics/ – A good source of articles on economics
http://money.howstuffworks.com/recession.htm – A discussion of recession
www.statistics.gov.uk – The Office for National Statistics; information on the latest economic indicators for the UK
www.tutor2u.net/economics/content/topics/macroeconomy/recession.htm – A discussion of recession
www.tutor2u.net/revision_notes_economics.asp – A good source of information about a range of economics topics
http://uk.finance.yahoo.com/ – A great source for share process and performance

Grading criteria	Outcome activity	Page number
To achieve a pass grade the evidence shows that the learner is able to:		
P1 Describe the likely effects on a selected business of variations in the economic environment	39.1	267
P2 Identify the impact of government spending on a selected business	39.2	273
P3 Outline how both fiscal and monetary policy decisions have affected a selected business	39.3	281
P4 Describe the impact on a selected business of developments in the global and European economies	39.4	299
To achieve a merit grade the evidence shows that, in addition to the pass criteria, the learner is able to:		
M1 Analyse the implications of government policies for a selected business	39.2	273
M2 Analyse the effects of fiscal and monetary policies for a selected business in terms of the market in which it operates	39.3	281
M3 Assess the impact of changes in the global and European business environment on a selected business	39.4	299
To achieve a distinction grade the evidence must show that, in addition to the pass and merit criteria, the learner is able to:		
D1 Evaluate the impact of changes in the economic environment on a selected business	39.4	299

Understanding retailing

Introduction

Retailing is a dynamic industry as it is constantly changing. The first part of the unit considers its current structure and highlights recent developments, such as hybrid stores where coffee and book retailing combine to produce a new sort of store environment.

Much innovation has taken place in the technology used to move products from producers to customers. This aspect of retailing, called logistics, is explored in the second part of the unit. It also considers the differing levels of service offered by retailers and the selling skills required in the retail sector.

Finally, the unit reminds you that the most effective retailers respond to changes around them, e.g. newly emerging product preferences to government policy affecting where stores can be built. The unit concludes by reviewing how the retail sector is responding to changes, such as an increasingly mobile population.

Visiting retailers is an everyday occurrence for many of us. This unit uses store visits and your experience of retailing to explore many of the topics.

What you need to learn

On completion of this unit you should:

1. Know the structure of the retail industry
2. Understand the role of retailing in the distribution of goods and services
3. Understand the sales and service functions in retailing
4. Know how the retail sector responds to internal and external change.

Consider this

Your family has run the local convenience store for many years. You have managed to compete with the local supermarkets by opening all hours, stocking products which reflect newly emerging tastes like convenience meals and keeping prices competitive by buying from the local cash and carry.

However, the market is changing very rapidly and the future is looking uncertain. A national supermarket has just bought a large site in the centre of town. At the same time it has opened two convenience stores both within three miles of your store. Even the students who bought their food and drink from you have started to order over the internet. You have noticed the supermarket delivery van in the area at all sorts of strange times.

You realise that you will have to make some crucial decisions in the very near future. Fortunately there are some options to be considered. The local airport is expanding and is building a new shopping mall to entertain the expected increase in passenger numbers. The local wholesaler is offering lower prices for many of the products you sell. In return, though, it requires you to invest in new 'Spar' signs inside and outside your store. Finally, you have noticed the development of hybrid stores in town and wondered whether a convenience store that incorporates an internet café would attract the large number of students in the area.

Which of these alternatives would you develop? Why not speak to your local convenience store owner about their view of the future?

Askham Bryan
College
LIBRARY BOOK

Organisation of the retail industry

Retailing is one of the most important industries in the UK and one that plays a role in everyone's life. It employs around 11% of the workforce in more than 200,000 businesses. The scope of the industry has steadily expanded. Retailers have grown into some of the world's largest companies, rivalling and in some cases exceeding manufacturers in terms of global reach. The industry has become concentrated in the hands of fewer retailers at the expense of many independent and small retailers. At the same time the average store size and employment has increased. The places where you can shop have become more diverse, with city centre, local and out-of-town shopping developments.

Definition of retailing

Retailers exist to provide service to customers at a profit. All the aspects of retailing – operating from an appropriate location, offering attractive product assortments, ensuring enough stock is available to meet demand – add value to the products they buy from suppliers and eventually sell to consumers.

Retailers cut their bulk deliveries from suppliers so individual consumers can buy the quantity they require – very often a single item. The term 'retail' comes from the French, meaning 'to cut' again.

Classification of types of store

There are several classifications of types of retail store, as shown in the table below.

Type of retailer	Example
Independent	Londis, Spar
Multiple chains	Matalan, WHSmith, Boots
Supermarkets	Morrisons, Sainsbury's, Aldi, Somerfield
Department stores	House of Fraser, John Lewis, Selfridges
Catalogue stores	Argos
Discount stores	Curry's, Superdrug, Comet

Practice point

Produce a timeline for retailing over the last 100 years. Pinpoint developments such as:

- the concentration of retailing in the hands of a few
- the increase in store size
- the growing numbers employed
- the increasing diversity of the retail industry.

Emerging store types

A number of new store formats have appeared recently such as:

- shopping villages
- factory shops
- television channels
- internet traders.

Shopping villages

These offer permanent discounts on a wide range of top brands and designer labels. The goods on sale are surplus stock from the high street or special buys and are typically sold through stores run by the brands themselves.

Take it further

- Do centres like these contain retailers that you would call a 'destination store'?
- What social changes have occurred to help such centres to be successful?

Factory shops

There is a difference between goods sold at shopping villages and the factory shops actually attached to a factory. A factory shop would normally be selling imperfect goods produced in the adjacent factory. Shopping villages are more likely to be selling last season's surplus stock that had to be removed from stores to make room for fresh goods.

Case study

The village people

McArthurGlen is careful to select the best possible locations for its designer outlets. When searching for a new site, visibility is key. The location must be no more than 10 kilometres from a quality road or motorway. The location should have a minimum of 3.5 million people living within a 60-minute drive time and 1 million within a 30-minute drive time.

At McArthurGlen it's not just about shopping. You find a whole host of activities taking place – from circus workshops to live jazz bands to home makeover days. Children can also enjoy a fun-packed school holiday thanks to a full calendar of events.

Each centre has a fully themed food court complete with a wide selection of cafes and food choices. They have everything from Prêt-à-Manger to McDonald's to Pizza Express to Coffee Republic. Ample parking is provided right next to the centre. Younger visitors can enjoy themselves in a safety-approved play area. Regularly cleaned and checked toilets include baby-changing facilities.

Centres are also wheelchair friendly with fully equipped disabled toilets. A free wheelchair loan service is also available.

1. Think about the features that make shopping villages attractive to consumers. ✓
2. What type of retailers do customers find in these centres? ✓✓

◄ **Shopping villages are home to top brand stores offering surplus stock at a discount**

■ Television sales channels

Cable or satellite television companies have dedicated shopping channels such as QVC and ExpressShop, but usually require separate telephone ordering. Recent technological developments concerning interactive digital television can allow the consumer to order instantly through their remote control.

The advantages of this kind of store are:

- they avoid the drudgery of queuing at stores and carrying heavy bags
- they relieve high street congestion and transport/parking problems
- they remove personal transport costs and increase leisure time.

Disadvantages include:

- the television is not available for normal viewing and the telephone not available for ordinary use
- there's a risk of error when ordering and difficulty of establishing responsibility for errors.

■ e-retailing

Selling and buying products over the internet continues to gain in popularity. The internet has three main advantages, as detailed below.

- *Convenience.* It shares this with other forms of home shopping. Shopping via the internet avoids the cost and time of making a journey, the chore of leaving the house, travelling along congested roads, sometimes paying for the privilege of parking and finally standing in a queue at the checkouts.

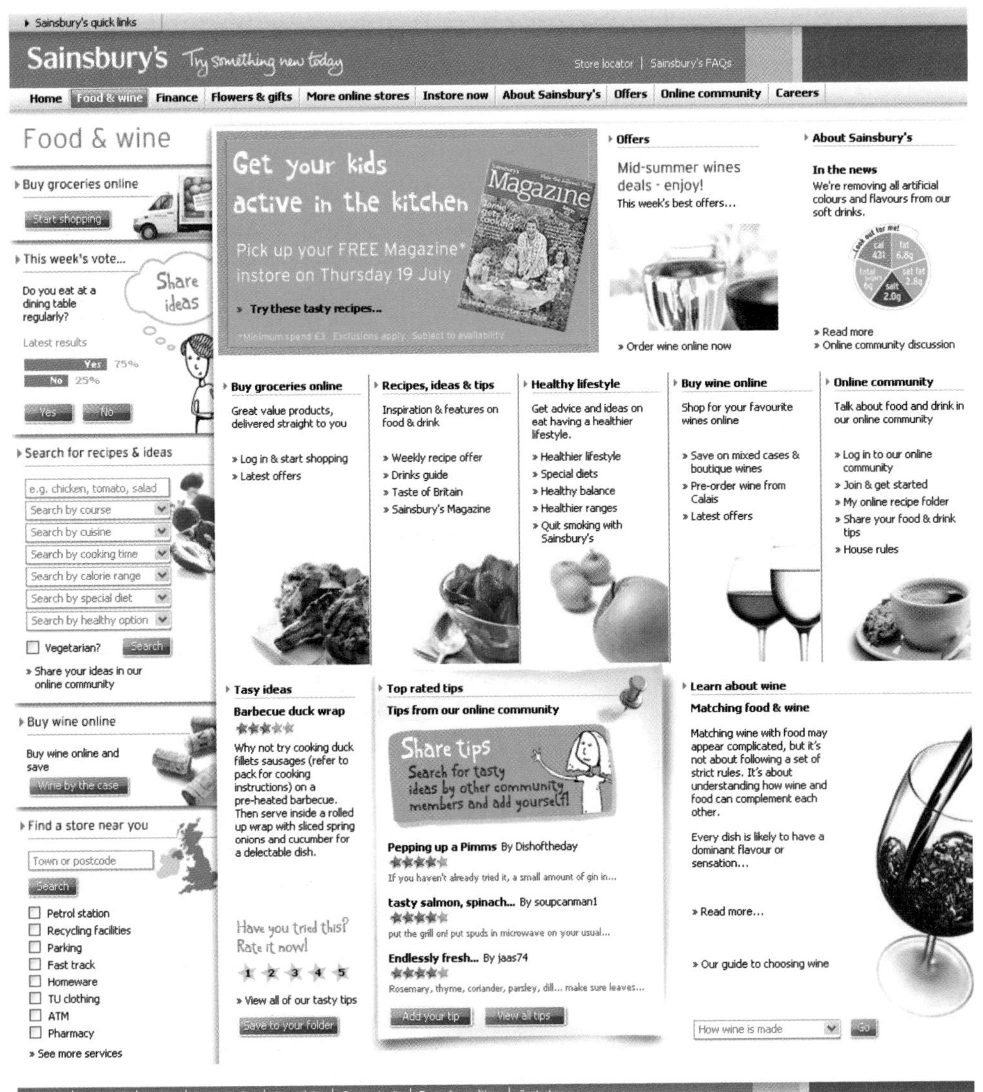

◀ e-retailing means many items, such as food and drink, can be purchased without the customer even having to leave their house

- *Choice.* This is by far the biggest advantage of the internet. It offers access to an enormous range of products from across the world. The advantage of choice also applies to the comparison with conventional shopping. No shopping centre can hope to match the range available on the Internet.
- *Cost.* In general, goods sold online are cheaper than those sold in shops. This is because the e-retailer does not have the expense of shop premises or sales staff. The e-retailer does, of course, have costs but these are generally less than the conventional bricks and mortar retailer.

Hybrid stores

Hybrid stores are beginning to appear which offer a 'new' combination of products in the same store. A good example would be where coffee and a bookshop have been combined. Coffee@Waterstones features a contemporary coffee shop situated in a Waterstone's book store. Visit www.ottakarscoffee.co.uk and enjoy the store experience yourself.

Online and physical stores

Bricks and clicks is a business model by which a company attempts to combine both an online web store and a physical store. For example, an electronics store may allow the surfer to order online, but pick up the order immediately at a local store. Alternatively, a furniture retailer may have displays at a local store from which a customer can order electronically for delivery.

The bricks and clicks approach has been used by retailers who already have a successful distribution network. It is considered far easier for a traditional retailer to establish an online presence than for a new internet business to establish a traditional presence. The success of this approach has destroyed the concept that the internet would make traditional retailers obsolete.

The advantages of bricks and clicks retailers are that they:

- utilise existing suppliers ensuring problem-free delivery and assured supply
- use established brands already trusted by the customer
- bring with them economies of size, such as being able to buy larger quantities and qualify for bigger discounts from producers
- other economies of size may also occur when buying, for example, advertising time on radio or in magazines
- have the benefit of **learning curve** gains which apply to organisations that have been in an industry for some time

A major disadvantage for these stores is that their website has the burden of costs associated with a 'bricks and mortar' business, meaning their prices are not always competitive.

Key Term

Learning curve The process of gaining experience and knowledge that result from learning from your mistakes.

Service vs. product retailing

Many shopping locations have a high proportion of service retailers, including banks, hairdressers, estate agents and cafés. These organisations are concerned with providing an effective extended marketing mix. Even product retailers now realise that they have to consider the three extra elements of the extended marketing mix – people, physical evidence, processes (see the table below).

Extended marketing mix	Implication for service retailers
People	• Should be naturally courteous, sincere and polite. • Must know about products and policies of the organisation. • Need to have excellent selling and negotiation skills.
Physical evidence	• Brochures available in attractive folders. • Give away gifts with some intrinsic value, such as diary or calendars. • Staff dressed in appropriate uniforms, with name badges.
Processes	• Various ways of processing payments or depositing money. • Immediate appointment booking system and in some cases on-demand consultation.

Remember

The traditional marketing mix, sometimes referred to as the 4Ps, includes product, price, promotion and place.

Classification of retailers

Retailers can be classified from a variety of viewpoints, each classification bringing something to the understanding of the sector. In the UK 11% of all enterprises are retailers operating from around 280,000 retail outlets.

Classification by store size and product strategy

Retailers can be classified depending on their approach to the products they stock, as the table below shows.

Store type	Description of product strategy
Supermarkets, superstores, hypermarkets	• Very large stores, such as ASDA and Morrison's, selling a full range of food and non-food products. • Supermarkets are stores with at least 200 sq m (about 2,000 sq ft) of selling space, using self-service methods and having at least three checkouts. • Superstores have 2,500 sq m of selling space and car parking facilities. • Hypermarkets are simply large superstores that have 5,500 sq m of selling space.
Discount stores	• Retailers such as Comet and Currys which concentrate on selling large quantities of consumer durables at discount prices.
Multiple stores	• Organisations like Marks & Spencer and House of Fraser which offer a narrow range of products. Multiple retailers have more than ten branches.
Multiple variety stores	• Stores like Boots and Woolworths which offer fast-moving lines, usually selling nationally advertised brand leaders or own brand merchandise.
Independent retailers	• Includes convenience store or C-stores such as Spar and Londis. They focus on selling essentials, fresh and convenience foods. Also features 'niche stores' which offer specialist products to a wide geographic area, e.g. snow boarding equipment. Independent retailers have fewer than ten branches.

Classification by number of employees and sales turnover

Overall there are just under 3 million people (11% of the labour force) employed in retailing in the UK in about 280,000 enterprises. The table below clearly shows how retailing in the UK is concentrated in the hands of a few major retailers with 34% of sales turnover being generated in just 1.25% of the enterprises.

Size of enterprise by people employed	Number of enterprises	%	Sales turnover (£ billion)	%
0–4	167,480	60	30.5	12
5–9	62,990	23	40.6	16
10–19	28,480	10	38.1	15
20–49	12,325	4.5	33.0	13
50–99	3,575	1.25	24.5	10
100 +	3,545	1.25	87.7	34

Remember

'Sales turnover' is another phrase for 'sales revenue' (the value of sales made within a trading period).

The table below shows the top ten retailers in recent years by turnover in the UK.

Company	Turnover (£ million)
Tesco	24,760
Sainsbury's	14,220
Morrisons	13,194
ASDA	13,098
Marks & Spencer	8,049
Co-operative	7,179
Argos	4,867
Dixons	4,698
Somerfield	4,521
John Lewis	4,499

Classification by type of activity

This classification groups retailers according to the type of merchandise they offer for sale. Using this classification, significant sector statistics are produced – especially by the government's Office for National Statistics (ONS). An example can be seen on page 313, where retail sales trends are considered.

Practice point

Visit your local shopping centre and undertake a survey of the retailers in that centre. Then classify them by type of activity and product strategy. Based on your analysis, what conclusions can you draw about local shopping centres?

Trading category	£ billion, 2006	%
Food stores	109.2	37.5
Non-food stores	131.59	51.75
– non-specialist stores	*21.49*	*8.45*
– clothing and footwear stores	*35.45*	13.95
– household goods stores	*34.66*	13.56
– other stores	*39.99*	15.75
Non-store retailing	13.61	10.75
Total retail sales	254.4	100

Location

The places where you can shop have become more diverse. These days there are local, city centre and out-of-town retail parks, plus regional shopping developments.

■ Local

Local shops serve suburban areas or smaller towns. They generally consist of a significant number of stores located around one main street. It is increasingly evident that product shopping is becoming a secondary reason for using local shopping centres. The main reasons for visits are to:

- go to the bank
- visit civic establishments such as your town hall or library
- socialise, e.g. meet friends for lunch.

There seems little prospect of local retailers in any location increasing their share of expenditure. The likelihood is that, faced with shopper attention from a diverse range of options (including electronic-based shopping), locally based retailers will have to face the prospect of a declining share of retail sales from shoppers.

Local shopping centres have been losing their attraction to shoppers for some time. Customers perceive these locations to lack a variety of stores. Fashion stores, fresh food stores and specialist fine food stores are not generally represented in local centres. Niche businesses such as craft and hobby stores, designer goods stores, specialist book shops and children's clothes stores are often suggested by consumers as the sort of stores that would enhance and be relevant in a local shopping centre.

■ In town stores and shopping centres

A typical high street has:

- department stores (such as Debenhams)
- multiples (such as Dorothy Perkins)
- service retailers (such as building societies and banks).

Up to the early 1990s there was a massive growth in out-of-town centres, but these can take away business from town centre stores. This prompted the government to insist that companies prove there is no suitable site in, or near, the town centre before allowing an outlet to locate to the outskirts. Recently, however, supermarket retailers have been opening stores such as Tesco Express in city centres. These are aimed at consumers who are working in city and town centres. These smaller supermarkets sell a limited range of goods but open for shorter hours, generally coinciding with office hours.

The bigger centres of population have town and city centre shopping centres, also known as malls, which are important shopping locations. The wide choice of types of shops to choose from is the most important perceived advantage of shopping centres. Centres that are going to be successful are the ones which pay particular attention to the mix of stores in the centres.

Shoppers do comment on some drawbacks to these locations because they can become very busy and overcrowded. Management needs to control shopper flow around the centres and try to eliminate congestion hot spots. Managers also need to ensure the stores are not too similar, highlighting the need to create an interesting and appealing mix of retailers within the centre. Free car parks and better in-centre facilities are other areas which influence shoppers when deciding where to shop.

■ Out-of-town retail parks and regional centres

Huge regional shopping complexes have been built in several out-of-town sites in the UK. These have the same types of attractions as shopping malls, but on a larger scale. These provide a wide range of facilities (restaurants, cinemas, cash points) and are close to main roads and/or motorways as well as train stations. Additionally, they provide large, secure parking areas. They contain a high proportion of destination stores, i.e. retailers that attract customers in their own right.

Major out-of-town shopping parks in Britain.

Rank	scheme	location	Size square feet (million)
1	Bluewater	Dartford	1.61
2	Metrocentre	Gateshead	1.58
3	Merry Hill	Brierley Hill	1.50
4	Trafford	Manchester	1.40
5	Lakeside	Thurrock	1.36
6	Meadowhall	Sheffield	1.35
7	Arndale	Manchester	1.30
8	Milton Keynes Centre	Milton Keynes	1.20

Other out-of-town retail parks feature stores such as Comet, Dixons, PC World, MFI and B&Q. The reason for their popularity with shoppers is that it is easy to park, prices are competitive and the size of the outlet means a great variety of goods is on sale.

Ownership

The ownership of retail stores reflects the diverse nature of the industry.

- *Independent retailers* are retail organisations with fewer than ten branches. The market share and number of independent retailers has been declining for many years, particularly in the food sector as supermarkets gained in strength. This trend seems set to continue, especially as supermarket chains are now opening neighbourhood convenience outlets to complement their bigger stores. Independent retailers tend to sell a specialist range of products (e.g. medicines), or they are general convenience stores that sell a range of products including groceries, household goods, wines and spirits. They try to offer a personal service and have a flexible approach to opening hours. Pricing, discounts and other trading policies are at the discretion of the owner.

- *Multiple retailers* are businesses with more than ten branches. Some multiples are classified as specialist stores, concentrating on a narrow range of items, such as Burtons for clothing. Multiple variety chains like Boots and Marks & Spencer offer a wider range of goods. They buy fast-moving branded product goods centrally and in bulk to obtain lower prices. They tend to be located in 'busy' shopping areas, clustered together with other well-known multiples. Prices are usually relatively low, generating volume sales. Their stores project a strong corporate identity, which makes them easily recognisable.
- *Voluntary chain retailers* choose to buy about 70% of their stock from a certain wholesaler whose buying power allows them to negotiate lower prices with key suppliers. The retailer invests in signs both in and outside the store to reflect a nationally agreed style. This style of trading is especially seen in the convenience store sector through organisations like SPAR, which has 2,600 stores in the UK.
- *Franchised retailers* are granted selling rights in a geographical area. In return, the **franchisee** pays a fee based on sales or perhaps agrees to buy supplies from the franchisor. It has become a popular method of trading in the UK. Well-known brands such as McDonald's and Kentucky Fried Chicken can be franchisee businesses. The benefits for the franchisee are as follows.
  – The trade name of the franchisor, plus all the associated goodwill with the name, can be transferred to the new business.

Case study

Would you join SPAR?

How to become a SPAR member

SPAR is looking for retailers whose stores are seen to have growth potential whatever their size. A membership fee is charged on a sliding scale dependent on the size of the store. Retailers are free to join or leave the group at any time.

SPAR key facts

SPAR is the world's biggest and most international retail food chain with 16,000 stores in 34 countries. SPAR is a symbol group, which means that individual SPAR members remain independent but enjoy access to the collective buying and marketing power plus all the added benefits of operating under a strong corporate brand.

SPAR UK has a turnover of more than £2 billion and is the leader of the convenience store sector. SPAR members in the UK are serviced by six Retail Distribution Centres (RDCs) which:

- offer special buying terms
- offer retailers loans to purchase equipment
- provide business development support.

The members benefit from weekly consumer promotions, as well as television, national and local press advertising.

SPAR retailers have access to the latest developments in retailing, including merchandising and category management ideas and store refurbishment. The SPAR Millennium Store Programme has already modernised more than 1,400 stores, producing increases in sales from between 10% and 70% year on year.

1. What might be the disadvantages of joining the Spar group? ✓✓
2. Under what circumstances might you consider joining a group like Spar? ✓✓✓

– The new business can be offered some pre-opening assistance such as site selection, staff training programmes, operating manuals and assistance in finding suppliers.
– Once trading, the franchisor can help with advertising, bookkeeping, supplies and general advice.

Take it further

- Have a look at the Londis website (www.londis.co.uk) and decide which group (SPAR or Londis) offers the best deal.
- If you were managing a business like SPAR, what would you offer independent retailers as an incentive to join?

Key Term

A franchisee Someone who owns and operates a franchise.

Structure of the retail industry

The structure of the industry has recently become more complex. Retailers have become more diverse with a large increase in different types of location and stores. The structure of the retail sector can be examined from a number of perspectives, including size and profitability, with each perspective adding to an overall understanding of the sector.

Size

UK retail sales are estimated to be £254.4 billion in 2006 – larger than the combined economies of Switzerland and Ireland. Retailing plays an important role in the UK economy, generating almost 6% of **Gross Domestic Product (GDP)**. More than a third of consumer spending goes through retailers.

Key Term

Gross Domestic Product (GDP) The sum total of the value of the country's output over the course of a year.

The table below shows the value and volume growth in total retail sales 2000–2006.

Year	Current price value (£ billion)	% annual change
2000	207.17	-
2001	219.39	+5.9
2002	230.16	+4.9
2003	235.76	+2.4
2004	246.32	+4.5
2005	248.6	+0.9
2006*	254.4	+3.5

Source: Office of National Statistics

*Estimate based on actual retail sales from January to September 2006

Trends in sales

Trends in retail sales have a direct impact on the health of the economy. Faltering retail sales can reduce the growth rates the UK is experiencing. The ONS reports monthly on trends in retail sales. Look at the extract from its August 2006 report shown in the case study entitled 'Retail sales growth slows in August 2006' (page 313).

Profitability

Recent reports by the marketing research company Mintel (www.mintel.com) suggest that around 60% of retailers have been enjoying improving **profit margins**. However, the profitability of individual retailers can vary significantly for a variety of reasons, as illustrated by the financial results of Tesco plc and Alexon plc (see case study entitled 'Contrasting fortunes' on page 314).

Case study

Retail sales growth slows in August 2006

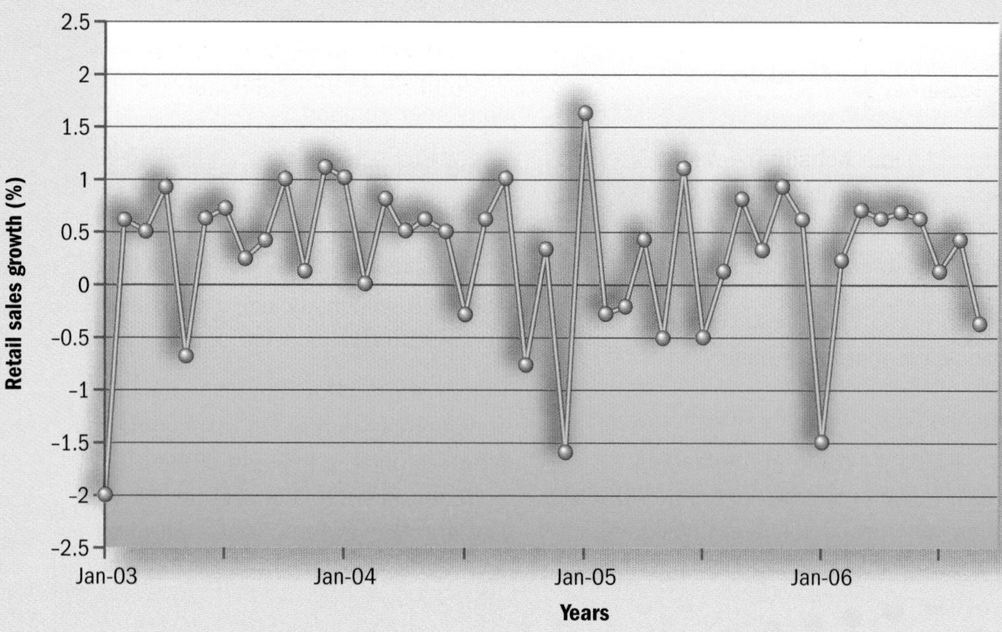

▲ **Retail sales growth (%) 2003–2006**

Underlying growth in retail sales slowed slightly in August, but was still strong when compared with the average in recent years, despite decreased sales in August by retailers of food and drink.

An analysis of monthly figures shows that the total sales volume increased by 0.3% between July and August. This follows zero growth in July and 0.7% in June. Food stores showed a decrease of 1.7%, the biggest fall since January 2003, compared with non-food stores which showed growth of 1.2%. Household goods stores showed growth of 3.3% following a decrease of 3.0% last month. 'Other' non-food stores showed growth of 1.0%. Sales growth in the non-store retailing sector was 6.3%, the highest since December 2002. The total volume of sales in August 2006 was 4.3% higher than in August 2005.

For the three months to August the value of retail sales was 3.7% higher than in the same period a year earlier. The average weekly value of sales in August 2006 was £4.7 billion, 4.2% higher than in August 2005. Food stores increased by 4.2% over the year compared with 3.9% growth for non-food stores.

1. What factors can you think of that might affect the sales in the product categories mentioned? ✓✓
2. Which retailers could be benefiting from the trends in retail sales? ✓✓

Take it further

- Visit the ONS website (www.statistics.gov.uk) and find the retail sales report for the latest month. How have retail sales developed over the period of the report?
- Would the strong growth in retail sales be considered a good or bad thing by the government?

Case study

Contrasting fortunes: Tesco and Alexon

▲ **'Sells everything, to everyone, everywhere'**

Tesco makes progress in four key areas

Sales and profits are up yet again at the leading supermarket chain. Tesco is on track to create 20,000 jobs worldwide this year. Group sales, excluding VAT, were up 12.6% to £20.7 billion in the 26 weeks to the end of July and pretax profits rose 10.3% to £1.1 billion.

Chief executive Terry Leahy reported progress in all four divisions of Tesco. UK sales were up 10.2% and trading profits 10.5%, with another 800,000 square feet of store space opened. International sales grew by 21.3% and trading profit by 21.1% as 3 million square feet were added to store space. UK non-food sales grew 12.6% and tesco.com grew sales 28.7%, increasing profits up 43.1%.

The improvement in UK sales was achieved despite price deflation of 0.4% as prices were cut to attract and retain customers in the cut-throat world of supermarkets. Leahy says that by controlling costs and increasing productivity, Tesco has absorbed costs that are outside its control, particularly energy and local business taxes.

The Tesco juggernaut shows no signs of slowing. It is winning more customers and persuading them to spend more in total despite – or perhaps because of – price cuts.

Alexon sales slump

First half profits slumped at the fashion retailer and the warm September was horrendous.

Alexon saw pre-tax profits crash from £7.9 million to £1 million in the six months to July. Total sales slipped from £197.7 million to £180.8 million, and margins suffered as the group stepped up promotional activity and cleared leftover stock. Chief executive John Osborn blamed the unseasonal warm September weather plus low consumer demand.

In the first half, the operating profit for Alexon brands slipped from £9.6 million to £6.6 million. The Mandolin brand, launched recently in 17 high street shops, lost £2.4 million in the first half. The full year loss will be about £5 million, including £2 million set aside to cover shop closures.

Osborn says: 'The Mandolin project placed a considerable burden on management resources within Alexon brands, and some of the other brands have suffered as a direct consequence. While Eastex, Dash and Ann Harvey fared reasonably well, Kaliko, Alex & Co and Minuet had poor seasons and will be similarly affected in the autumn.'

The operating loss for Dolcis shoe shops increased from £900,000 to £2.4 million. Sales were 7% down on lower **margins** and autumn sales have been slow as women shunned boots in the warm weather.

The operating loss for menswear increased from £1.5 million to £3.5 million. Attempts to sell own branded merchandise at the expense of known brands backfired spectacularly. Because of the lead time between ordering and the goods arriving, this mistake has only just been rectified.

Bay Trading saw profits fall from £1 million to £100,000. Sales were 3.9% down, reflecting the absence of any strong trends in the young fashion market.

Overall, this is a pretty dismal set of results and with the high street environment remaining tough any improvements may be hard to achieve.

1. What factors distinguish the successful performance of Tesco compared with Alexon? ✓✓
2. Can you identify any features of the Tesco performance that might be worrying? ✓✓✓

Take it further

- What might you do if you were asked to improve the performance of Alexon?
- What does this tell you about how to be a successful retailer?

Key Term

Margin Sometimes referred to as profit margin, this is the difference between the retail price and cost of production and selling of an item.

Store size and location

A variety of store sizes can be found in the retail sector. Each size has a particular role to play in the market. The store size has a significant effect on its location. For example, superstores are found on large out-of-town retail or regional parks, while convenience stores are found in housing neighbourhoods. The types of stores operated by Tesco show the link between store size and location, as the table on the next page shows.

Independent retailers and multiple retailers

These days, retailing is concentrated in the hands of a few. A trend that has emerged in recent years is the dramatic decline of independent retailers.

Case study

Once they were open all hours

They have been the backbone of communities for hundreds of years, dispensing local gossip, local knowledge and groceries for millions of loyal customers. But the corner shop could soon become extinct within ten years as multiple retailers threaten to take away their customers and destroy their supply chain.

The decline in the number of smaller shops at a rate of 2,000 a year for the past five years has coincided with the expansion of Tesco, Sainsbury's and Morrisons. There were 30,000 small shops in 2000 and now there are only 20,000. If the trend continues, they will all be gone in ten years. This reinforces a recent report from the New Economics Foundation, which found that between 1995 and 2000 the UK lost 20% of some of its most vital institutions – corner shops, grocers, high street banks and post offices – amounting to a cumulative loss of more than 30,000 retail outlets.

The future of the corner shop is in serious doubt. Supermarkets claim they are providing the convenience stores required by consumers, but for the independent operator the future is bleak. This is a sector that multiple chains were not even in more than five years

▲ If current trends continue, corner shops may soon be a thing of the past

ago and now they operate more than 600 stores. Tesco has recently announced that it expects to double the number of convenience stores it operates to 1,200 within the next ten years.

1. Why can organisations like Tesco make a profit operating a convenience store whereas the independent retailer is struggling for survival? ✓✓
2. Does the new breed of convenience stores have features that make them attractive to customers? ✓✓✓

Store type	Description and location
Extra	Extra is Tesco's largest store format. It serves large, densely populated catchment areas such as city suburban areas. It sells a full range of food and non-food products. It is located in large out-of-town areas.
Superstore	These are large specialist food outlets, though the larger ones do carry clothing as well as non-food categories such as books, stationery and electrical goods. They serve smaller residential areas and are located on retail parks
Metro	Metro is the format developed for busy high street city centres. This store type is significant in size and sells a range of everyday products catering for the increasing number of city dwellers and professional people looking to do important shopping near their workplace.
Express	Express is a C-store format. This store type focuses on a local residential neighbourhood selling fresh and convenience foods. Some are located in petrol forecourts and are the smallest of Tesco's store format.

▲ Types of Tesco stores

Take it further

- What might happen once competition no longer exists from the convenience store sector?
- Which groups of consumers are perhaps more vulnerable to the loss of independent retailers?

Practice point

Choose a local shopping centre of reasonable size and complete a store survey. Then calculate the proportion of stores that you would describe as not-for-profit before commenting on the results.

Not-for-profit and public place retailers

Some shopping areas, such as local centres, have seen a growth in not-for-profit retailers – especially ones run by charities such as Oxfam, Help the Aged and Cancer Research. They sell goods brought in by donors and use mainly volunteer staff. The revenue is used to support the aims and objectives of the charity concerned.

Public place retailers are also a common sight at a variety of diverse venues, as the table below shows.

Public place retailer	Characteristics
Kiosks	Main rail stations have self-contained units on their concourses selling, for example, fast food or newspapers, magazines, books and confectionery for travellers. A WHSmith retail kiosk is a common sight at many UK rail stations.
Museums	Tourist attractions have realised the potential to sell visitors mementoes of their visit, to raise funds for restoration or expand the exhibits at the location.
Street vendors	The pedestrianisation of many of our city centres has allowed street vendors to trade effectively. These vendors can be seen selling products such as flowers, fruit and even socks. They can also be found in shopping mall concourses offering gifts, sweets and lottery tickets. Major sporting events attract street vendors selling programmes and team supporter merchandise.
Vans	These are a common sight at outdoor events such as country fairs, concerts and sporting events. Perhaps the most familiar are ice cream retailers who signal their arrival in a tuneful manner.
Vending machines	For many years, selling from machines has been associated with cigarettes, drinks and confectionery. However, in recent years there has been a noticeable rise in the products available from vending machines (e.g. hot drinks). They provide consumers with service seven days a week, 24 hours a day.

Third places

Work environments other than a central head office or a home office are called 'third places'. Research indicates that an increasing number of people will shortly be using third places, and that many individuals will spend 25–35% of their total work time in these new kinds of locations. Examples of third places include coffee shops, public libraries or even a borrowed office.

Third place developments are expected in rural environments and in the outer suburbs of larger metropolitan areas. That said, they will all have some common characteristics such as:

- access to tools (e.g. computers)
- access to knowledge (e.g. from technicians)
- support services (e.g. catering services).

Additionally, the space in these developments can be used for several different things, including:

- to work in
- to learn in
- civic activities.

Third places are likely to become anchor locations for economic development in our increasingly global, knowledge-based economy. They might offer a new retailing opportunity, with possibly a new retailing format.

Employment characteristics

- The retail industry employs approximately three million people. This equates to 1 in 9 (11%) of the total UK workforce. Over the last five years, employment in retailing has grown by 141,000.
- Average gross weekly earnings in the retail sector are about £250, although in London it is nearly 30% higher than in other areas of the UK.
- The retail industry accounts for about 20% of all part-time jobs and 6% of all full-time jobs. It is heavily dependent on part-time employees – especially in London.

Thinking point

Having studied the structure of the retailing industry, what evidence can you provide to support the claim that the retail industry is dynamic, flexible and responsive?

Outcome activity 41.1

Pass

Describe the structure and organisation of the retail sector.

Merit

Compare the function of four different retail formats and shopping locations.

Grading tips

Pass P1

Include a paragraph on the following topics:

- size and trends in sales
- location and size of stores
- types of retailer including not-for-profit and public place retailers
- trends in the number of retailer types
- employment characteristics of the sector.

Merit M1

Compare means to highlight the similarities and differences. Retail format and store location are closely linked. The various types of store operated by Tesco clearly illustrate this relationship.

Distribution channels

A channel of distribution is a network of organisations that, in combination, perform all the functions required to link producers with customers.

Availability of products

For retailers, the situation of being able to offer the right product in the right place at the right time for the right price remains frustratingly elusive, even with the enormous amount of data that retailers and e-retailers can gather about the buying patterns and tastes of consumers.

The problems e-retailers have had delivering products that customers have ordered over the web have been widely reported in the news. In all probability you have gone to a store only to find that it does not have the item you want – even though the store has plenty of stock. Price reductions have grown from 8% in 1985 to 33% in 2005. These numbers include promotional price reductions as well as forced price reductions that are the result of retailers having too much stock. But the increase is so large that business people take it as a sign that retailers are having trouble matching supply to customer demand. Take a look at the table below.

How does the customer react to out-of-stocks?
31% buy the item at another store. 26% substitute for a different brand. 24% either delay purchase or never purchase the product.

Movement of goods from manufacturer to retailer to consumer

There are many possible distribution channels with varying characteristics. For most products it is sensible to use more than one of them.

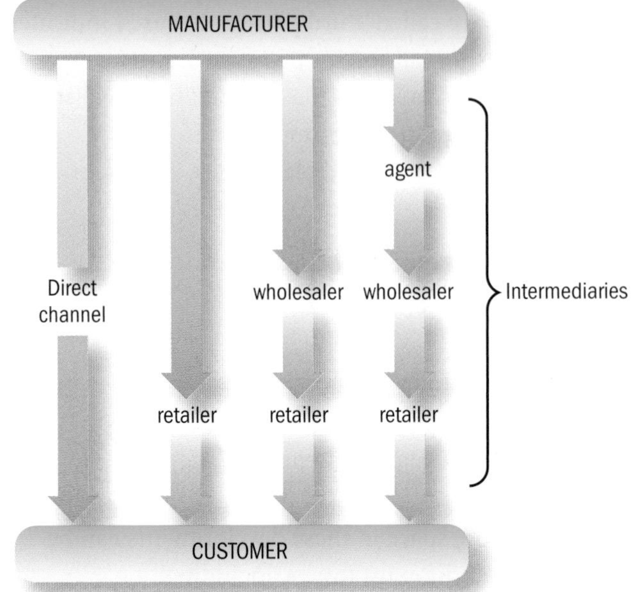

▲ **Products reach consumers in a variety of ways**

Organisations between the producer and customer are called intermediaries. The most common intermediaries are as follows.

- *Retailers.* These may be owned by the produ ed by the producer (e.g. The Body Shop) or independent of the producer (e.g. Iceland).
- *Wholesalers.* These range from cash and carry outlets (e.g. Makro), which offer a minimal service to 'full function' wholesalers which provide credit, delivery and technical advice (e.g. Bookers the catering wholesaler).
- *Agents.* These may represent the producer, retailer or the wholesaler. Agents obtain orders for producers, retailers and wholesalers but they are not employed by the organisation. They are self-employed.

Remember

A franchise is a business established using the name, logo and trading methods of an existing successful business.

Distribution channels for different types of goods

The distribution channels used to deliver a product to the consumer can be quite different. The table on page 320 illustrates the difference between food and clothing distribution.

Wholesaler as intermediaries

Wholesalers stock a comprehensive range of goods. They sell these products to other organisations such as retailers, who intend to resell them. They may provide a range of services for their customers including:

- **breaking bulk**
- packing and labelling
- supplying promotional materials
- quick delivery.

The most recent development in this area has been the growth of cash and carry units such as Makro. Retailers who buy from this type of organisation are responsible for transporting the stock and paying in cash, but prices are lower than those obtainable generally at the traditional wholesaler.

Key Term

Breaking bulk Breaking into smaller amounts. This is an important job for a retailer – buying large quantities from a producer or wholesaler and offering smaller quantities to consumers.

Retail control of the supply chain

Own brands

A major development of retail marketing in recent years has been the development of the retailer's name as a brand rather than simply a name over the shop. The name of many major retailers is better known to consumers than many producer brands. This has increased the control of retailers over the supply chain by enabling them to decide the features, quality, packaging and price of such products. Retailers use **own-brand** items to offer their customers different and better value products.

Key Term

Own brand This can be a name, a symbol or a design used to identify a specific retailer and make it appear different from its competitors.

e-retailing

Retailers were quick to understand the potential of the internet. Many 'bricks and mortar' retailers quickly established websites to sell their goods. They realised that if they did not develop such facilities they might find themselves facing new internet-based-only retailers.

Of more concern is that it offered producers the opportunity to deal directly with their customers, making the role of the retailer redundant. This process is called 'disintermediation'. It is attractive to producers because in many instances they can offer lower prices to customers while making higher profits. This process is becoming a reality for some products such as music, films, software and tickets. The retailers most under threat are ones where the internet can accept payment and almost instantaneously deliver the product. The retailer's control over the supply chain is severely weakened under such circumstances.

Thinking point

Compare and contrast the characteristics of the retailers WHSmith and Amazon.

▼ The difference between food and clothing distribution

Channel feature	Clothing	Food
Geographic areas from which products obtained.	Abroad, especially the Far East.	Mostly from the UK but some from abroad.
The time between a retailer placing an order and receiving deliveries.	Long time – can sometimes take up to a year (see case study on Augulla, below).	Short time – fresh goods especially.
Responsiveness to consumer demand.	Generally not so responsive – products available in store change on a seasonal basis rather than on what consumers are buying.	Responds quickly to changes in demand – hot weather can dramatically alter demand for food products.
Special shipment requirements.	Arrives flat packed in cartons or ready for hanging in store.	Special vehicles deliver fresh, chilled and frozen products. Other food products delivered in general purpose vehicles.
Intermediaries.	Shipped in containers from abroad to the regional distribution centres (RDCs) of large retailers, to wholesalers or direct to stores.	Deliveries also to RDCs of large retailers who have special chilled and frozen goods storage facilities. Fresh products delivered direct to store or are crossed docked at RDCs – goods moved directly from supplier's truck into store delivery vehicle for immediate shipment to store.

Case study

Augulla Limited

In its Bombay factory, Augulla Limited makes a range of basic clothes. The process is fairly straightforward, but it takes a product a long time to reach the customer. The company is considering buying other companies in the supply chain in order to reduce the time taken. To help make a decision, information has been collected about the average time taken by different activities, starting with the purchase of fibres and ending with delivery to the final customer.

- Fibre stored in commodity warehouses before purchase 140 days
- Fibre moved to spinners 11 days
- While at spinners:
  - fibre in stores 21 days
  - spun into yarn 13 days
  - finished yarn stored 11 days
- Yarn bought by knitters and moved to factory 8 days
- At knitters:
  - store yarn 6 days
  - knit to form fabric 9 days
  - store work in progress as grey (not coloured) stock 12 days
  - dye in standard colour 7 days
  - store fabric ready for sale to garment producer 8 days
- Augulla buys fabric and transports to factory: 7 days
  - store fabric 12 days
  - cut to form garment components 5 days
  - store garment components before manufacture 6 days
  - sew components to form garments 14 days
  - store garments as finished goods 12 days
- Deliver to regional distribution centre in UK 21 days
- Deliver to wholesaler 17 days
- Deliver to retail store 19 days
- Sold to customer 6 days

1. What are the major issues within this supply chain? ✓✓✓
2. What other companies in the supply chain could Augulla buy hoping to improve overall performance? ✓✓✓
3. What might be the other benefits of reducing the length of the supply chain? ✓✓
4. If this is a typical supply chain for products produced abroad, why do so many clothing retailers source their products from such places? ✓✓✓

▼ **Amazon has become a major competitor for WH Smith**

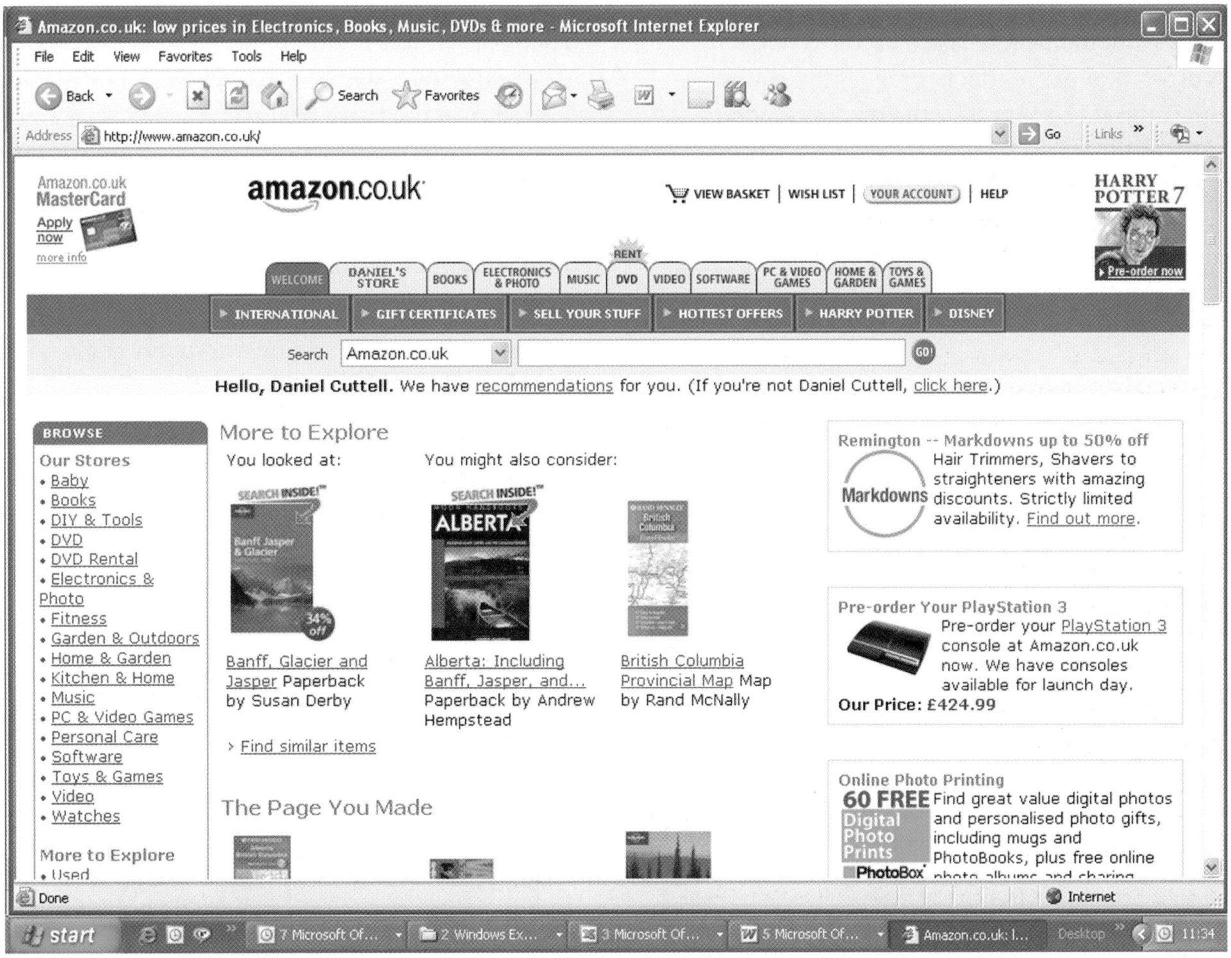

Amazon.co.uk: low prices in Electronics, Books, Music, DVDs & more - Microsoft Internet Explorer

File Edit View Favorites Tools Help

Address http://www.amazon.co.uk/

Amazon.co.uk MasterCard Apply now more info

amazon.co.uk

VIEW BASKET | WISH LIST | YOUR ACCOUNT | HELP

HARRY POTTER 7 Pre-order now

WELCOME | DANIEL'S STORE | BOOKS | ELECTRONICS & PHOTO | MUSIC | DVD | VIDEO | SOFTWARE | PC & VIDEO GAMES | HOME & GARDEN | TOYS & GAMES

INTERNATIONAL | GIFT CERTIFICATES | SELL YOUR STUFF | HOTTEST OFFERS | HARRY POTTER | DISNEY

Search Amazon.co.uk

Hello, Daniel Cuttell. We have recommendations for you. (If you're not Daniel Cuttell, click here.)

BROWSE

Our Stores
- Baby
- Books
- DIY & Tools
- DVD
- DVD Rental
- Electronics & Photo
- Fitness
- Garden & Outdoors
- Home & Garden
- Kitchen & Home
- Music
- PC & Video Games
- Personal Care
- Software
- Toys & Games
- Video
- Watches

More to Explore
- Used

More to Explore

You looked at: Banff, Glacier and Jasper Paperback by Susan Derby

You might also consider: Alberta: Including Banff, Jasper, and... Paperback by Andrew Hempstead; British Columbia Provincial Map Map by Rand McNally

› Find similar items

The Page You Made

Remington -- Markdowns up to 50% off Hair Trimmers, Shavers to straighteners with amazing discounts. Strictly limited availability. Find out more.

Pre-order Your PlayStation 3
Pre-order your PlayStation 3 console at Amazon.co.uk now. We have consoles available for launch day.
Our Price: £424.99

Online Photo Printing
60 FREE Digital Photo Prints PhotoBox Find great value digital photos and personalised photo gifts, including mugs and PhotoBooks, plus free online

Done Internet

start 7 Microsoft Of... 2 Windows Ex... 3 Microsoft Of... 5 Microsoft Of... Amazon.co.uk: l... Desktop 11:34

Provision of product-enhancing functions

Transport and storage

A delivery service is an important way of adding value to the product and for retailers to differentiate themselves from competition. The provision of a delivery service is essential for certain types of merchandise such as furniture or large electrical durables such as washing machines. For others, it can provide a competitive advantage. Some fast food operators such as Domino Pizza have chosen to offer a delivery service as one way of setting themselves apart from the competition.

Effective storage techniques, whether in the warehouse or the store stockroom, can enhance and add value to the product by being available when the customer requires it.

- Vertical storage and minimising aisle width provides the space to stock the right quantities of a product.
- The layout should help to speed up the collection and despatch of the products. Frequently required products should be kept near the stockroom door adjacent to the store.
- Handling of the product should be kept to a minimum to reduce the potential for damage. Roll cages can be moved from the warehouse to the store shelf without any additional handling.

After-sales service

This recognises the fact that customer needs do not end when a sale has been made. Efficient after-sales service may be the vital factor in encouraging a high level of repeat purchase. Look at the following table.

After-sales service elements
• Commonly required spare parts or consumables (e.g. vacuum cleaner bags) available. • Repair (e.g. mobile phone unlocking) and servicing facilities (e.g. for scooters) provided. • Technical advice either in-store or through an appropriately and adequately staffed telephone helpline. • Commitment to the guarantee provided when the product was bought. • Providing a delivery, installation and removal of replaced item service at a time convenient for customers.

Distribution process

A retailer may have an enticing store, well trained staff, and a distinctive and relevant brand reputation. However, these things count for nothing if the products are not actually on the shelf when the consumer is shopping. Moving products to customers effectively is a vital process for retailers. That certainly seems to be the view of Ian Canadian, the director of the Institute of Logistics. Recently, he has made these comments.

- 'The biggest expense in the retail business is the cost of moving goods.'
- 'The principal element of customer service is the availability of product.'
- 'Many retailers could treble net margins if they managed the supply chain more efficiently.'

Supply chain

The primary function of the supply chain is to provide goods or services required by end consumers. The chain essentially starts with the extraction of raw material. Each link in the chain processes the material in some way or supports this processing. The supply chain extends from raw materials through many processes to the ultimate sale or delivery of goods or services to the final consumer. It can also arguably include the disposal of any associated waste.

A more efficient and responsive supply chain will:

- improve stock availability
- improve choice
- offer up-to-date products
- reduce stock levels and mark-downs.

In overall terms, costs will fall while sales and profits increase.

Sourcing in the UK and internationally

The benefits of domestic sourcing includes:

- shorter lead and transit times
- the ability to monitor closely the total production process
- lower costs in terms of management time and communications.

▲ **A traditional supply chain**

In general, a retailer may accept higher prices in exchange for the lower risk and costs associated with UK sourcing. Clearly, sourcing costs from a distant and underdeveloped country may be far greater than those from a geographically closer country. Many companies adopt a policy of sourcing from several countries. Nike, for example, has shoes produced in South Korea, Taiwan, Thailand and Hong Kong.

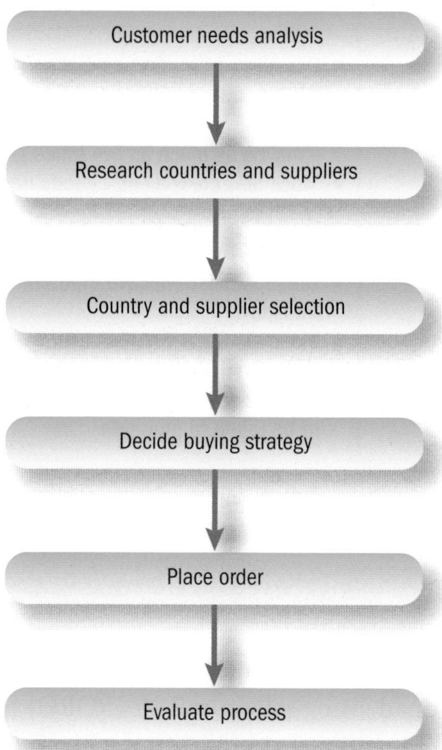

▲ **International product sourcing process**

Suppliers

There are many potential sources of supply for most retailers. Some, such as the Co-operative, manufacture the products themselves. Other sources are wholesalers and distributors who represent producers. Many retailers buy specific key products from a few, established suppliers. However, some buy from many suppliers based on the best opportunity at any given moment.

Concentration of purchases with a few suppliers has a number of advantages.

- It fosters a long term co-operative relationship between a retailer and its suppliers.
- Such co-operation can lead to a more active retailer–supplier interaction in the design of new products and improved retail marketing activity.
- Furthermore, suppliers are likely to favour their established customers in distributing a limited supply or popular item.
- Finally, it can lead to cost savings due to quantity discounts and better stock management.

Whether a firm decides to deal with a few or many suppliers, it must carefully research the strength and weakness of all prospective suppliers before selection takes place. The selection of suppliers by the retailer must take into account several important factors, as the table below shows.

Factor	Relevance
Reputation of supplier	For ethical reasons retailers must deal with reputable suppliers.
Brand name	The merchandise must be suitable for the store's customers.
Brand image	The image of the brand must fit the store's product strategy.
Price and payment terms	Prices, delivery terms and payment arrangements must be acceptable.
Supplier reliability	Suppliers must be able to deliver on time to the agreed quality.
Support provision	Suppliers who provide promotional help are generally preferred.

Distributors

Distributors normally represent an international producer in one of their important overseas markets. Consequently they will:

- be situated in the market for which they have distribution rights
- have the financial strength to carry adequate stock levels
- be prepared to purchase in large quantities to minimise the expense of international transport
- be wholly or partly involved in promotion and any after-sales service requirements of the product
- be responsible for the business transactions in their market for the exporter's products
- accept the risks that are associated with trading in a particular market.

Logistics process

Logistics is the management of resources within the supply chain to ensure the right product is available, in the right quantity at the right time.

Types of transport

Although there are often a lot of costs incurred by the transport operation, it also adds value by moving goods to the place desired at the time desired by the customer. The choice of transport mode for freight within the UK is road. This is clearly shown in the table below.

Mode	Tonnes (millions)	Tonnes (%)
Road	1,660	81.5
Rail	94	4.6
Water	132	6.5
Pipe	151	7.4
total	2,037	100

Selecting a mode of transport is determined by cost, reliability, accessibility, transit time, capability and security. The table below gives more details of these factors.

Transport mode	Characteristics
Road	• Key virtue is access as all producers, warehouses and retail stores have access by road. • Some legal restrictions such as driver hours and weight limits.
Rail	• Cost effective – perhaps one-tenth of the cost of road transport. • Much slower than road transport and rougher for the goods. • Much less convenient, with collection required from rail head.
Air	• Considered very fast, taking one-tenth of the time of a road journey. • Much more expensive than road transport – maybe as much as five times greater. • Much less convenient – goods have to be taken to airport.
Water	• The most cost-effective mode of transport. • Much slower, with boats averaging 20 mph on inland waterways. • Much less convenient, with goods having to be taken to quayside.

Moving goods in Europe and internationally

Much of the freight that enters or leaves the UK travels by road, using roll on/roll off (RORO) ferries to cross the English Channel to continental Europe. The use of RORO ferries is inefficient for long sea journeys mainly because of poor space utilisation on a ferry. The advent of the Channel Tunnel has made rail a practical alternative for international transport. Another development that is making rail increasingly attractive is the development of 'piggyback' systems, where a trailer can be carried on a railway wagon. This minimises the amount of double handling, reducing the journey time. Look at the table on page 325, which lists the factors relating to freight travel to and from the UK.

▼ **Freight travel to and from the UK**

Mode of transport	Characteristics
Road	• Quick service where ferry services are frequent. • No double handling of goods – saving time and minimising likelihood of damage. • Shipments from virtually anywhere in Europe can reach the UK. • Reasonable security because drivers stay with vehicles. • Extra costs are incurred if vehicle returns empty.
Rail	• Provides a economical method of transport. • Beginning to offer similar journey times to road transport. • Goods have to be brought to and from rail head. • Security may be an issue because no driver is with the load.
Air	• Air transport is quick, which allows retailers to hold smaller stock levels. • Cost for most products is very expensive – except for emergency stock or to meet a deadline like Christmas. • Delays at airports as goods have to be loaded and unloaded.
Water	• Provides a slow but economical method of transport. • Delays may occur waiting for suitable sailing conditions. • Time needed to load and unload goods.
Containers	• Most consumer products transported by container. • Good level of security and therefore lower insurance costs. • Need special equipment to handle containers – limits number of transfer points. • Containers are initially expensive to produce. • Empty returning containers increase cost.

Storage locations

A variety of storage facilities are required to link the flow of goods to retailers.

■ Stockrooms

The need for stockroom space varies from one retail trade to another and between various methods of retailing. Stockrooms should be as conveniently located as possible to selling areas. However, they should not take up valuable selling space. A stockroom should be used as efficiently and as infrequently as possible. The important factors determining stockroom organisation are as follows.

- *Use of space.* Wall areas should be used to the maximum while full use of floor-to-ceiling height should be attempted.
- *Accessibility.* All stock should be as accessible as possible and the faster-selling items should be nearest to the sales area.
- *Grouping.* Lines should be stacked so that they follow the same pattern and layout as the store.

■ Warehouses

Warehouses add value because rather than being purely somewhere to store goods they are increasingly places to do crucial jobs. Modern warehouses can therefore:

- break bulk when large deliveries are received from producers
- create bulk by consolidating small quantities of individual products into a bulk delivery to a single store or location
- smooth out demand by organising deliveries to and from the warehouse in an orderly manner (stores do not want all their supplies arriving at the same time, nor do warehouses)
- combine goods, such as special promotional packs where a free product (e.g. a cereal bowl) has to be attached to a packet and promotional labels applied to the combined item.

Case study

Hams Hall: an automated fulfilment factory

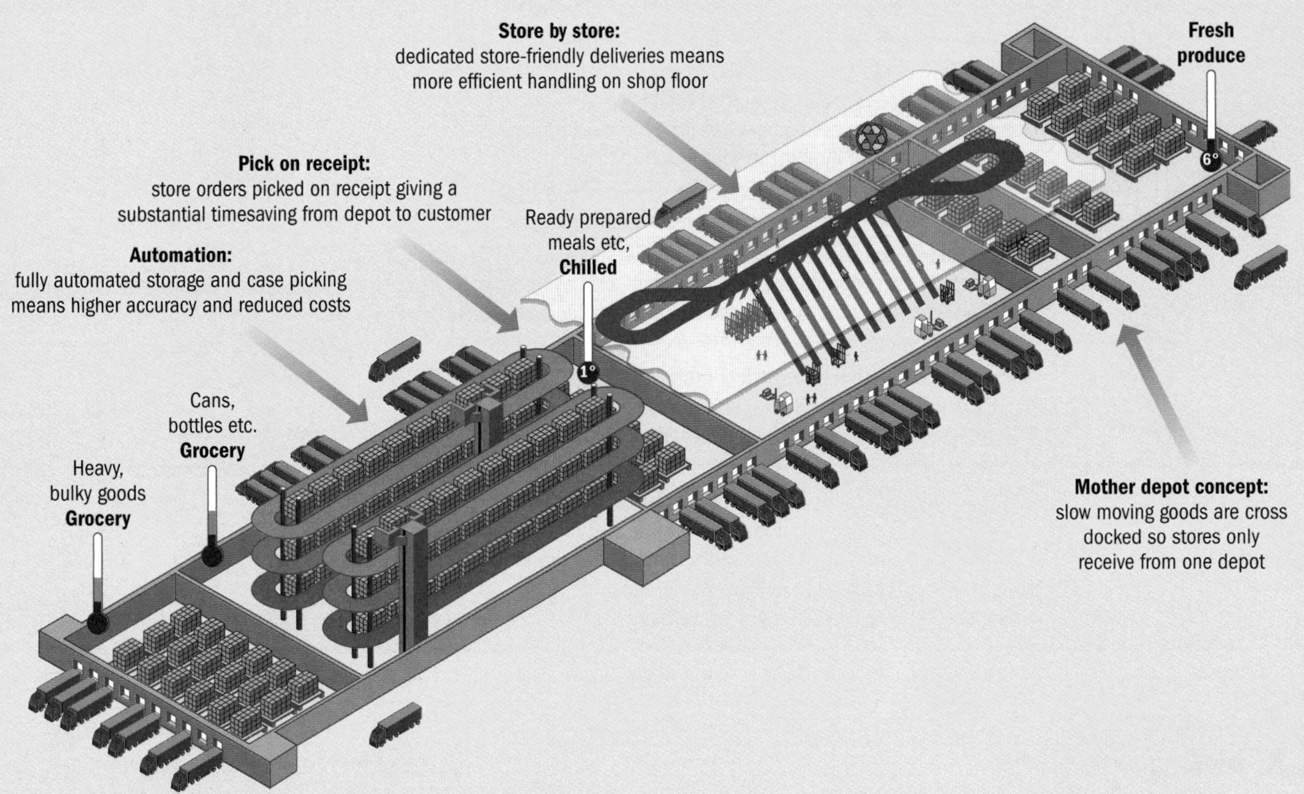

By any standards Hams Hall is impressive. The 700,000 square feet fulfilment factory can handle more than two million cases a week. The facility situated at the centre of the motorway system in the West Midlands has special unloading areas for fresh produce, slow-moving goods arriving from other Sainsbury's warehouses, heavy bulky grocery goods and one for cans and bottles.

The site has space for manoeuvring Sainsbury's large vehicles, although one of the benefits of the fulfilment factory is that eventually the company will need 150 fewer vehicles at depots and on the road. The facility and its associated technology means fewer and more accurate deliveries to each store. Stores will now receive all the products they need in one delivery. Previously, chilled products and standard produce were delivered separately.

Hams Hall is one centre of a distribution system that will see the number of depots reduced from 21 to nine regional, two national and two frozen food facilities – all located near major transport routes. Already, two national centres have been opened near the M6 in Stoke-on-Trent and on the M25 at Rye Park, Essex, along with a regional centre at Waltham Point also next to the M25 in North London.

1. What are the benefits Sainsbury's are hoping to obtain from their fulfilment factories? ✓
2. What factors would you take into account when deciding where to build such a facility? ✓
3. Can you identify anything that might influence the development of such facilities? ✓✓
4. Which food retailers do you think are experts in ensuring the products customers want are always in the store? ✓✓

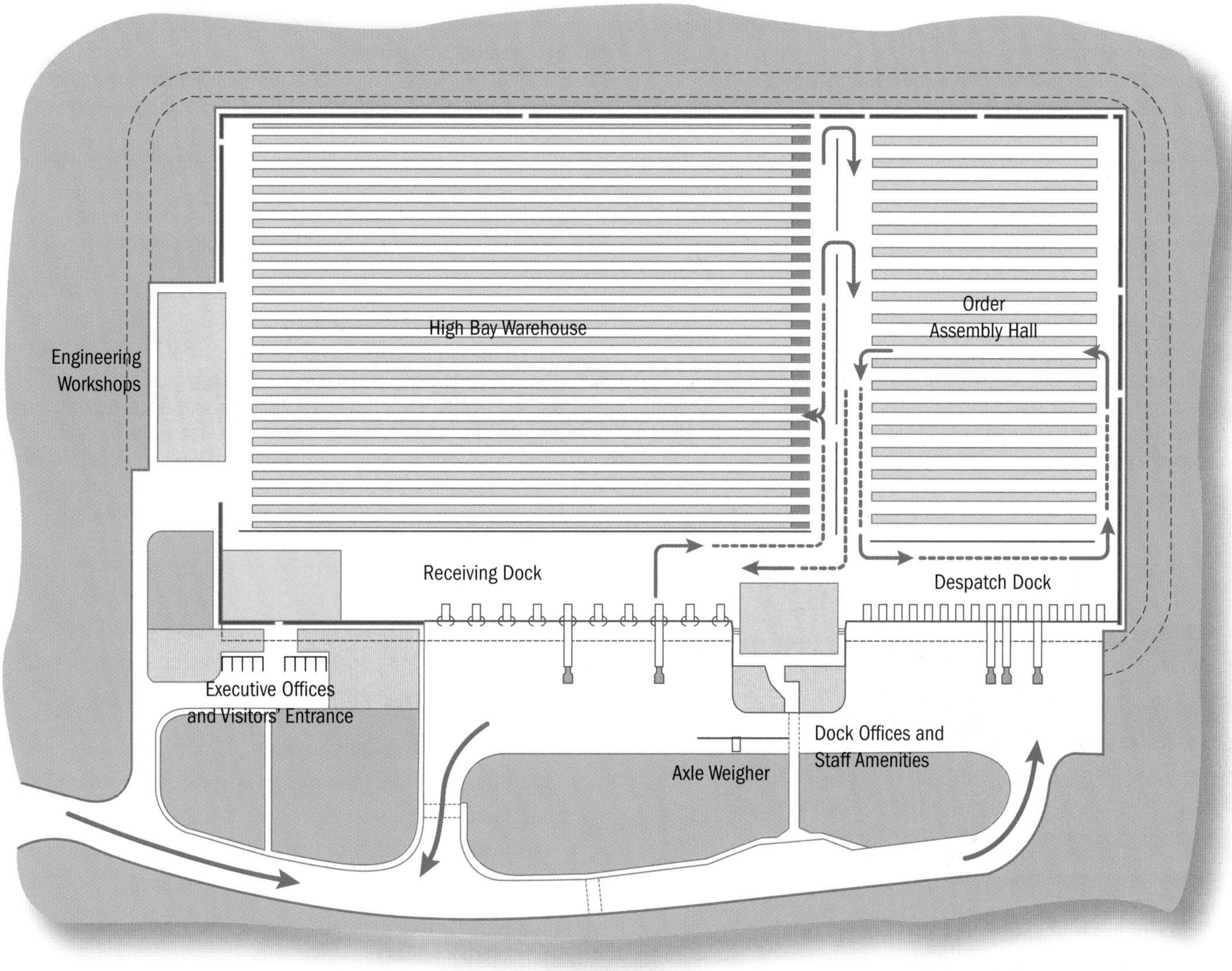

▲ A typical warehouse design

■ Distribution centres

Regional Distribution Centres (RDCs) are a recent development in logistics. The most modern facilities are called fulfilment factories. Proximity to major transport routes, space for manoeuvring large vehicles and plenty of loading/unloading facilities characterise these locations. Sainsbury's automated fulfilment factory at Hams Hall, near Birmingham, has all these things, as the case study (page 326) shows.

Use of IT in the supply chain

IT has a growing and increasingly influential role in the supply chain. Many of the developments can possibly be classified as being designed to increase the responsiveness of the supply chain to customer needs (see the table on page 328).

Thinking point

Retailers use a variety of distribution channels to source their products. Using retailer information, data from logistics organisations, textbooks and your own observations, examine first the channels used by independent retailers, then multiple retailers.

▼ The influence of IT in the supply chain

Bar-coded merchandise Enabling the unique identification and tracking of all goods throughout a supply network.	**POS data sharing with suppliers** This will allow suppliers to react to actual demand patterns rather than trying to meet demand by forecasting the demand – always a difficult activity.
Electronic reordering The ordering and reordering of goods, especially during a sale season, are performed electronically to increase speed and accuracy.	**Consumer information systems** Through the use of POS data and developments such as loyalty cards, more data than ever is being collected on consumer preferences.
Sharing with trading partners This involves not simply sharing stock data throughout the supply chain but data on, for example, planned promotions and new products. IT systems will allow this to occur in a secure manner with the intention of improving the efficiency and effectiveness of the supply chain.	**Radio Frequency Identification Tags (RFID)** Retailers expect to use RFID to track products on planes, trucks and ships through ports and warehouses, on to shop shelves, through tills, and into homes and offices. Accurate tracking should eventually save millions of pounds as it improves distribution, reduces theft, cuts labour costs and reduces stock levels. For instance, it is expected to reduce the time it takes to perform a stock count from around two hours to about 20 minutes and without the need to disturb the stock.

Practice point

Visit a number of retailers and produce a short report on how they use information technology in their marketing and stock control activities.

Distribution of e-retail products and services

Online shopping with home or office delivery is fast becoming a way of life throughout Europe. Increasingly, customers are using these services because they don't have the time to shop or dislike grocery shopping.

For the retailer, fulfilling such orders is one of the largest costs apart from being one of the hardest aspects to get right. Two methods are being used by retailers.

- *Store picking.* Orders are assembled in store by picking products off the supermarket shelves using low levels of technology. Tesco Direct and Sainsbury's Orderline both currently operate in this way.
- *Dedicated warehouses.* Orders are assembled in central dedicated facilities, often using labour-saving devices such as scanners and conveyor belts.

Store picking has its advantages.

- It allows fast, low-risk expansion of the service in the early growth stages.
- Delivery distances are generally shorter because stores cover a small, local catchment area.

It also has some disadvantages, such as:

- out of stocks
- high picking costs
- capacity constraints
- store customer disruption.

Additionally, it is costly at higher volumes than dedicated warehouses because stores are designed to trap customers and are not laid out for picking stock quickly.

By contrast, the advantages of dedicated warehouses are as follows.

- Out-of-stocks are considerably reduced.
- There are no capacity constraints, whereas stores have limited storage space locally.
- There is no disruption to or from customers shopping in the facility.
- A consistent range is delivered by warehouses, whereas stores have local range variations.

Remember

The internet can accept payment, then almost instantaneously deliver some products such as music, films, software and tickets.

Practice point

Try to find a family member, friend or acquaintance who has ordered a product over the internet (e.g. a computer from Dell) and track its progress until it is delivered.

Non-conventional channels

The grey market refers to the flow of new goods through distribution channels other than those authorised or intended by the producer. Only new products fall into the legal and accepted definition of a grey market.

Unlike those on the black market, grey goods are not illegal. Instead they are being sold outside the normal distribution channels by companies that may have no relationship with the producer of the goods. Frequently this form of parallel import occurs when the price of an item is significantly higher in one country than another. This situation commonly occurs with cigarettes and electronic equipment such as cameras. Entrepreneurs will:

- buy the product where it is available cheaply (often at retail but sometimes at wholesale prices)
- import it legally to the target market
- sell it at a price that provides a profit, but that is below the normal market price there.

Outcome activity 41.2

Pass

Describe the process of distributing goods through different channels from the manufacturer to the customer.

Merit

Compare the methods used to distribute two selected products and services.

Distinction

Evaluate the system used in delivering goods and services for a retailer such as ASDA.

Grading tips

Pass 

Use textbooks, company literature (including websites), logistics organisation information and even perhaps retailer interviews to gather information to describe the distribution methods used by two contrasting retailers.

Merit 

Distinguish between the similarities and differences of the distribution processes of two companies in different sectors.

Distinction d1

'Evaluate' means to make a judgement after looking at the positive and negative aspects of an issue. In this case the evaluation could consider such issues as:

- responsiveness to consumers' needs
- costs incurred
- the use of international or domestic suppliers
- the use of intermediaries
- the shipping arrangements involved.

Askham Bryan College LIBRARY BOOK

Customer focus

Organisations that have a customer focus realise the best way to meet their objectives is by concentrating on customer needs and satisfying those needs better than the competition. For retailers this is probably best measured through customer satisfaction.

Customer satisfaction

Customer satisfaction measures how well an organisation has lived up to the expectations of its customers. Nowadays price and value plus good service equals customer satisfaction. Yet it is becoming hard to create any meaningful differences simply based on price and value. Developing a reputation for delivering good service could be the deciding factor between retailers with very similar offers.

The majority of shoppers report that they have walked out of a shop without buying because of poor service. Even more damaging for stores hoping to encourage repeat purchases from among its customers is that a large number have experienced such poor service they have never used that store again.

Collections and uses of customer information

Retailers nowadays invest a lot of money in collecting and using customer information, as the table below shows.

Uses of IT in communication with customers

Powerful databases are now available to help retailers communicate effectively with customers. This type of communication is being personalised, enabling individual messages to be sent to customers. This style of marketing is called micro-marketing. Databases are being used for the following functions.

- To match new products and new offers to customers who are likely to be interested. For example, Amazon notes the books customers have previously bought and alerts them when a similar title is published.
- To strengthen customer loyalty through, for example, reminders about key events. Websites ask surfers to register to access special information areas. This can involve giving some key details (including areas of interest) which are then used to communicate with that customer. This is called 'permission marketing'. It is considered a more effective way to deal with customers because they have actively asked you to send them certain sorts of information to which they are more likely to respond. As a consequence the messages sent are individualised to that customer.
- To re-activate customer purchasing by providing something special to regain a customer. Databases can be used to send out materials just before a lapsed customer is about to purchase a product such as insurance once again.

Collection method	Uses of the customer information
Marketing research	Used in developing new retail services and the assessment of advertising messages.
Loyalty cards	Provides insights into characteristics of customers and their buying habits.
Complaints	Helps to improve retail services. Data helps to establish and assess appropriate store standards such as acceptable queue lengths at checkouts.
Web site 'browser' data	Indicates which products customers are buying and perhaps, more interestingly, which ones they consider before buying. Customer reviews onsite can be very revealing, such as on amazon.co.uk.
Sales assistants	Help retailers to identify which sales promotions work and which advertising activities are genuinely effective. Usually a discussion point for staff meetings.

▲ Methods of collecting customer information and the use this information is put to

▲ Are you happy to provide personal data to organisations?

Customer Relationship Management (CRM)

Relationship marketing focuses on maximising the lifetime value of desirable customers. It can be defined as identifying, establishing, maintaining, enhancing and where necessary terminating the relationship with customers at a profit. Its focus is on maintaining and enhancing customer relationships. The table below may help to identify the distinguishing features of different retailer approaches.

Transactional approach (e.g. buying from Argos)	Relationship marketing approach (e.g. being a car dealership customer)
• Focuses more on single transaction. • Emphasis on product features. • Some emphasis on customer service. • Limited customer commitment. • Little customer contact – but when it occurs there is the expectancy of a sale. • Quality concentrated on product.	• Focuses more on customer retention. • Emphasis on product benefits. • High emphasis on customer service. • Higher customer commitment. • Regular customer contact – without expecting an immediate sale. • Quality is a concern for all employees, especially ones that impact on customer-buying experience.

Customer service

Customer service covers all the activities that affect the customer's experience of dealing with an organisation. This encompasses the impressions created by the manner, appearance and training of staff, including the reality of how well the customer's needs and wants were satisfied. Businesses offering a high level of customer service will add value to their products, enabling them to charge a higher price, while ensuring customer loyalty.

Customer service as an objective

In many retail sectors, price as a point of difference is losing its edge. However, being price competitive remains essential for success. Retailers are turning to customer service as a means of providing additional points of difference. The long-term challenge is to maintain and sustain any competitive advantage a retailer can acquire for itself through customer service. Standards, it seems, need to continually improve to maintain a competitive advantage.

■ Advantages

Although service standards are always important and may well be given a higher profile in the near future, shopping decisions comprise a combination of factors. However, the advantage of delivering excellent customer service is that retailers can create an emotional barrier to prevent customers switching to a competitor.

■ Problems

The greatest problem for retailers is the need for greater consistency in delivering the service levels demanded by customers. Factors preventing this consistent delivery include the following.

- High staff turnover adversely affects standards, with staff constantly learning the job.
- Moves to reduce staff costs affect the training and development of staff.
- Ever-increasing length of the trading week hinders creating a consistently effective customer service.

- Staff sometimes lack the commitment and motivation to deliver high customer service standards.
- Not all retailers have a high quality customer service culture

Target marketing

Different organisations offer different levels of service. Department stores make it an important part of their overall appeal. Other stores such as T.K.Maxx place less emphasis on customer service. The overall objectives of the organisation set the approach to customer service. Carefully communicating to consumers what they can expect once in store is a key function. Retailers choose the level of customer service demanded by their target market.

Identifying needs

Retail sales people should help buyers to select products that meet their needs. What suits one buyer may not suit another. Product selection tends to be influenced by the following factors.

- *Source.* Some sources have a strong selling appeal, such as Swiss watches and Japanese cameras.
- *Durability.* Many buyers are prepared to pay more for articles that are likely to last longer without replacement. This is important in the case of consumer durables, but less so for clothing.
- *Low running costs.* What may be cheap to buy may be expensive to use. A consumer may be persuaded to choose a product that is economical to run, even if it costs a little more.
- *Economy.* Price is invariably an important factor and not just with the lower income groups. Customers balance price with the subjective idea of value.

Before, during and after a sale

The standard of customer service offered before, during and after a sale (transaction), is important not only for the sale itself but also whether that customer returns to purchase again (see the table below).

Product offer

Unique selling points (USPs) distinguish a product or a retailer from its rivals. Retailers sell many products from their suppliers (e.g. Panasonic) which have USPs. Retailers also need USPs to distinguish themselves from competitors. Competition is so intense between retailers that they sometimes need a number of USPs to project a distinctive image. It is these USPs that enable sales staff to convince consumers to buy from their store. The table opposite gives some examples.

Pre-transaction	Transaction	Post-transaction
• Store provides customer phones, cafes, banking machines, toilets, trolleys and kiddy rides. • Treat customers effectively – remember first impressions are important. • Provide information as requested. • Agree to make an appointment if requested. • Explain the product features and benefits-matching them to the needs of the customer.	• Answer questions honestly and truthfully. • Demonstrate product. • Help customers find the product they might be looking for. • Assist customer in making fast and efficient payment. • Help to complete any documentation such as guarantee registration. • Thank customers for purchasing the product and reassure them they have made the right decision.	• Handle complaints effectively. • Deliver and install properly while removing and disposing of replaced product. • Ensure the customer is happy with product. • Contact to reassure customers they made right purchase. • Remind customers that the product is due for a service. • Suggest buying a complementary product such as product care item. • Any wrapping requirements identified and undertaken.

▲ Customer service before, during and after a sale

Retailer	Unique selling points (USPs)
Toys "R" Us	Great product choice, plenty of car parking and helpful staff.
ASDA	Every day low prices [EDLP], excellent locations, large car parks and helpful staff.
Evans	Clothes for the larger woman – size 16+, high street locations.
Argos	Low prices, easy order process, quick service.
Vision Express	Glasses available that very day.
Ikea	Innovative and stylish design.

▲ **Unique selling points of some well-known retailers**

Thinking point

Identify some well-known retailers and consider their unique selling points (USPs). They must have some, otherwise they would not survive the tough competition they face everyday.

After-sales service

Sales staff are intimately involved in after-sales service. Most retailers recognise that customer service does not end when the customer leaves the store. Customers can have a variety of after-purchase requirements. By responding to after-sales needs, retailers encourage further purchases and foster long-term customer relations. Each retailer must decide on which aspects of after-sales are important to their customers. Sales staff should be aware of what is available and use such support to secure sales. See the table below for some examples of after-sales service.

After-sales service: the options

- Fitting service for kitchens, bathrooms and bedrooms.
- Technical help line for products like computers.
- Installation service for washing machines and computers.
- Removal of product being replaced, e.g. cookers and refrigerators.
- Repair and servicing facility for products like bikes and cars.
- Stock of commonly requested spare parts.
- Extended warranty or guarantee option for household appliances.

Service quality

Many retail sales people naturally emphasise the quality of the products they are selling. However, from a retailer's point of view it is the quality of its customer services that is important. Retail customer service should:

- be reliable
- be responsive to the needs of customers
- be undertaken competently
- empathise with the consumer.

But how do such concepts translate into performance on the store floor? Exactly what do customers perceive as good service quality? A number of research projects have begun to explore the factors that make up the operational dimensions of service quality. Look at the table below which explores these issues.

Customer service: some of the issues

- Stores should:
  - be clean
  - have correct signage
  - have tidy displays
  - have good lighting
  - have trolleys that work
  - have clear aisles.
- Checkout queues need to be short. Even two or three people ahead of you is becoming unacceptable.
- Staff should be more visible
- Staff responsiveness to queries needs to be improved.
- The procedures for returning and exchanging goods should be considered excellent.
- The time taken to resolve price queries at the checkout is a source of dissatisfaction among shoppers.
- Out-of-stock products contribute negatively to the opinion a customer forms of the service offered by a retailer.

Take it further

Visit a range of stores such as Debenhams, Woolworths and Argos, which you suspect offer differing levels of customer service. Obtain additional customer service information from textbooks, company literature and websites. Then for each store observe the level of customer service being offered. Record your findings in tabular format. Comment on why consumers accept these differing service levels. If they didn't, these stores would quickly close.

Sales process

The customer's first impression of the sales person is important. A smile from the sales person is always a good start. The most common approach used by sales people is 'Can I help you?' and the most common answer is 'No, I'm just looking.' A better introduction would be, e.g. 'That camera is the latest in the range and is on special introductory offer at present.'

The retail sales assistant should try to deliver a persuasive and personable presentation, discussing the benefits of the product that are important to that buyer. These benefits should be communicated effectively in a manner that is pleasant and courteous, by sales staff appropriately dressed.

The penultimate stage in the selling process is to conclude with a sale. Several closing techniques are available to help sales people make a sale.

- *Asking for the order*: 'Would you like to order one?'
- *The indirect close*: 'Would you like the red or blue model?'
- *Summarising the key benefits, then asking for the order*: 'This car meets your requirements in terms of miles per litre and service charges. Shall we go ahead and order it?'

The final stage is to re-assure buyers that they have made a sound choice in purchasing the product.

Selling skills

Several different types of buyer enter a selling environment. It is important that sales staff learn to recognise the reasons a potential buyer may be considering a purchase. This is generally referred to as the 'buying motive'. The skill is to identify and select the product information that will appeal to the buying motive of the buyer, as the table below shows.

Buying motive	Implications for retail selling
Imitation	Consumers buy products to imitate those they admire. This is especially true of cosmetics and clothing. This is often referred to as 'aspirational marketing'.
Exclusiveness	Some customers are willing to pay high prices for durables or clothing that underline their self-proclaimed leadership through ownership of exclusive products.
Family affection	A great deal of money is spent on children in the shape of toys and clothes; this is part of the general pleasure of giving.
Other motives	These can include health, recreation, habit, security, curiosity, novelty, possession and pride.

Sales staff should also attempt to pay full attention, remembering that listening requires self-discipline. They need to listen carefully and not interrupt buyers. Sales staff should not speak over buyers, as it is impossible for either party to listen properly. Active listening helps sales people concentrate on customers' interests and needs while allowing them to think about how they might be met.

Retail sales staff need to listen to the comments, remarks and questions that reveal whether a buyer is beginning to take the product seriously and becoming increasingly interested in making a purchase. Such remarks are called 'buying signals'. Sales people should be listening for buying signals because they should attempt to close the sale when the buyer indicates a readiness to buy. Take a look at the signals in the table below.

Examples of verbal buying signals
• 'Do you accept credit cards?' • 'Do you have my size in stock?'
Examples of non-verbal buying signals
• The way the customer flexes the shoe to judge the flexibility of the leather. • The way a buyer tries the item alongside something else (such as an accessory), which says: 'This will go with something I already have at home.'

Sales support

Some tranactions require important administration duties from the retailer. These can include:

- processing an order for the customer if the goods are out of stock
- ordering replacement stock from the warehouse if levels are becoming low
- organising delivery to a customer at the requested time on the right date
- recording the details of a customer complaint and the action needed to be taken
- processing a store charge card application.

Sales techniques

In many retail selling environments sales staff do not enter into negotiation because the prices, delivery policy and payment terms are laid down in company policy. However, in some markets (e.g. car retailing or replacement window selling) negotiation is part of the process. There are three key aspects to any negotiation.

1. Sales staff must find out the limits to which they can negotiate such prices and changes to product features.
2. Sales staff should try to find out the precise needs of the buyer. This information can be used to identify the crucial factors in the buyer's mind and estimate the value to them of a concession. Many negotiations have been concluded successfully after agreeing to some minor concession.
3. Sales staff should keep as many concessions in reserve as possible. Concessions should only be given when necessary to achieve the order.

Retail sales assistants need to have the discipline to sell the customer the right product rather than the one that provides them with the highest commission payment. The sales techniques employed must ensure that the needs of the customer are satisfied by the product sold, otherwise retailers risk losing customers forever when they discover the product does not provide them with the benefits they were seeking.

Outcome activity 41.3

Pass

Outline how focusing on the customer by providing good customer service is essential to effective retailing. 

Merit

Explain the ways in which sales techniques and customer service have developed in PC World. 

Distinction

Assess the impact of the different sales techniques and customer service offered by Dell computers. 

Grading tips

Pass 

Explain the key elements of customer service and discuss its importance. The key elements should be classified and discussed in terms of what happens before, during and after a purchase.

Merit 

PC World started by selling desktop computers. Over time, it has expanded its product range to mirror the developments in computing technology. Consider how the selling techniques of PC World's staff have changed to cope with these developments. Then consider how the customer service aspect of this retailer has also evolved to deal with the technology advances.

Distinction 

Dell offers the consumer an alternative way to buy computer technology. How do the sales techniques and customer service they offer impact on the customer?

41.4 How the retail sector responds to internal and external change

The retail environment

Macro environment

Retailers are subjected to external events and developments over which they have no control such as:

- changes in consumer and business confidence
- changes in the housing market
- developments in employment levels.

The more successful retailers are the ones that react and in some cases anticipate these changes. They cannot be ignored without threatening the long-term survival of the organisation.

The key **macro environmental** factors that affect retailers are considered below.

Key Term

Macro-environment Includes the economy, technology, society, government and the competitive environmental factors that can influence an organisation but that are outside its direct control.

Government policy

■ Trading hours

The Sunday Trading Act 1994 is the law governing a shop's right to trade on a Sunday. Buying and selling on Sundays had been banned in the UK by the Shops Act 1950, but after the accession of the UK to the European Economic Community (now called the European Union), the ban may have been in breach of Article 30 of the Treaty of Rome as amounting to an unlawful restraint on the free movement of goods.

The Act allows stores to open, but restricts opening times of larger stores of more than 280 square metres to a maximum of six hours. Most shops that open on a Sunday, except in Scotland, open 10am to 4pm. Shops in Scotland where Sunday trading was already fully deregulated, retained the right to open at any time. However, the right for workers in Scotland to refuse to work on a Sunday was later conferred by the Sunday Working (Scotland) Act 2003.

The legislation met with considerable opposition. However, the shop worker's trade union USDAW (Union of Shop, Distributive and Allied Workers) finally agreed to support six-hour Sunday trading in return for a promise that Sunday working would be strictly voluntary and premium pay would be offered.

■ Planning guidance

The Country Planning Act 1990 directs local authorities to produce local structure plans. These plans show how shopping areas are likely to be developed over a ten-year period.

Nowadays retailers have to follow a particular sequence when seeking permission to build out-of-town centres. If a retailer puts forward a proposal, it must consider its accommodation options in this order.

- First, the town centre.
- Next, an established edge of town centre.
- Then a local centre.
- Finally an out-of-town location that is, or can be made, readily accessible by a variety of transport options.

This makes it much more difficult for developers to gain planning permission for out-of-town developments. Local planners are particularly concerned that:

- the development should not harm the vitality and viability of any nearby town centre
- any proposals should not give rise to unacceptable vehicle or pedestrian traffic conditions.

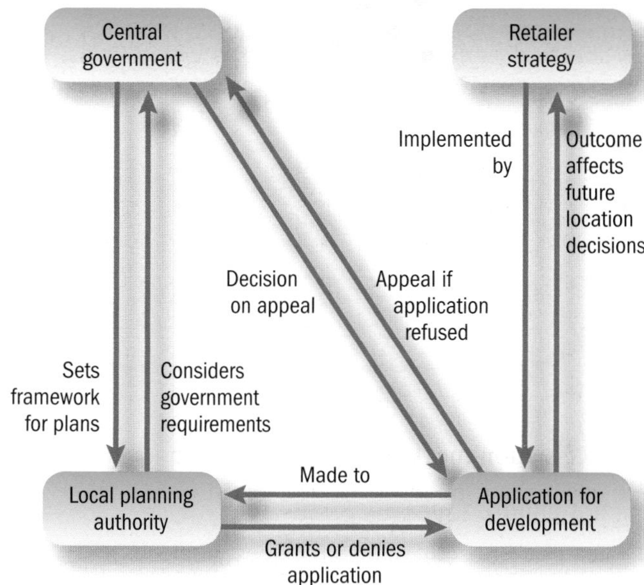

▲ **The planning process**

Local authority development plans weigh the importance of industrial and commercial development with that of maintaining and improving environmental quality. Government planning guidelines found on the Communities and Local Government website (www.communities.gov.uk) make special reference to modern distribution facilities:

> Some types of modern distribution facility have a low density of employment and are served by a very large number of lorries. Retail distributors depend on efficient distribution systems and require locations capable of serving regional, national and European markets. Sites for such developments are best located away from urban areas to minimise congestion. The sites should also be capable of access by rail and water transport.

Source: Communities and Local Government: Planning Policy

Implementation of legislation

The Office of Fair Trading (OFT) is a body established by the Enterprise Act 2002, which enforces both consumer protection and competition law. The OFT's goal is to make markets work well for consumers by ensuring vigorous competition.

The OFT has three main operational areas:

- competition enforcement
- consumer regulations enforcement
- markets and policies initiatives.

All three aspects of the OFT's work affect retailing, as the table below shows.

OFT operational area	Impact on retailing
Competition enforcement	Enforces the Competition Act 1998. Has recently investigated the merger between Morrisons and Safeway. One of the recommendations was that Morrisons sold some former Safeway stores to other supermarket operators.
Consumer regulations enforcement	In response to concerns raised by the OFT, Dell Corporation Ltd changed its terms and conditions to make them fairer to consumers. The online retailer of computers, software and IT services co-operated with the OFT and agreed to improve its consumer agreements.
Markets and policies initiatives	OFT has been asked by groups representing independent retailers to investigate the movement of supermarkets such as Sainsbury's into the convenience store retail market.

Take it further

Produce a summary of the report produced by the Office of Fair Trading (www.oft.gov.uk) into school uniform retailing. Conclude with your views on the current practice among schools and retailers.

Social change

Many of the retail opportunities appearing in the marketplace are connected to social change, as the following table shows.

Social factor	Changes and implications for retailing
Demographics	UK society is ageing. The 2001 **census** recorded that, for the first time, there are more people aged over 65 than under 16. This is a trend that will help local shopping centres, as older customers are less inclined to travel very far for their shopping.
Household structures	The structure of UK households has changed significantly in recent years. There has been a decline of the traditional family. Meanwhile, single-person households and co-habitation have risen. Retailers have to offer pack sizes suitable for single-person households
Mobility	Greater mobility has broadened the repertoire of locations and retailers that people can chose from. Retail parks have captured a substantial share of the expenditure. Interest in and acceptability of shopping as a leisure activity demands that people travel to more distant destinations rather than shop locally.

Key Terms

Census An official survey of a country's population. The census surveys throughout the UK usually take place every ten years.

Economic growth The way incomes per head increase over time.

Recession A period of rapidly declining economic circumstances characterised by falling levels of demand, very little investment, low business confidence and rising levels of unemployment (see Unit 39 for further explanations).

Thinking point

Have a look through an Argos catalogue (or look at the Argos catalogue online at www.argos.co.uk) and identify products that have emerged in response to social change.

The impact of economic growth, recession, social change and new technologies

The case study below shows how all the issues referred to have an impact on toy retailing.

Case study

Not children for very long

Economic growth: Although disposable income might not have a direct bearing on the toy market, rising households incomes are having a positive indirect influence on the amount of money that parents are devoting to their children. This is both in terms of money set aside for presents and also money given on a regular basis as pocket money.

Recession: Unemployment levels in 2003 stood at 1.5 million while consumer confidence in the future weakened even for people still in employment. Yet demand for toys remained remarkably strong. Families seemed determined to ensure that the children were the last members of the family to suffer.

Social change: The number of under-fives actually fell by more than 7% between 1998 and 2003. There will be a fairly significant fall in the number of five to nine year-olds in the next few years, while the number of under fives will rise slightly. Products such as fashion dolls, action figures and collectible cards are likely to be adversely affected.

New technologies: Traditional toys have come under threat from a number of external factors. Apart from the growing tendency to stop playing with toys at an earlier age, another threat has been competition from video and computer games. In addition, the internet has had an effect in terms of opening up new leisure options for children.

1. How would you describe the overall prospects for toy retailers? ✓✓
2. How might a toy retailer capitalise on the opportunities generated by new technology? ✓✓

Information management

Information management in the macro environment generate both threats and opportunities for retailers, as the table below shows. Customers can influence the information they receive while retailers must carefully manage the collection, storage, analysis and use of information.

Opportunities	Threats
• Customer able to select promotional messages they want to receive (called permission marketing). Thought to be more effective than traditional promotional methods. • New ways of gathering important customer data (e.g. loyalty cards) and ways of analysing customer data (e.g. **data mining**).	• Consumers may object to giving away so much personal information for organisations to use for promotional reasons. • Greater potential for fraud using, e.g. cloned credit cards. • Retailers must ensure they abide by the Data Protection Act guidelines for collection, storage and use of customer data.

Key Term

Data mining The technique that describes the process of exploring these large amounts of data with the objective of revealing hidden relationships or patterns that provide an insight into customer behaviour.

The competitive environment

Retailing is probably more competitive than many other industry sectors, although it is worth looking at different categories of retail activity and making a judgement. Sometimes you might find the answer surprising! You might notice that the sectors with the greater amounts of competition have also been the sectors experiencing the most change. Unit 3 (Book 1) discusses Michael Porter's theories of competition.

Remember

Competition is the driving force behind change.

Practice point

Porter's Five Forces analysis helps marketing managers assess the amount of competition and to understand the factors producing it. Simply answer 'Yes' or 'No' to the questions below. They are all about clothing retailers. If your answers are mainly 'Yes', the market is probably very competitive. If the answers are mainly 'No', the likelihood is that competition is low key.

- Is the market declining in terms of unit sales or value?
- Is there a significant number of clothing retailers?
- Is the number of clothing retailers in the market increasing?
- Do customers tend to show loyalty to a particular retailer?
- Could the retailers easily serve more customers?
- Would it be difficult for retailers to convert their stores quickly and inexpensively to serve another market?

Competitors and market position

The clothing sector covers a wide range of retailers, from the price-led, value retailers through young fashion specialists to the more aspirational or older focused brands. Superficially they may all appear to be competing with each other. But each has its particular appeal – Primark for prices, T.K.Maxx for bargains, M&S for quality, Topshop for young fashions.

Case study

Serendipity: today's fashion shopper

This market positioning chart shows that only certain sectors of the market are genuinely competitive.

1. Which area of this retail market looks likely to be very competitive? ✓✓
2. Can you guess what happened to the Marks & Spencer customer profile when it recently suffered a downturn in sales? ✓✓✓

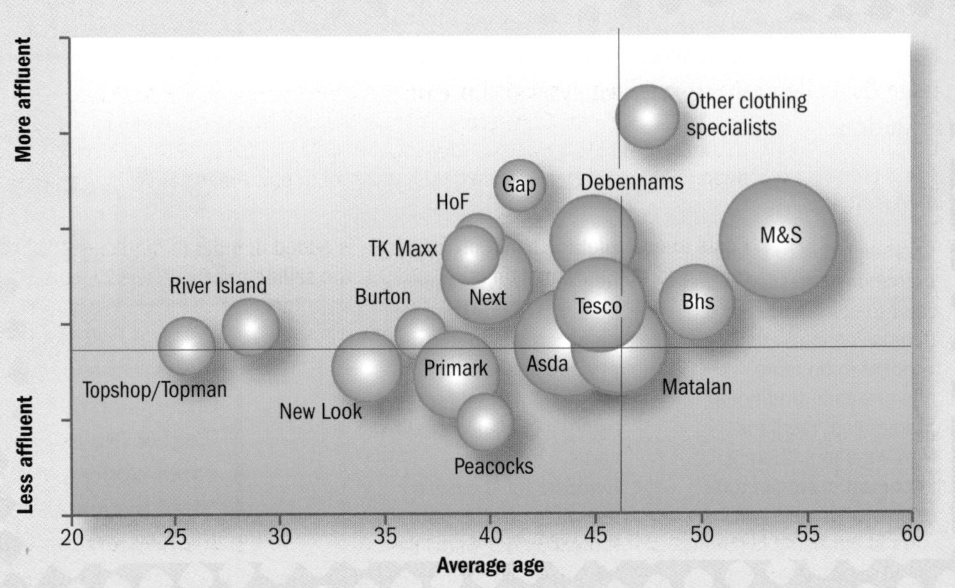

Thinking point

- Do stores such as Primark and T.K.Maxx appeal to the poorest elements of society or have they changed the customer's attitude to prices?
- Should Next be satisfied with becoming a 'younger version of M&S'?

Barriers to entry

Barriers to entry are obstacles put in the way of new organisations entering a market. The ability of existing firms to maintain such obstacles will depend on their marketing and financial power. Clearly some sectors of retailing are easier to enter than others.

Take, for example, hairdressers. The market is easy to enter because capital requirements are low and the training can be achieved fairly quickly. Compare this with supermarkets. The size of current competitors means they benefit from economies of size, making it difficult for others to enter the market. Wal-Mart, the world's largest retailer, decided it would be too expensive to build stores in the UK so it entered the market by buying ASDA.

Pricing

Retailers can adopt a variety of approaches to pricing. Pricing strategies are discussed fully in Book 1 (Unit 9, pages 254–55). The approaches outlined in the table opposite may be appropriate for retailers.

Product development

The appearance of new products creates opportunities for new stores or for stores to alter the product mix they offer. Look at the examples in the table on page 341.

▼ Pricing approaches

Pricing approach	Market conditions
Competition	Prices are set on the basis of what competitors are charging. This method is used mostly by organisations facing fierce competition. Generally, if there are several organisations in a market selling a similar product, then the tendency will be towards competitor-based pricing. This is the situation for many retailers.
Demand	'Demand pricing' considers the conditions prevailing in the market before setting prices. For example, a retailer might look at the amount of disposable income the potential customers have, or whether it is becoming socially important to own a particular product. A popular method is to charge 'what the market will bear'. This means setting prices depending on what the consumer is prepared to pay. Pricing of DVDs is an example of this approach.
Costs	Costs are calculated, then a profit margin is added in order to determine the price. For example, if an item costs £10 to make and the profit margin is set at 25%, the selling price will be £10 + £2.50 = £12.50. The cost plus approach leads to price stability with prices changing only to reflect cost changes. This is rarely the case in many retail markets and consequently is not a popular pricing policy for retailers.

Retailer	Product opportunities for retailers
The Link	Mobile phones and accessories.
PC World	MP3 players, wireless technology products, mobile phones.
iTunes	New type of store – downloading your favourite music.
HMV	From records and cassette tapes to CDs and DVDs.
Dixons	Significant digital camera sales have persuaded Dixons not to stock 35mm cameras any longer. The popularity of the DVD player and recorder has forced them to stop offering the video (VHS) recorder.

▲ Product opportunities for retailers

New products and services

Retailers are constantly looking at new products and services they could effectively offer their customers, as the table below shows.

Retailer	Additional products and services
Sainsbury's	Banking services – savings accounts and mortgages.
ASDA	George – the fashion clothing brand.
Tesco	Insurance and travel bookings.
Carphone Warehouse	Landline and broadband services.

Take it further

Carphone Warehouse is a retailer that has introduced a variety of innovative developments in its stores and online sites. Investigate the Carphone Warehouse to identify examples of innovative retailing.

New retailing formats

The search by customers for quality time is beginning to re-shape product and service retailing. Customers are looking for new experiences and life-changing activities. Starbuck's coffee, for example, has turned the ordinary activity of coffee drinking into an exciting experience. This suggests that stores will have to keep re-inventing themselves to maintain and retain their customers. This trend is already noticeable in the world of clubs and bars, which change their image and decor at regular intervals.

Remember

The internet can be regarded as a new retailing format now that organisations like amazon.co.uk are trading very successfully.

Thinking point

Consider the impact of competitive trends on retailing by copying and completing the table below. Several points might be included for each trend. For each point think about whether it has short- or long-term implications for retailers.

Macro and competitive environment trends	Impact on retailing
Increasing power of multiples	Increase in profits for multiples – long term.
Concentration of retailing	
Lower barriers to entry	
Innovative practices	
Difficult to obtain superstore planning permission	

Case study

Aerotropolis: airports are developing into hubs of commerce

In today's speed-driven global economy, the airport is developing into a hub for commerce. Similar to a traditional city and its outlying suburbs, the airport is becoming the focus for a sprawl of businesses in what is being called the 'aerotropolis'. Airport shops are no longer solely for duty free gifts and indulgences. Instead, they contain a diverse range of shops to cater for workers and even residents surrounding the 'city'.

Amsterdam's Schiphol Airport is a prime example of an aerotropolis. Around 58,000 people are employed daily at the airport and the surrounding business district. Aerotropoli are not just centres for commerce; they are increasingly becoming home to the thousands of employees who work in the area. Schiphol's passenger terminal, containing an expansive mix of shopping, dining and entertainment arcades, doubles as a suburban mall that is accessible to air travellers and the general public.

1. How might the product range offered by cosmetic and toiletry stores change in an aerotropolis? ✓✓
2. Name some retailers who might think about opening stores in an aerotropolis. ✓✓

Development of shopping for a mobile population

The increase in the mobility of the population is creating retail opportunities for organisations, as the table below shows.

Retail format	Development features
Motorway service area (MSA)	Car ownership continues to rise, as does the number of people with a licence. Currently about 90 MSAs which are open 365 days a year, 24 hours a day, serve this market. The retail outlets within these MSAs are restricted on the size of their stores on these sites; they cannot sell alcohol; nor can they advertise their brands. A revision of these rules would allow these outlets to develop in line with customer needs and wants.
Railway stations	Passenger numbers on the national rail network are rising rapidly. Convenience stores, confectionery and tobacconist shops are enjoying increasing demand, while teenagers are keen on DVD, music, electrical, accessories, clothing and gift purchase at stations. Stations are attracting some retail experimentation with health and beauty operators such as Boots, The Body Shop and Superdrug opening stores. In addition, higher value accessory retailers such as Swatch and Tie Rack have expanded with Vodaphone and the stationer Paperchase joining the market. Some of the busier ferry ports are developing in a similar fashion.

Thinking point

- What do you think is the long-term future for airport retailers?
- What other locations might develop along similar lines?

Take it further

Using a variety of sources, such as newspapers, news programmes, store visits, interviews with retail employees and customers, identify the current trends and state of the retail industry.

Outcome activity 41.4

Pass

Identify the level of competition faced by Carphone Warehouse.

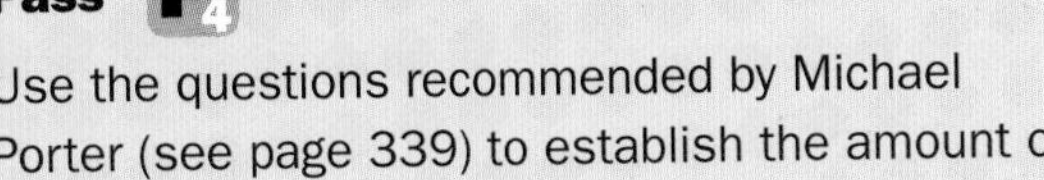

Grading tips

Pass P4

Use the questions recommended by Michael Porter (see page 339) to establish the amount of competition facing Carphone Warehouse.

End of unit test

1. What percentage of the workforce is employed in retailing?
2. What is the difference between a shopping village and a factory shop?
3. How has the local shopping centre changed in recent years?
4. Explain why independent retailers have been declining in numbers very recently.
5. Describe the three main advantages of shopping on the Internet.
6. Explain how a grey or parallel market works.
7. Draw a flow diagram showing the supply chain of products sourced abroad.
8. Describe the various carriers retailers can use.
9. List the key features of a relationship marketing approach.
10. Devise two effective closing techniques.
11. What must a retailer consider before seeking permission to build an out-of-town shopping centre?
12. What retail sectors might prosper during a recession?
13. Name four opportunities or threats that information technology presents to retailers.
14. How would you assess the amount of competition in a particular retail sector?
15. What sort of barriers to entry operate in the sandwich bar sector?

Books

Brittain, P and Cox, R, 2004, *Retailing: An Introduction*, FT Prentice Hall
Kent, T and Omar, O, 2002, *Retailing*, Palgrave Macmillan
Varley, R and Rafiq, M, 2003, *Principles of Retail Management*, Palgrave Macmillan

Websites

www.brc.org.uk – The British Retail Consortium
www.retail-week.com – *Retail Week* magazine
www.statistics.gov.uk – Office for National Statistics

See also the websites of well-known retail outlets.

Grading criteria	Outcome activity	Page number
To achieve a pass grade the evidence shows that the learner is able to:		
P1 Describe the structure and organisation of the retail sector	41.1	317
P2 Describe the process of distributing goods through different channels from the manufacturer to the customer	41.2	329
P3 Outline how focusing on the customer by providing good customer service is essential to retailing	41.3	335
P4 Identify the competitive factors faced in the retail environment by a selected organisation	41.4	343
To achieve a merit grade the evidence shows that, in addition to the pass criteria, the learner is able to:		
M1 Compare the function of four formats and locations of retailing	41.1	317
M2 Compare the methods used to distribute two selected products and services	41.2	329
M3 Explain the ways in which sales techniques and customer service have developed in a selected retail organisation	41.3	335
To achieve a distinction grade the evidence must show that, in addition to the pass and merit criteria, the learner is able to:		
D1 Evaluate the distribution systems in delivering goods and services for a selected organisation	41.2	329
D2 Assess the impact of different sales techniques and customer service in a selected organisation	41.3	335

Glossary

Acceptance A formal agreement to accept an offer.

Accessibility The ease and comfort with which websites can be used by those with disabilities.

Administration (going into) A step taken before a company becomes completely bankrupt. The firm is taken over by a team of administrators, possibly accountants, who try to save the business by finding a buyer or selling off bits of the firm to raise money on behalf of creditors.

Aggregate demand The total amount of demand for goods and services in an economy.

Authentication Proving that you are who you say you are.

Authoring tools Software packages that offer a WYSIWYG user-friendly environment allowing for website design without knowledge of HTML.

Balance of payments The difference between the level of exports from a country and the level of imports into that country.

Boom A period of very rapidly improving economic circumstances.

Brand image The creation of an easy-to-spot identity that consumers get to know well.

Break-even analysis Comparison of a firm's revenue and its fixed costs to identify the minimum sales level needed to break even.

Breaking bulk Breaking into smaller amounts – for example buying large quantities from a wholesaler and offering smaller quantities to customers.

Business cycle Changes in the levels of economic activity in a country, normally featuring alternating periods of growth and slump.

Capacity The legal ability or authority to make a valid contract.

Capital intensive A production process that requires a lot of machinery and technology.

Cashflow forecast A technique for estimating the future bank balance of a company and anticipating overdraft requirements.

Caveat emptor Latin term meaning as a buyer you should be aware of defects in a product when you buy it.

Census An official survey of a country's population, usually taking place in the UK every ten years.

Channel conflict Where the introduction of an internet sales channel threatens relationships with businesses working in existing channels.

Clicks and mortar business A business that has physical buildings and an internet presence.

Completing the transaction Actually making sales from a website.

Conditions Essential parts of a contract.

Consideration Something of value done by the parties.

Consumer contract Contract made between a business and members of the public for consumer goods such as food, clothes and furniture.

Contract An enforceable agreement made between parties.

Convergence criteria The conditions a potential member needs to meet before being allowed to join the Eurozone.

Co-operative A business owned by, and operated for, the benefit of those using its services.

Corporate governance The people and procedures for taking the major decisions within a business.

Corporate social responsibility The policy of a business towards all stakeholders that takes their interests into account.

Corruption Not following fair and equal procedures to make decisions; attempting to persuade by using cash or opportunity.

Creditor A business or person the firm owes money to.

Cultural imperialism Where local ways of life are being influenced and altered through the effects of Western values and practices spreading all over the world.

Customer profile The characteristics of a typical person or business that buys from your business.

Customer retention Keeping customers so that they choose to come back to your site to make repeat purchases.

Customisation Opportunity for the customer to manipulate and change the online presentation of a product.

Cyclical trend A change or pattern that recurs on a regular basis.

Data mining The process of exploring large amounts of data with the objective of revealing hidden relationships or patterns that provide an insight into customer behaviour.

Deficit funding Finding the money to pay for an overspend by the government.

Direct marketing Sending marketing messages directly to customers (e.g. by email, post).

Direct taxes Taxes paid according to a person's income or wealth.

Disintermediation The removal of 'middle men' from the process of purchasing products.

Dow Jones index An index that records changes in the value of share prices on the US stock exchange.

Duress Where a person enters into a contract against their will.

Dynamic pricing The facility of the web that enables online businesses to adjust prices quickly, according to market conditions.

Economic growth Increases in GDP that lead to improvements in standards of living for the country's citizens.

Entrepreneur A person who takes a risk to set up and run a business venture.

Ethical values The standards that are set by a business or individual that control their behaviour.

Euro The single currency now being used by many of the countries that are members of the EU.

Excess capacity When an organisation has too many goods or services on offer compared to the number of customers.

Executed consideration An act in exchange for a promise.

Executory consideration Set of promises yet to be fulfilled.

Express terms Clauses in an agreement actually agreed by the parties.

Fiscal policy Refers to changing government spending and taxation levels.

Flat-structured organisation An organisation that has fewer levels of management.

Franchise A small business that buys the right to use a larger firm's name, advertising and products.

Franchisee Someone who owns and operates a franchise.

Free enterprise An economic system in which people are free to offer goods and services to meet demand.

Globalisation Where the economies of the world are becoming more dominated by a few multi-national businesses.

Global warming The gradual warming of the planet's surface caused by carbon dioxide build-up in the atmosphere.

Goodwill The amount paid by a buyer to the seller of a business that exceeds the value of the assets of the business; it represents the value of the business' reputation, brand image, workforce skills and customer base.

Gross domestic product The total market value of all the goods and services produced by a country in one year.

Gross salary Salary before any deductions, such as tax or national insurance, are made.

Growth A period of improving economic output and circumstances.

Hierarchical or pyramid-structured organisation An organisation that has many hierarchical layers.

HM Revenue and Customs The government department responsible for collecting taxes as well as paying tax credits and child benefits.

Hosting A website needs to be held on a server, i.e. 'hosted'.

Hypertext Text available on the web that contains hyperlinks to other web pages.

Implied term Parts of the contract not necessarily included by the parties but automatically included by law to protect the parties.

Indemnity clause Term in a contract between two parties in which one of the parties agrees to indemnify the other party for liabilities in respect of a third party.

Indirect taxes Taxes added to the prices of goods and services sold.

Inflation An increase in the general price levels in a country. This is generally regarded as problematic for a country's economy.

Information fatigue Having so much information that it becomes meaningless and impossible to use.

Invitation to treat Indication that a person might be open to receive an offer. Not legally binding.

Knowledge-based economy An economy that is based upon the creation of advanced information services.

Labour intensive A production process that requires a lot of human resources.

Leakages Savings and taxes paid. These reduce the effect of the Multiplier.

Learning curve The process of gaining experience and knowledge that results from learning from your mistakes.

Leasing Renting a capital item such as a car or machinery.

Limited company A business that is owned by shareholders, all of whom have limited liability for the firm's debts.

Limited liability Shareholders lose no more than the value of their shares if the business should fail.

Liquidated damages Damages agreed at the negotiation stage.

Malpractice Any occasion when someone does not follow accepted normal practice (usually to gain advantage).

Margin Sometimes referred to as profit margin, this is the difference between the retail price and cost of production of an item.

Market diversification Expanding a business by offering new products or services.

Marketing mix A combination of blended tactics used in delivering a marketing strategy.

Market segment A subgroup, within an overall market, that has similar characteristics.

Marketing strategy The general direction in which marketing decisions take a business.

Misrepresentation A set of untrue facts made by one party relied on by the other when entering into a contract.

Mistake Where a person enters into a contract after getting the facts in the negotiation wrong.

Mitigation To reduce your loss.

Monetary policy Refers to changes in money supply and levels of interest rates.

Money supply The total purchasing power in the economy.

Mortgage A large loan for an extended period (often 25 years) normally given for the purchase of property.

Multimedia elements The facility on a web page to show streaming video or sounds to back up textual information.

Multiplier The number of times that additional government spending on the economy is re-spent and the resulting overall increase in spending.

National insurance A tax paid according to the size of a person's income; it goes towards paying for the NHS, social security and state pensions.

Net salary Salary after deductions are made.

Objectives Specific and measurable targets that lead to a particular overall goal.

Offeree The person receiving the offer.

Offeror The person making the offer.

Organisation of the Petroleum Exporting Countries (OPEC) The group of countries that produce the majority of oil exports for the world.

Outsourcing Paying another firm to take on some of the functions of your business in order to reduce costs and increase company flexibility.

Own brand This can be a name, a symbol or a design used to identify a specific retailer and make it appear different from its competitors.

Payment security Setting up online payments systems so that customers' details remain hidden.

Pension A payment that is given to a person when they retire. Pensions can come from a company scheme, a private scheme, or the state pension which people pay into through national insurance contributions.

Personalisation Adjusting the web page that is returned to a visitor so that it offers information that is personal, based upon their previous visits to the website.

PESTLE analysis An analysis of the environment in which a business operates, looking at Political, Economic, Social, Technological, Legal and Environmental influences.

Portal A gateway site that offers many links into other sites related to the same theme.

Pressure groups Voluntary organisations that exist to create a case that will be listened to by decision makers everywhere. This includes business leaders and politicians.

Price transparency When everyone who visits yours website can see all your prices.

Privacy The level of security of personal information – a crucial factor in a website's status in the eyes of the users.

Privity of contract The relationship between parties to a contract. It is a legal concept denying third parties the right to sue on a contract.

Product development Taking an existing product and adding new features.

Promisee The person receiving the promise.

Promisor The person making the promise.

Public sector net borrowing The amount the government has spent above the level of tax raised.

Quota A limit to the number of imports allowed.

Recession Officially, two consecutive quarters of negative growth in the economy. This is a period of rapidly declining economic circumstances.

Remedy Solution for the victim of a breach of contract.

Reservation of title Retaining ownership of the goods until the contract is completed.

Rogue traders A trader operating as a legitimate business without the required skills and ability to do the job.

Search engine advertising Paid-for links that are presented by a search engine when a user requests a particular search.

Service industries Industries not dealing in physical products.

Skills audit An identification of the skills required and held by the entrepreneur and his/her employees.

Skill sets Groups of competencies and skills that employees need in order to be able to carry out a job.

Slump A period of declining economic circumstances and output.

Spam Unsolicited emails, often referred to as junk mail.

Standard form contract A contract made between parties using their standard set of terms.

Stakeholders Individual or group with any sort of interest in the activities of a business.

Stock exchange The market where stocks and shares are bought and sold.

Subsidy Non-repayable money paid by the government to a company.

SWOT analysis Analysis of a business to find its strengths and weaknesses and to identify the opportunities and threats facing it.

Tangible Something you can physically touch.

Target market The segment that marketers aim for when they create their marketing message.

Tariff A tax on imports.

Terms Parts of the contract agreed by the parties.

Testing Trying out the website to make sure it is capable of use by both staff and customers.

Title The legal right of ownership.

Trade deficit A period where imports exceed exports.

Trade description A description made by sellers about the goods they are selling.

Trade journals Regularly published magazines which contain the latest thinking from people who work in specific industries.

Trade surplus A period where exports exceed imports.

Trade union A group of workers who join together to negotiate pay and working conditions – for example, the National Union of Teachers.

Trading bloc An agreement between countries that are often geographically close. It enables its members to co-ordinate their foreign trade policies for the benefit of all bloc members.

Ultra vires To act outside one's powers.

Undue influence Where one party exerts pressure on another to enter into a contract due to the nature of the relationship or position.

Unlimited liability Business owners are personally responsible for all the debts of the firm and their personal possessions can be seized to clear company debts.

Unliquidated damages Damages awarded that were not agreed.

Usability The ease with which staff and customers can use a website.

USP (unique selling point) The features of a business that make it different from, and more attractive than, its competitors.

Value added Where value is added to something through work and application of skills and understanding.

Venture capital Venture capitalists invest money into businesses that are high risk.

Visual appeal A pleasant and appropriate look and feel that is fitting in the context of the organisation.

Warranties Important terms of the contract but not so important as to be classed essential.

Website functionality What the customer can do on a website and the functions the site offers.

Website scalability The capability of a website to grow alongside the growth of the business.

Website stickiness The capacity of a website to make people stay on the site and eventually make a purchase.

Whistleblowing Informing managers or other authorities about unethical practices going on within an organisation.

Index

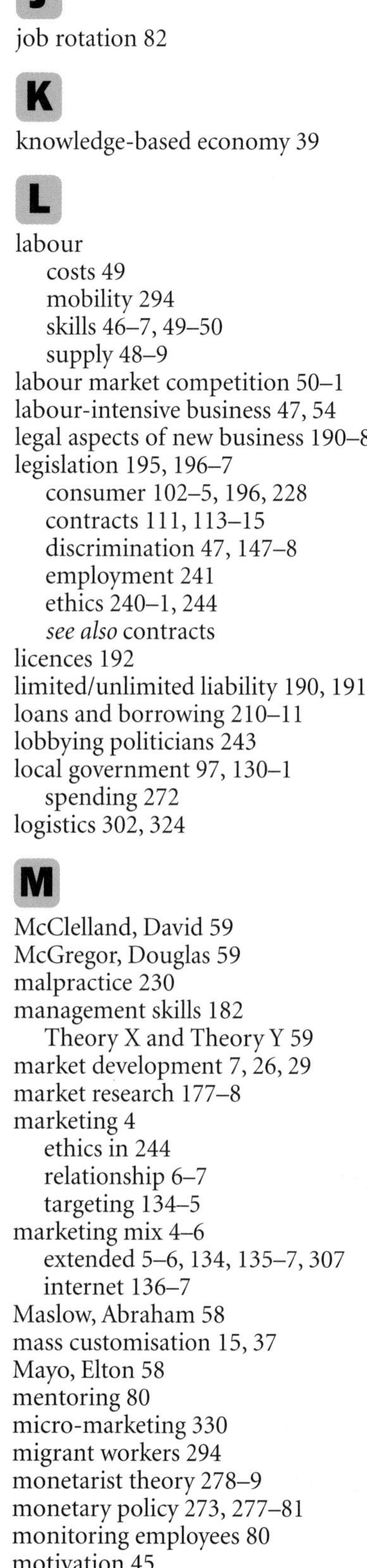

N

O

T

Askham Bryan
College
LIBRARY BOOK

Let the web do the work!

Visit our website today for details on all our products and much more...

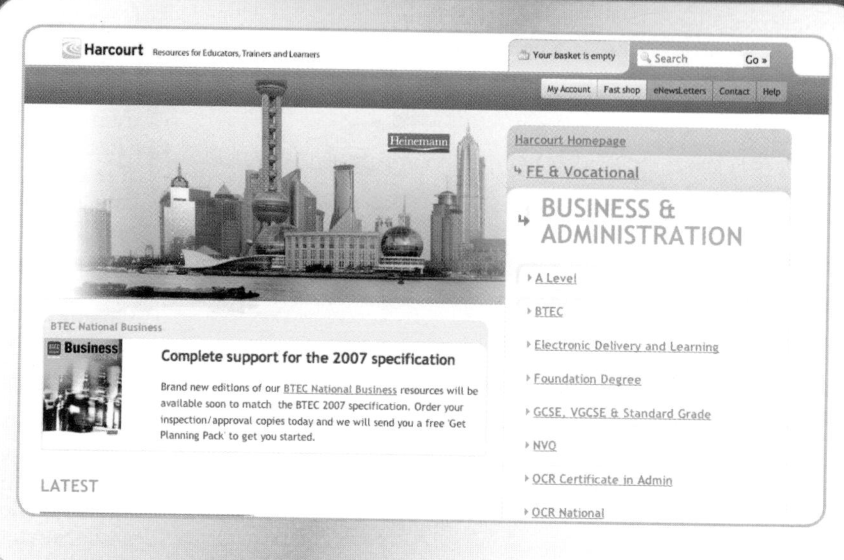

✤ Access FREE support materials

Use our website to download free sample material.

✤ Register for our FREE Business eNewsletter

Our termly eNewsletter will keep you up-to-date on the latest publications, offers and industry news. Register online today!

✤ Order online – 24 hours a day

It's quick and simple to order your resources online, and you can do it at a time that suits you – day or night!

✤ Write your own review

We love to hear what you think of our books.
Simply find the title on our website and click on 'submit review'.

www.harcourt.co.uk/business

(T) 01865 888118 (E) orders@harcourt.co.uk

(F) 01865 314029 (W) www.harcourt.co.uk

M769